Major Cities of
Europe

Great Stay Guide

Major Cities of
Europe

Little Hills Press

Text by Fay Smith and LHP Editorial Staff
© Little Hills Press, February 2001
Photographs © Little Hills Press

Editor & Internal Designer: Mark Truman
Publisher: Charles Burfitt

Cover Design by Artitude
Printed in Hong Kong

Major Cities of Europe
Great Stay Guide
ISBN 1 86315 153 2

Little Hills Press
Sydney, Australia
www.littlehills.com
info@littlehills.com

DISCLAIMER

Whilst all care has been taken by the publisher and authors to ensure that the information is accurate and up to date, the publisher does not take responsibility for the information published herein or the consequences of its use. The recommendations are those of the writing team, and as things get better or worse, with places closing and others opening, some elements in the book may be inaccurate when you arrive. Please inform us of any discrepancies so that we can update subsequent editions.

Contents

Part Three

Preface

W ELCOME TO EUROPE! This amazing continent is made up of many countries, each with its own special identity, culture and lifestyle. Each has a rich history and will provide you with unique experiences never to be forgotten.

Many people undertaking their first trip to Europe book a package tour and cover most of the continent in a couple of whirlwind weeks. *Wow! What was that?* At the end of it all, each significant sight of Europe occupies a small pocket of the traveller's memory. Together they flash through the mind like images in a music video whenever the traveller attempts to recall his or her trip. Thankfully there is usually an abundance of photographs - taken on a camera worn out by two weeks of constant use - to refresh the memory. Although the traveller has barely survived the physically-demanding experience, this type of trip remains a good introduction to a diverse part of the world packed with many famous things to see.

The photographs that you have taken can be used to plan for the next trip - the one when you don't wish to do everything, but would prefer to return to a number of your favourite European spots and indulge in them a little longer. The one when you make sure that the alarm clock which woke you up before 6am on your last visit during the package tour is safely deactivated this time around. Then you can rise at your leisure, spend some time getting to know the local scene, the people and the attractions. Find your favourite restaurant, club or park, or a delightful little bookshop where you can browse endlessly.

This book is designed for people who plan to visit particular European cities, whether or not they are on a whirlwind tour. It assumes that you have not had a lot of time in these cities, and provides thorough details of their main attractions so that you may head directly to the places that interest you. It therefore lists what are in our opinion the most important sights to see.

There are suggested tours for you to undertake on foot. Whilst exploring European cities, cars are really an encumberance, even in a vast city such as London, where it is best to take advantage of the tube and then hail a cab. Going on foot with a light rucksack means that you are more flexible and can adapt your plans without unecessary hassles, such as finding parking, paying for parking, having to return to the car constantly whenever you wish to move on, and worrying about it being broken into or damaged while you are away.

How To Use This Book

Symbols

Throughout the text you will find that symbols have been used to denote the information that follows, whether it be an admission price, opening time, phone number, email or web address. This will aid you in locating the specific details you desire more quickly.

Here is a list of the symbols used with an explanation of each:

C   indicates a phone number

✪ indicates a price
🕓 indicates opening times
👁 indicates a web site
✉ indicates an email address

Taxes

Taxes vary throughout Europe. Where possible we have included the tax for a specific country or service within a country, and at the very least, warn you of possible additions to your bill so you have some idea of what to expect.

Accommodation and Eating Out

The *Accommodation* and *Food and Drink* sections contain by no means an exhaustive list of what each European city has to offer. We have tried to cater for a range of tastes and provide suggestions for your selection. Place listed are designed to give you a basis for comparison and to act at the very least as a starting point for the planning of your holiday. All budgets from lavish to limited have been considered and included.

Layout

The chapters of this book are laid in alphabetical order by country. They begin with an introductory overview of important basic facts about each country. The selected major cities then follow as separate featured sections within the chapter.

Internet Information

For your convenience you will find throughout this book relevant websites and email addresses, which can be used for the preliminary planning of your European holiday.

PART ONE

Introduction

THIS CHAPTER OUTLINES some travel tips which you may find helpful. Specific details for each city regarding currency, electricity, appliance information, tips on shopping, sightseeing, and more, are contained in each chapter for the particular countries we have covered.

Passport

You need a passport to travel. For first time travellers the following are some of the documents required before you can be issued with a passport - birth certificate and/or proof of citizenship, photographs of which at least two are passport-size, your drivers license and so on. Normally you will have a face-to-face interview with a government official.

Generally speaking you are looking at paying over A$130 (US$65) for a passport valid for 10 years. In most cases passports are valid for 10 years, however they are useless if they have less than 6 months left on them unless you are an Australian going to New Zealand and vice versa. This does not apply to any other countries. Though the European Union has its own rules for member countries, both UK and Irish citizens need a valid passport with at least 6 months left on it, as do citizens of other members countries of the EU.

Here are some important contacts who will tell you exactly what you need and where to lodge the application:

Australia: ✆131232
             ✇www.dfat.gov.au/passports

Canada: ✆800 567 6868
             ✇www.dfait-maeci.gc.ca/passport/passport.htm

New Zealand: ✆0800 225 050
             fax 64 4 748 010
             ✇www.passports.govt.nz/

United Kingdom: ✆0870 521 0410
             ✇www.ukpa.gov.uk

USA: ✆1 900 225 5674 or 1 888 362 8668
             ✇www.travel.state.gov

Money

Some of us still like to have a few travellers cheques just in case, however the way of the present is the credit card or the bank card, which you can activate at any ATM in most towns in Europe.

If you have a credit card make sure it also has a pin number. This may seem like a superfluous comment, however some credit cards are only secured by a password, which is useless if the ATM in Europe requires you to enter a pin number for your card.

Make sure the account your card accesses is cashed up before you travel. Also check to see if the money is accessible before you leave, just in case the bank or the financial organisation you deal with has made a mistake or is suffering technical problems. Try making a simple withdrawal and check the balance.

You might like to get the phone numbers you will need to call if you have credit card hassles in each of the countries you plan to visit. If you want to, test them from home before you leave. At night it will probably cost you $2 in total and save you making frantic calls to dead ends in the unfortunate event that a problem arises.

Web Sites for the Major Credit Cards

These sites can provide you with the location of offices and ATMs in Europe.

- www.americanexpress.com.au/atm/atm.asp
- www.thomascook.com (a confusing site but you may be able to find your way around it)
- www.mastercard.com/atm
- www.visa.com/pd/atm/main.html

When changing money at either a bank or a Bureau de Change it is important to check the commission fee to avoid being overcharged. Ask beforehand or check the notices near the counter carefully (look for the fine print!). Fees should be no more than $5.00 or L5000.

Make sure you always keep the receipts. When you are leaving a country and want to change your money from the currency of the country you are leaving into the currency of your next destination, you will invariably be asked to produce a receipt to prove that you purchased the currency whilst in the country you are in - otherwise you will be denied.

Contact Details and Valuables

The following tip is something that any travel agent and decent guidebook will advise.

It is worthwhile to have two copies of each of the documents listed below.

Passport - the front two pages which have your identification details and photograph, and also pages where Visas appear.

Your ticket/s

Driver's license

Insurance documentation

Travellers Cheque numbers

Credit Card details - just the numbers, not any identifying marks showing what card it is. Write them in a jumbled up way that doesn't look specific except to you.

Put these at the bottom of your suitcase where you will hopefully not see them until you return and unpack your bags. Forget about them for now. If you need them you will know where to find them.

Leave the second lot of copies with family back home. This will save you a lot of problems if disaster strikes.

Insurance

It is advisable to take out comprehensive insurance for the duration of your stay. Your travel agent can handle this for you and it normally covers you for loss of personal belongings, specific flight cancellations or rerouting, medical costs including all hospital and doctors' fees and any emergency transport associated with this, injury, death (not suicide - sorry to sound so gory). Payment is made for the number of days you are away. Of course, the rates vary as does the coverage, so shop around.

Driving Through Europe

Camper vans and mobile homes (RVs in the US) are common in Europe. Using one makes it obvious that you are a tourist, not only by the number plate. It is a convenient way to travel but be warned that when you leave the vehicle it can become a target for thieves, since by theory is that travelling tourists have their valuables centred in one place: the vehicle. So it is a good idea to have your passport, credit cards and money on you. Any other valuables you do not plan

Part of the Swiss Alps

to take with you should be hidden somewhere in the vehicle and not exposed if someone peers through the window.

Some people opt for a van or a station wagon, in which they can put a fold-down mattress. These are not obvious tourist vehicles and so may have less chance of being tamperered with, although in some cities it is essential to hide everything from view regardless of the type of vehicle, otherwise a break-in is guaranteed.

Remember, in budgeting for travelling around Europe, you should keep in mind the cost of fuel in your different ports of call. As a rule of thumb the country areas will be more expensive than the city. Diesel will be more expensive per gallon or litre but will take you much further per litre or gallon and is more efficient.

Trains

Eurail is definitely the way to book and organise your tickets. It allows you to develop some flexibility with regard to where you want to travel. In addition to the basic travel component of the fare you must pay an additional charge for your individual seat. Depending on the country and the type of train, seats must be booked in advance, although this is not always necessary and you should check first.

The two web sites listed below have good information and allow you to book and pay online:

Rail Pass Express: 👁www.eurail.com

RailEurope: 👁www.raileurope.com (info and commercial)

Note that if you travel at off peak times the prices are much cheaper. This is especially the case if you book a certain number of days in advance. The same applies to the tube in London and in other cities, so if you are going to be there for a week or so and plan to do a lot of travel by train, enquire at the rail information centres for their special passes giving you cheaper fares. This is certainly true in Frankfurt am Main.

Taxis

In certain cities this is the most effective way to get around. However, in places like Rome you can be assailed by unofficial taxi drivers at the airport and end up in an unlicensed cab, paying a fortune. It is always important to make sure that if you are going to go by cab you travel in a cab with a proper meter. Insist that the driver turns the meter on.

If your destination is not too far away from where you get the cab, the driver may not bother switching on the meter and will not mind arguing with you if in the end you hand over $10 instead of the $20 he was after, since the fare should really have been only $5 anyway.

In London the big black cabs are pretty obvious and the fare is preset. Most taxis do not take credit cards. In the UK you have to spend over £11.50, otherwise they will charge this price as the minimum. You should take it as given that cabs require cash.

Also, it can sometimes occur that your hotel is not far from the station or airport where you have just arrived - but it is raining and the distance is too far to cart your luggage. If you are in the queue and discover that the drivers aer enquiring about your destination then waving you away and moving onto the next person, it is because you do not have a decent fare to offer them. Should you find yourself in a similar situation, head into the street and hail a taxi - once you are settled comfortably inside with all your gear, break the news to the driver in a confident, matter-of-fact tone.

Force yourself to shrug off the travel fatigue and have presence of mind when you arrive in a new city. Watch what the locals are doing - it may take some minutes - but you will soon find the nearest taxi stand and line up like everyone else. You will always find drivers with excellent English offering you their cab, but these fellows normally charge exhorbitant fares. Remember the official colours and the running meter.

Buses/Trams

At the airport information centre and normally in the popular tourist spots in a city you will find maps with city bus routes on them.

On many buses the locals can get away with not paying, but for a visitor it is not a good idea. Normally the tickets are purchased from a local kiosk, on the bus itself, or at a tram or bus stop via a vending machine. It depends on the city. "Always pay" is the best advice as you never know what can happen. In Rome, for example, you must validate your ticket at the back of the bus when you board, and it is valid for 75 minutes. If you do not validate it you can end up being served with an on-the-spot fine, for which a receipt will be issued by the inspectors to the value of $100 (there goes lunch and dinner) - and they do swoop. Once, when caught in this predicament, two enterprising young Australians managed to convince the inspectors in dreadful Italian that in *their* country, tickets were validated when they left the bus, not when they got on - and were let off the fine.

What to Take

Europe for Australians, United States citizens from southern California, and anyone living below the 35th parallel, is cold and wet. Only in July and August does it approach anything like 30C (90F) degree heat. As always there is a caveat - Rome and other places on the Mediterranean in summer can be stifling. However, for almost everywhere else it means taking the following items:

A warm overcoat. As far as this is concerned, treat it as an investment for the family. Have one in the house - a great big 'Europe Coat' - so every man, woman or child can wear it when they go to Europe. Who cares what you look like as long as you are warm?;

A water and rain resistant coat including head cover - not one that is just damp resistant.

An umbrella that you can fold up.

A scarf.

A hat or beanie, preferably one that covers the ears.

A thick jumper (pullover).

A winter suit (if you are going on business).

Sturdy shoes - if you have a look at what you normally wear, they are probably thin soled leather shoes, or some sort of synthetic material that is not particularly thick. You may have to invest in a pair of thick soled shoes that will have you walking a couple of extra inches off the ground. As for pricing - check locally, and also whether they are water resistant. Then go on the web and check the cost of a similar pair of shoes in say, London or whereever your journey is going to commence. Past experience has shown that it is better to shop at home first as you may find that the shoes you want could be on special, and that they are priced according to what the local market can stand. In California, for example, the brand may be quite inexpensive because of competition, and in Australia the brand may also be inexpensive (relatively speaking) as the market will not pay any more for it, whereas in London it could be three times the amount because that is what the market can tolerate there. Shop around.

Walking shoes - a comfortable pair of well cushioned walking shoes are perfect for traversing the staggering number of cobblestone streets to be found throughout Europe. Level bitumen or beautiful soft grass is something apparently belonging only to the New World.

Socks - warm and woollen.

Gloves - indispensable.

If you are travelling throughout Europe in summer you can always dispense with the pullover and other bulky items, and wear shorts and a T-shirt instead.

Health

Fitness

It is hopeless to set off on this holiday without being in some sort of reasonable physical shape. It is a good idea to have a regular routine of physical exercise.

If you are going to be doing a lot of walking, and you should be, then before you go, walk every day or every second day for an hour or so, and do some other exercises that take care of the muscles in the back and the arms. Practice lifting by bending your knees, strengthening the muscles around you thighs, as you may have to cart your luggage for uncomfortable distances across arduous uphill terrain. Decide thoroughly what you must take and what are optional extras. Calculate the weight you will be carrying and remember: "If in doubt leave out". Younger travellers may find this a little amusing, but it is amazing how many 20 year olds suddenly find that they are out of shape and worse off than the oldies, believing that natural physique and youth will get them through. No matter what your age, if you do not do regular sport, start engaging in some regular exercise so you can develop the stamina to stay enthusiastic for the duration of your trip.

Adjusting

As far as Australians are concerned, a trip to Europe is an endurance-test just to get there. 25 hours in a plane is no fun, especially if you are not travelling business or first class. Even then, it is still something of an ordeal: change of time zones, disruption of sleeping patterns, and your tour begins the very day you arrive! After two weeks you are shuffling back onto a plane, heading home while suffering the flu and other related ailments - and this was a holiday?

Normally the adrenaline is pumping, but as you are so tired after the long flight, you will tend to sleep well on the first night. If you arrive in the day, try to stay up until nightfall and go to bed at a similar time, if not a little earlier, than is the local custom. Then the next day you should be ready for action. Force your victimised system to adjust and run on European time. That way you can take advantage of the daylight hours. This is a holiday, so the stress of a normal working day routine is temporarily absent - be vibrant, energetic, and enjoy.

Medicine

Your medicine bag should include those medicines you may not only need to take, but also what you may need.

Paracetemol. Do not assume that the local paracetemol in Germany is the same as what you get back home, you may have an allergy to one of its constituents and end up with a rash.

Tinea cream

Antiseptic

Needle

Cotton

Tissues

Tweezers

Introduction

Something for an upset stomach (One aunt of the contributors recommends half a glass of brandy followed by half a glass of port wine to cure an upset stomach).

Ear plugs, for both the plane and hotel. They are also handy if you want to go swimming.

Remember that the old inhalation method can help a fluey cold. All you need for this is a towel, boiling water and a basin. Some may wish to add eucalyptus oil. Then get a good night's sleep and maybe a day's rest if necessary.

On the Plane

Sleeping

Most airlines do not give **eye patches** to economy class passengers on long haul flights. Exceptions to this are Qantas and British Airways. So take them with you. Ask your travel agent for a pair or ask where can you purchase them. A $3 purchase will be well worth it. For sleeping on long flights, eye patches are essential, otherwise your journey will feel that much longer and whatever sleep you do get will be at best fitful.

Some people prefer to use medicinal drugs, but there are at least a couple of good reasons to avoid them and try to get some natural sleep instead. Though the trip may seem shorter because you are out of it for hours, what happens when two hours after takeoff the plane needs to divert to another destination because of a minor problem with an O ring in the starboard engine? In your sleeping-pill induced stupor you must now attempt to clamber off the plane. Then there are the very rare cases when an emergency occurs. At such times you want to be at your most alert, especially if you need to disembark quickly. And we have not even mentioned the possible side effects. So avoid pills if you can.

An extra pair of socks may come in handy. Over extended periods of inaction, when you are riveted to your seat, your feet are likely to

Gartenstrasse, Frankfurt

become targets for the plane's air-conditioning and will feel the cold most acutely. You want to preserve them for all that walking you will be doing once you touch down in Europe. Also, on a 25 hour flight, it is amazing how comfort becomes critically important among a person's priorities of survival.

Alcohol

Alcohol does not really help either. The constant air-conditioning dehydrates the body and you end up with swollen feet - try putting your shoes back on if you have not moved your feet for hours. Beer can have you running backwards and forwards to the smallest room on the plane - so if you want to have a few drinks, do your fellow passengers a favour and get a seat on the aisle.

Where to Sit

Fortunately now most airlines have a no smoking policy throughout the aircraft for long haul flights. For most travellers this development was not too soon coming. The bronchia's tend to end up less clogged on a flight where smoking is not permitted than on those with a smoking section. Watch out for this on European-owned airlines such as Iberia. Also, European airlines tend to overbook and you may be shuffled into the smoking section if there are problems with seat allocation. Or you might end up in the smoking section because all the non-smoking seats are now occupied by a group of tourists on a package tour who booked in four hours before you did. Since you only have a ruby frequent flyer card and not an emerald diamond, you will be ushered to the seat down the back next to the toilets. But you can't complain because you are lucky to have made the flight at all!

To try and avoid all this, it is best to have your seat allocated to you before you fly and make sure this is done for each leg or sector of your trip. If this cannot be achieved, try and check in early and see what the airline staff can do for you. It also helps to fly with an airline from your country of origin. They tend to realise that one benefit of accommodating you in Europe is that you might choose to fly with them domestically. After all, airlines developed frequent flyer programs precisley to give you that little extra perk which makes you feel important and persuades you to fly only with them. Use this marketing strategy to *your* advantage.

Give some consideration to where you prefer to be seated as it can contribute to being comfortable during the flight. Some people prefer to be seated in the back of the plane, others the front. The window is always the most popular. The emergency exit rows give you more leg room but you cannot spread out as the arms of the seats are fixed, whereas those in other rows can be moved up to increase your personal space. Also, in emergency exit rows luggage must be put in the overhead lockers, so you cannot have your carry-on luggage tucked into the pouch on the back of the seat in front of you for easy access. The aisle is fine as long as the person on the window or the middle does not get up too often during the flight. If you *are* stuck in the middle, politely ask the flight attendant if there is a chance you may be moved to either an aisle or a window seat. If not, console yourself with the thought that the flight will not last forever.

Airlines now advertise the pitch between the seats in economy class. Check these out, especially if you have long legs. This may determine your choice of airline, along with price, flight time to your destination, entertainment provided, and so on. Find out as much as you can about your intended airline and strive to tailor the flight to your needs.

Travel Agents

Booking on the web can be fine but certainly in the last couple of years travel agents have become much more professional - perhaps because they are competing with the web. Generally speaking they keep up-to-date by going on *famils* organised by airlines and travel wholesalers - the kinds of tour groups with whom you may end up. Some airlines see the agent as a vital link in their distribution channel. So when booking a flight or tour, the agent can put in a request for you; window seat, front of the plane, plenty of leg room, etc. An airline, if they can will, endeavour to accommodate the request. Agents can get good deals for you, sort out your wish list in half an hour and give you extra food for thought, whereas a convoluted web site may take a lot longer to navigate successfully. In addition, if you miss your flight they can put in a word for you and you may end up not having to pay a penalty fee. Remember that the web is closing in, but human contact remains alive and well.

Your Accommodation

It is important to set priorities based on your budget. For example, in Venice we are going to splurge and give the credit card a work out - $700 for one night at the Gritti, whereas in Firenze (Florence) we are content to stay in an inexpensive *pensione* not far from the *Stazione* (railway station).

The travel agent can book your accommodation for you. If you have no idea where to stay or the quality of accommodation that places offer, then get the travel agent to pursue this in detail for you. You can

Piazza Navona, Roma

give your travel agent a budget and an idea of what sort of accommodation you want, what you expect from a hotel and where you want it to be located. A couple of extra dollars for a room will be more than compensated for by location, as you may not have to use public transport to reach the places you want to visit. Indeed, you will have more time for sightseeing if you are in the city centre.

This book gives you a range of hotels that vary in quality from excellent to ordinary, but all are clean and central. You can always go on the web and check out their prices there, or fax the hotel and ask for a quote, then compare this to what your agent can get for you. One thing about accommodation - try to get a room a way from the street. Noise is a wonderful source of irritation for so many people.

Remember that you are in a foreign land that has a totally different *modus operandi*. It's time for you to go to bed and you notice the locals are just starting to head off to the restaurants. You front at a restaurant for some dinner at 7.30pm and you wonder why the place is empty and the chicken half-done. You ask for water with your lunch and they give you wine!! Well, welcome to Europe.

When you do manage to jolt your body into a mode of local assimilation and it becomes time to get some sleep, discard the eye patch and head over to the window. Many European hotels have a wonderful invention above the eaves - shutters. Pull them up to block out any sunlight. If you are someone who is used to rising with the sun and doesn't need an alarm, make sure the shutters are open or you might still be snoozing at 11am. It is a good idea to get the hotel reception to give you a wake up call - you're not here to sleep! Don't trust the alarm clock because both of you may be running on different time zones, and daylight saving may be a factor.

Web Addresses

To help with familiarising yourself with the countries you want to visit we have included web addresses of many of the official national tourism sites plus a couple of others you may find useful, such as Eurail.

Austrian National Tourist Office ☞www.austria-tourism.at
Belgian Tourism ☞www.visitbelgium.com
British Tourist Authority ☞www.bta.org.uk
Automobile Association of Great Britain ☞www.theaa.co.uk
Danish Tourism Board ☞www.visitdenmark.com
French Government Tourist Bureau ☞www.francetourism.com
German National Tourism Office ☞www.germany-tourism.de

Greek Tourism 👁www.greektourism.gr
Irish Tourist Board 👁www.itb.ie (www.ireland.travel.ie)
Italian Tourism Office 👁www.enit.it/Eng/ 👁www.christusrex.org
Netherlands Tourism 👁www.visitholland.com
Portugese Tourism 👁www.portugal-info.net
Scottish Tourist Board 👁www www.holiday.scotland.net
Tourism Office of Spain 👁www.okspain.org
Switzerland Tourism 👁www.myswitzerland.com
Vatican 👁www.vatican.va

General Sites for Europe

Rail Pass Express 👁www.eurail.com
RailEurope 👁www.raileurope.com (info and commercial)
Europe Online 👁www.europeline.com
European Travel Commission 👁www.visiteurope.com

Language

Here are some 60+ words in four major European languages which should assist basic communication and may get you out of some trouble or help you to find your way around.

Spanish

Travel

airport	*el aeropuerto*
bus	*bus*
railway station	*estación ferrocarril*
taxi	*taxi*
ticket	*un billette*

When you get there

bathroom	*cuarto de baño*
beer	*ceveza*
chair	*una silla*
credit card	*tarjeta de credito*

elevator	*ascensor*
hotel	*hotél*
how much does it cost?	*¿cuanto cuesta?*
key	*llave*
luggage	*equipaje*
my room	*mi quarto* or *mi habiacion*
restaurant	*restaurante*
street	*la calle*
table	*una mesa*
to bed	*a la cama*
toilet	*el servicio*
travel agency	*agencia de viajes*
wine	*vino*

Communicating

my name is	*mi nombre es*
excuse me please	*perdóneme por favor*
good evening	*buenos tardes*
good morning	*buenos dias*
goodbye	*adios*
hello	*hola*
I want	*yo quiero* (stronger)
I would like	*me gustaria*
I have a problem	*tengo un problema*
no	*no*
please	*por favor*
please help me	*ayudame por favor*
see you later	*hasta luego*
sorry or pardon	*perdon*
thank you	*gracias*
this afternoon	*esta tarde*
this morning	*esta manana*

tonight	esta noche
where is...?	¿donde esta...?
yes	si

Days

Monday	Lunes
Tuesday	Martes
Wednesday	Miercoles
Thursday	Jueves
Friday	Vienes
Saturday	Sabado
Sunday	Domingo

Numbers

one	uno
two	dos
three	tres
four	quartro
five	cinco
six	seis
seven	siete
eight	ocho
nine	nueve
ten	diez
eleven	once
twelve	doce
thirteen	trece
fourteen	catorce
fifteen	quince
sixteen	dieciséis
twenty	veinte
thirty	treinte

Italian

Travel

airport	*l'aereoporto*
bus	*auto*
railway station	*la stazione ferroviaria*
taxi	*taxi*
ticket	*un biglietto*

When you get there

bathroom	*il bagno*
beer	*birra*
chair	*una sedia*
credit card	*carta di credito*
elevator	*ascensore*
hotel	*un albergo*
how much does it cost?	*cuanto costa?*
key	*la chiave*
luggage	*bagaglio*
my room	*una camera*
restaurant	*un ristorante*
street	*trada*
table	*la tavola*
to bed	*a un letto*
toilet	*il gabinetto*
travel agency	*agenzia di viaggi*
wine	*vino*

Communicating

my name is...	*mi chiamo...*
excuse me please	*mi scusi* or *permesso*
good evening	*buonascera*
good morning	*buongiorno*
goodbye	*arrivederci* or *ciao*
hello	*buongiorno* or *ciao*

I want	*vorrei*
I would like	*mi piace*
I have a problem	*il problema*
no	*no*
please	*per favore*
please help me	*per favore aiutare me*
see you later	*a pùi tarde*
sorry or pardon	*mi scusi* or *mi perdone*
thank you	*grazie*
this afternoon	*cuesta pomeriggio*
this morning	*stamattina*
tonight	*stacera*
where is...?	*Do'vè...*
tes	*sì*

Days

Monday	*Lunedì*
Tuesday	*Martedì*
Wednesday	*Mercoledì*
Thursday	*Giovedì*
Friday	*Venerdì*
Saturday	*Sabato*
Sunday	*Domenica*

Numbers

one	*uno*
two	*due*
three	*tre*
four	*quattro*
five	*cinque*
six	*sei*
seven	*sette*
eight	*otto*
nine	*nove*

ten	*dieci*
eleven	*undici*
twelve	*dodici*
thirteen	*tredici*
fourteen	*quattordici*
fifteen	*quindici*
sixteen	*sedici*
twenty	*venti*
thirty	*trenta*

French

Travel

airport	*l'aéroport*
bus	*un bus*
railway station	*la gare*
taxi	*taxi*
ticket	*un billet*

When you get there

bathroom	*salle de bain*
beer	*biéres*
chair	*chaise*
credit card	*les cartes de crédir*
elevator	*ascenseur*
hotel	*un hôtel*
how much does it cost?	*combien es-cie?*
key	*la clé*
luggage	*les bagages*
my room	*je suis chambre*
restaurant	*le ristorante*
street	*la rue*
table	*la table*
to bed	*se coucher*

toilet	les toilettes
travel agency	une agence de voyage
wine	vin

Communicating

my name is...	je m'appelle...
excuse me please	excusez-moi
good evening	bonsoir
good morning	bonjour
goodbye	au revoir
hello	bonjour
I would like...	je voudrais...
I have a problem	un probléme
no	no
please	s'il vous plaît
please help me	pouvez-vous n'aider?
see you later	a bientôt
sorry or pardon	pardon
thank you (very much)	merci (beaucoup)
this afternoon	ceci aprés-midi
this morning	ceci matin
tonight	ce soir
where is...?	où est...
yes	oui

Days

Monday	Lundi
Tuesday	Mardi
Wednesday	Mercredi
Thursday	Jeudi
Friday	Vendredi
Saturday	Samedi
Sunday	Dimanche

Introduction

Numbers

one	*un*
two	*deux*
three	*trois*
four	*quartre*
five	*cinq*
six	*six*
seven	*sept*
eight	*huit*
nine	*neuf*
ten	*dix*
eleven	*onze*
twelve	*douze*
thirteen	*treize*
fourteen	*quatorze*
fifteen	*quinze*
sixteen	*seize*
twenty	*vingt*
thirty	*trente*

German

Travel

airport	*flughafen*
bus	*bus*
railway station	*bahnhof*
taxi	*taxi*
ticket	*fahrkarte*

When you get there

bathroom	*baderzimmer*
beer	*bier*
chair	*sthul*
credit card	*kreditkarte*
elevator	*lift*

hotel	*hotel*
how much does it cost?	*wieviel kostet es?*
key	*schlüssel*
luggage	*gepäck*
my room	*ein zimmer*
restaurant	*ein restaurant, ein gaststätte*
street	*strasse*
table	*tisch*
to bed	*zo bett*
toilet	*toilette*
travel agency	*reisbüro*
wine	*wein*

Communicating

my name is...	*ich heisse..., mein name ist...*
excuse me please	*entschuldigung*
good evening	*guten abend*
good morning	*guten morgen*
goodbye	*auf wiedersehen*
hello	*guten tag, hallo*
I want	*Ich möchte*
I've a problem	*Ich habe problem*
no	*nein*
please	*bitte*
please help me	*bitte helfen*
sorry or pardon	*entschuldigung*
thank you	*danke*
this afternoon	*heute tag*
this morning	*heute morgen*
tonight	*heute abend*
where is...?	*wo ist...*
yes	*ja*

Introduction

Days

Monday	*Montag*
Tuesday	*Dienstag*
Wednesday	*Mittwoch*
Thursday	*Donnerstag*
Friday	*Freitag*
Saturday	*Samstag*
Sunday	*Sonntag*

Numbers

one	*ein*
two	*zwei*
three	*drei*
four	*vier*
five	*fünf*
six	*sechs*
seven	*sieben*
eight	*acht*
nine	*neun*
ten	*zehn*
eleven	*elf*
twelve	*zwölf*
thirteen	*dreizehn*
fourteen	*vierzehn*
fifteen	*fünfzehn*
sixteen	*sechzehn*
twenty	*zwanzig*
thirty	*dreissig*

European Time Zones

City	Hours from AEST	from GMT	from NY time
Amsterdam	-10	+1	+6
Athens	-9	+2	+7
Barcelona	-10	+1	+6
Berlin	-10	+1	+6
Brussels	-10	+1	+6
Copenhagen	-10	+1	+6
Dublin	-11	+0	+7
Frankfurt	-10	+1	+6
Lisbon	-11	0	+7
London	-11	0	+5
Madrid	-10	+1	+6
Manchester	-11	0	+5
Paris	-10	+1	+6
Rome	-10	+1	+6
Venice	-10	+1	+6
Vienna	-10	+1	+6
Zurich	-10	+1	+6

Clothing Sizes And Conversion Chart

Women's Clothing

Coats, Skirts, Dresses, Slacks, Jerseys, Pullovers

Aust/NZ	8	10	12	14	16	18
Europe	38	40	42	44	46	48
UK	8	10	12	14	16	18
USA	6	8	10	12	14	16

Shoes

Aust/NZ	4	5	$5^{1/2}$	6	$6^{1/2}$	7	$7^{1/2}$	8	$8^{1/2}$	9	$9^{1/2}$	10
Europe	34	36	37	37	38	38	39	40	40	41	41	-
UK	3	$3^{1/2}$	4	$4^{1/2}$	5	$5^{1/2}$	6	$6^{1/2}$	7	$7^{1/2}$	8	$8^{1/2}$
USA	$4^{1/2}$	5	$5^{1/2}$	6	$6^{1/2}$	7	$7^{1/2}$	8	$8^{1/2}$	9	$9^{1/2}$	10

Introduction

Men's Clothing

Suits, Coats, Trousers, Jerseys, Pullovers

Aust/NZ	14	16	18	20	22	24
Europe	46	48	50	52	54	56
UK	36	38	40	42	44	46
USA	36	38	40	42	44	46

Shirts (Collar Sizes)

Aust/NZ	15	$15^{1/2}$	16	$16^{1/2}$	17	$17^{1/2}$
Europe (cm)	38	39	41	42	43	44
UK	15	$15^{1/2}$	16	$16^{1/2}$	17	$17^{1/2}$
USA	15	$15^{1/2}$	16	$16^{1/2}$	17	$17^{1/2}$

Shoes

Aust/NZ	8	9	10	11	12	13
Europe	42	43	44	46	47	48
UK	8	9	10	11	12	13
USA	$8^{1/2}$	$9^{1/2}$	$10^{1/2}$	$11^{1/2}$	$12^{1/2}$	$13^{1/2}$

European Behaviour

Good manners have common characteristics wherever you go. Every European country has its own culture and mannerisms and the visiting traveller should respect them.

If we may be permitted to indulge in sweeping generalisations - distilling years of travel and conversational opinions - one could say the following about Europeans. The British are usually polite but can sometimes be perceived as being unpersonable. Certain travellers may mistake this aloofness for rudeness. The French are flamboyant, proud and individualistic. Those in Paris can give the impression of being tired of visitors, whereas as in Rome you have more chance of encountering charming and patient individuals. The Italians are charismatic, smart, wear their wealth on their back and make a fortune off the rest of us. The Spaniards are earthy, tough and helpful to travellers, though their police can sometimes be rather unpleasant. The Germans are sentimental, resourceful and exceedingly organised.

These are of course personal observations and you will always find exceptions. They can be treated as a taste of what you might expect, but the best advice when confronted with a new social situation is to ask and thank and learn.

Tipping

Generally speaking the cost of services involves a 10% tip to be added to the bill. Where a service charge is already imposed, there is no need to leave a tip unless the service is exceptional. With taxis one normally rounds the fare up to the next 50p or pound (£) in the UK or 1,000Lire in Rome.

Cameras and Film

For travellers to Europe it is normally far cheaper to buy the film at your favorite camera shop duty free and have all the films processed when you return home. X-ray security machines in airports can be damage photo film when it travels through them, if the film is exposed to this treatment too often on your trip. Better to keep the film roll tucked safely away in its little cylinder. One suggestion is to put all your film in a plastic bag and have it passed through the security check outside the machine.

Be sure to take spare batteries, since the duration of your trip and the fact that you can't remember when you last replaced them may mean a camera dies on you at the most inappropriate sightseeing time.

Mail and Contacting Home

The best way these days to let everyone at home now how your trip is progressing is to get an email address on a free email service such as

Yahoo or Hotmail. Teach those in your family who don't know how to access emails before you leave. Addresses can be accessed in any cyber cafe - and there are plenty in Europe. Or you may be staying with family or friends who are hooked up to the web.

Phone cards are an alternative that allows you to cap the cost of your calls and control your expenditures. VISA has a system which utilises access through a phone company and all you need is to find a public phone.

You can send mail care of an American Express office as long as the recipient has an AMEX card. You should check if they accept parcels. American Express offices will hold the mail for 30 days and this service is free. For most post offices the service is free also, though there may be a holding fee of a couple of dollars in some countries. If you are sending material or having it sent make sure the sender puts a return address on the letter or parcel.

Post offices also have the same system the world over. Just include as much information as possible on the parcel/package/postcard that your are sending.

Keeping Up-To-Date

Please note that because some places close and others open quite frequently, we would greatly appreciate hearing about it. Travel information must always be updated, developed and improved, so if over time any facts in this book have become incorrect, please let us know about it to help make your next Little Hills Press guide book accurate.

Have a great trip. We hope our guide enhances your European experience.

Introduction

PART TWO

Austria

L AND-LOCKED AUSTRIA is situated in Central Europe and has an area of 83,849 sq km. It is a democratic federal republic of nine provinces, with a total population of 8,000,000. The capital is Vienna, where approximately a fifth of the population live, and the language of the country is German.

Austria is very mountainous with peaks reaching up to 3800m. It is a popular skiing venue with snow from January to the end of April in some parts.

Climate

Austria has a moderate climate, temperatures varying according to altitude. Generally winter extends from December to March, and average temperatures are 24C in July and 1C in January.

Entry Regulations

Visitors must have a valid passport, but a visa is not required for visits of up to three months (six months for holders of European passports).

The duty free allowance for travellers over 17 years of age from non-European countries is 200 cigarettes or 50 cigars or 250 grams of tobacco, 2 litres of wine and 1 litre of spirits. The tobacco allowance for travellers from European countries is 400 cigarettes or 100 cigars or 500 grams of tobacco. Non-Europeans are entitled to these if they have *stayed* in Europe prior to travelling to Austria. Changing planes or spending time in a transit lounge does not count as a stay.

There is no restriction on the import or export of local or foreign currencies. No vaccinations are required for any international traveller.

Currency

The currency of the land is the Austrian Schilling (AS), which is divided into 100 Groschen. Approximate exchange rates, which should be used as a guide only, are as follows.

A$	=	8.50AS
Can$	=	10.00AS
NZ$	=	6.82AS
S$	=	8.75AS
UK£	=	22.35AS
US$	=	14.73AS
Euro	=	13.76AS

Notes are in denominations of 5000, 1000, 500, 100, 50 and 20 Schillings, and coins are 20, 10, 5 and 1 Schillings, and 50 and 10 Groschen.

From 1 January 2001, the official currency will be the Euro (E), and to facilitate the changeover prices have been in both currencies since 1999.

Shopping

Banks are generally ⊙open 8am-12.30pm, 1.30-3pm Mon, Tues, Wed and Fri, 8am-12.30pm, 1.30-5.30pm Thurs. All banks are closed Sat and Sun. Exchange counters at airports and the main railway stations are usually ⊙open 8am-8pm (Vienna until 10pm) daily.

Shopping hours are ⊙Mon-Fri 8am-6pm, Sat 8am-1pm, although many stay open until 5pm. Many shops close for two hours in the middle of the day.

Credit cards are widely accepted in the major cities, but not in the smaller towns even at petrol stations.

Telephone

International direct dialling is available and the International code is 00, the country code 43. The area code for Vienna is 01 or 09, that for Salzburg is 0662. Payphones have slots that take 1, 5, 10 and 20 schilling coins, and an audible tone warns that time is running out.

It is expensive to make international calls from hotels, particularly in Vienna where there is often a surcharge of 200% of the cost of the call.

Driving

An International Driving Licence is necessary to hire a car, and third party insurance is obligatory. It is compulsory to wear a seat-belt, and children under 12 years of age are not permitted in front seats.

Speed limits are:

Cars

built-up areas	-	50kph
open roads	-	100kph
motorways	-	130kph

Cars with Trailer over 750kg

open roads	-	60kph
motorways	-	70kph

You should expect to pay tolls on expressways, multi-lane highways and city highways.

Miscellaneous

Local time is GMT + 1 (Central European Time) with daylight saving in force from late March to late September.

Electricity - 220v AC, with round, two-pin plugs.

Health - Austria has good health services but they are very expensive. It is recommended that visitors have adequate medical insurance.

Sales Tax (VAT) - Citizens of non-European countries who purchase goods in excess of AS1000 in one store at one time can apply for a refund of the VAT they paid. Ask the shopkeeper to complete the tax-free cheque form, and present it, along with the merchandise, to customs officials upon leaving the country by air or by car and travelling into a country that is not part of the European Union. People travelling by train should send their purchases as registered luggage, then the customs clerk at the railway station at point of departure will validate the tax-free cheque. More information can be obtained at any Tourist Information Office.

Vienna

Gateway to eastern Europe and capital of Austria, Vienna (Wien) lies on the banks of the Danube, near the borders of Hungary, Slovakia and Czechia.

It is very much a city of music, having been home to such composers as Mozart, Bruckner, Beethoven, Schubert, Brahms, Haydn and Johann Strauss.

History

The site of Vienna was occupied by the Celts long before the birth of Christ, and it was known to have been a Roman military camp called Vindobona in the year 1AD.

In 1155, the Babenbergs, the first dynasty to reign over Austria, chose Vienna as their residence. During the reigns of Leopold V and Leopold VI, the city underwent considerable expansion, financed in part by the ransom the English were forced to pay the Babenbergs for the return of their captured King Richard the Lionheart.

Rudolf I of Habsburg took control of Austria after victory in the Battle of Durnkrut in 1278, but the people were not too thrilled about him and subsequently rebelled. However, it is the Habsburgs that Vienna has to thank for her reputation as one of the great cities of the world - particularly Charles VI and Maria Theresia in the 18th century and Francis Joseph in the 19th.

Tourist Information

Tourist information offices are located at 38 Karntner Strasse (Opera House), and 40 Obere Augarten Strasse, ✆(01) 211 14-222, fax (01) 216 84 92 (👁www.info.wien.at).

Local Transport

Vienna has an excellent public transport system. The U-Bahn (underground railway) has three lines, and there are bus, trolley and rail services to all parts of the city.

For an interesting way to visit the old parts of the city, hire a *fiaker* and listen to the driver's tales of Viennese life in olden days. Allow plenty of time.

Worth looking into is **The Vienna Card (Die Wien Karte)** which costs ◐AS210 and offers 72 hours travel on the underground, buses or trams, reduced entry fees to several attractions, and discounts on guided tours, shopping, and meals in certain cafes, taverns and restaurants. The Card is available at most hotels, Transport and Information Offices, or outside Vienna with credit card by phone ✆43-1-798 44 00-28.

Accommodation

Following is a small selection of hotels in Vienna, with prices for a double room per night, which should be used as a guide only. The telephone area code is 01.

City, Bauernmarkt 10, 1010 Wien, ✆01/533 9521, fax 01/535 5216. A pension on the third floor of the building which offers 19 plainly

DETAIL OF THE PUBLIC TRANSPORT SYSTEM OF VIENNA

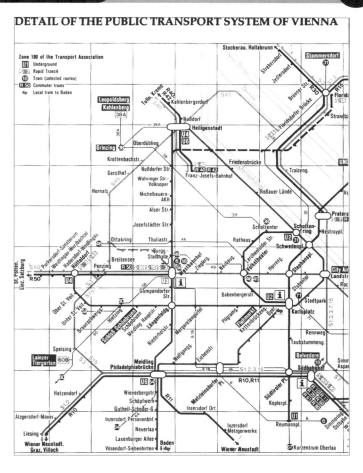

furnished rooms well located in the old part of the city. All you can eat breakfast included in the price of the room. Cheaper in winter - ✪from 990S.

Kugel, Siebensterngasse 43/Neubaugasse 46, 1070 Wien, ✆01/523 3355, fax 01/523 3355. A run down family owned hotel of 38 rooms located just to the west of the ring (old city). Continental breakfast included in the price of the room, but no credit cards are accepted - ✪780S.

Hotel Karntnerhof, Grashofgasse 4, A-1010 Vienna, ✆01/512 1923, fax 01/513 22 28 33. A comfortable small hotel advertising itself as family friendly and located a few minutes walk from the cathedral. 44 rooms, some available without private bathroom for a substantial saving (double without bathroom ✪860S). Breakfast is included - ✪1,720S.

Hotel Cryston, Gaudenzdorfer Gürtel 65, (✉cryston@hotels.or.at). 3-star hotel with individually furnished rooms. Centrally located, close to public transport and a short trip to the Ring and the Old Town - ✪990AS (73E).

Hotel Royal, Singerstrasse 3, A-1010 Vienna, ✆01/51 568, fax 01/513 9698. A pleasant hotel furnished with reproduction antiques, good-sized rooms and all the comforts of a decent, though not expensive hotel. St Stephens Cathedral is nearby and some rooms have views overlooking it - ✪from 1,600S.

Hotel Schneider, Getreidemarkt 5, A-1060 Vienna, ✆01/588 380, fax 01/588 38 212. A good choice for families as suites contain kitchenettes. The hotel is well appointed, tastefully decorated and centrally located. A buffet breakfast is included - ✪from 1,750S.

Hilton Vienna, Am Stadtpark, ✆717 00-0, fax 713 06 91 (✉rm_vienna@hilton.com). A deluxe hotel in the downtown area. Facilities include restaurants, bars, coffee shop, health club and shops - ✪3100-3700AS (225-268E).

Holiday Inn Crowne Plaza Vienna, Handelskai 269, ✆727 77, fax 727 77-199 (✉crowneplaza@aon.at). A superior first class hotel. Facilities include restaurants, bars, coffee shop, health club, sauna and shops - ✪1970-2550AS (144-185E).

Parkhotel Schoenbrunn, Hietzinger Hauptstrasse 10-20, ✆878 04, fax 878 04-3220 (✉ parkhotel.schoenbrunn@austria-trend.at). A first class hotel in the midtown area. Facilities include restaurants, bars, coffee shop, health club, swimming pool, shops and a beauty salon - ✪1700-2950AS (124-215E).

> **Hof Hotel Wien**
>
> Kulmgasse 22, 1-488-05, (fax) 1-488-05-8 (✉ hof@hotels.or.at). This modern 4-star hotel is located between the Schonbrunn Palace and Grinzing - ✪1590 (116E).

For those on a budget there are the following **Youth Hostels**:

Jugendgasterhaus Wien Brigittenau, Friedrich Engelsplatz 24, ✆(1) 330 0598, fax (1) 330 8379.

Jugendherberge Wien, Myrthengasse 7, Neustiftgasse 85, ✆(1) 523 63160, fax (1) 523 5849.

Hostel Ruthensteiner, Robert Hameringgasse 24, ✆(1) 893 4202, fax (1) 893 2796 (✉ hostel.ruthensteiner@telecom.at).

Food and Drink

The most famous dish from this city is Wiener Schnitzel, but there are many more national dishes to tempt the taste buds, including various types of sausage.

Any stay in Vienna should include a visit to a Coffee House, and one of the best known is **Sacher**, Philharmonikerstrasse 4, ✆51 456-0 (✉ hotel@sacher.com), home of the Sachertorte that has found its way onto menus all over the world. The Sacher is ☉open daily 5pm-midnight.

Your hotel, or the Tourist Information Office, can provide you with a booklet listing over 100 coffee houses in the city, and you are sure to find something that appeals.

In the suburbs of Grinzing, Sioevering, Heiligenstadt and Nussdorf, a cluster of fir twigs hanging above the door of an inn means that the year's wine is ready to be enjoyed. These are known as Heurigen localities, and the wine can only be from the innkeeper's own vineyards. There is also Heurigen music to accompany the wine and food, and it usually consists of a quartet of two violins, an accordion and a guitar, who play traditional Schrammel tunes. It is great fun, and very popular with the locals.

Sightseeing

The Ring is an avenue that was created after the city wall was removed in 1857. It has several names as it circles the old city - Schotten Ring, Dr Karl Lueger Ring, Dr Karl Renner Ring, and so on.

The **Stock Exchange** is on Schotten Ring, and to the south are the main buildings of the **University**, the new Gothic **Rathaus** (Town Hall - guided tours available), and opposite is the famous **Burg Theatre** (Palace Theatre - guided tours available).

To the south is the much-loved **Volksgarten** (people's gardens) with the **Theseus Temple**. On the other side of the Ring is **Parliament House**, which is built like a Greek temple. In front of the building is a monumental fountain topped by a 14m statue of Pallas Athene, and the poles on each side of the fountain fly flags when parliament is sitting. When there are no flags guided tours are available. It is a very photogenic building. Next are the **Alte Hofburg** and the **Neue Hofburg** (Old and New Imperial Palaces) on Helden Platz, the seat of the Habsburg family and centre of a world empire. Nowadays they are open to the public and contain the **National Library** and the **Ethnological Museum**.

In Michaeler Platz, in the direction of the city, is the **Looshaus** and unsurpassed views of the sprawling Old Hofburg. Also in the Hofburg is the world famous **Spanish Riding School** whose Lipizzaner horses have morning work-outs ☉late Feb-June, Sept-Dec (10am), and tickets are available at the entrance. At the end of the Hofburg is the **Albertina** which houses the world's largest collection of graphic arts. Near here in Philharmoniker Strasse is the famous **Hotel Sacher** which sells the original Sacher's Torte.

Turn left and walk along Neuer Markt to the **Kapuziner Church** and the **Habsburg Crypt**, which contains the sarcophagi of 147 members of the royal family, including twelve emperors and sixteen empresses. The tomb of the beloved Maria Theresia is considered by some to be one of the most beautiful examples of rococo art.

Go through the **Burgtor** (gate) and cross the Ring to the **Natural History Museum** and **Museum of Fine Arts**, both of which started off with the emperors' collections. In the middle of the park between the two buildings is the **Maria Theresia** memorial. Along the Opern Ring behind the New Hofburg are the Hofburg Gardens which have many memorials: Emperor Franz Joseph, Mozart, Goethe and others.

From here it is just a short walk to the **Opera House** the first of the monumental buildings erected on the Ring. Although it is very much the centre of cultural life in Vienna, it was not well received either during its construction or upon its completion. Built in the French Renaissance style, people likened it to a railway station and made other derogatory statements to the point where one of the architects committed suicide. The opera house opened on May 25, 1869, with a presentation of Mozart's *Don Giovanni*. Guided tours are available.

Following Karntner Strasse from the Opera House towards St Stephen's Cathedral, the main shopping area is on the left, and it stretches past Neuer Markt to Kohl-markt. The streets here are pedestrian malls, and contain a wide variety of shops from up-market boutiques to souvenir stalls. There are also many coffee shops and restaurants.

St Stephen's Cathedral was originally consecrated in 1147, and was a Romanesque structure. The Gothic reconstruction commenced in 1304, and was consecrated 36 years later. At the end of the 16th century a Renaissance-style octagonal capped roof and a belfry were added. It is one of the great churches of Europe and well worth a visit.

Sights Further Afield

The **Belvedere Palace** is situated on a rise south of the city centre. It was built for Prince Eugene of Savoy at the beginning of the 18th century, and is a masterpiece of sophisticated Baroque architecture. Prince Eugene played a major part in Vienna's liberation from the Turks, and consequently became very popular with the Emperor and the local people. The Emperor had the Belvedere built in gratitude, and the local people made sure the Prince kept control of the army when he was threatened with dismissal.

The State Treaty that released Austria from its 10 years of occupation by the four Allied powers was signed in the Belvedere Palace on May 15, 1955. The upper belvedere can be reached from Prinz Eugen Strasse and the Gurtel, and it has a gallery of 19th and 20th century paintings, including works by Gustav Klimt and Egon Schiele. (☉Open Tues-Sun 10am-5pm, ☎795 57-134). The lower belvedere is off the Rennweg. There you will find a museum of medieval and baroque art.

The **Schonbrunn Palace** is on the west side of the city, and is one of Vienna's most famous sights. The name means 'beautiful fountains' after those that were built over the natural springs in the 17th century, when the Emperor Matthias had his hunting lodge on the site. The

lodge was burnt down by the Turks in 1863, and Leopold I decided to build a new summer residence for his family. The Gloriette (triumphal arches) was completed in 1775, and was used in those days for innumerable social events.

The palace was the favourite residence of Maria Theresia, whose daughter Marie Antoinette, of French Revolution fame, spent her childhood here. Mozart performed here for the Empress at the age of six. Napoleon had his headquarters here in the early 1800s, and his son, whose mother was Archduchess Marie-Louise, was raised here by his grandfather Emperor Franz. Emperor Franz Josef was born here and died here, after 68 years on the throne, and it was at Schonbrunn that Emperor Karl I abdicated, bringing an end to 636 years of Habsburg rule.

Today 40 rooms of the palace are open to the public and are not to be missed. Allow plenty of time for a visit as there is so much to take in, and time is needed to wander through the gardens, and visit the Gloriette for a magnificent view of the city.

Austria

The Best of Vienna in Brief

Hofburg Palace. The winter home of the Habsburgs has 2,600 rooms and an amazing history of survival since its construction in 1279. Within the complex is the famous Spanish Riding School with their Lippizaner stallions.

Museum of Fine Arts (Kunsthistorisches Museum). Displays the stunning art collection amassed by the Habsburg family along with additional ancient and classical peices. *Maria-Theresien-Platz, Burgring 5.*

Augustinian Church (Augustinerkirche). Built in the 14th century, this church was the venue for imperial weddings. Its architecture underwent a reverse transformation from baroque back to its original gothic style. *Augustinerstrasse 3.*

Lipizzaner Museum. The Spanish Riding School in Vienna attracts hundreds of thousands of visitors each year who marvel at the classic equestrian skills (dating back four hundred years) of the riders and their steeds. Visit the Lipizzaner Museum in the Renaissance building to see its collection of uniforms and paintings which trace the history of the horses. Then move on to the stables themselves. *Reitschulgasse 2.*

Kaisergruft. This crypt contains 147 bodies from the Habsburg family, with details of the family tree and tombs with intruiging artwork. *Neuer Markt.*

Vienna Boys' Choir. Perform during the Sunday morning mass at the Palace Chapel (Die Burgkapelle) in Hofburg.

Opera (Staatsoper). An inherent part of Vienna's history and culture. Each year there are over 300 performances here, offering plenty of opportunties for you to immerse yourself in the atmosphere. *Opernring 2.*

St. Stephan's Cathedral (Dompfarre St. Stephan). A magnificent restored gothic building with a 450-foot-high steeple. *Stephansplatz 1.*

Carinthia Street (Karntnerstrasse). This pedestrian street is known for its shopping and sidewalk entertaiment.

The Danube. Seeing the river on a cruise or while cycling leisurely along its shores are two relaxing delights.

Academy of Fine Arts (Gemaldegalerie Akademie der Bildenden Kunste). Houses Bosch's *Last Judgement* and works by Botticelli and Rembrandt. *Schillerplatz 3.*

Wine Tasting. Vienna Woods is the place to sample the freshly-produced wines from the *heurigen* (wine taverns) dotted across the vineyards overlooking the Danube Valley.

Schonbrunn Palace. Summer residence of the Habsburgs whose stunning architecture and interior decoration rivals but does not quite surpass Versailles. *Schonbrunner Schlosstrasse.*

Salzburg

The beautiful city of Salzburg is the capital of the province of the same name, and has a population of 145,000. The picturesque Salzach River flows through the centre of the city, which is famous as the birthplace of the composer Wolfgang Amadeus Mozart. It also was the location for the movie classic *The Sound of Music*, as the Trapp family were residents of Salzburg.

The old town is on the left side of the Salzach, dominated by the Fortress Hohensalzburg; the new town on the right of the river nestles beneath the Kapuzinerberg (the Capuchin monastery/fortress).

History

Historians agree that parts of Salzburg were inhabited as far back as 3000 BC. At various times during its history the town was home to Illyrians, Celts, and then Romans, who called it Juvavum. The town became an important trade centre, and was raised by the Romans to the status of a municipium, but during the migration of Germanic tribes, the settlement was destroyed.

It was the 7th century that saw the beginnings of today's city, when Bishop Rupertus founded the Benedictine monastery of St Peter,

View of the Alstadt (Old Town)

which became the seat of the bishops, later archbishops, for many centuries. The first cathedral was erected by Bishop Virgil in the 8th century, and work on the present cathedral began in 1614 under Archbishop Markus Sitticus.

This religious importance has resulted in a wealth of ecclesiastic architecture, as well as palaces, museums and many interesting period houses.

Tourist Information

The information office is in Mozartplatz, and has all the information, maps, brochures, etc, that are available, ✆(662) 889 87-330 (👁www.salzburginfo.or.at)

Local Transport

The city has a good public transport system, but for the visitor walking tours are the way to go. If you run out of energy in the old city, continue your tour in a fiaker (horse-drawn cab). Their starting point is in the Residenzplatz.

Accommodation

Following is a small selection of accommodation venues, with prices for a double room per night, which should be used as a guide only. Usually a continental breakfast is included in the room rates. The telephone area code is 662.

Kobenzi-Vitalhotel, Am Gaisberg 11, ✆641 510, fax 642 238 (✎info@hotel-kobenzi.co.at). A superior first class hotel in the midtown area. Facilities include restaurant, bar, health club, swimming pool, shops and beauty salon - ✪2200-5900AS.

Stadtkrug, Linzer Gasse 20, ✆873 545, fax 873 545-54 (✎lucian@ping.at). A first class hotel in the midtown area. Facilities include restaurant, bar and swimming pool - ✪1600-2450AS.

Markus Sittikus, Markus-Sittikus-Strasse 20, ✆871 121-0, fax 871 121-58 (✎markus-sittikus@austria.at). A medium range hotel in the midtown area - ✪980-1400AS.

Lechner, Rainerstrasse 11, ✆872 740, fax 879 380. A budget hotel, but close to most things - ✪880-990AUS.

There are several **Youth Hostels** in Salzburg:
Jugendgastehaus Salzburg, Josef-Preis Allee 18, ✆842 6700, fax 841 101 (✎oejhv-sbg-jgh-nonntal@oejhv.or.at).
Eduard-Heinrich Haus, Eduard Heinrich Strasse 2, ✆625 976, fax 627 980.
Haunspergstrasse, Haunspergstrasse 27, ✆875 030, fax 883 477.

Food and Drink

Coffee houses and restaurants abound in Salzburg, especially along the banks of the Salzach. The city even has its own special dish - Salzburger Nockerin which translates roughly as 'souffle style of Salzburg'. It is lemon-flavoured and delicious.

Austria

Sightseeing

A walking tour of the old city begins at the information office in Mozartplatz.

The platz has a large statue of Mozart, but apparently it is not true to life because his sons were not too impressed with the likeness when it was unveiled in 1842. The tour then winds its way to the **Alter Markt** (old market), a photogenic square formed by old houses that is home to: **St Florian's Fountain**; the **Smallest House of Salzburg**, now owned by an optician; **Cafe Tomaselli** (1703) the oldest coffee house in the city; and possibly a few stalls reminiscent of the square's original function.

The tour then enters the pedestrian Getreidegasse and passes the **old town hall** (1407), a suitably chastened McDonald's sign, and **burghers' houses** from the 15th to 18th centuries. Many little lanes and alleys run of the street near this section, and they contain interesting shops and coffee houses. Also note in this street and many others in the old city, the hanging shingles outside the buildings. These are mostly descriptive of the profession or trade of the owner, and were designed before most people could read and write. Some of them are quite amusing.

The most visited house on Getreidegasse is no. 9, **Mozart Geburtshaus**, where Mozart was born on January 27, 1756, and lived

until 1763. The house now contains a museum of Mozart memorabilia, including his childhood violin, many other instruments that he played, letters, manuscripts and more - very interesting. Salzburg is very proud of

Mozart and has several yearly events that celebrate his music - Mozart Week in late January, festivals at Easter and through all of August, and the famous Salzburger Kulturtage in October.

Continuing to the right at the end of Getreidegasse brings you to **Anton-Neumayr Platz**, where there is a statue of the Virgin Mary dating from 1691. On the left is the **Monchsberg lift**, which ascends inside the rock to a terrace that offers a fantastic view over the city. It is also the entrance to the **Cafe Winkler** and its gambling casino.

Next on the tour is Museumplatz, where there are a couple of museums, then around the corner is **St Mark's church** (1699). Follow the map for a few twists and turns then stop at the traffic lights on Sigmundsplatz to admire the **Horse-Pond**. The paintings on the rear wall were restored in 1916, but the main attraction is the *Horse Tamer* which was sculpted by Michael Bernhard Mandl in 1695.

The walk then visits Universitatsplatz, where there is a food market every day except Sunday, and the **Church of the Immaculata** (1707), which has to be one of the most beautiful Baroque churches. Follow directions to the Hofstallgasse and there is the **Festspielhaus** (playhouse), which is actually two playhouses, the new containing a 2000+ auditorium, and the old seating 1300 people. Nearby is the open galleried theatre that was the venue for tournaments and animal baiting in the olden days. Continue on into Franciskanergasse to the **Franciscan Church**, consecrated in 1223, and well worth a look-see. Exit by the south door and walk under an arch into the courtyard of **St Peter's Abbey**, founded in 690 by St Rupert. Be prepared now to be overwhelmed and educated as you wander from church to tomb to chapel, to cemetery to mausoleum, ending at **St Margaret's Chapel** with its beautifully cared-for graves.

Next stop is the **Hohensalzburg fortress** (1077) which can be reached by taking the funicular from its lower station in Festungsgasse. There are great panoramic views of the city from the fortress, but there are also interesting guided tours available that include the state apartments, the cells and torture chamber, and the fortress and Rainer museums.

The **Cathedral** (Dom) is in Domplatz and can seat 10,000 people. There have been several cathedrals on this site, and the present church was consecrated in 1628. The dome was completely destroyed and the interior badly damaged during World War II, so it was restored and reconsecrated in 1959. Its bells are the largest in Europe. The cathedral has much for those interested in art and sculpture, and there is a museum that was inaugurated on the 1200th anniversary of the cathedral that has an unusual collection of religious memorabilia. Heading now towards the **Residenzplatz**, watch out for the **Excavations Museum** which has artifacts found on the cathedral site that range from early Roman times to the Middle Ages.

Residenzplatz is the largest of Salzburg's squares and it contains the largest baroque fountain in the world. It is also home to the **Residence**, completed in 1619 and the seat of the archbishops until 1803. Conducted tours are offered and it is the best way to view the place. The building contains some wonderful works of art.

On the other side of the square is the **New Residence**, erected in 1602. It has the **Glockenspiel Tower** which plays works by Mozart every day at ☉7am, 11am and 6pm.

The only place left on this walking tour is **St Michael's Church** on the north side of Residenzplatz. It dates from the year 800 and is the oldest parish church in the city.

It might be a good idea to take time out now to enjoy a stroll along the river before crossing one of the bridges over the Salzach to the new town.

First stop is the **Mirabell gardens**, which are very formally laid out and include a large fountain with sculptures that are supposed to represent the four elements. At one end of the gardens stands what's left of the **Schloss Mirabell**, which was mostly destroyed by fire in 1818.

In the Makartplatz is the **Landestheater**; next door is the **Salzburg Marionette Theatre**; adjacent is the **Mozarteum**, an international music academy; outshining them all is the **Church of the Holy Trinity**; and just off the square in Theatergasse is the **Cafe Bazar**, which is a popular artists' haunt. There are two more churches in this area - **St Sebastian's** in the Linzergasse, and the **Loreto Church** in Paris-Lodron Strasse.

Finally, there is the **Capuchin Monastery**, and a magnificent panoramic view is available from the bastion below the monastery.

The Best of Salzburg in Brief

Mozart's Birthplace (Mozart Gerburtshaus). Home of the Mozart family, containing valuable art and instruments used by the young musical genius. *Getreidegasse 9*.

Mozart Residence (Mozart Wohnhaus). The original house was destroyed during WWII and this replica was built and opened as a musem in 1996. It is the place to go for a complete record of Mozart's life and work. *Makartplatz 8*.

Salzburg Cathedral. One of Salzburg's gems, this 17th century marvel presents an unmatched testament to Renaissance architecture, with a baroque interior that takes in the best of this style. The cathedral's organ has no fewer than four thousand pipes. *Residenzplatz, south*.

Stiftskirche St. Peter. Another church crafted in the baroque style, this former Romanesque basilica contains a wealth of art. *St-Peter-Bezirk*.

Glockenspiel. Head into Mozartplatz to hear the 35 bells of this carillon ring out their tunes three times daily. *Mozartplatz 1*.

Mirabell Gardens. A combination of natural features and man-made figures carefully arranged by Fischer von Erlach spread across this public park. *Off Markatplatz*.

Part of the Mirabell Gardens

Mirabell Palace (Shloss Mirabell). After all the architectual changes that have been made in rebuilding the palace, not much of the original is left to appreciate. *Mirabell Square*.

Getreidegasse. This is the expensive but visually-attractive shopping district of Salzburg.

Residenz. Apart from its rich and fabulous State rooms, this old palace of the Archbishops is famous for its large and lavish baroque fountain and for the fact that Mozart often entertained guests here with his music. *Residenzplatz 1*.

Museum Carolino Augusteum. An interesting collection of various pieces spanning archaelogical rarities to Romantic-period paintings. *Museumplatz 1*.

Sound of Music Tour. Filmed on location, this classic film brought some of Austria's best scenery to the silver screen. Popular tours take you to all the sites - from the mansion to the gazebo - which have been burnt into your memory by endless re-runs.

Monchsberg. Good views back over Salzburg can be enjoyed from this natural ridge bearing old defence fortifications.

Hohensalzburg Fortress. Complete construction of this impregnable stronghold took a staggering 604 years. The castle is still preserved in its entirety. Highlights include the medieval art, the torture chamber, the residential quarters of the Archbishops, and the best views over Salzburg, which on a clear day stretch all the way to the Alps. *Monchsberg 34*.

Driving Through Austria

A Scenic Tour of Austria by Road

Itinerary - 7 Days - Distance 760kms

Enter from Switzerland at **Feldkirch**, with its medieval market square. From the west to get to the rest of the country, travel through the **Alberg**. You can take the toll tunnel or drive over the pass to **St Anton**. In winter this is one of the world's top ski areas, in summer a delightful holiday centre. Travelling further east towards **Ehrwald** is an area known as **Ausserfern**. This is ideal for hiking and cycling. Driving towards **Innsbruck** you pass through **Seefeld**, a resort area. The Brenner pass and the Achen pass provide entry into Austria from the north. The Achen pass leads down to **Jenbach**, where a steam cogwheel train runs in summer.

Through the Brixen valley, you reach **Kitzbuhel**, another famous resort, then drive down to **Zell Am See**, a historic mountain town by the lake. The Salzach river takes you towards **Salzburg**, through the Gastein valley and the ski/spa resorts of **Bad Hogastein** and **Badgastein**. **Eisriesenwelt** has the largest ice cave system in the world while **Hallein** has a working salt mine where visitors can tour the mine.

From Salzburg, head towards **Gmunden**, passing through **St Wolfgang** and **Bad Ischl**. At Gmunden you can take the expressway towards Vienna, detouring at **Melk**. This part of Austria is known as the Wachau, an extremely scenic and historic section of the country. The **Danube** between **Melk** and **Krems** is picturesque. From here, you can head towards **Vienna** through **Stockerau**.

Austria

Belgium

B ELGIUM IS A DEMOCRACY under a limited monarchy. It is a very densely populated country, with more than 10 million people living in its 30,497 sq km. Belgium still has the boundaries won by the revolution of 1930, in spite of the cultural differences between the Walloons and the Flemish citizens.

Language, though, is the chief distinction between the two groups - the Walloons speak French, and the Flemish speak Dutch. Both languages are regarded as official and equal, and people who deal with the general public are required to speak both. People in the hospitality industry usually speak English as well, so assistance will not be far away should you need it.

Today Belgium, together with Holland and Luxembourg, is a part of the Benelux, or Low Countries, with practically no border control between the members. The headquarters of the EU (European Union) is located in Belgium's capital, Brussels.

Climate

There are seasonal extremes, although the climate is mainly temperate. The hottest month is July and the coldest is January.

Entry Regulations

A valid passport of at least six months is required by all visitors. Visas are not required for periods of less than three months, and no vaccinations are required for any international traveller.

The duty free allowance is 200 cigarettes, 100 cigarillos, 50 cigars or 250 grams tobacco, 1 litre of spirits or sparkling wine, and 2 litres of non-sparkling wine.

There is no restriction on the import or export of local or foreign currencies.

Currency

The currency of the land is the Belgian Franc (BEF), which is divided into 100 centimes, but the smallest coin in circulation is 50 centimes. Approximate rates of exchange, which should be used as a guide only, are:

A$	=	24.50BEF
Can$	=	29.33BEF
NZ$	=	20.00BEF
S$	=	25.00BEF
UK£	=	65.51BEF
US$	=	43.16BEF
EURO	=	40.34BEF

Belgian francs are accepted in Luxembourg, but there is no reciprocal arrangement.

Banks are generally ☉open 9am-4pm Mon-Fri, and *Post Offices* are open 9am-5pm Mon-Fri.

Shops are normally ☉open 9am-6pm Mon-Sat.

Belgium

Credit cards are widely accepted in the major cities, but not in the smaller towns.

Telephone

International direct dialling is available and the International code is 00, the country code is 32. The area code for Brussels is 02. Emergency numbers are - Police ℰ101; Ambulance and Fire Brigade ℰ100.

Driving

Motorways connect most cities and towns in the country, and there are no toll charges. Driving is on the right and the speed limits are:

Built-up areas	-	50kph
Outside built-up areas	-	90kph
Motorways	-	120kph

The Royal Automobile Club of Belgium (RACB) is at rue d'Arlon, 53 - 1040 Brussels, ✆(02) 287 0980.

Miscellaneous

Local time is GMT + 1 (Central European Time) with daylight saving in force, late March to late September.

Electricity is 220v AC, with round two pin plugs. In old houses it may be 120v but they are changing to 220v.

Health - Belgium has good health services, but they can be expensive. Health insurance is highly recommended.

Belgium

Brussels

Brussels is a small Walloonic-Flemish city that has become an administrative centre of Europe with excellent railway connections and Common Market Offices. It is a charming city of contrasts, and offers much to the traveller.

History

Belgium was a prosperous part of the Frankish Kingdom under Charlemagne, and Flemish cloth was much sought after abroad. After his death the country was partitioned, leading to the rise of powerful local lords, such as the Counts of Flanders.

Nevertheless the country flourished, until it became involved in European affairs. Belgians became subject to the Kingdom of France, then to the Dukes of Burgundy, then to the Spanish and Austrian Habsburgs. In the 16th century, Brussels was the political capital of the emperor Charles V, who had been born in Belgium.

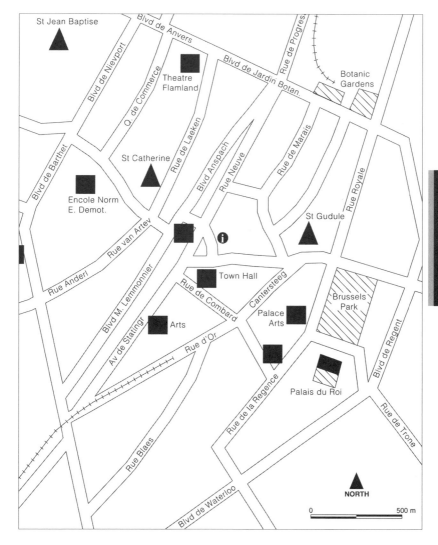

The Revolt of the Netherlands, although successful in the north was defeated in Belgium, and Habsburg rule was reinstated. The country became the scene of the warring Bourbons and Habsburgs. A time of French rule followed, then a brief reunion with Holland, before the revolution of 1830 gained independence.

Tourist Information

The Brussels Information Centrum (TIB), Grand Place 1, 1000 Brussels, ✆(02) 513 8940.

Local Transport

Brussels has a metro (underground) system, buses and trams. For information on schedules or prices, ✆(02) 515 3064.

The metro stations have works of art for sale, and a catalogue can be obtained from the information offices.

Accommodation

It is recommended that if you like taking the risk and prefer to organise your accommodation when you arrive in Brussels, the Tourist Information Centres both at the airport and the central railway station can organise great deals for you in summer, and can invariably get you a bed at other times of the year.

The prices here are for a double room, and include the VAT tax. These hotels take credit card. You may assume that rooms have a phone and ensuite. Some of the hotels in Brussels survive by taking in attending delegates of the diplomatic missions and meetings throughout the year. During July and August it is the summer holidays, so hotels tend to be fairly empty and offer better rates.

Crown Plaza Hotel, Rue Gineste 3, Brussels 1210, ✆32-2 203 6200, fax 32-2 203 5555, email ✎crowneplazabrussels@skynet.be. 358

rooms, cocktail lounge, fitness centre, business centre, laundry facilities on site - washer/drier. 1km from the Grand Palace. Art deco styled hotel with superb service. The location is first class - ✪212Eur.

Holiday Inn, Chaussee de Charleroi 38, Brussels 1060, ✆32-2 533 6666, fax 32-3 538 9014, email ✉kverstreken@121tele.com. 200 rooms, cocktail lounge, restaurant - La Papelotte, parking (not included in tariff). This is a Holiday Inn, so you can expect to be comfortable in Belgian-styled Americana in Europe. 3km from Grand Palace - ✪132Eur.

Ibis Brussels off Grand Place, rue du Marché aux Herbes 100, Brussels 1000, ✆32-3 514 4040, fax 32-2 514 5067, ✪www.ibishotel.com. 184 rooms, bar, everything that you would normally find in an Ibis hotel. Excellent location - ✪120Eur (5000Bfr).

Ibis Brussels Centre Ste Catherine, rue Joseph Plateau No2, Brussels 1000, ✆32-3 513 7620, fax 32-2 514 2213, ✪www.ibishotel.com. 236 rooms, restaurant, 10 minutes from the Grand Palace - ✪100Eur (4000Bfr).

Amigo, Rue de l'Amigo, 1-3, 1000 Brussels, ✆(02) 547 4747, fax 513 5277 (✪www.hotelamigo.com, ✉hotelamigo@compuserve.com). This 5-star hotel has 183 rooms, a bar/lounge and a French restaurant - ✪7700-11,500BEF (190-285EUR).

Bedford Hotel, Rue du Midi, 135, 1000 Brussels, ✆(02) 507 0000, fax 507 0010. The Bedford is a 4-star hotel containing 321 rooms. Facilities include a bar/lounge and restaurant - ✪7900-17,000BEF (195-421EUR).

City Garden, Rue Joseph II, 59, 1000 Brussels, ✆(02) 282 8282, fax 230 6437. A 96 room, 2-star hotel with a combined bar and lounge - ✪6000-7350BEF (148-182EUR).

Belgium

Montgomery

Avenue de Tervueren 134, Brussels 1150, ✆32-3 741 8511, fax 32-2 741 8500, ✎ hotel@montgomery.be 63 rooms, restaurant - La Duchesse, bar (Monty's), library. A civilised hotel that has a library. Rooms are spacious and elegantly furnished helping one to feel more at home than in rented premises. Service is superb as directed by Julie Bolander-Derede. Try this place when the EU are not in session - it is within walking distance of their headquarters and likely to be full during such times. July-August is the time to go to this hotel if you want a good deal - ✪12,500Bfr.

Mozart (Grand Place), Rue Marche aux Fromages, 15A, 1000 Brussels, ✆(02) 502 6661, fax 502 7758 (☞hotel-Mozart.be, ✎hotel.mozart@skynet.be). The Mozart has 47 rooms and a bar/lounge - ✪2800-4500BEF (69-111EUR).

Welcome, Rue du Peuplier, 5, 1000 Brussels, ✆(02) 219 9546, fax 217 1887 (☞www.hotelwelcome.com, ✎info@hotelwelcome.com). This 3-star hotel has good facilities including a restaurant and bar. There are 10 rooms, although not all of them are air-conditioned. The character of the hotel and the attention to detail makes it a popular one - ✪2600-3600BEF (53-89EUR).

Sun Hotel, Rue de Berger, 38, 1050 Brussels, ✆(02) 511 2119, fax 512 3271 (✎sunhotel@skynet.be). A basic 2-star hotel with 22 rooms, a restaurant, and bar/lounge area - ✪1950-4350BEF (48-107EUR).

For budget hotels try the web page:
☞www.bub-brussels.be/eng/bnbeng.htm

Food and Drink

The main meal is eaten in the middle of the day, and consists of very generous portions. Afternoon coffee, usually with a pastry of some kind, is around 4pm, with supper at 7pm.

The national drinks are coffee and beer, and there are over 350 brands of beer available. This is not counting the local ales available in some of the villages. There are no licensing hours, but the sale of spirits in cafes and restaurants is forbidden. The obvious national food item would have to be Brussels Sprouts, but some typical Belgian dishes are: asparagus a la flamande, chicken stew (waterzoei) and rabbit cooked with prunes.

La Truite d'Argent, 23 Quai au Bois à Brûler, Brussels 1000, ✆32-3 219 9546. A fancy restaurant which specialises in the local cuisine. Meats and vegetables are combined in clever and inventive dishes. Main course ✪1000Bfr.

Following are a few eateries that won't dig too deep into your wallet:

Le Ble Noir, 470 Chaussee de Boondael, ✆(02) 644 3574 - specializes in pancakes.

Le Foyer, 1 Rue Infante Isabelle, ✆(02) 512 0245 - near the Grand Place, specializes in Belgian dishes.

La Grande Porte, 9 Rue Notre-Seigneur - popular with the locals.

La Maree, 99 Rue de Flandre, ✆(02) 511 0040 - 25 years in the business of serving wonderful seafood, especially the fish soup.

Rugantino, 184-186 Boulevard Anspach, ✆(02) 511 2195 - a very good Italian restaurant that is usually very crowded; what better recommendation than that?

Sightseeing

The **Grand Place**, the centre of social, economic and political activities from the 12th century, was almost entirely destroyed in 48 hours in August 1695, by order of Louis XIV. However it was rebuilt in less than four years in a blend of Italian and Flemish Baroque style. From ☺June to September, from 9pm, there is a sound and light show. The most prominent building on the Place is the **Town Hall** (Hotel de Ville), which is ☺open to visitors Mon-Fri 9am-4.30pm. The other buildings are houses of the various Guilds (associations of craftpersons); for example, the King House (Maison du Roi), which now houses a **Communal Museum**, was the Bread House in the 13th century.

To the left past the Town Hall, a short walk leads to the corner of rue de l'Etuve and rue du Chene, and the well-known but slightly vulgar **Manneken-Pis Fountain**. The small bronze statuette, which dates back to 1619, is called 'the oldest citizen of the city' and represents a young hero from Brussels' folklore. The figure owns a varied and abundant wardrobe that is housed in the Communal Museum in the Grand Place.

Another small part of the old town is found on the way to the cathedral, around Petite rue de Bouchers, with its elegant restaurants and St Hubert Galleries. The beautiful, gothic **St Michael's Cathedral** dates from the Middle Ages, and contains the graves of the Dukes of Brabant, the Archdukes Albert and Isabelle, and Charles of Lorraine.

The **Saint-Hubert Royal Galleries** were built in 1846, and were the first covered shopping arcades in Europe. (Many people thought that Bern had the first.) They are made of up three distinct parts - the King's Gallery, the Queen's Gallery and the Princes' Gallery. The other main shopping area is around rue Neuve.

The Palace of the Nation, in Parc de Bruxelles, on rue de la Loi was built in 1783 for the sovereign Council of Brabant. Called the Palace of

Town Hall, Brussels

the States General in 1817, it became the Palace of the Nation after 1830 and is where both houses of Parliament sit. The **Parc de Bruxelles** was formerly the hunting ground of the Dukes of Brabant, and was converted to a French garden in the 18th century. In 1830 it was the main battlefield in the war between Dutch troops and the Belgian insurgents.

La Place des Palais (Palaces' Square) is bordered by the **Palais des Academies**, the **Royal Palace**, and the **Palais des Beaux-Arts**. The first was the former residence of the Prince of Orange, and was built between 1823 and 1826. It has housed the Belgian Royal Academy since 1876. The Royal Palace is the most important of the trio, and it owes its Louis XVI appearance to King Leopold II, who had alterations to the facade carried out in 1904. It is the official residence of the present king, Albert II. The **Palace of Fine Arts** is west of the square and is a spacious building, mostly underground. It has many exhibition rooms, a movie theatre and a concert hall. It was built in 1930.

The nearby **Place Royale** was built in the 18th century during the reign of Charles of Lorraine. The equestrian statue in the centre is of Godefroid de Bouillon, and behind it is the St Jacques-sur-Coudenberg Church.

The **Congress Column**, off Konings Sraat, rises to a height of 47m and is topped by a statue of Leopold I, the first king of the Belgians. There is access to a lookout that provides a panoramic view of the city. At the foot of the column are the tombs of two unknown soldiers from the World Wars.

Rue de la Loi runs south-east from the city centre to the **Parc du Cinquantenaire** which is home to the **Cinquantenaire**, a monumental arched structure inspired by Leopold II and completed in 1905. The **Army Museum** and the **Royal Museum of Art and History** are housed either side of the arch.

Belgium

The Best of Brussels in Brief

Grand-Place. Another legacy of the Habsburgs, this dazzling square showcases Brussels' best in a nutshell. A piece of medieval Europe has been charmingly trapped within its decorated streets, where everything seems to be happening at once. Visit the Museum of the City of Brussels inside the King's House, and the Brewers Museum, but keep in mind that the real attractions here are outdoors. There are a number of outlets here where you can sample delicious offerings of creamy Belgian chocolate.

Museum of Ancient Art (Musee d'Art Ancien). Here you will find many artistic treasures created at the hands of Bruegal, van der Weyden, Rubens, Bosch, van Gogh and others. *Rue de la Regence 3.*

Museum of Modern Art (Musee d'Art Modern). Connected to the Museum of Ancient Art and featuring the talents of Rene, Magritte, David, Dali, Delvaux and others. *Rue de la Regence 3.*

Town Hall (Hotel de Ville). Situated in the Grand Place, this building is worth a look for the sculptures on its exterior and the intricate tapestries hanging from the walls inside.

Cathedral of Saint-Michel (Cathedrale des Saints Michel et Gudule). Noteworthy aspects of the cathedral are its stained-glass windows and the stonework involved in its elegant arches and enormous columns and - a supreme example of the gothic style. *In Parvis Sainte-Gudule.*

Place du Grand-Sablon. This attractive area is the place for antiques, which have really become the hub around which activity in Grand-Sablon spins, with markets and traders displaying their valuable wares.

Royal St Hubert Galleries. This shopping arcade was opened back in 1847 and is worth a pleasant stroll past its shops, cafes and buskers if you have some time on your hands. *Near ru de Bouchers*.

Manneken-Pis. This statue depicts a young boy mischievously succumbing to the call of nature. The effigy has become a symbol of the city and its cheeky irresistability continues to disarm passers-by. *Corner rue du Chene and ru de l'Etuve.*

Place Royale. There are a number of attractions here at this busy street intersection, one of which is the Church of St. Jacques-sur-Coudenberg.

Royal Museum of Army and Military History. See various mem- 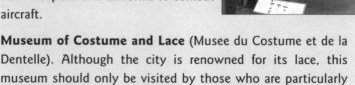 orabilia of nineteenth century warfare, from weapons and uniforms to combat aircraft.

Museum of Costume and Lace (Musee du Costume et de la Dentelle). Although the city is renowned for its lace, this museum should only be visited by those who are particularly passionate about the subject. *Rue de la Violette 6*.

Bruparck! This theme park features 'Atomium', a giant atomic molecule, 'Oceade', a water park, and 'Mini-Europe', scaled-down replicas of famous European buildings. It is located in the city's north.

Driving Through Belgium

A Scenic Tour of Belgium by Road

Itinerary - 6 Days - Distance 513kms

From **Ostend**, a port city and seaside resort, head towards **Bruges**. This is one of the most medieval cities in Belgium, with many canals, and which is famous for its lace. From Bruges, drive towards **Ghent**, the centre of the Flemish flower industry. It also has an impressive number of historic buildings.

Bruges

Antwerp, on the border with Holland, is the home of Rubens and Flemish Baroque. It is also the centre of Belgium's diamond industry. Driving towards Brussels, you pass through **Mechelen**, and **Leliven**, the former capital and site of the oldest university of the Low countries. From there you reach **Brussels**, the capital of Belgium and the European community. Brussels has many fine museums and historic buildings, as well as great shopping. South of Brussels, **Beloeil** has a 14th century castle with 25 acres of 17th century gardens, while **Mons** is another historic town.

Head east towards **Namur**, at the meeting point of two rivers - the Meuse and the Sambre. Namur has a famous citadel. The Meuse valley, south of Namur leads to the gardens at **Anneuoie**. These unique 18th century gardens have an intricate water and fountain system. Travelling north again, you reach **Han-sur-lesse** with 3 kilometres of underground caves and a spectacular sound and light show. Further north again is **Liege**, another historic city with beautiful buildings and galleries.

Belgium

Denmark

D ENMARK IS A CONSTITUTIONAL MONARCHY, with a total area of 43,069 sq km, made up of 407 islands and a large peninsula, Jutland, bordered by northern Germany. The population is 5.2 million, one-quarter of whom live in the capital Copenhagen.

Considered by many to be the prettiest of the Scandinavian countries, Denmark is also the most prosperous, which is evidenced by the many manor houses of various architectural styles and periods.

Denmark has been settled since prehistoric times, and there are many passage graves, particularly in the south, that are open for inspection.

The language of the country is Danish, but English is widely understood and spoken.

Climate

Denmark is situated in a temperate zone, and the weather is often wet and windy. Winter brings snow and rain.

Average temperatures in Copenhagen are: January max 3C, min -1C; June max 21C, min 13C.

Entry Regulations

Visitors must have a valid passport, but visas are not required. It is always a good idea, though, to check with an embassy or consulate in your own country before departure.

The duty free allowance is 200 cigarettes or 50 cigars or 250g tobacco, 50g perfume or 250ml eau de toilette, 500g coffee; 100g tea; and other goods to a maximum value of Dkr350.

No vaccinations are required.

Currency

The currency of the land is the Krone (plural Kroner), and Dkr1 = 100 ore. Approximate rates of exchange, which should be used as a guide only, are:

A$	=	4.50Dkr
Can$	=	5.42Dkr
NZ$	=	3.70Dkr
S$	=	4.30Dkr
UK£	=	12.10Dkr
US$	=	7.97Dkr
Euro	=	7.45Dkr

Notes are in denominations of Dkr1000, 500, 100 and 50, and coins are Dkr20, 10, 5, 2 and 1, 50 and 20 ore (amounts of ore are rounded off when paying cash but remain on cheques).

Banks are ☉open Mon-Fri 9.30am-4pm, Thurs until 6pm, and some currency exchange offices are open until 10pm. Keep in mind that the banks may refuse to exchange large foreign bank notes.

Visa and *MasterCard* are widely accepted, but not so *American Express*, except in major hotels and shops.

Post offices are ☉open Mon-Fri 9am/10am-5pm/5.30pm, Sat 9am-noon.

Generally *shops* are ☉open Mon-Wed 9am-5.30pm, Thurs 9am-7pm, Fri 9am-8pm, Sat 9am-noon, but some do not open until 10am and then stay open longer. Department stores close at 7pm or 8pm, and on the first and last Sat of the month they stay open until 5pm. In the country areas most shops close for lunch (noon-2pm). Shops in the tourist areas, and all bakeries and kiosks are open on Sunday.

Telephone

International direct dialling is available and the International code is 009, the Country code 45. In Denmark there are no area codes - all parts of the country have an eight digit number.

Driving

Traffic drives on the right-hand side of the road, and passes on the left. Headlights have to be on 24 hours a day.

Speed limits are:

Expressways	-	110km/h
Dual carriageways	-	80km/h
Single carriageways	-	80km/h
Town areas	-	50km/h

When driving in the countryside it is best to avoid the smaller side-roads which are mostly used by cyclists, many travelling in family groups.

The maximum blood alcohol limit allowed when driving is .05.

Miscellaneous

Standard time is GMT + 1.

Electricity is 220 volts AC. It is advisable to carry an adaptor for your appliances.

Health - It is advisable to have private medical insurance, especially if you are travelling from a country that is outside the European Union.

Tipping - As a service fee is included in hotel and restaurant bills, it is not necessary to tip unless you feel that you have been given very good service.

Denmark

Copenhagen

Copenhagen is situated on the island of Sjaelland, in the north-eastern part of Denmark, across the Sound from Sweden's industrial city of Malmo. It is the country's capital and main city, the residence of the monarch, the seat of government, parliament and the supreme court.

The city is also the centre of trade and industry in the country. It is also a colourful city with a rather relaxed ambience.

History

The inner town of Copenhagen has been inhabited for at least 6000 years. A thousand years ago it was a small fishing village called Havn (harbour), but it was important because of its great natural harbour and its position on the main trade route. In 1167 Bishop Absalon, Bishop of Roskilde, built a castle on a small island and fortified the town. Soon it became known as Kiobmaennehavn (the merchants' harbour), which lead to Kobenhavn, its present name in Danish.

In the 15th century the city passed to the Crown of Denmark, and a university and a naval base were established. Copenhagen prospered and was the principal city of a realm that included Norway, Iceland, southern Sweden, Schleswig-Holstein, as well as Denmark.

The city's importance made it a target and, in the civil and religious strife of the Protestant Reformation, it was often sacked. In the 17th century it prospered under the energetic builder King Christian IV and foreign trade grew enormously. Buildings from this period include the Borsen, the Holmens Church and the Palace of Rosenborg. The 17th century brought a devastating war with Sweden, and for two years Copenhagen was besieged by the Swedish King Charles X Gustavus - unsuccessfully.

Great tracts of the city were destroyed by fire in 1727 and 1795, but these were only temporary setbacks in a period of rapid growth that came to an end with the Napoleonic Wars.

In 1801, the British fleet attacked Copenhagen without a declaration of war, to keep the Danes from closing the Baltic Sea. That ferocious battle, one of Horatio Nelson's great triumphs, ended in a truce, but the British bombarded the city again in 1807 and left much of it in ruins.

It took some time for Copenhagen to recover, but the 19th century brought increasing wealth. In a break with the past, the city's walls were pulled down in 1856, and expansion began into the surrounding districts. In the 1870s industrialisation began in earnest, and a free port was set up in 1894.

During World War II, Copenhagen was occupied by German forces, but the city suffered little damage. The widespread popular resistance to the occupation forces is commemorated in the Museum of the Danish Resistance Movement. In recent years, Copenhagen has become one of the leading cultural and artistic centres of northern Europe.

Tourist Information

There is a tourist information office at 1 Bernstorffsgade (near the Tivoli Gardens), ✆3311 1325. It is ⊙open Mon-Fri 9am-2pm, Sat 10am-2pm.

Copenhagen 'This Week' is a free monthly magazine that lists everything a visitor needs to know about the city.

Local Transport

Copenhagen has efficient bus and subway systems. The subway is called S-tog, ✆3314 1701, and accepts Eurail passes. Bus fares are paid as you board, and the driver will have change. City maps have bus and subway routes marked, but when in doubt ask one of the locals. They are always happy to help. If you wish to enquire about bus timetables, ✆3645 4545.

There are plenty of taxis in the city, and they can be flagged down anywhere. If you are travelling in a group of, say, four people, it will often be cheaper to hire a taxi than take a bus.

Accommodation

Following are a few hotels in the city centre, with prices for a double room per night in Dkr, which should be used as a guide only. These hotels accept credit cards.

It is recommended that if you like taking the risk and prefer to organise you accommodation when you arrive at a city the Tourist Information Centre both at the airport and the central railway station can organise great deals for you in summer, and can invariably get you a bed at other times of the year.

Hotel Danmark, Vester Voldgade 89, DK-1552 Copenhagen V, ✆45-3 311 4806, fax 45-3 314 3630. 51 rooms, restaurant, garage not included in tariff, laundry. Very close to Tivoli Gardens and Town Hall Square - ✪1000Dkr.

Hotel Kong Arthur, Noerre Sogada 11, 1370 Copenhagen K, ✆45-3 311 1212, fax 45-3 332 6130. 107 rooms, bar, 3 restaurants, laundry service, parking (free). The decoration includes antiques which gives it a certain charm. Centrally located by Peblinge Lake it is within walking distance of the main shopping areas. Classed as a 4 star hotel and is family run - ✪1020Dkr

71 Nyhavn Hotel

Nyhavn 71, 1051 Copenhagen K, ✆45-3 343 6200, fax 54-3 343 6201, email ✉ 71nyhavnhotel@arp-hansen.dk. 83 rooms, restaurant - Pakhuskaelderen. This is a heritage building scenically situated on the water - ✪1300Dkr.

Plaza Hotel, Bernstorffsgade 4, 1577 Copenhagen V, ✆45-3 314 9262, fax 45-3 393 9362. 93 rooms, bar, restaurant. Family run hotel with a quality of decor that makes it very comfortable. Opposite Tivoli Gardens, next to 'Stroget', the main shopping area, and a couple of minutes walk from the main railway station and the airport shuttle - ✪1400Dkr.

Glostrup Park Hotel, Hovedvejen 41, DK2600 Glostrup, ✆45-4 396 0038, fax 45-4 343 301, email ✉ glostruop@parkhotel.dk. 85 rooms, games room, bar, well regarded restaurant - La Cocotte - laundry service, some 15 minutes by car from the centre of Copenhagen, part of the Hansen chain, ensuring a comfortable stay - ✪525Dkr.

> **Hotel Phoenix**
>
> Bredgade 37, 1260 Copenhagen, ✆45-3 395 9500, fax 45-3 333 9833, email ✉ phoenixcopenhagen@arp-hansen.dk. 212 rooms, 2 restaurants, bar. Located in the city centre. Elegant decor in a seventeeth century building. Chandeliers and marble give it an Italian feel - ✪1435Dkr

Hotel Palace, Raadhuspladsen 57, ✆3314 4050, fax 3314 5279. Has a restaurant and cocktail bar - ✪Dkr1200-1700.

Hotel Alexandra, HC Andersens Boulevard 8 (on Town Hall Square), ✆3314 2200, fax 3314 0284. Restaurant and cocktail bar - ✪Dkr1200.

Komfort Hotel, Loengangstraede 27 (near the Town Hall), ✆33 12 65 70, fax 33 15 28 99. Restaurant, cocktail bar - ✪Dkr972.

Other hotels can be found on 👁www.hotels-in-denmark.dk

Food and Drink

Restaurants include a 25% tax plus a 15% tip, so eating out is an expensive experience. Danish specialties are pastries (*wienerbrod*), open sandwiches (*smorrebrod*), and hot dogs (*polse*), but don't expect those in their native land to look exactly the same as the ones you love back home.

If you want to sample all the traditional Danish dishes in the same meal, visit the **Bistro Restaurant** in the Central Station, ☏3314 1232, and enjoy a *koldt bord*. This is the local version of the Swedish smorgasbord.

Pakhuskaelderen, Nyhavn 71, ☏343 6200. Part of the hotel 71 Nyhavn and is in the cellar of a restored former warehouse. The specialty here is seafood and the restaurant boasts a fine wine cellar. Danish cooking and international dishes also feature. Pricey.

Restaurant Brochner, Noerre Sogade 11, 1370 Copenhagen K, (Hotel Kong Arthur), ☏45-3 311 1212. Specialises in Danish and French cuisine and has won respectable awards. Good value.

Library Bar in the Plaza Hotel, Bernstorffsgade 4, 1577 Copenhagen V, ☏45-3 314 9262, is world famous. Voted by *Forbes Magazine* as one of the five top bars in the world. One drinks in an enticing environment of leather bound volumes, classic period pieces and paintings from some of Europe's masters.

Shopping

The main department stores are **Illum**, ☏33 14 40 02, and **Magasin**, ☏3311 4433, and both are on Stroget (pronounced stroyet), the pedestrian shopping mall.

Scala is a complex of boutiques, restaurants and entertainment venues, and is worth a visit. It is on Vesterbrogade, across from the Tivoli.

Shops are ☉open Mon-Fri 9.30am-7pm, Sat 9am-2pm.

Sightseeing

A walking tour of Copenhagen begins at **Radhuspladsen** (Town Hall Square), which was once the west end of town. Built in the Italian Renaissance style, there is a statue of the city's founder above the hall's portal. The Town Hall is ☉open to the public Mon-Fri 10am-3pm, and admission is free. The walk up the 300 steps to the tower and the best view of the city, however, will set you back ✪Dkr12, ☺3366 2582.

Look up the walls of the building on the square that is opposite the Stroget, and you will see the city's 'weather girls' - riding a bike if it is going to be fine, armed with an umbrella if it is not.

Nearby are the **Tivoli Gardens**, which were built in 1843 outside the city walls. The first public amusement park in Europe, the Tivoli was built to appease the people's discontent with their lot, and it succeeded. Covering 20 acres, the gardens offer rides, games, marching bands, roulette wheels, funny mirrors, restaurants and many happy hours. There are also many free concerts, puppet shows, and more. The park is ☉open Sun-Wed 11am-midnight, Thurs-Sat 11am-1am (late April to mid-September), closed off-season, ☺3315 1001. Admission high season (mid-June to mid-August) is ✪Dkr45, low season Dkr39, children 4-12 Dkr20-25 depending on the season. 'Tivoli Passes' offer admission and unlimited use of the 27 rides and cost ✪Dkr195-205 adults, Dkr175-185 children. Individual rides require 1 to 3 tickets which cost ✪Dkr10 each.

It should be kept in mind that this amusement park is over 150 years old, and was around a long time before Walt Disney began opening up his 'lands' and 'worlds'.

The **Tivoli Museum**, which has exhibits about the history and workings of the Gardens is ☉open daily during the season 11am-6pm, off season Tues-Sun 10am-4pm.

The **train station**, behind the Tivoli, was obviously also built outside the city walls.

To the right of the Town Hall is a statue of Copenhagen's favourite son, **Hans Christian Andersen**, and to the left of the Hall is the **Lur-**

Blowers sculpture. Original lurs, which were popular instruments three and half thousand years ago, are on display in the National Museum.

The **Ny Carlsberg Glyptotek**, cnr Hans Christian Andersens Boulevard and Tietgengade, has the largest collection of antique art in Northern Europe, along with many 19th century French and Danish sculptures and paintings, that include works by the Impressionists. ⊙Open Tues-Sun 10am-4pm (winter noon-3pm) and admission is ✪15Dkr, ✆3341 8141.

The **National Museum** is at Vestergade 10, and has a very good collection of Danish history from the earliest times presented in chronological order with English explanations. The museum is ⊙open Tues-Sun 10am-5pm and admission is ✪30Dkr, ✆33 13 44 11.

The northern boundary of the museum is the Frederiksholms Canal, which you cross via the Marble Bridge, which was built in 1775. This leads to **Slotsholmen** (castle island), which has much to offer the visitor. Firstly there is the **Christiansborg Palace**, the fifth to be built on this site, which has housed since 1928, the Parliament, the Supreme Court, the Foreign Office and the Royal Chambers. Guided tours of 22 of the Queen's reception rooms are available ⊙Tues-Sun at 11am, 1pm and 3pm (May-September); Tues, Thurs and Sun 11am, 3pm (Oct-April), and cost ✪30Dkr, ✆33 92 64 92. There are tours of the parliament.

In the basement of the palace tower are the foundations of the **original castle** built by Bishop Absalon. The exhibit is ⊙open daily 9.30am-3.30pm (closed Mon and Sat in the off-season) and entry is ✪17Dkr.

Other parts of the palace that can be visited include the **Royal Mews** with its coach museum, a **Theatre Museum**, and the **Palace Chapel**. Next door to that is a museum housing the works of **Bertel Thorvaldsen**, 1770-1844, and in fact it also houses the tomb of the great neoclassical sculptor himself. The museum also offers one of the best views of the city, across the **Gammel Strand**, the departure point for harbour cruises.

Still on Slotsholmen are: **Christiansborg Slotsplads**, with its equestrian statue of Frederick VII; the **Royal Library**, built in 1906; the **Royal Brewery**, commissioned by Christian IV; as was the **Arsenal**; and the Renaissance **Exchange**, with its dragon tail spire. Still there is more to see.

From the Palace Chapel, walk along Kobmagergade to the **Stroget** and the **Amagertorv**, the square in the centre of the city. House no 6 on the square is the main exhibition and sales rooms of **Royal Porcelain**.

The next attraction you can take or leave, depending on your point of view. At Kobmagergade 24 is the **Museum of Erotica**, which has as its theme the role Denmark played in the 1970s in the legalisation of pornography. There are other exhibits on sexual practices down through the ages, and similar items of bad taste, and the admission price is ✪50Dkr.

The next stop is also not compulsory, unless you are travelling with children. The **Toy Museum** is at Valken-dorfsgade 13.

Following the Stroget to its end at **Kongens Nytorv** (King's New Square), which dates from the 17th century. Buildings here include the **Royal Theatre** and **Charlottenborg**, which houses the Royal Academy of Fine Arts. The pretty centre of the square is called the **Krinsen**, and the man on the horse is Charles V.

Now we come to a very colourful part of the city, a harbour extension called **Nyhavn**. Apart from the old sailing ships, there are plenty of pubs and people that combine to make a visit worthwhile. Hans Christian Andersen was enamoured of this area and lived for a time in three different houses - Nyhavn 18, 20 and 67.

At the end of the canal, turn right and walk past the ferry docks to the **Harbour Promenade**. Continue past the 6m bronze copy of Michelangelo's *David* to the **Amalienhave Park**, which is between the harbour and the **Amalienborg Palace**, the home of the Danish royal family. There are actually four identical rococo palaces: Queen Margrethe II and family live in the one to the left of the harbour side entrance of the square. Prince Frederik, the heir apparent to the throne lives directly opposite.

There is a changing of the guard at noon when the queen is in residence, but frankly, it is not worth organising everything to be there then.

The **Christian VIII Palace** is open to the public and has exhibits from the time of Christian IX (1863-1906).

The statue in the centre of square is Frederick V, and locals like to think that he is riding towards the Marmorkirken, which took 150 years to build.

Continuing north onto the Bredgade, the next stop is the **Museum of Decorative and Applied Arts**, which has the best collection of Japanese arts and crafts outside of Japan.

At the end of the Bredgade, turn right into the Esplanaden, and you will be able to see the **Freedom Museum** (Frihedsmuseet), which details the Danish Resistance against the Germans during World War II. It is ☺open daily 10am-4pm (May to mid-September), Tues-Sun 11am-3pm (rest of the year), ☏3313 7714.

There are two attractions remaining on our walking tour. The first is the **Gefion Fountain**, and the last is the **Little Mermaid**, the symbol of Copenhagen. The statue is, of course, based on a character from a Hans Christian Andersen fairy tale. The sculptor was Edvard Eiksen, whose wife posed for him, and the work was finished in 1913. I would rate this statue as one of life's disappointments. Whoever heard of a mermaid with two legs that ended in flippers? We all know that they have a fishtail.

After all this walking, it might be a good idea to return to the city by taxi, or by bus 1, 6 or 9 from Kastellet Park near the Freedom Museum.

There are a few other interesting places to visit in Copenhagen, but they do not fit comfortably into a walking tour.

To the west of the main station is the **Carlsberg Brewery**, and there are free tours and tasting sessions available ☉Mon-Fri 11am and 2pm, ✆3327 1314 ext 1312. To get there take bus 6 to 140 Ny Carlsberg Vej.

Also this way is the **Royal Copenhagen Porcelain Manufactory**, Vestergade 10. It has tours on weekdays and 'seconds' available to keen-eyed purchasers.

Last, but not least, is the **Rosenborg Palace**, which can be reached by taking the subway to Norreport Station, then walking in a northerly direction. The palace was built between 1606 and 1617, and visitors can see apartments relating to the various kings from Christian IV (1588) to Frederick IV (1863). Also on display are the **Danish Crown Jewels**. Guides are available, and the palace is ☉open daily 10am-4pm (June-August); 11am-3pm May, September and October; and Tues-Fri and Sun 11am-2pm in the off-season. It is best to visit Rosenborg in the middle of the day, however, as there is no interior electricity, ✆3315 3286.

The Best of Copenhagen in Brief

Tivoli Gardens. An amusement park in the heart of the city, Tivoli opened back in 1843 and has been popular ever since. Its main theme of entertaining fun manifests itself in a range of ways, from Hans Christian Andersen rides to Viking ships to Arabian palaces. *Vesterbrogade 3.*

National Museum (Nationalmuseet). Wander through the Stone Age, the Bronze Age, the Classical Age, the Middle Ages, the Renaissance and into the Modern Age. An outstanding collection of rune stones, relics, weapons, coins, instruments and all manner of art traces the history of Civilisation and fascinating fragments of earlier times. *Ny Vestergade10.*

The Little Mermaid statue (Den Lille Havfrue). The popular character of Hans Christian Andersen's fairy tale is immortalised in bronze on the shoreline, a fair distance north-east of the city centre.

Ny Carlsberg Glyptotek. This marvellous collection spans centuries, with displays of Egyptian, Greek, Roman and Etruscan art right up to French masterpeices of the nineteenth century. *Dantes Plads 7.*

Rosenborg Castle. First among the many valuable treasures stored in the castle are the Crown Jewels kept in the Treasury. The surrounding royal gardens make for a pleasant spot to relax. *Oster Voldgade 4A.*

Town Hall (Radhus). Houses the World Clock and a statue of Hans Christian Andersen. *Radhuspladsen.*

Christiansborg Palace. Stroll through the elegant rooms after slipping on the soft shoes provided to help preserve the floor.

Take in the centuries of Danish royal history. *Christiansborgs Slotsplads, Prins Jorgens Gard 1.*

Royal Museum of Fine Arts (Statens Museum for Kunst). Rubens, Rembrandt, Matisse and Picasso feature among this extensive collection representing French artists of the last century and also the Dutch golden age. *Solvgade 48-50.*

Stroget. The best pedestrian shopping mall in Scandanavia, some say in Europe. This is where you'll find the premier department stores.

Danish Resistance Museum (Frihedsmuseet). Recounts the effects of the Nazi regime on Denmark and the story of Danish efforts to oppose it. There are accompanying exhibitions of various wartime items. *Churchillparken.*

Open-Air Folk Museum (Frilandmuseet). A recreated village of farmsteads, windmills and workshops in Danish architecture. *Kongevejen 100.*

Royal Arsenal Museum (Tojhusmuseet). An impressive array of historical weapons in all shapes and sizes. *Tojhusgade 3.*

Amalienborg Palace. Residence of the Danish Royal family since the turn of the eighteenth century. This building was created in the baroque style and has some internal rooms open for public viewing. *Slotsplads.*

Copenhagen Cathedral (Vor Frue Kirke) and **Marble Church** (Frederik's Church). Copenhagen's two most impressive churches, each built in different architectural styles. *Norregade and Frederiksgade 4 respectively.*

Round Tower (Rundetarn). Climb this tower for expansive views over Copenhagen. *Kobmagergade 52A.*

Denmark

Driving Through Denmark

A Scenic Tour of Denmark by Road

Itinerary - 2 Days - Distance 337kms

Copenhagen is the capital of Denmark. There are many things to see and do here. Two sights on most peoples lists are a visit to the Tivoli Gardens (open in summer only), and to the statue of the Little Mermaid, on the harbour foreshore. Driving north from Copenhagen you reach **Helsingor**. This town is an important departure point for ferries to Sweden. The Kronborg Castle here is often the setting for *Hamlet*.

Travelling southwest you reach **Hillerod**, with its renaissance period castle, now a national historical museum. **Roskilde** is one of the oldest towns on the island, with a Viking museum containing five ships retrieved from the fjord.

Through **Slagelse** you can catch a ferry to the island of **Funen**, and **Odense**. This is the birthplace of Hans Christian Anderson, and is also the third largest town in Denmark. Head south from Odense to **Svendborg**. The route is very scenic with coastal views, small villages, and imposing castles to see. The town is an old shipping port, and is an interesting and picturesque place. There are many small islands around here.

Take the road to the island of **Langeland** and then the ferry to **Lolland**. This island is Denmark's prime farming area, and also has a safari park, and an automobile museum for visitors. From Lolland travel to the islands of **Bogo** and **Mon**. Mon has spectacular scenery, with cliffs, woods and beaches. Drive north from here along the east coast of **Sjaelland** and you will arrive back in Copenhagen.

Denmark

France

F RANCE IS THE SECOND LARGEST country in Europe, with an area of 547,026 sq km, and a population of about 55 million. The French Fifth Republic has a constitution that was adopted in 1958 and amended in 1962. There is a President, elected for a 7-year term, a Prime Minister appointed by the President, and a parliament of two houses.

The capital is Paris where approximately 4 million people live. The language of the country is, of course, French, but English is spoken in big stores, banks, hotels and tourist offices.

Climate

There are wide variations in the climate, depending on the region. Inland has hot summers, and there is usually heavy winter snow in the Alps.

The averages for Paris are 13-24C in July, and 0-6 in January.

Marseille, on the Mediterranean coast, averages 18-28C in August, 3-12C in January.

Entry Regulations

Visitors must have a current passport, and people from member countries of the EU, Canada, the United States and New Zealand, amongst others, do not require visas. Australians and Singaporeans, however, do require visas.

The duty free allowance is 200 cigarettes or 50 cigars or 250 gm of tobacco, 1 litre of spirits (more than 22% alcoholic strength) or up to 2 litres of spirits (maximum of 22% alcoholic strength).

There is no restriction on the import of local currency, however it is only permissible to convert French Francs into foreign currencies up to the equivalent of F5,000.

No vaccinations are required for any international traveller.

Currency

The currency of the land is the French Franc, abbreviated to F or FRF, which is divided into 100 centimes. Approximate exchange rates, which should be used as a guide only, are:

A$	=	4.00FF
Can$	=	4.77FF
NZ$	=	3.25FF
S$	=	4.15FF
UK£	=	10.65FF
US$	=	7.02FF
Euro	=	6.56FF

Notes are in denominations of 500, 200, 100, 50 and 20 Francs, and coins are 20, 10, 5, 2 and 1 Francs and 50, 20, 10 and 5 centimes.

Banks are usually ☉open 9am-noon and 2-4pm weekdays, but closed either Sat or Mon. They also close early on the day before a public holiday.

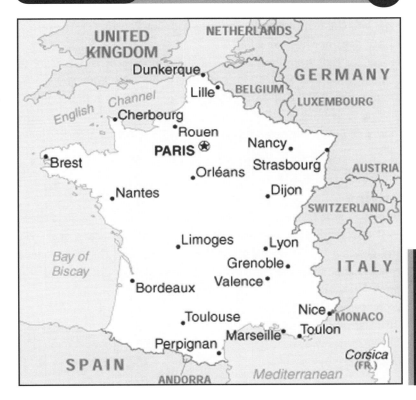

Post Offices in the main cities are usually ☺open Mon-Fri 8.30am-7pm, and Sat 8.30am-12.30pm.

Shops in Paris are usually ☺open Mon-Sat 10am-7pm, but outside of Paris they tend to close for a couple of hours around lunch time, and may be closed on Mon afternoon.

Credit cards are widely accepted in the major cities.

Telephone

International direct dialling is available and the International code is 19, the country code 33. The telephone system has only two regions -

Paris and the rest of France. The area code for Paris is (I), the rest of France does not have an area code.

Note: For calls from Paris to any of the provinces, it is necessary to dial 16, then the local 8-figure numbers; for calls from any of the provinces to Paris, dial 16 (I) then the local 8-figure number. But, if dialling Paris from, say Sydney, you would dial 0011 + 33 + I + the local 8-figure number. In other words, the 16 is not used for overseas calls.

Emergency numbers are: Police ✆17; Fire ✆18; Operator ✆13.

Driving

To hire a car it is necessary to have a valid driving licence, held for at least one year, and a passport. It is compulsory to wear a seat belt, and children under 10 years old may not travel in the front. Speed limits change with the weather, and are as follows:

Road System	Dry	Wet
Expressways	130	110
Dual Carriageways	110	100
Single Carriageways	90	80
Town Area	45-60	35-50km/h

Miscellaneous

Local time is GMT + I (Central European Time). In the summer it changes to daylight saving. Daylight saving operates from late March to late September.

Electricity - 220v AC, with round-pin plugs.

Health - France has no specific health warnings, but adequate medical insurance is recommended.

France

Paris

If there were to be a capital of Europe, it would have to be Paris. Whereas London caters for young people, Paris is for everyone.

Even though the twenty inner suburbs (arrondissements) are influenced by customs from other lands, Paris remains very French.

History

Before the time of Christ there was a small town in the middle of a river, and it was called Lutetia. Here lived a tribe called the Parisii. The Romans, led by Julius Caesar, conquered the Parisii, extended the town onto the left bank of the river and fortified it. This town became Paris.

In 496, Clovis, the Christian leader of the Franks, defeated the German tribes and established a new hereditary dynasty, the Merovingian. He selected Paris as the capital, and succeeding rulers added to and beautified the city.

In 886, Norman invaders sacked Paris and it was reduced to a small island town once more. This is now the Ile de la Cite. The Normans were given Normandy as a consolation prize, and things returned to normal.

Kings came and went, and at one stage were almost abandoned in favour of feudal lords, and then came Hugh Capet, who was crowned King of all France in 987. There followed 400 years of stability, with Paris becoming established as the political, economic and cultural capital of the country. The Sorbonne, the Louvre and Notre Dame were built during the reign of Philip Augustus (1180-1223).

The Golden Age of the French monarchy was during the reigns of Louis XIII, Louis XIV (the Sun King, who built Versailles) and Louis XV. Then came Louis XVI and his Queen Marie Antoinette, and in 1789, the Revolution, and then Napoleon.

Following Napoleon there was a restoration of the monarchy, then the 2nd Republic lasted from 1848 until 1852. This was followed by the 2nd Empire, then the 3rd Republic, then the Vichy Government during the Second World War.

When Paris was liberated in 1944, General Charles de Gaulle's government was recognised by the Allies, and a new constitution was drawn up in 1946. There followed a period of instability, then a new constitution saw the beginning of the 5th Republic, under which the present government operates.

Tourist Information

The Office de Tourisme de Paris, 127, ave des Champs-Elysees, ℂ(01) 4952 5354, fax (01) 4952 5300, is ⊙open daily 9am-8pm (closed May 1, Dec 25 & Jan 1).

There are offices at the following train stations: Gare du Nord, ℂ(01) 4526 94 82; Gare de L'Est, ℂ(01) 4607 1773; Gare de Lyon, ℂ(01) 4343 33 24; Gare d'Austerlitz, ℂ(01) 4584 9170; Gare Montparnasse, ℂ(01) 4322 1919. From May 1 to September 30 there is also an office at the Eiffel Tower, ℂ(01) 4551 2215.

In addition there is a 24 Hour Tourist Information phone line ℂ(01) 4952 5356.

Local Transport

The first thing to do when you arrive in Paris is get hold of a copy of *Paris par Arrondissement* which has good maps of Paris, the subway system and the bus routes. It is available from bookstores and major newsstands.

Buses are an economical way to get around, as ✪16 Francs (2 tickets) will cover the whole metropolitan area. Single tickets are available on the bus, or books of ten, which work out cheaper, can be obtained from Metro stations and some tobacco shops.

The Metro (underground) can be a bit confusing at first, but if you read your map, and the maps on the street and inside the station, you will soon get the hang of it.

There are around 14,500 taxis in Paris, but as usual this is an expensive way to get around. Taxis can be hailed in the street, picked up a taxi stand, or summoned by phone.

Accommodation

Following is a selection of accommodation with prices for a double room per night, which should be used as a guide only.

Paris Hilton

18 avenue de Suffren, Paris, ✆(01) 4438 5600, fax 4438 5610. A modern 5-star hotel on the Left Bank, close to the Eiffel Tower. Facilities include restaurants, bars and shops - from ✪1500FF. (Metro Bir Hakeim, RER Champ de Mars).

California Champs Elysees Best Western, 16 rue de Berri, Paris, ✆(01) 4359 9300, fax 4561 0362. Very conveniently located. 173 rooms, bar, restaurant (not open for dinner) - from ✪1500FF (Metro George V, RER Charles de Gaulle-Etoile).

Acadia Best Western, 4 rue Geoffroy Marie, Paris, ✆(01) 4022 9999, fax 4022 0182. A 3-star hotel close to museums and monuments. 36 rooms and breakfast room for meals - ✪900-1500FF (Metro Montmartre, RER Auber).

Bedford, 17 rue de l'Arcade, Paris, ✆(01) 4494 7777, fax 4494 7797. A 3-star hotel close to museums with 148 rooms and a breakfast room - ✪900-1500FF (Metro Madeleine, RER Auber).

Celte La Fayette, 25 rue Buffault, Paris, ✆(01) 4995 0949, fax 4995 0188. A small, but comfortable hotel close to sightseeing. 52 rooms - ✪600-900FF (Metro Cadet, RER Auber).

Etoile Friedland, 177 rue du Faubourg Saint-Honore, Paris, ✆(01) 4563 6465, fax 4563 8896. A hotel with 40 rooms situated one block from the Champs Elysees - ✪600-900FF (Metro Charles de Gaulle-Etoile, RER Charles de Gaulle-Etoile).

There are five youth hostels in Paris:

Le D'Artagnan, 80 rue Vitruve, ✆(01) 4361 0875, fax 4361 7540.

Cite des Sciences, 1 Rue Jean-Baptiste Clement, ✆(01) 4843 2411, fax 4843 2682.

Jules Ferry, 8 Boulevard Jules Ferry, ✆(01) 4357 5560.

Rue Marcel Duhamel, rue Marcel Duhamel, 91290 Arpajon, ✆(01) 6490 2885.

Relais Europeen de la Jeunesse, 52 avenue Robert Schumann, 91200 Athis Mons, ✆(01) 6984 8139, fax 6984 7848.

Food and Drink

People have been known to visit France simply to partake of the food and wine, and if there was any time left, to take in the sights. This would be a very expensive visit, because meals in French restaurants and restaurant-bars are not cheap, in fact they are often very expensive. Nevertheless, the food is usually very good, and it goes without saying that French wine is magnifique.

All restaurants in France are required to display outside their premises a full bill of fare, with prices. It is a good idea to study this before entering, and to look for some of the *menus* or fixed-price meals. These usually offer three or four courses at a much more reasonable price than choosing from the a la carte section.

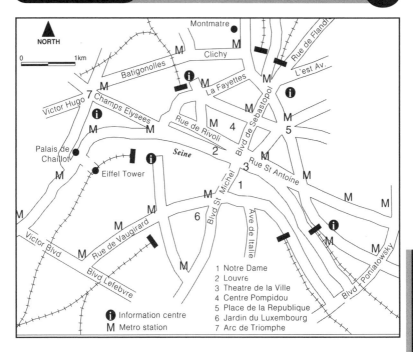

NORTH

0 1km

Montmatre

Clichy

Rue de Flandr

L'est Av.

Batignolles

La Fayettes

Blvd de Sebastopol

Victor Hugo

7 Champs Elysees

Rue de Rivoli   4

5

Palais de Chaillot

Seine

2

Eiffel Tower

Rue St Antoine

3

1

Blvd St Michel

6

Ave de Italie

Victor Blvd

Rue de Vaugirard

Blvd Poniatowsky

Blvd Lefebvre

1 Notre Dame
2 Louvre
3 Theatre de la Ville
4 Centre Pompidou
5 Place de la Republique
6 Jardin du Luxembourg
7 Arc de Triomphe

ℹ Information centre
Ⓜ Metro station

France

Sightseeing

Following is a walking tour of the city, which would be quite difficult to achieve in one day, but which covers all the main sights. One thing to keep in mind, Paris is not called the City of Lights for nothing, and every visitor should ensure that they take a tour, grab a cab, or catch a bus at night time to see the city illuminations. An evening trip down the Avenue des Champs-Elysees is truly unforgettable.

A tour should begin where it all started, the geographical centre of Paris.

Ile de la Cite

Go across the Pont d'Arcole, which spans the Seine's arm, and on the left is the **Town Hall**. In 1871 it was the barracks of the Paris Commune who fought their last battles in the 20th arrondissement.

Also in the 20th arrondissement around metro Belleville and metro Menilmontant is the international quarter, with its worldwide charm. On the Ile de la Cite, is the cathedral of **Notre Dame**, arguably Paris's greatest and most famous building. Of French Gothic architecture, the cathedral was built between 1163 and 1345, and is one of the most beautiful churches in the world. It has an archaeological vault/tomb and museum that are well worth a visit.

Other buildings on the island are the **Palais de Justice**, the legal headquarters of France, and the **Conciergerie**, which was the 'Antechamber of the Guillotine' during the Revolution. It was here that Marie-Antoinette and many others spent the night before their appointment with Madame Guillotine. Visitors can see her chapel and crucifix, a guillotine blade, Robespierre's cell and the Cour des Femmes, where the condemned said their last farewells to their loved ones. Behind the Palais de Justice is the **Sainte-Chapelle**, which was built by St Louis (Louis IX) in 1248.

Next to the Ile de la Cite is the **Ile St Louis** which is usually overlooked, but it is where you can buy the best ice cream and sorbet, at *Berthillon*.

Take Pont Sully to the north bank of the Seine, then follow Boulevard Henri IV to the **Place de la Bastille**, a large square that is all that is left of the famous prison. Relatively new to this square is the **Opera de la Bastille**, which has performances mainly for the people who live in the suburbs to the east of here. The tickets are affordable, unlike the other opera venues, and it is not necessary to dress up for the occasion.

A short walk from here is the **Place des Vosges**, which was the Place Royale. It has thirty-eight town houses built over long arcades. It has been restored, and House 6, where Victor Hugo once lived and worked, has been turned into a museum dedicated to him. Continue along rue des Francs-Bourgeois and after a few blocks the **Pompidou**

Centre presents itself. It has to be one of the ugliest buildings of all time, but this in itself guarantees hundreds of visitors each day. The centre contains a library, a children's workshop, a theatre workshop, a music laboratory, and the **National Museum of Modern Art**, ℂ(01) 4478 1233. It is ☉open Mon, Wed, Thurs, Fri noon-10pm, Sat-Sun 10am-10pm.

The next stop is **Forum des Halles**, a vast, sunken multi-level complex sprawled over Les Halles Metro and RER stations. This was the site of the city's food market since the 12th century, but modern traffic and lack of space forced the market out into the suburbs (near Orly Airport). The complex is mostly covered at ground level with gardens and tree-lined footpaths, and it would take a few visits to fully appreciate all the gardens as well as the plethora of shops below, the **Grande Epoque** waxworks museum, the **Musee de Holographie**, and the olympic-size swimming pool.

The Louvre
Walk down to rue de Rivoli, turn right, and a short way ahead is the **Palais du Louvre**.

The Louvre was a medieval fortress built in 1200 during the reign of Philippe Auguste. The site was called Lupara, and the fortress was where Paris's defences were the weakest. Now this location is at the south-west quarter of the Square Courtyard, where there are remains of several towers unearthed between 1984 and 1985. In the 14th century, Charles V added to the building and it became a royal residence, but then came the Hundred Years' War, and royalty became enamoured with the Loire valley for over 150 years, deserting their capital.

The 16th century saw Francois I demolish the keep and replace the rest with a Renaissance style building. This style of architecture was continued with additions and renovations through the various reigns. The Louvre Museum came into being at the end of the 18th century during the French Revolution, when it was decided that the royal collections should be on display for everyone.

Now the Louvre is the largest complex in Paris, and it contains the world's richest collection of art. It is impossible to see it all in one day, or even to take in what you have seen in one day, but if you are not really into art and just want a quick look-see, the following will help. The *Mona Lisa* is behind glass in the Italian Gallery; the *Winged Victory of Samothrace* and the *Venus de Milo* are in the Greek and Roman section; and Rembrandt's *Bathsheba at her Toilet* is in the Dutch collection.

The Louvre is ☺open Wed-Mon 9am-6pm, and until 10pm on Mon, and guided tours are available. Admission is ✪45FF before 3pm, 26FF after 3pm and all day Sunday, and free for the under 18s. It might be wise to mention now that there are 62 museums and monuments in Paris and the greater metropolitan area, so if you intend to visit a few it might be a good idea to enquire about the **Carte Musee et Monuments** pass. It is available from museums, monuments, tourist information offices, and main Metro stations, and costs ✪80FF for one day (which would have to be a very long day to fit in several museums), 160FF for three days, and 240FF for five days.

Near here, along rue de Rivoli, is the Place du Palais Royal, and the **Palais Royal** itself. This was originally owned by Cardinal Richelieu, but today its arcades have shops selling all sorts of odds and ends. From the corner of the Palais, the Avenue de l'Opera leads off at an angle and finishes at the Place de l'Opera and the **Opera House**, now called the Opera Paris-Garnier in honour of its architect (or one could say that somebody had to take the blame).

Meanwhile, back on the tour the next stop is the **Jardin des Tuileries**, at the east end of which is the **Arc de Triomphe du Carrousel**, a small version of the real thing. The Tuileries gardens are about 1km long, are well set out with statues, pools, fountains and

France

playgrounds and make a very pleasant distraction from sightseeing. At the west end of the gardens, though, is the **Orangerie**, a museum devoted to the works of the Impressionists. It has two oval basement rooms covered with murals of Monet's water-lilies - incredible! The exhibition also has 14 Cezannes, 24 Renoirs and works by Modigliani, Matisse and Picasso. ☺Open Wed-Mon 9.45am-5.15pm, admission is ✪27FF .

From there it is only a few steps to the **Place de la Concorde**, the central square of Paris, with its Egyptian obelisk. Now it is time to stroll down the **Champs-Elysees**, firstly past the **Grand** and **Petit Palais** (on the left) and the presidential **Palais de l'Elysee** (right), then past department stores, restaurants, cinemas, and the fountains of the Rond-Point des Champs-Elysees, finally reaching the **Place de l'Etoile** (now Place Charles de Gaulle) and the magnificent **Arc de Triomphe**.

This monument to France's military victories was conceived by Napoleon and is built on a raised platform. It is 50m high and 45m wide, and is covered with statuary and bas-reliefs denoting victories in various wars and battles. Underneath the arch is the Tomb of the Unknown Soldier from World War I, on which a flame is continually burning. It is a very moving monument, and should not be missed. There is also access to the top for fantastic views of the city.

The Champs Elysees becomes the Avenue de la Grande Armee, and then the modern **Palais de Congres** is on the right and the **Bois de Boulogne** is on the left. The Bois is a beautiful park, but not recommended at night.

From the Arc de Triomphe take Avenue Kleber to the **Palais de Chaillot**, best known for the view from there to the Eiffel Tower, but also home to the **Museum of Mankind** and the **Cinema Museum**.

France

France

The Eiffel Tower

Anyway, there it is, the **Eiffel Tower**, and as you get closer to it, and it seems to get larger, you will notice the thousands of people milling around its foundations. There are people in long queues waiting to board the elevators that take visitors up to any of the three viewing stations; there are quite a few hardy types who are starting/finishing the 1652 stairs that rise to the top station; and there quite a few who are

saying, "No way. I'm not going up there, it doesn't look sturdy enough." And it does look a bit fragile, just like scaffolding.

Designed by Gustave Eiffel, and built for the World Exhibition in 1889, the tower is 300m high (the temperature causes this figure to vary by about 40cm - higher when hotter), and the views from the stations are magnificent. The best time is supposed to be about an hour before sunset.

In front of the tower is the **Champ de Mars**, which leads to the **Hotel des Invalides**, built by Louis XIV as a hospital for 4000 war veterans. In the hospital is the **Musee de l'Armee**, probably the finest military museum in the world, and in the grounds is a Baroque domed church that contains Napoleon's tomb.

North of the City

Take the Metro to Blanche and come face to face with the famous **Moulin Rouge** complete with windmill. The area around Boulevard de Clichy and the **Place Pigalle** was made famous by Toulouse-Lautrec, and it is still the scene of the sleazy side of Paris nightlife. During the day it looks extremely tacky, but at night it does tend to take on a glamorous air. There are a few street markets that may grab the attention.

With the Moulin Rouge on the left, continue along Boulevard de Clichy to rue de Steinkerque, turn left and follow the street up to the long flight of stairs that leads to **Montmartre**. This hill has had a very long and colourful history. The Romans built a temple to the god Mercury here; in the 3rd century AD it was renamed Mont des Martyrs in honour of the execution of St Denis; in 1871 hundreds of rebels were massacred in the caves; in the late 1800s, it became an artists' colony and earned the title of the birthplace of modern art; and today it is teeming with tourists. But don't let that you put you off. The artists are still there, and you can have your portrait sketched while you wait (but settle on the price first); or you can wander around the narrow cobbled streets, visiting the art and craft shops; or you can pop into a bistro and try some real French Onion Soup, which is a meal in itself. A visit to the **Basilique du Sacre-Coeur** might not be high on your list, but there is a great view of the city from the walkways around the domes.

If you decide to take the funicular down the hill, check out the souvenir shops to the right of the top station. Sometimes they have stock that is unavailable anywhere else in Paris.

Versailles

A trip to Versailles should be compulsory for every visitor who lands in Paris, and it can be reached by RER route C.

Versailles was built by Louis XIV, the Sun King, and was completed in 1682. Louis made it the official residence of the court and the seat of royal power. As the court consisted of the royal family, all their close relatives, the king's advisors, and everybody's personal servants, as well as the household staff, it is no wonder that the Palace of Versailles is so large. The western face of the building measures over 600m.

Amazingly, back in its early days the palace was open to the general public, though obviously not to the extent that it is today. Now visitors are admitted to the Sun King's private quarters above the official suite, but in those days Louis would not have appreciated a crowd dropping in (especially if he was entertaining Madame du Barry).

Versailles is ☉open Tues-Sun 9am-6.30pm (May-Sept), 9am-5.30pm (Oct-April), ✆(01) 3084 7400. The park and gardens are ☉open daily from dawn to dusk. Fireworks displays are held once a month, and the Grands Eaux (fountains display) is held on some Sundays from May to mid-October.

Attractions not to be missed are:
The Hall of Mirrors
The Chapel
The Opera Royale
The Grand Trianon
The Petit Trianon
The various apartments
The beautiful gardens.

Euro-Disneyland

Situated 30km east of Paris, off the A4 motorway, this theme park is a very expensive way to spend a day. It has an area of more than 2000ha, and is modelled on the original Disneyland in California. Some of the US rides have been duplicated, but they can't duplicate the continual sunshine offered by Anaheim, so the weather can cause a problem. Nevertheless, the park is attracting thousands of visitors each day, and it is wise to arrive early, or stay till the death, to avoid long queues.

France

The Best of Paris in Brief

Louvre Museum (Musee du Louvre). Home to an overwhelming number of masterpeices, this is unquestionably Europe's greatest museum. The enigmatic *Mona Lisa* lives here among unrivalled company. Joining a tour is the best way to appreciate the ample artistic genius without straying off on a time-consuming tangent. *Pyramid, 1er.*

Eiffel Tower. The 7,000 tons of metal comprising this famous structure have stood above Paris since 1889. Forget the cost, forget the crowds and make sure you go all the way to the third and topmost level, which provides the most rewarding views of Europe's premier city. *Champ-de-Mars, 7e.*

Notre-Dame. Apart from its architecture, this 700-year-old gothic cathedral contains some fine flourishes of biblical art and sculpture. This place has a wonderful, significant history and should make its way promptly onto your Paris itinerary. *6 place du Parvis Notre-Dame, 4e.*

Orsay Museum (Musee d'Orsay). Exhibits Realist, Art Nouveau and, of course, Impressionist styles. The extent of the latter makes this museum most noteworthy. *1 rue de Belle-chasse.*

Napolean's Tomb and Army Museum (Hotel des Invalides). Contains, of course, an extravagent crypt for the French conquerer and a superlative Army museum. *Place des Invalides.*

Arc de Triomphe. Napolean's great Arc of Triumph overlooks the mayhem of the traffic surrounding it, with twelve roads feeding into the one area and everybody working in widening concentric circles to break free of the near-gridlock. The tomb of the Unknown Soldier is located here. *Place Charles-de-Gaulle-Etoile, 16e.*

Champs-Elysees. Take time to walk down this busy and historical boulevard, particularly at night.

Sainte-Chapelle. The stunning gothic design, a marvel of its time (1248), is characterised by the use of plenty of glass to allow radiant light to pass into every holy corner. This is where the Crown of Thorns was once kept, the relic in fact inspiring the creation of the church that was to be its resting place. *Palais de Justice, 4 bd. du Palais, 1er.*

Ile St-Louis. A stroll through this small island residential area will take you past the quaint homes and haunts of some famous historical figures, including Madame Curie and literary greats Voltaire and Baudelaire.

Montparnasse Tower. Good views from the top of this 59-floor structure, particularly of the Eiffel Tower.

Latin Quarter. Known for its cafes, restaurants and jazz clubs. Students spread out from the University of Paris to sip coffee and discuss philosophy. Activity hovers around the trendy strip of place St. Michel.

Basilique du Sacre-Coeur. Completed in 1871, the church is noted for its unusual Byzantine style and its views over Paris. Nearby avenues of Montmartre have become a centre for street artists. *Place St.Pierre, 18e.*

Picasso Museum (Musee Picasso). A must for Picasso fans, this museum is totally dedicated to the master's life and the evolution of his work on many mediums. *5 rue de Thorigny, 3e.*

France

Cluny Museum (Musee National du Moyen Age). The best collection of medieval art from the Middle Ages. *6 place Paul-Painleve, 5e.*

Pere Lachaise Cemetery (Cemetiere du Pere-Lachaise). A distinguished list of occupants rest here, from Oscar Wilde to Jim Morrison as well as some the city's famous sons and daughters.

Palace of Versailles. The envy of Europe - and commissioned by Louis XIV to be exactly that - the awe-inspiring Palace of Versailles requires a day-trip to visit, which is well-worth organising. There are few disappointments within this staggering creative acheivement, and the highlights are the immense palace gardens and the Hall of Mirrors inside.

Nice

Situated in the south-eastern corner of the country in the *departement* of Alpes-Maritimes, Nice is known as the Queen of the Riviera. It is a very pretty part of the world, and the departure point for trips to Corsica.

Nice is a popular holiday resort to which thousands flock every year, despite the fact that its plentiful beach is all pebbles.

History

Nice belonged to Italy until it was given to France in 1860 by the House of Savoy. It has always been a favourite with English tourists, and until World War II it had that 'Oh So English' trademark, a long pier jutting out into the Mediterranean. Still, Nice must have appreciated this annual English influx because the waterfront street is called Promenade des Anglais.

Tourist Information

There is an information office in Avenue Thiers, at the railway station, ©9387 0707, ©open daily 8am-7pm (later in the summer season), and another near the airport at 5 Promenade des Anglais, ©(04) 9383 3264, ©open Mon-Sat 8.45am-12.30pm and 2-7pm.

Local Transport

There is a regular bus service from the Promenade des Anglais to the airport, and long distance buses to Cannes, Toulon and Marseille. Between Gare de Provence in Nice and Digne in the coastal alps there is a private railway - *Chemins de Fer de Provence*. It winds through the romantic Var Valley.

Accommodation

Following is a selection of accommodation with prices for a double room per night, which should be used as a guide only.

West End Hotel, 31 Promenade Des Anglais, Nice, ©(04) 9214 4400, fax 9388 8507 (✔travelweb@hotelbook.com(14137)). A superior first class hotel in the downtown area. 125 rooms with facilities including a restaurant, bar, coffee shop and private beach - standard room ✪600-1200FF.

Sofitel Nice Hotel, Parvis De L'Europe, Nice, ©(04) 9200 8000, fax 9326 2700 (✔travelweb@hotelbook.com(14174)). Opposite the Acropolis Trade Fair Centre in the middle of town with a view of the Bay of Angels. 152 rooms, restaurant, bar/lounge, pool - ✪760-1200FF.

Atlantic Hotel, 12 Boulevard Victor Hugo, Nice, ©(04) 9388 4015, fax 9388 6860 (✔travelweb@hotelbook.com(04094)). In the heart of Nice, 500m from the railway station. 123 rooms, restaurant, bar/lounge - ✪500-1000FF.

Primotel Suisse, 15 Quai Rauba Capeu, Nice, ✆(04) 9217 3900, fax 9385 3070. 42 rooms, close to Old Town and flower market. Contains a restaurant and bar/lounge - ✪285-560FF.

Nice Rivoli Hotel

45 Rue Pastorelli, Nice, ✆(04) 9392 6960, fax 9392 6222. (✉travelweb@hotelbook. com(28796)). Situated near the Old Town, and a five minute walk from the beach. 122 rooms, bar, heated pool, sauna - ✪470-1100FF.

There are two **Youth Hostels** in Nice:

AJ Nice, Route Forestiere du Mont Alban, ✆(04) 938 92 364, fax 920 40 310.

Summer Hostel - for details contact the AJ Nice hostel above.

Food and Drink

The food is called *Nicoise* and the local specialty is *bouillabaisse*, a very tasty fish stew. There are many eateries within walking distance of the Promenade des Anglais, from the expensive restaurants in the first class hotels, to small coffee shops and self-service places.

Sightseeing

The **Promenade des Anglais** is 7km long, runs along the waterfront, and is lined with palm trees and flowers. It is also lined with expensive hotels, including the famous Hotel Negresco, and casinos and expensive cafes.

At the intersection of the Promenade and the Quais des Etats Unis, broad boulevards branch off to Place Massena. They are the connections between the old, or lower, part of town at the foot of Chateau Hill and the new city centre around Avenue Jean Medecin (in the direction of the railway station) and the Boulevard Victor Hugo.

France

Then there is the harbour area, **Lympia**, east of the Chateau and west of Mont Boron.

In the old town area, walk along the Boulevard Jean Jaure from Promenade du Paillon to the Port Fosse steps, then turn right into rue du Marche, past the Palais de Justice, Place du Palais, to the Marche aux Fleurs (flower market) and the Fruits et Legumes (fruit and vegetable market) on Cours Saleya. The **Galerie de Malacologie** is at no. 3 Cours Saleya, and has exhibits of the fauna of the Mediterranean.

There are some beautiful buildings in the old town. East of the markets is a building which was the old Savoy Senate building until 1792, and later the Law Court until 1860. One street further on is **Adam and Eve House**. A little further on is the baroque **Eglise de Jesus**, and across the street of the same name is the cathedral of **St Raparate** on Place Rossetti which was named in honour of the martyr. Walk through the lanes - Halle aux Herbes, Place Entrale, rue du Collet, until you get to the rue St Augustin/rue Pairolliers - for some very picturesque old town scenery.

From here rue de la Providence climbs up to Le Chateau, a former fort, from where there are panoramic views. On the other side are: **Place Garibaldi**, an early extension of the town; the **Quai des Etats Unis** has the **Museum of Contemporary Art**; a bit further on is the **Naval Museum** in the 16th century Bellanda Tower.

There are a few interesting places to visit in the suburb of **Cimiez** - the **Archaeological Site and Museum**, with the **Matisse Museum** in the same building; and the **Marc Chagall Museum** in Avenue Dr Menard.

Principality of Monaco

To the east of Nice, further along the sea front, is the **Principality of Monaco**, a sovereign state surrounded by the *departement* of Alpes-Maritimes. It has been ruled by the Grimaldis since 1308.

Monaco consists of three parts: the capital Monaco, the resort of Monte Carlo, and the commercial centre of La Condamine - although one flows into the other and a visitor would not notice any distinct areas.

Although the name 'Monte Carlo' is almost synonymous with the word 'gambling', only a small percentage (about 3%) of Monaco's revenue comes from the casinos. But, if you are in the neighbourhood, why not try your luck? It is necessary to show your passport to participate in any gambling. If, on the other hand, you are a people watcher, grab a table in one of the outdoor places opposite the casino, and see how the other half live.

Driving Through France

There are so many places to see in France, that it is possible to only describe a few short tours.

Versailles and the Loire Valley

Itinerary - 6 Days - Distance 844kms

Head southwest out of Paris until you reach **Versailles** and the famous palace and surrounding park. This is near **Rambouillet**, a small town in the forest of Rambouillet. Here is the hunting lodge of the President of France. When it is not being used, visitors may tour through the lodge.

Further south is **Chartres**, a medieval town famous for its cathedral. Drive through **Bonneval** and **Chateaudun**, old towns, until you reach **Blois**. There is a huge chateau here, dating from the 13th century. The town is also famous for its chocolates. At **Chaumont Sur Loire**, the chateau is situated in a beautiful park, while at **Amboise**, it overlooks the river Loire. There is also a residence where Leonardo da Vinci lived, with models he constructed, on display.

Tours is in the centre of the chateaux region, with many historic buildings. The chateau is now a silk industry museum. Driving west, you reach **Angers**, a noted textile and wine producing town. There are also many interesting buildings. Turn back at Angers, and drive east to **Saumur**. This town is noted for its chateaux, wines and Calvary school. **Chinon** is a very medieval town with a huge castle, and chateaux, including one where Joan of Arc once lived.

Travelling east you pass through the chateaux towns of **Azay Le Rideau** and **Chenonceaux**. The chateau at Chenonceaux is built out over the river Cher. At **Cour Cheverny**, the chateau has been in the same family since it was built, and has not been extended. The largest of the Loire chateaux is at **Chambord**.

Heading north again you reach **Orleans**, an ancient town which is best known for its association with Joan of Arc. Closer to Paris, the **Forest of Fontainebleau** is one of the most picturesque places in the region, with its palace. The state apartments are open to visitors. From Fontainebleu drive back to Paris.

The French Riviera, Monaco and Verdon

Itinerary - 5 Days - Distance 635kms

From Nice, drive south to **Antibes**, the centre of the local flower growing industry. The Grimaldi Chateau is now a Picasso museum. **Juan-Les-Pins** and **Golfe Juan** are fashionable resorts along this coast. The most famous resort is **Cannes**, with its world renowned festivals and casinos. The harbour of **St Raphael** is used for fishing and pleasure boats, and also has a museum of underwater archeology.

Nearby is **Frejus**, originally established by Julius Caesar (49BC) and has many artefacts from that era. **Carrefour-de-la Foux** is the turn off point for **St Tropez**, another fashionable resort.

Travelling further south you reach **Hyeres**, the oldest of the resorts along the coast, and then **Toulon**. Toulon is an important naval base. The old town still remains in original condition despite being bombed in World War II.

Bypassing **Marseille**, you reach **Aix-En Provence**, the old capital of Provence. It has many historic buildings, and is now well known as a spa resort. There is an open air music festival held every July and August.

Following the road north you reach **Manosque** where you turn off towards the **Grand Canyon Du Verson**, leading to **Grasse**. On the way you pass through medieval towns such as **Riez** and **Castellane**. **Grasse** is famous as the centre for perfume production, and the flower beds are nearby. You can visit some of the perfume factories. Making your way back down from the hills you reach **Nice**, a city dating from Roman times. There are many historic buildings and museums here, as well as being the premier resort of the Riviera.

Bordeaux and the Dordogne

Itinerary - 6 Days - Distance 700kms

Bordeaux is the fifth largest city in France, and is a famous wine producing area. It is possible to tour many of the vineyards. The surrounding area is noted for its beaches and forests.

Drive east to **Libourne**, situated at the junction of the Dordogne and Isle rivers. This is an old town with buildings dating back to the 14th century. One hundred kilometres north of Libourne, you find the town of **Cognac**. Cognac is the home of the brandy trade, and it is possible to visit some of the brandy warehouses (by appointment). From

Cognac, drive east to **Angouleme**. This was once the largest fortress in France, and remnants of the medieval walled city still remain.

Further south, lies **Brantome**, which is situated on an island in the river Dronne. The abbey (which is now a musuem) and the town hall date from the 7th century. From here, drive south to **Perigeux** which is world renowned for its truffles and foie gras. This is an ancient town with archealogical finds dating back to Neolithic, Roman and Gallic settlements. Another ancient town nearby, **Montignac**, is famous for the Lascaux caves, showing prehistoric drawings. Although the caves are closed for preservation purposes, replicas may be viewed. Montignac is also known as the walnut growing centre of France.

Driving further east you reach **Brive-La-Gaillarde**, which is an important fruit and vegetable growing region. Again this is an ancient town, dating from the 12th century.

Directly south of Brive-la-Gaillarde is **Rocamadour**, a fortified medieval town which is famous for its situation - it is built up a cliff face. Some of the buildings are partly set into rock. **Souillac**, on the Dordogne river is a popular base for exploring the limestone caves and regions.

The town of **Bergerac**, still on the Dordogne river, is an important wine and tobacco growing centre. There is a Tobacco museum in the Town Hall. Heading back to Bordeaux, stop at **La Reole**, situated above the Garonne River. Again this town dates from medieval times. The tour finishes back in Bordeaux.

Germany

THE FEDERAL REPUBLIC OF GERMANY is situated in central Europe and has an area of 356,910 sq km. The population is around 82,000,000 and the official language is German. English is taught in schools, and most people in the hospitality industry are fluent in English.

Climate

The climate is generally mild, with harsher winters in the Bavarian Alps. The July average is 21C, and the January average -1C.

Entry Regulations

Visitors must have a valid passport, and a visa is not required for visits of up to three months.

The duty free allowance is 200 cigarettes, 100 cigarillos or 50 cigars or 250 gm of tobacco; 1 litre of spirits (more than 22 degrees proof) or 2 litres of spirits (up to 22 degrees proof) and 2 litres of sparkling wine and 2 litres of still wine, or a proportional assortment of these products; and 50 grammes of perfume. There is no restriction on the import or export of local or foreign currencies.

No vaccinations are required for any international traveller.

Currency

The currency of the land is the Deutsche Mark (DM), which is divided into 100 Pfennigs.

Approximate exchange rates, which should be used as a guide only, are:

A$	=	1.20DM
Can$	=	1.42DM
NZ$	=	0.97DM
S$	=	1.25DM
UK£	=	3.18DM
US$	=	2.09DM

Notes are in denominations of 1000, 500, 200, 100, 50, 20 and 10 Deutsche Marks, and coins are 5, 2 and 1DM, and 50, 20, 10, 5, 2 and 1 Pfennigs.

Since 1.1.1999 the Euro has been in circulation, and 1 EUR = 1.95583DM.

Banks are ☉open Mon-Fri 9am-noon, 2-4pm. The Reisebanks at Zoo Station and Ostbahnhof are ☉open daily from 7.30am.

Shopping hours are ☉Mon-Fri 9am-6.30pm (Thurs until 8.30pm), Sat 9am-2pm (until 4pm on the first Sat of each month). Shops are closed on Sundays. The big stores in Berlin are ☉open Mon-Fri 9am-8pm, Sat 9am-4pm.

Post Offices are ☉open Mon-Fri 8am-6pm, Sat 8am-noon.

Credit cards are widely accepted.

Telephone

International direct dialling is available and the International code is 00, the country code 49. International calls can be made from booths marked 'Auslandsgesprache', or from post offices.

Payphones have slots for 10 Pfennigs, 1DM and 5DM, or phonecards (Telefonkarten) are available at post offices. Booths where these can be used are marked 'Kartentelefon'. Reverse charge (collect) calls can only be made to the United States.

It is very expensive to make international calls from hotels.

Driving

Germany has nearly 11,000km of toll-free motorways (autobahn), as well as highways that are famous worldwide for their scenic countryside.

UK, American and Canadian citizens can hire a car with a valid driving licence from their own country, other nationalities require an international driver's licence. Traffic drives on the right, seat belts are compulsory, and children under 12 years are not permitted to travel in the front seat.

Speed limits are:

Built-up areas -	50kph
Open roads -	100kph
Motorways -	130kph

Miscellaneous

Local time is GMT + 1, and there is daylight saving in the summer time.

Electricity - 220v AC 50 Hertz, with round ended two-pin plugs.

Health - Visitors from EC countries are covered for medical costs, but all other travellers should have health insurance.

Germany

Berlin

Berlin lies in the north German lowlands, on the banks of the Spree River, and its name comes from a Slovakian word meaning 'built on a marsh'. The city has an area of 892 sq km, and it is the third largest in Europe (only London and Paris are larger). It measures 45km from east to west and 38km from north to south, and is divided into 23 districts, each one a city in itself. The population is around 3.5 million.

Although the Wall came down in 1990, Berliners still think of themselves as either Ossis (East) or Wessis (West), as a large proportion cannot remember life before the Wall.

History

History first records Berlin as a city in 1251, in competition with the city of Colln, on the left bank of the Spree. The two cities combined in 1307, under the name of Berlin.

Berlin has had a colourful history ever since the elector of Brandenburg made it his official residence in 1447. It was involved in the Thirty Years War that began in 1618, was invaded by Napoleon in 1806, warred with Austria in 1866, and France in 1870, and was made the capital city of the German Empire in 1871. In 1914, the first world war commenced when Germany invaded France, and in 1918 it concluded with Germany's defeat. Kaiser Wilhelm II abdicated, and the Weimar Republic was established in the same year.

1933 saw Hitler elected, and under his leadership Germany headed for the Second World War, invading Poland in 1939. Once again Germany was defeated, and in 1945 the Allied armies entered Berlin and divided it into four sectors.

The communist DDR (German Democratic Republic) built the Wall in 1961, dividing Berlin into East and West. After the demolition of the wall, all-German elections were held in 1990 and the Christian Democrat coalition was voted into power. Berlin once again became the seat of parliament in 1991.

Tourist Information

The Berlin Tourist Office has several branches: on the ground floor of the Europa Center, Budapester Strasse entrance, ☼open Mon-Sat 8.30am-8.30pm, Sun 10am-6.30pm, ✆(030) 250 025; Tegel Airport Main Hall, ☼open daily 5am-10.30pm; KaDeWe, Travel Centre, ground floor, ☼open Mon-Fri 9.30am-8pm, Sat 9am-4pm.; Brandenburg Gate, South Wing, ☼open daily 9.30am-6pm.

The Berlin Information Centre, Hardenbergstrasse 20, 1000 Berlin 12, has plenty of free maps and brochures.

Local Transport

Public transport in Berlin consists of the U-Bahn (underground), S-Bahn trains, single and double-decker buses. The East is serviced by trams.

Unfortunately, using the **underground system** in the city is confusing and time consuming, with several transfers often necessary to get from A to B. Many U-Bahn stations are inundated with signs that only add to the confusion, as they tell of transfers, exits, transit directions, but there is a shortage of signs telling travellers where they are. Also, there are few stations that have local maps to aid orientation.

Electric **trams** were invented in Berlin, with the first one going into service in 1881. The trams in East Berlin have rattley old carriages, but those in Potsdam are in good repair. Tram stops have HH signs.

Buses can be just as confusing as the underground, but if you enjoy the double-decker variety, why not try to come to grips with the system. **Remember the front stairs are for going up, the back for going down**. Bus stops have a green H on them.

There are different kinds of reduced fare tickets available from ticket offices or, more conveniently, from machines. It may pay you to invest in a *WelcomeCard* book of vouchers for ✪DM29. It offers three days travelling around Berlin and Potsdam on all buses and train operating within the A, B and C fare zones of Berlin, plus discounts of up to 50% for entry to many attractions. The Card is a bonus for families because it entitles every adult to take up to three children under the age of 14 for free. The Cards are available from all BVG ticket offices, tourist information points and some hotels.

A tip for finding your way around Berlin: street numbers run up one side of a street, then down the other, so that no. 2 may be opposite no. 300, depending on the length of the street. The street numbers for each block are indicated on signs on street corners.

Germany

Accommodation

As mentioned previously, Berlin is a big city, so you can expect to find plenty of accommodation. Following are a few of the inner city accommodation outlets, with prices in DM that should be used as a guide only. The telephone area code is 030.

Alsterhof Ringhotel Berlin, Augsburger Strasse 5, ✆212 420, fax 218 3949. 200 rooms, a restaurant, bar/lounge and swimming pool - ✪225-390DM including buffet breakfast.

Hotel Am Zoo

Kürfurstendamm 25, ✆884 370, fax 8843 7714. There are 136 rooms, some of which have good views overlooking the Kurfürstendamm. Trendy bar and an adequate dining area - ✪328-485DM including buffet breakfast.

Hotel Avantgarde, Kurfurstendamm 15, 10719 Berlin, ✆882 6466, fax 882 4011. 27 rooms and a combined bar and lounge - ✪230-380DM, including breakfast.

Best Western Hotel Boulevard, Kurfurstendamm 12, ✆884 250, fax 8842 5450. 114 beds and a bar - ✪204-320DM, including buffet breakfast.

Berlin Plaza Hotel, Knesebeckstrasse 63, ✆884 130, fax 9941 3754. 221 beds with facilities including a restaurant and bar - ✪199-339DM including buffet breakfast.

Hotel Berliner Hof, Tauentzienstrasse 8, ✆254 950 fax 262 3065. 80 beds - ✪240-280DM including buffet breakfast.

Food and Drink

Traditional Berlin fare, such as blockwurst and meat balls, is in small supply, but there are still a few places that stick with the originals. Here is a selection.

Wilhelm Hoeck, Charlottenburg, Wilmersdorfer Strasse 149, ✆341 8174 - ◷open Mon-Sat 8am-midnight. Home made meat rissoles, gherkins and pickled eggs near the draught beer taps. This is as Old Berlin as you can get.

Laternchen, Charlottenburg, Windscheidstrasse 24, ✆324 6882 - ◷open Mon-Fri 6pm-midnight, Sat-Sun 6pm-1am. The decor is definitely Old Berlin, but sometimes the menu can have a few imports.

Marjellchen, Charlottenburg, Mommsenstrasse 9, ✆883 2676 - ◷open Mon-Sat noon-midnight, Sun 5pm-midnight. Believed by some to have the best Konigsberg dumplings in town, this eatery also has alcoholic Danzig Goldwasser on offer.

Zur letzten Instanz, Mitte, Waisenstrasse 14-16, ✆242 5528 - ◷open daily noon-1am. This is one of, if not the oldest pub in Berlin, dating back to 1621. In keeping with this reputation there is always "Eisbein" (pickled pork shank) on the menu.

Germans are prolific beer-drinkers, so it is not difficult to locate a pub, in fact there seems to be one on every corner.

Shopping

The best known department store in Berlin is the Kaufhaus des Westens, better known as *KaDeWe*, in Wittenbergplatz. It opened in 1907, and is the largest department store in Germany, and the third largest in Europe - Galeries Lafayette in Paris is the largest, followed by Harrods in London.

KaDeWe has seven floors, but it is the sixth floor that almost puts the store in the sightseeing category, for this is where the legendary giant delicatessen is found.

The **Europa Centre** at Breitscheidplatz has a shopping centre, and shopping streets are: Kurfurstendamm and its side streets; Schloss Strasse in Steglitz; Wilmersdorfer Strasse in Charlottenburg; Savigny-platz; Savignybogen; and Under den Linden between Brandenburger Tor and Alexanderplatz.

Forms for reclaiming VAT are issued with the purchase, and the refund is issued when leaving Germany.

Sightseeing

Charlottenburg

The centre of unified Berlin is in the district of Charlottenburg, and this is the best place to begin a tour.

The **Kaiser-Wilhelm-Gedachtniskirche** (Emperor William Memorial Church) on Breitscheidplatz, ©245 023, was almost completely destroyed during World War II, due to its proximity to the strategically important Zoo station. The powers that be wanted to raze the ruins, but Berlin magazines aroused public interest in the project and a new complex has risen from the ashes. Guided tours are available on ©Thurs and Fri at 1.15pm, 3pm and 4.30pm, and it is worth visiting for the beautiful mosaic ceiling in the small hall. This is as beautiful as the original church, which is not what some think about the rest of the building.

Kurfurstendamm, affectionately called Ku'damm, branches off opposite the church. This street is 3.5km long and 60m wide, and Otto von Bismarck, the first German chancellor, decided to make it into a shopping and amusement avenue. Apparently he had become enamoured of the Champs Elysees during a trip to Paris in 1871, and wanted to make the Ku'damm as famous, if not more so. All buildings were to be four storeys, and the facades had to be decorated with stucco. English gardens were to be laid out in the front of the houses, and those on the corners had to have a dome on top. It was magnificent but, unfortunately, World War II destroyed 202 of the original 250 buildings.

Fasanenstrasse runs off Ku'damm, and at no. 79-80 is the **Judisches Gemeindehaus** (Jewish Community House), ℂ883 6548. This modern centre for Berlin's 6000 Jews was built on the foundations of a Byzantine synagogue that was burned to the ground on infamous Kristallnacht, November 9, 1938. The present building has fragments of the former portal in the entrance. A bronze sculpture by Richard Hess stands in front of the building and has an inscription from the book of Moses.

Back on Breitscheidplatz is the **Europa Centre**, the building with the Mercedes symbol on the top. This twenty-three storey building has more than one hundred shops and restaurants, a casino, *La Vie en Rose* nightclub, the Tourist Office and various airline offices. A **Panoramic Lookout** is a few steps up from the 22nd floor, and access is on Tauentzienstrasse between the Dresdner Bank and the cinema. This tower is ☺open daily 9am-midnight, and admission is ✪DM5, but it is worth it on a clear day.

The Europa Centre stands where the famous Romanische Cafe stood before it was destroyed in the war.

Opposite the Europa Centre and the Memorial Church is the **State Art Gallery**, which is sometimes used for exhibitions.

The **Bahnhof Zoo** (Zoo Train Station) was completely renovated for the 750th anniversary of Berlin in 1987. It is both a mainline and S-Bahn station as well as a U-Bahn station in the annex. The station has an information counter, a hotel reservation display, a bookstore and lockers, and because it is in the middle of the zoo complex, every other kind of shop is in close vicinity.

The **Zoologistche Garten** (Zoo) is across from the station in Hardenbergplatz, ℂ2540 1255, and it is ☺open daily 9am-6.30pm (winter 5pm). Home to 11,000 animals, this zoo claims to have more species than any other. Admission is ✪DM10. When Berlin was a divided city a second zoo was established in Friedrichsfelde, the **Tierpark**. It is not as large as the West Berlin establishment, but it does have the largest polar bear collection in the world.

While at the zoo, in West Berlin, you might consider visiting the **Aquarium** which is in the building next to the Elephant Gate. Admission is ✪DM8, or you can get a combined zoo/aquarium ticket for ✪DM12.

From the Zoo underground station take a train to either Sophie-Charlotte Platz, or the more convenient Richard-Wagner Platz, then follow the signs to the Charlottenburg Palace (Schloss), the most beautiful baroque building in Berlin.

Charlottenburg Palace was originally built as an eleven window summer house for Sophie Charlotte, the wife of the future King Friedrich I. It was completed in its present form, with the cream-coloured facade measuring 505m, in 1790.

The palace was severely damaged during the bombing raids of World War II, but there has been much careful restoration. The gardens were originally in the French style, but in the early 19th century they were remodelled into a somewhat disorganised English style. The most recent restoration has preserved the best of both. Interesting buildings in the park include the **Schinkel Pavilion**, a Neapolitan style villa built by Friedrich Wilhelm III and his second wife Princess Liegnitz. It is ☉open Tues-Sun 10am-5pm. Near the banks of the Spree, at the north of the park is the **Belvedere**, built in 1788 as a teahouse for Friedrich Wilhelm II. It is ☉open Tues-Sun 10am-5pm.

At the end of a line of fir trees on the west side of the park is the **Mausoleum**, ☉open Tues-Sun 10am-5pm. This temple was built by Friedrich Wilhelm III for his Queen Liuse. Several other royals have been interred here.

The **Historical Rooms** (Historische Raume) of the Palace are ☼open to the general public Tues-Sun 10am-5pm, Thurs until 8pm, and admission for all buildings and rooms is ✪8DM. This is another opportunity to see how royalty spent their waking and sleeping moments, but don't expect this tour to be another Versailles.

The **Orangerie** at the west end of the palace was built as a hothouse, became a theatre during the late 1780s, and is now a coffee shop.

Museums

Whilst in this area there are a few museums to visit. The **Egyptian Museum**, 70 Schloss Strasse, ✆320 911, was built as barracks for the royal bodyguards. It now has one of the best Egyptian collections in the world, with two really outstanding pieces - a 3400-year-old bust of the beautiful Nefertiti, wife of Pharaoh Akhenaton, from the Tel el-Amarna period; and the Kalabasha Monumental Gate built around 20BC for the Roman Emperor Augustus. The latter was presented to the museum by the Egyptian government when its site was flooded by the Aswan High Dam; the former was unearthed by a team of German archaeologists in 1912, and, like so many of Egypt's treasures, was "souvenired".

Across from this building is the **Antikenmuseum**, ✆320 911, with a good collection of ancient Greek, Etruscan and Roman art, and the Treasury in the basement has a silver and gold collection dating from around 2000BC.

The **Brohan Museum** is opposite the Palace, ✆321 4029, and is ☼open Tues-Sun 10am-6pm, Thurs till 8pm. It has a large collection of Art Deco paintings, sculptures, arts and crafts and furniture, collected between 1889 and 1939.

In Sophie-Charlotte Strasse, no. 17-18 is the **Plaster Cast House**, ✆321 7011, ☼open Mon-Fri 9am-4pm, Wed till 6pm. A bit different from ordinary museums, this is a branch of the Prussian Cultural

Germany

Foundation, and visitors can buy plaster casts of about 7000 of the foundation's exhibits (even including Nefertiti).

Heading away from Charlottenburg, travel along Otto-Suhr Allee to Ernst Reuter Platz, named for the first mayor of Berlin after the Second World War, then on to Strasse des 17 Juni, which bisects the **Technical University**. Follow this street to the **Charlottenburger Tor**, over the Landwehr Canal. This was the entrance to Charlottenburg from the Tiergarten district, and was built in 1905, the 200th anniversary of the death of Sophie Charlotte. On the left of the gate is Friedrich I (originally Elector Friedrich III), and on the right is his wife Sophie Charlotte, pointing the way to the Palace. The original gate was larger than at present because in 1937, the size of the columns was reduced to enable Hitler's architect Speer to have enough room for his grand avenue for Nazi victory parades - Charlottenburger Chaussee. The present name of the street is derived from the workers' uprising in East Berlin on June 17, 1953.

Brandenburger Tor

Probably the best way to get to the gate from Charlottenburger is to catch double-decker Bus 100, which begins its journey in front of *McDonald's* at the Zoo train station. Although this is a normal part of the local transport system, it has become popular with sightseers as its route takes in all the important attractions between east and west.

The first stop is the **Europa Center**, then the bus makes its way to Spreeweg, and the stop marked **Grosser Stern** (Big Star). This large roundabout has a **Victory Monument** which can be climbed for a good view of the surrounding area. The bus then continues past Schloss Bellevue, along John Foster Dulles Allee, for a stop in front of the **Kongresshalle** (locally called the Pregnant Oyster, for obvious reasons). The next stop is the Reichstag, then Reichstag Sud (south) in front of the Gate, then past what was the Wall, then a left turn onto **Unter den Linden** (under the lime trees), probably the best-known street in Berlin.

The first **Brandenburg Gate** was part of the walls of the old city, and it was demolished in 1788. The present gate was opened on August 6, 1791, and it is 65.5m wide, 11m thick and 26m high. The central opening is 5.5m and was originally reserved for the use of royal coaches. The 6m quadriga, drawn by four horses, was built in 1794. Originally the winged charioteer was the Greek goddess of peace, Irene. In October 1806, Napoleon took the complete quadriga to Paris, and when it was returned in 1814, the driver had become Victoria, the victory goddess, and she had a laurel wreath and an iron cross. The quadriga was destroyed in World War II, and the East Berlin magistrate had a replica erected in 1958.

Another interesting building in this area is the **Reichstag**, built between 1884 and 1894 as the seat of the German parliament. During World War II it was almost completely ruined, and it stayed that way until the 1960s when the West German parliament decided to rebuild it as a symbol of the desire to reunite the country. There are guided tours ☉daily at 2pm, and an audio tour.

Germany

Outside Berlin

Potsdam

The city of Potsdam is south-west of Berlin, and begins across the Glienicke Bridge.

It is the capital city of the state of Brandenburg, and home to a world-famous tourist attraction, the **Sanssouci Palace**.

Built between 1745 and 1747 for the Prussian King Friedrich II, nicknamed 'the Great', the then twelve room castle was used as a summer residence. Friedrich liked to model himself on Louis XIV, the Sun King, so French was often spoken in his court, and one of his courtiers suggested the name 'Sans souci' (French for 'without care') for his new palace.

In 1763-64, after the seven-year war, King Friedrich oversaw the building of the Neues Palais, the Picture Gallery, the New Chambers and the Chinese Teahouse, gathering a lot of his ideas from the Palace of Versailles.

Between 1851 and 1861, Friedrich Wilhelm IV decided to extend the complex, and he was influenced by anything Italian, so his buildings - the Great Orangerie, Charlottenhof Palace and the Roman Baths - reflect this different style.

Whether or not it compares with Versailles is up to each visitor to decide, and unfortunately, entry is not always guaranteed, as curators fear the damage that crowds can inflict on the buildings. As tour groups are given priority, the best thing independent travellers can do is to arrive early, pick up a numbered card, tour the gardens, then return in the afternoon to tour the palace complex.

The opening times (which may change, so check with the information offices) are:

Sanssouci Castle, New Chambers, New Palace, Chinese Tea House, Charlottenhof Castle, Roman Baths:

  ⊕ February-September -   9am-5pm
    October -   9am-4pm
    November-January -   9am-3pm (Lunch break 12.30pm-1pm)
    Closed every 1st and 3rd Monday of the month.

Ladies' Wing and Orangerie Castle:

  ⊕ Middle of May to the middle of October only.

Admission is from ✪5DM (Ladies' Wing) to 10DM (Sanssouci).

Note that some parts may only be visited with a guide.

To get there by car: Autobahn Berliner Ring, Bundes-strasse 1 or 273.

By train: Regional train R3 to Potsdam Kaiserbahnhof. S-Bahn from Berlin to Potsdam Stadt, then by tram to Luisenplatz, or the Bus line A to Sanssouci.

For further information contact Potsdam Information, Friedrich Ebert Strasse 5 D-14467 Potsdam, ✆(0331) 275 580, fax 275 5899 (👁www.potsdam.de).

The Best of Berlin in Brief

Egyptian Museum (Ägyptisches Museum). The jewel of this treasure-packed museum is seeing the bust that depicts the ancient Queen Nefertiti. *Schloss-strasse 70.*

Charlottenburg Palace (Schloss Charlottenburg). This baroque palace used to be a residence of Prussian royalty. Some works from the baroque period which were collected by the royals are on display in the publicly-accessible rooms. *Luisenplatz.*

The Museum of the Wall (Museum Haus am Checkpoint Charlie). Traces the history of the Berlin Wall from its sudden construction to its heady demise, detailing escapes, both successful and failed, and outlining the pervading consequences its existence had on the city. *Friedrichstrasse 44.*

Tiergarten. This landscaped public park occupies a large portion of central Berlin. In its midst is the giant Victory Column (Siegessaule), from the top of which you can take in a panoramic view of Berlin.

Berlin Zoo (Zoologischer Garten Berlin). Located in Tiergarten, the Berlin Zoo houses a wide array of animals. The pandas are the most popular exhibit.

Germany

Gemaldegalerie. Fine German, Italian and Dutch paintings, from the talented hands of Rembrandt, Bruegel, Bosch, Bottiecelli, Raphael and others. Over 600 works are display on this celebrated gallery. *Mattaiskirchplatz 4.*

Kurfurstendamm. A shopping district with up-market boutiques and trendy cafes serving coffee to keep you on your feet.

Kaiser Wilhelm Memorial Church (Gedachtniskirche). This church is still in ruins after its bombing during WWII, and has an interesting exhibit of the event. *Kurfurstendamm.*

Kaufhaus des Westens ("KaDeWe"). A massive department storing selling everything including the kitchen sink - a staggering variety of merchandise, and a noteworthy food section. *Wittenbergplatz.*

Natural History Museum (Museum fur Naturkunde). The highlight is the huge complete dinosaur skeleton, the world's largest.

German Cathedral. Contains an interesting history of Germany.

Deutsche Guggenheim Berlin. Contemporary modern art with an emphasis on encouraging young artisits. There are also works from more better-known people like Cezanne. *Unter den Linden 13-15.*

Pergamon Museum. The focus here is on ancient enxhibits, and the most coveted piece is the enormous Pergamon altar, more than 2100 years old, which depicts figures from Greek mythology. *Kupfergraben, Museumsinsel.*

Bonn

In the days of The Wall and a divided country, Bonn was the capital of West Germany and the seat of government. Now it is no longer a centre of power, and has reverted to being simply the birthplace of Beethoven.

Bonn sits on the west bank of the Rhine River, approximately 30km south of Cologne.

History

Called Castra Bonnensia by the Romans when they had a full-strength legionary post on the site, Bonn was the residence of the Prince-Bishops of Cologne for about five hundred years.

During the Napoleonic era the city was occupied by his armies, and after his defeat it became part of Prussia in 1815. Shortly after this the University came into being.

Before the Second World War, Bonn was a quiet, attractive university town, but during the war the town centre was heavily bombed and suffered almost complete destruction. In 1949 Bonn was made the seat of the Federal Government, which caused its population to double. The town has been almost completely restored in the post war period.

Tourist Information

The Tourist Information Centre, Cassius-passage, Munsterstrasse 20, 53103 Bonn, ✆(0228) 773 466, is ☺open Mon-Fri 9am-6.30pm, Sat 9am-5pm, Sun and public holidays 10am-2pm. (✆www.bonn-regio.de)

There is a branch of the German National Tourist Office at Niebuhrstrasse 16b, ✆(0228) 214 071-72.

Sightseeing

Most of the old town is a pedestrian zone enclosed by a ring road, and the centre is the **Marktplatz**, a triangular-shaped area that has on one corner the 18th century **Town Hall**. An annex of the town hall can be entered from Rathausgasse, and it contains the city's **art collection**.

From the western corner of Marktplatz, Bonn-gasee branches off, and at no. 20 is the **Beethovenhaus** where the great composer was born in 1770. The house is now a museum dedicated to Beethoven and has been completely restored. It is ⊙open Mon-Sat 10am-5pm, Sun 10am-1pm.

South-west of the Marktplatz is the **Munster St Martin**, in Munsterplatz. A Romanesque style basilica of the 12th-13th century, the church is worth visiting for its original wall paintings. Take Remisius-strasse which runs off Munsterplatz, then turn right into Furstenstrasse and continue to Am Hof, part of the ring road. Opposite are the main buildings of the **Friedrich Wilhelms Universitat**, the university of Bonn. These buildings formed the residential palace of the Prince-Electors of Cologne.

South-west of the Munster is the main railway station, and not far from there, at 14-16 Colmantstrasse, is the **Rheinisches Landesmuseum**. It has a good collection of sculptures, paintings and antiquities, and is ⊙open Tues, Thurs 9am-5pm, Wed 9am-8pm, Fri 9am-4pm, Sat-Sun 11am-5pm.

Most of the important government buildings, including the home of the President of the Federal Republic, are in Adenauerallee. It runs parallel to, but not alongside, the Rhine.

Bad Godesberg, about 7km to the south, is a spa resort and home to several diplomatic missions. It can be reached by rail or by the B9 road. The town dates back to Roman times, but its dubious claim to

Germany

fame is that it was where Adolf Hitler and Neville Chamberlain, the then Prime Minister of Britain, met in 1938 to discuss the fate of Czechoslovakia. While in Bad Godesberg, look out for Godesburg, a ruined 13th century castle that has been restored as a hotel.

The Best of Bonn in Brief

Beethoven House. A museum has been established inside the famous composer's birthplace.

Town Hall. A good example of the Rococo style.

The Royal Palace. Created late in the baroque period.

Bonn's Museums. Visit the German History Museum (Haus der Geschichte), the Art and Exhibition Hall (Kunstund Ausstellungshalle), the Art Museum (Kunstmuseum Bonn), and the Alexander Koenig Museum, all of which are in close proximity to each other.

Cologne

Cologne (Köln) is situated on the left bank of the Rhine, 40km south of Dusseldorf, and is over 2000 years old. Cologne was badly damaged during World War II, but most of the very old buildings have been carefully restored.

Many people visit Cologne during Fastelovend (Carnival) which begins on New Year's Eve and continues until the Monday before Ash Wednesday! Originally held to celebrate the end of winter it is now more of a time to let your hair down, with more than 300 balls held during the festival. It climaxes with a procession on Rosenmontag (Rose Monday).

The Cathedral - the famous Dom - that in part was the only thing standing after the Second World War - is the centre of town. Not far away is the famous address of 4711 (Eau de Cologne).

In many ways this city is off the beaten track as far as international visitors are concerned. Most people go to Cologne (Köln) by rail or car, though there is an international airport nearby. Bonn, the former capital, is just down the road, so to speak.

History

Cologne was founded by the Romans in 38BC, and many remains from this period are still in situ. The cultural and commercial capital of the Rhineland, Cologne was guaranteed an important part in world affairs, because of its strategic position where the trade routes from the four compass points met. Today it is well known world-wide for its trade fairs, something of a carryover from the markets of earlier times.

Tourist Information

There is a very helpful information office opposite the cathedral at Untere Fettenhenen 19, D-50667, Köln, ℂ(0221) 221 23345, fax 221 23320. (☞www.koeln.org/koelntourismus, email ✎koelntourismus@stadt-koeln.de). Their ☉opening hours are:

Winter (1 November to April 30th) 8.00am-9.00pm Monday to Saturday, Sunday and Public Holidays 9.30am-7.00pm.

Summer (1 May to 31 October) 8.00am-10.30pm Monday to Saturday, Sunday and Public Holidays 9.00am-10.30pm

Local Transport

The widely spread network of U-Bahn (underground), trams and buses that connect with the S-Bahn (city train) traffic of the Ruhr network, gives optimal public transport coverage.

Accommodation

Here the prices are for a double with an ensuite. Credit cards are accepted, and both heating and air-conditioning are part of the package. When booking a hotel room in Germany, especially on the web, browse the range of the booking agencies that come up when you conduct your search. Check out the prices and go for the cheapest as they are not always the same and you can always get a deal.

Note that on the day you arrive you can also book at the Tourist Information office for accommodation that night.

Ambassador Hotel, Barbarossaplatz 4a, ©49-211 568 900 for bookings. 50 rooms, family run, restaurant, rooms are relatively large - ✪240DM.

> *Antik Hotel Bristol*
>
> Kaiser-Willhelm Ring 48, ©49-221 12 0195, fax 221-13 1495. 44 rooms, city centre. A private hotel that affords a very pleasant stay in quality surroundings. The decor is replete with antiques and the friendly service makes this a very nice hotel. Restaurant, bar, parking, concierge, currency exchange - ✪230DM.

Sofitel Mondial Am Dom, Kurt Hackenberg Platz 1, 50667 Cologne, ©49-221 2 0630, fax 221 206 3522, email ✉H1306@accor-hotels.com. 205 rooms, Pacific Bar, Beer Pub Prost, 2 restaurants. Opposite Cathedral, Ludwig Museum and Philharmonic Hall - ✪250DM.

Mercure Severinshof is a first class hotel in the downtown area. Facilities include restautant, bar and health club.

There are three **Youth Hostels** in Cologne:
Deutz, Siegestrasse 5a, ©(221) 814 711, fax (221) 884 425.

Germany

Riehl Jugendgastehaus, An der Schanz 14, ©(221) 767 081, fax (221) 761 555.

Station-Backpacker's Hostel, Marzellenstrasse 44-48, ©(221) 912 5301, fax 912 5303.

Food and Drink

Surprisingly, because Cologne is set on a river famous for its wines, the city has some of the best local beer in Germany, called *Kolsch* (which means 'belonging to Köln').

There is no special dish that is associated with Cologne, but you can be guaranteed a hearty meal in any establishment serving local food, rather than international.

Sightseeing

The obvious place to begin a tour is the **Cathedral** (Dom). Work on the building began in 1248, but it was not completed until 1842. Fortunately, though, no one lost the plans because the Gothic style was carried through to the end. During World War II, 90 per cent of the old town area was destroyed, but the Cathedral, though sustaining much damage, was still standing.

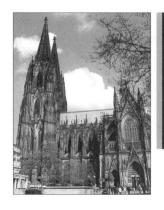

The inside of the church is very peaceful, even though it is in the middle of the hustle and bustle of the city. There is a viewing platform 97m above the city in the south tower, but there are 509 steps to be dealt with to get there. Many works of art are to be found inside, among them a wooden crucifix carved in 969, the Bible window in the choir, the Shrine of the Magi (pictured) which is said to hold relics of the Three Kings, a mosaic floor in the choir. The cathedral treasury is also worth a visit.

The main railway station (hauptbahnhoff) of the city is centred next to the Dom. This area is the transport hub of the city.

The square building on the left, facing the cathedral's east end, is the **Romisch-Germanisches Museum**, which was built over the Roman Dionysus Mosaic. The mosaic was found when workmen were excavating to build an air-raid shelter during the second world war. The museum has many other exhibits of life in Cologne from Roman times to the reign of Charlemagne.

Along Unter Goldschmied strasse is a 100m long Roman drainage channel that you can walk along (the new Town Hall is also here), and the remains of the **Roman town wall** around the corner of Komodien and Tunis strasses and the corner of Zeughaus and Auf dem Berlich strasses. On the left of the new **Town Hall** is the centre of the old town, which is a pedestrian zone, and nearby is **St Martin's Church** which is surrounded by new buildings that blend in with the old (an early example of the present day interest in preserving the past). This part of the old town is the **Alter Markt** (old market) and there are several ale houses and eateries in and around, such as Papa Joe's Biersalon, Alter Markt 50-52, where non-traditional New Orleans jazz features, and the Gaffelhaus traditional restaurant at Alter Markt 20-22. Then head for Heumarkt (Haymarket), and at no. 60 there is Altstadt Paffgen, where you can grab a bite to eat, and maybe try some of the Kolsch beer.

Take Gurzenichstrasse from Heumarkt, then turn right into Unter Goldschmied and you will see the **Gurzenich**, a Gothic festival hall that was completed in 1444, and rebuilt after the Second World War. From here take Obenmarspforte to Hohe strasse, a pedestrian mall that leads back towards the cathedral.

Alternatively, stay on Obenmarspforte until you reach the Offenbachplatz, then take special notice of the large Renaissance style building, or more importantly, its street number - **4711**. This is where the chemist who produced the formula for Kölnisch Wasser, or as it is better known, Eau de Cologne, lived. The house is now a perfume museum, and it has an interesting clock that puts on a performance ⊙every hour from 9am to 9pm.

The streets in Köln or Cologne, however you want to pronounce it, are fairly wide and graced with many trees. An efficient tram service operates throughout the city, and the local people are most helpful in the main in giving directions.

For attractions further afield, the northern edge of the city has the Zoological Gardens and Aquarium, and in summer an aerial cableway operates across the Rhine from the zoo, offering fantastic views of the city and the cathedral. Next to the zoo is the Botanical Gardens.

The Best of Cologne in Brief

Cathedral. Germany's largest cathedral, 600 years in the making, has many points of interest and definitely should be visited if you are in Köln.

Roman Churches. Twelve picturesque churches erected in the Roman period are to be found in the inner-city area.

Wallraf-Richartz and Ludwig Museums. More art from the famous greats in the Wallraf-Richartz is balanced by the twentieth-century works featured in the neighbouring Ludwig.

Romisch-Germanisches Museum. Wonderful collection of Roman antiquities somewhat diminished by the fact that details of the displays are only recorded in German.

Kölner Philharmonie. A famous concert hall.

Imhoff-Stollwerck Chocolate Museum. Situated on the banks of the Rheine, this modern museum explains the process of chocolate making with a history of the pratice and, of course, a taste of the product.

Town Hall. A treasure from the medieval era.

Rheingarten. Head here for a taste of beer from the local brewers.

Germany

Frankfurt am Main

The city of Frankfurt is situated at the crossroads of Germany. It has a population of around 625,000 and is one of the world's great financial centres.

This city possesses the most dynamic and professional event organisers in the world. It has become the hub for many international airlines who bring millions of people to Frankfurt every year to attend a conference, convention or fair - industrial or commercial - held at the famous Messe. The Messe stretches for kilometres with at least 10 convention halls and is some 3 floors high. Mini buses run all day to transport fair-goers from one part of the complex to another.

Most of the old part of the city was destroyed by bombing during the Second World War, so much of what is seen now is not original.

Tourist Information

Information centres are found at: the main railway station, opposite track 23 - ☉open Mon-Fri 8am-9pm, Sat-Sun 9am-6pm, ℂ(069) 212 388 00, fax 212 378 80; Romerberg 27 - ☉open Mon-Fri 9.30am-5.30pm, Sat-Sun and public holidays 10am-4pm. (☜tct.frankfurt.de)

Local Transport

Frankfurt has rail, underground, bus and tram services, with the latter being the most efficient way of getting around the city.

Accommodation

Several hundred hotels live off the Messe, as do the countless restaurants, bars and shops in the area.

It is best to book and visit Frankfurt when a fair is not on, especially the Book Fair normally held in October. Every available room is booked out at this time and the prices are not cheap.

Prices are for a double and include the VAT of 10%. The hotels tend to be functional rather than glamorous, and those listed here are around or near the Hauftbanhof - Central Railway station on Baselerstrasse, or nearby streets. Running south from the Railway station you can find yourself very quickly in the Red Light district of the city.

There is a web site that is excellent for information on accommodation in Frankfurt called ☜www.dunia.org/germany/city/hotels. You will have to book your hotel through them, as they give you no information on phone numbers, faxes or actual street address, though each hotel is accompanied with a map to give you some idea of where it is located. Another web address well worth checking on is ☜www.frankfurt-online.net/hotel

Carlton Hotel

Karlstrasse 11, 60329 Frankfurt, ©69-232 093, fax 66306-600. This small, stylish, boutique hotel has 27 rooms on 5 storeys and is located in the middle of the business district. Excellent facilities and family-run service will ensure a pleasant stay, particularly for business travellers. ✪130-300DM.

Hotel Europa, Baseler Strasse, 17, ©69-236 013, fax 236 203. 50 rooms with ensuite, tourist class hotel - ✪150-200DM.

Along Baseler Strasse there are countless tourist class hotels - the *Imperial*, the *Hotel Wiesbaden*, the *Excelsior*, the *Manhattan* - all sorts of name that you can imagine. Accommodation is not the problem but the price may be. Either the Tourist Office at the Hauphtbanhof, Airport or the Messe can find you accommodation. Do not be shy in approaching these centres.

Best Western Imperial Hotel am Palmengarten

Sophienstrasse 40, 60487 Frankfurt, ©069-793 0030, fax 069-793 03888. 150 rooms, restaurant, garage, near a park, rooms have all the necessary modcons - ✪190DM.

Hotel Apollo, Mücheneer Strasse 44, 60329 Frankfurt, ©069-23 1285, fax 069-23 2909. 70 rooms, restaurant. This is a two star hotel that is near the centre of town and it is clean and comfortable. Decent prices - ✪60DM in off season.

Pension Adria, Neuhaub Strasse 21, 60322 Frankfurt, ©069-59 4533, fax 069-55 8284. 13 rooms with garage(extra), ensuites, very simple, no phone - ✪60DM.

Germany

Arabella Sheraton Grand Hotel Frankfurt is a first class hotel in the midtown area. Facilities include restaurant, bar, coffee shop, health club, swimming pool and shops -

Dorint Hotel is a first class hotel in the midtown area. Facilities include restaurant, bar, coffee shop, health club and swimming pool.

Frankfurt's **Youth Hostel** is:
Haus der Jugend, Deutscherrnufer 12, ✆(069) 619 058, fax 618 257.

Depending on what time of year the prices vary considerably. Best to buy through a tour operator before departure.
You can organise private accommodation at the Messe which is the main reason why a lot of people from overseas visit Frankfurt during the year.
Accommodation Service - Messe Frankfurt GmbH, fax (069) 7575 6352, Torhaus Service Centre, Level 3.
Telephone for enquiries, not for reservations:
Hotel Accommodation: ✆(069) 7575 6222, ✆7575 6695.
Private Accommodation: ✆7575 6296, ✆7575 6696.

Food and Drink
In the district of Sachsenhausen apple cider is sold at the world famous Apfelweinlokale. This area of Frankfurt is dotted with many restaurants.

Around the Opera House and along the main avenues there are some excellent restaurants. Across the river along Gartenstrasse, and around the Dom (old Cathedral - recently restored) and Town Hall (Romer) there is a delightful selection. Many people gravitate to the ubiquitous McDonald's, and Movenpic are also well represented in Frankfurt.

Sightseeing

Frankfurt's favourite son is Johann Wolfgang von Goethe, the famous author, and he was baptised in **Katharinekirche**, which is opposite the **Hauptwache** (Guard House), a junction for the above ground and underground rail systems. The Guard House was built in 1730, and is a good place to begin a tour of the city.

There are a couple of other churches in this vicinity - the **Lieb-frauenkirche** and the **Paulskirche**. St Paul's was built 1789-1833, but was burnt to the ground in 1944. Because of its historical significance as the meeting place of the German National Assembly in the 1840s, people from all over the country donated the money to have it rebuilt.

Not far from St Paul's, at 23 Grosser Hirschgraben, is **Goethehaus**, where the great man was born and lived. It is now a museum, and is ☉open Mon-Sat 9am-6pm, Sun 10am-1pm (April-September); Mon-Sat 9am-4pm, Sun 10am-1pm (October-March).

On the nearby Romerberg is the city's restored landmark - the Romer, the town hall complex of buildings. Of them, the **Kaidersaal** (Imperial Hall) in the Zum Romer is ☉open to the public Mon-Sat 9am-5pm, Sun 10am-4pm. The tourist information office is at Romerberg 27, and they have good free maps of the city.

To the left of the Romer is the **Imperial Cathedral** (Kaiserdom), where the German emperors were elected and crowned. The building

Germany

is from the 14th-15th centuries, and has many works of art including a life-size stone Calvary scene by Hans Backoffen (1509).

From here head towards the river and the **Historisches Museum**, with a varied collection that includes a model of Frankfurt of 1912 and replicas of the crown jewels of the Holy Roman Empire. The museum is ☉open Tues 10am-5pm, Wed 10am-8pm, Thurs-Sat 10am-5pm, and there is no general admission fee.

Other Museums

On the other side of the river from here are seven museums. The **Museum of Arts and Crafts** (Museum fur Kunsthandwerk) has four sections - Far Eastern, European, Islamic, and Books and Writing. It is ☉open Tues-Sun 10am-5pm, Wed until 8pm, and admission is free.

The **Ethnological Museum** (Museum fur Volkerkunde) has a very large collection from the world over. It is ☉open Tues-Sun 10am-5pm, Wed until 8pm, and admission is free.

The **German Film Museum** (Deutsches Filmmuseum) has a good exhibition of cinematographic history. It is ☉open Tues-Sun 11am-6.30pm and admission is free. In the lower ground floor there is a very good cafe.

The **German Architectural Museum** (Deutsches Architektur-museum) is the only one of its kind in the world, and is only of interest to people involved, or interest in the profession. It is ☉open Tues-Sun 10am-5pm, Wed until 8pm, and admission is free.

The **Postal Museum** (Bundespostmuseum) is only for people with special interests. It is also ☉open Tues-Sun 11am-5pm, Wed until 8pm. Admission is free.

The **Art Institute** (Stadelsches Kunstinstitut) has a collection of 13th to 20th century art that includes works by Rubens, Durer, Rembrandt and Botticelli. It is the only museum in the group to charge admission. ☉Open Tues-Sun 11am-5pm, Wed until 8pm.

Liebighaus is a sculpture museum with exhibits dating back to 3000BC.

These museum are only a 15 minute walk from the old centre of Town. A footbridge across the Main near the old centre of town brings you to the museum area in no time. On the Museum side there is a very pleasant walk along the river bank.

Places Further Afield

Frankfurt has a very modern **Zoo** that can be reached by the underground. The main entrance on Alfred-Brehm-Platz is ☉open March 16 to September 30 daily 8am-7pm; October 1 to October 15 daily 8am-6pm; February 16 to March 15 8am-6pm. The entrance on Rhonstrasse is ☉open daily September 16 to March 15 8am-7pm; March 16 to September 15, 8am-6pm.

The **Palmengarten** is to the north of the city and has entrances on Siesmayerstrasse, Bockenheimer Landstrasse, Palmengartenstrasse, Siesmayerstrasse and Zeppelinallee. It has a large greenhouse that simulates tropical jungle conditions; other greenhouses containing tropical and sub-tropical plants; a children's playground; a train ride; and a restaurant. It is ☉open daily Jan-Feb 9am-4pm, March 9am-5pm, April-Sept 9am-6pm, Oct 9am-5pm, Nov-Dec 9am-4pm, and there is an admission fee.

The town of **Darmstadt** is south of Frankfurt on the Bundesstrasse 3, and it was home to Hesses' grand dukes until 1918. The town's **Castle** was modelled on Versailles and is worth a visit. In the castle museum is the *Darmstadter Madonna* painted by Hans Holbein in 1526, and the Porcelain Museum has the grand dukes' collection of 18th and 19th century porcelain and earthenware.

Another attraction in the town is the **Mathildenhohe**, an artists' colony started by the last grand duke, Ernst-Ludwig. It has several interesting buildings including the Russian Chapel, built in 1899 as a present from Czar Nicholas II to his wife Alexandra, and the Marriage

Tower, built in 1905. Alternatively, you can go to the university (1386 founded) town of **Heidelberg** for the day by car. Situated on the River Neckar. Recommended.

The Best of Frankfurt in Brief

Imperial Cathedral (Kaiserdom). Ten German emperors and kings were crowned here.

Imperial Hall (Kaisersaal). This is where the royals held their lavish banquets, and its doors are open to the public.

St Paul's Church (Paulskirche). Germany's first democratically-elected parliament operated from here.

Guard House (Hauptwache). Once the outpost of the City Guard and also used as a prison.

Town Hall (Romer complex). Completed in the fifteenth century, this building is still the city's Town Hall.

Goethe House (Goethehaus). The home in which the prolific German poet was born.

Old Opera House (Alte Oper). The centre of the city's cultural sphere.

Historical Garden (Historischer Garten). Excavations here among these historical gardens uncovered Roman artifacts dated back to the first century AD.

Commerzbank building. This is Europe's tallest office building at 257.7m in height.

Historical Museum (Historisches Museum). A good collection of various artifacts.

Heidelberg

This amazing university town sits on banks of the river Necker, which is spanned by the Bridge of Worms. Heidelberg is dominated by the incredible ruins of the castle of Ludwig. The castle was destroyed in 1689 by French troops in one of this city's celebrated fights with other principalities. In this case it was against Louis XIV who laid claim by inheritance to this beautiful part of the world.

The town is a delightful place with small cobblestone squares and streets, pubs and eateries, bookshops, students digs, churches, halls, and an environment that is simply very pleasant for an afternoon amble. Do not forget to take the funicular up to the old destroyed castle of Ludwig, part of which is still useable. The stonework and construction is impressive. There are beautiful gardens and you can walk in the park along pleasantly winding paths. The view of the city from the castle is spectacular.

Heidelberg is less than 2 hours by car from Frankfurt, making it perfect for a day trip or overnight stay.

History

Heidelberg's fame extends to Martin Luther and the Calvinists who had a number of celebrated stouches here in the sixteenth century. Its rulers came and went, oscillating between the protestant elector Friedrich V, then Maximilian of Bavaria, then Tilly, then Karl Ludwig, until Louis XIV of France claimed it.

Meanwhile the populace wanted some say in administration, so rebellions broke out regularly in the city. It was a place of coming and going for armies, scholars and religious notables.

In the 18th century the city was rebuilt based on its old Gothic layout, but in the new Baroque style. In 1815 the Emperor of Austria, the Tsar and the King of Prussia, signed the Holy Alliance here. It was the site of the German National Assembly in 1848. The university has a reputation for scholarship, and escaped bombing during the Second World War. It has many notable Noble Prize winners, and boasts a student population of 28,000 in a population of 135,000. Perhaps for many American's especially, the film *The Student Prince* has made it a popular place to visit and stay.

Accommodation

Prices are for a double room. When booking accommodation it is important to ask if the hotel has a lift, central heating, and an ensuite. The places listed below do have these facilities. The following internet address is a good one for finding a place to stay and planning your trip ☞www.cvb-heidelberg.de

Best Western Rega Hotel Heidelberg, Bergheimer Strass 63, 69115 Heidelberg, ✆062 21 5080, fax 062-2150 8500, ☞www.rega. bestwestern.de. 236 rooms, garage, restaurant, comfortable but not your average Heidelberg student hangout, central heating - ✪250-270DM.

Achat Hotel, Karlsruher Strasse 130, 69126 Heidelberg, ✆062 21 31 0300, fax 062 21 31 03 33. 80 rooms, restaurant, central heating (rather important in this area). A good location in the old part of town towards the river - ✪165DM.

Classic Inn, Belfortstrasse 3, 69115 Heidelberg, ℭ062 21-13 8320, fax 062 21-1 38 3238. 40 beds, telephone. This is a simple hotel which is a 3 minute walk at most to the train station - ✪140-165DM.

Elite, Bunsenstr.15, 69115 Heidelberg, ℭ062 21-2 5734, fax 062-21 16 3949. 23 rooms, not far from the university clinic and various govenment offices - ✪100DM.

Munich

Munich, the largest city in, and capital of, Bavaria, is a very interesting place to visit that is often overlooked by visitors to Germany. Not only does it have some very interesting attractions of its own, it is a good starting point for exploring the Bavarian Alps.

History

Bavaria was an independent state for centuries before it became part of the German Empire in 1871. Bavaria had been ruled for over 700 years by the Wittelsbach family, who had overseen the town plan of Munich and had many fine buildings erected. Even today, the people of this area think of themselves first as Bavarians, then as Germans.

Tourist Information

The Munich Tourist Office, 1 Sendlinger Strasse 1, 80331, Munich, ℭ(089) 2333 0234, fax 2333 0337 (◉www.muenchen-tourist.de). There is a tourist information office at the Railway Station, platform 2, that is ☉open Mon-Sat 8am-8pm, Sun 10am-6pm; and another at the Town Hall in the Marienplatz.

Local Transport

Munich has an excellent public transport system that incorporates train, underground, trams and buses. It is best to enquire at one of the information offices about timetables and methods of buying tickets and passes. There are plenty of ticket machines available, but these can be difficult to use if you don't understand the instructions, so get that advice.

Accommodation

Prices given are for a double room per night with an ensuite, and are in the local currency. Major credit cards are accepted at these establishments. Rooms are airconditioned and central heating is the norm. Prices are higher during Oktoberfest and conventions in September. The area code for Munich is 089.

Hotel Europäischer Hof, Bayerstrasse 31, D-80335 München, ☏89-55 1510, fax 89-55 15 1222, email ✎info@heh.de. 150 rooms, three tiers of accommodation. The hotel has a high quality collection of paintings, from Van Gogh and Picasso to Gaughin. There is a breakfast room and restaurant. It is modern, comfortable and located across the road from the Hauptbanhof (central railway) and airport shuttle - standard room ✪216-306DM.

Hotel Jedermann, Bayerstrasse 95, 80335 München, ☏89-54 3240, fax 89-54 32 4111, ☞www.hotel-jedermann.de. 34 rooms, breakfast room, a smallish central hotel that is family owned and only 5 minutes walks from the Hauptbanhof - ✪130-240DM.

Arabella Sheraton Bogenhausen Hotel, Arabellastrasse 5, 81925 Bogenhausen, ☏89-9 2320, fax 89-9232 4449. 644 rooms, shop, games room, nightclub, restaurants, lobby cafe and bar, fitness centre, swimming pool, parking, not located near the city, shuttle to the airport. Underground station is a 3 minute walk from the hotel then a 10 minute ride to the centre of the city. Near the new Munich

Exhibition Center. Parking available and taxi rank at the entrance - ✪280DM.

Hotel Splendid, Maximilianstrasse 54, 80538 München, ✆89-29 6606, fax 89-291 3176. 40 rooms. A small hotel that offers excellent service with very pleasant rooms. Great location near the Opera House with the underground station, Lehel, close by. There is a scenic terrace for drinks and breakfast - ✪182-322DM

Hotel Exquisit

Pettenkoferstrasse 3, 80336 München, ✆89- 55 1 9900, fax 89-55 19 9499, email ✎info@hotel-exquisit.com. 50 rooms, garage, breakfast room, delightful inner courtyard, (though if you are renting a maisonette you may wish to have it on your own (✪340DM), which you may prefer over the impersonal atmosphere of a large international hotel). Located in a quiet side-street near Munich's centre. The Marienplatz, Stachus and Oktoberfest site can easily be reached on foot - ✪280-340DM.

Food and Drink

Bavarians eat a great deal of pork, so you won't see much in the way of beef or lamb dishes on the menu, but liberal use of the word 'schweine'. Also there will be more dumplings (which are rather delicious, although fattening) than potatoes. Sausages are a German favourite and the one associated with Munich is the Weisswurst, literally white sausage. It is made from a mixture of bacon and veal, parsley and pepper, and should be eaten with a sweet mustard.

The traditional Bavarian drink is beer, which comes in helles (light) or dunkels (dark). Special, stronger brews are made for important occasions, for example the Oktoberfest. If you can't stand the strong stuff, the word for 'shandy' is 'Radler'.

Sightseeing

A walking tour can start from the railway station.

Go along the extension of the platforms to the pedestrian zone, Schutzenstrasse, then Neuhauser Strasse and **St Michael's Church** (Michaelskirche). It is built in the Renaissance style, and is the crypt of the Wittelsbach family. The crypt is ☺open Mon-Fri 10am-1pm, 2-4pm, Sat 10am-3pm.

Next stop is the **Frauenkirche**, the cathedral, which dates from the 15th century. It has twin towers capped with copper domes that are a city landmark, and the southern one has an elevator which only operates from ☺April to October, Mon-Sat 10am-5pm, adults ✪4DM, children 2DM.

Nearby is **Marienplatz**, the centre of the city since its foundation in 1158. Here is the 15th century **Old Town Hall** (Rathaus) and the beautiful, Gothic-revival, 19th century **New Town Hall**, which has a mechanical show (automata) in the clock tower at ☺11am each day, and from May to October also at noon, 5pm and 9pm. The tower of

Germany

the new town hall is ☉open Mon-Fri 9am-7pm, Sat-Sun 10am-7pm, and the elevator ride is adult ✪3DM, child 1.50DM.

On the right, in Rindermarkt, is the **Peterskirche** (St Peter's), the oldest and most loved church in Munich. The tower called Alter Peter can be climbed and is ☉open Mon-Sat 9am-6pm, Sun 10am-6pm, adults ✪2.50DM, child 0.50DM.

Keep left from here and you will come to the **Victualienmarkt**, a large food and vegetable market. From here you can go two ways. Either keep going along Rosen Tal Strasse to the **Stadt Museum** on St Jakobs Plats (☉open Tues-Sun 10am-6pm), and then visit the **Asamkirche** in Sendinger Strasse, with its Bavarian Rococo creations, then along the Ring to Sendingertor Platz.

OR, go in the opposite direction along Sparkassen Strasse and on the right is the square with the famous **Hofbrauhaus**.

On the left is the **Alter Hof**, the first residence of the Wittelsbach rulers. Further along is Max Joseph Platz, with the **Nationaltheatre** (Opera House) and the **Residenz**, a complex of buildings that has grown over the centuries. Courtyards link the various buildings which include the **Residenzmuseum** with its fine art collection. It is ☉open Tues-Sun 10am-4.30pm. On the left is the **Feldherrnhalle**, built by Ludwig I in 1844 and copied from the Loggia dei Lanzi in Florence. And behind here on Odeons Platz is the **Theatinerkirche**, with its impressive dome and towers.

Once again there are choices to be made.

You can turn left into Brienner Strasse and go along to the **Platz der Opfer des Nationalsozialismus** (Square of the Victims of National Socialism), the area of the former Fuhrer and the Nazi party buildings. Then go past the obelisk covered in granite tiles to the Konigsplatz, which became the National Socialist Party's Square. On the northern side is the old **Glyptotek** (Greek and Roman sculptures, ☉open Tues,

Wed and Fri-Sun 10am-5pm, Thurs 10am-8pm), on the western side is a reproduction of the **Propylaon** on the Acropolis in Athens, and on the right hand side is **Lenbach House**. Once the home of the 19th century portrait artist, Franz von Lenbach, the house is now a gallery exhibiting a selection of his paintings as well as a fine collection of 19th century Munich landscape painters. It also has a good cafe and restaurant, and is ⊙open Tues-Sun 10am-6pm. At the end of Brienner Strasse is Stiglmaier Platz with the Lowenbrau Keller and beer garden.

OR, you can go straight ahead along Ludwigsstrasse, which has the national library and St Ludwig's church on the right and the university on the left.

At Geschwister Scholl Platz, turn into Leopold Strasse and continue on to the Siegestor (victory arch), where the residential area of Schwabing begins. Near here is the **Cafe Stephanie** where great names of literature, such as Thomas Mann and Erich Muhsam, met for a bite, and where the postcard painter, Adolf Hitler began his career.

OR, if you turn right at Odeonsplatz and go across the **Hofgarten**, you will pass the art gallery that was built during the Third Reich and is an example of the architecture of that era. Continue past there and you will come to the very long and narrow **Englischer Garten**, which has a lake, a Greek temple, a Chinese pagoda, restaurants and cafes, and lots and lots of grass. To the left is **Schwabing**, the traditional students' quarter, but things are becoming a bit expensive there for them.

There are plenty of other interesting sights, but one that stands out is to the west of the city and that is **Schloss Nymphenburg**, the Baroque summer palace of the Bavarian royal family. It can be reached by U-Bahn to Rotkreuzplatz and then tram 12, and it is ⊙open Tues-Sun 9am-12.30pm, 1.30-5pm April-Sept, 10am-12.30pm, 1.30-4pm Oct-March. There are guided tours, especially to Ludwig I's Gallery of Beautiful Women, and beautiful pavilions in the grounds.

Another place that may be of interest to some is **Dachau**. It can be reached by train, and has been preserved in memory of those people who were treated so inhumanely and who died there.

The Best of Munich in Brief

Old Town (Altstadt). The place for cafe's, churches, shopping and street entertainment of all kinds. Stroll through Mary's Square (Marienplatz) and take in the Gothic architecture and the Glockenspiel.

Alte Pinakothek. This is a huge museum with many important works. Over 900 paintings are on display spanning six centuries of the craft. *Barer Strasse 27.*

Neue Pinakothek. Located on the other side of the Square from the Alte Pinakothek, this museum pick up roughly where the other leaves off, in chronological terms. *Barer Strasse 29.*

Bavarian National Musem (Bayerisches Nationalmuseum). A great museum featuring much more than paintings. Many eras are covered in its three exhibition floors. *Prinzregentenstrasse 3.*

German Museum of Masterpeices of Science and Technology (Deutsches Museum). Dedicated to the history of technology with working displays and interactive exhibits. *Museumsinsel 1.*

Residenz. This is where Bavaria's rulers resided, collecting art and making architectural additions to their palace over the centuries, which accounts for the distinct variety of styles. Highlights of the complex are the Treasure House (Schatzkammer), Residenz Museum and Cuvillies Theatre, but the palace itself is generally considered poor by Europe's standards. *Max-Joseph-Platz 3.*

Nymphenburg Palace (Schloss Nymphenburg). Only slightly more interesting than the Residenz, Nymphenburg is where the Bavarian royalty, the Wittelsbach family, resided during the summer. The palace architecture is of the baroque style. *Schloss Nymphenburg 1.*

Cathedral of Our Lady (Frauenkirche). This gothic cathedral was built in the fifteenth century and destroyed during WWII bombings. After the war, the city's largest church was restored with impressive results to become the Munich's most famous landmark.

St Michael's Church. A rare Renaissance church. *Neuhauser Strasse 52.*

St Peter's Church. Built in the twelfth century, this is the oldest church in Munich, with good views from its steeple. *Rindermarkt 1.*

Munich City Museum (Munchner Stadtmuseum). Four floors of very different collections. *St Jakob's Platz 1.*

Haus der Kunst. An interesting offering of modern twentieth century art. *Prinzregentenstrasse 1.*

English Garden (Englischer Garden). 3.7 square kilometres of landscaped gardens make this the biggest of its kind in Europe.

BMW Museum. Headquarters of the famous automobile manufacturer, with displays and tours. *Olympia-zentrum.*

Hofbrauhaus. Munich's best beer hall, and indeed the world's best known, is open long hours every day and is very popular with tourists and locals alike. It has an astonishing capacity of 4,500 people.

Olympic Park and Stadium. The Olympic Games were held in these impressive grounds back in 1972. Apart from the stadium and swimming pool, there is a sports theme park worth visiting for its 40 interactive attractions.

Driving Through Germany

It is only possible to describe a few tours around Germany, as there are so many places to see.

The Rhine and Moselle Valleys

Itinerary - 5 Days - Distance 660kms

From Frankfurt, drive south to **Darmstadt**. This town is a cultural and art centre. There are many interesting museums, and a pretty artist's quarter. Further south, drive through **Heppenheim** with its 11th century observatory ruins, to **Heidelberg**, a university town in the Neckar Valley. In the ruins of the castle dating from the 14th century, concerts are held during the summer. Heading west from Heidelberg you reach **Bad Durkheim**, noted for its spa, and centre of the largest wine growing region in Germany. The biggest wine festival in Germany is here every September. North west of Bad Durkheim is **Idar Oberstein**, a town in a narrow valley. This town is well known for its jewellery trade.

Bernkastel-Kues, **Traben-Trarbachr** and **Zell** are important wine growing centres on the Moselle river. North through the Moselle Valley you come to **Bonn**, a major city. Bonn was the capital of the Federal Republic, and has many historic buildings. Beethoven was born here, and his house is open to the public. From Bonn, head south east to **Neuwied**, a town founded by religious refugees, and now known for its pumice industry. **Koblenz** nearby, is at the junction of the Rhine and Moselle rivers. This town is the commercial heart of the wine industry. Koblenz also has a famous wine festival in August.

Along the Rhine, **Lahnstein** and **Braubach** are old towns with historic buildings. **St Goar** and **St Goarshausen** stand on opposite banks of the Rhine, and are linked by ferry. Castles overlook these towns. **Kaub** also has historic castles nearby, with the Pflaz Fortress on an island in the middle of the river. **Rudesheim** is a popular tourist destination, set near the Rheingau vineyards and the Rhine Gorge. There is a wine making museum in the castle.

Heading back towards Frankfurt, you pass through **Weisbaden** and **Mainz**. Weisbaden is noted for its spas, cultural facilities, parks and gardens. Mainz is an old industrial and university city with historic buildings and a printing museum. The tour finishes in **Frankfurt**, which is one of Germany's most important cities. It is situated on the river Main, and is known for its Motor Show and other trade fairs.

The Black Forest
Itinerary - 6 Days - Distance 682kms

From Stuttgart, head south to **Tubingen**, an old university town, situated on the Neckar river. **Hechingen** and **Sigmaringen** are pretty towns with ancient castles. Further south, you reach **Lindau** which is built out into Lake Constance (the **Bodensee**). It is joined to the mainland by the Sea Brucke, and is a popular tourist destination. Driving along the northern shore of Lake Constance you pass through the holiday towns of **Friedrichs-Hafen** and **Meersburg**, which are very picturesque. At **Unter-Uhldingen** you can see reconstructions of Stone and Bronze Age buildings.

By making a short detour into Switzerland, you can see the spectacular waterfall (rheinfalls) at **Neuhausen**. The best place to see this sight is from the grounds of the Laufen Castle. Back into Germany, **Titisee** is a popular sporting town. It is near Mt Feldberg, the highest peak in the Black Forest.

Freiburg is the largest town in the Black Forest region, and is noted for its university and historic buildings. Driving north from Freiburg, you pass through the health spas of **Alpirsbach**, **Freudenstadt**, and the famous **Baden-Baden**. As well as the spas, there are many other things to see and do here, including visiting the Casino, the vineyards or taking a cable car up the nearby mountain. Heading back towards Stuttgart is **Pforzheim**, the gateway to the Black Forest, and well known for its jewellery and watch making industry. **Stuttgart** is the largest city in the south west of Germany, and as well being a commercial centre is also very scenic.

Germany from West to East

Itinerary - 3 Days - Distance 240kms

From the Dutch border drive east. **Osnabruck** is notable for its cathedral, dating from medieval times. Further east you arrive at **Hannover**, another old city. Hannover is an important art and cultural centre, with many galleries and museums. Of note is the Herrenhausen Palace, with its gardens. **Braunschweig**, and **Magdeburg** feature castles and cathedrals from the 12th and 13th century, as well as some examples of Roman architecture.

Driving towards Berlin, you pass through **Brandenburg**, which although is a modern city, has many ancient manuscripts held in the cathedral. **Potsdam** is a very scenic city, with castles, parks and galleries well worth visiting. From Potsdam, you reach **Berlin**. There are many things to see and do in this city, now the capital of Germany. As well as the ruins of the Berlin Wall, there are many galleries, historic buildings and palaces to see.

South of Berlin, **Wittenberg** and **Dessau**, lies Worlitz Nature Park on Warlitz Lake. Dessau is the home of the Bauhaus movement, and has a museum dedicated to design. Many of the buildings have been restored. Heading south from Dessau you reach **Leipzig**, a famous university, publishing and cultural centre.There is much to see and do here. Through **Merseburg**, you reach **Halle**, Handel's birthplace, and you can visit the cathedral where he played. The tour finishes here, and you can either explore more of Germany or head into the Czech Republic.

Greece

GREECE WAS THE CRADLE OF CIVILIZATION, and the birthplace of democracy, drama and philosophy. It was home to legendary figures such as geometricians Euclides and Pythagoras, philosophers Aristotle and Plato, and Aesop, whose fables have delighted children for centuries. The influence of Greek architecture spread throughout the world, and has been the model for many famous buildings, including America's White House. And, let us not forget one of the country's other innovations - the Olympic Games, which will return to their homeland in 2004.

The Greek language has left its mark on other languages as well. Words such as *metropolitan*, *aristocratic*, *gymnastics*, *sophisticated*, *philanthropy*, *harmony*, *music*, *architecture* and *ecology* are among thousands that have come to us from the Greeks.

Situated on the southern tip of the Balkan Peninsula, Greece has a land area of 131,944 sq km, and a population of around 10 million. The capital is Athens, which is in the province of Attica.

Greece

Climate

The weather is relatively mild and dry, although summers are hot. The heaviest rainfall is in December and January. Average temperatures for Athens are 6-13C in January, 20-30C in June.

Entry Regulations

Valid passports and on-going travel documents are required for a stay of up to three months. Visas are not necessary, but it is best to check with your travel agent when making your reservations.

The duty free allowance is 200 cigarettes, or 100 cigarillos or 50 cigars or 250gm of tobacco, 1 litre of spirits and 2 litres of wine. There is no restriction on the import or export of foreign or local currencies.

No vaccinations are required for any international traveller.

Currency

The currency of the country is the Drachma (dr). Approximate exchange rates, which should be used as a guide only, are:

A$	=	205.73drs
Can$	=	245.34drs
NZ$	=	167.29drs
S$	=	210.64drs
UK£	=	547.90drs
US$	=	361.01drs
EUR	=	337.39drs

Notes are in denominations of 500 (green), 1000 (brown), 5000 (blue) and 10,000drs (purple), and coins are 5, 10 (silver), 20, 50 and 100drs (bronze).

Business hours are flexible, and most smaller establishments ☉close for siesta from 2-5pm during the summer months.

Banks are usually ☉open Mon-Fri 7.30am-1pm. The following banks in Athens are open after hours for currency exchange:

The National Bank of Greece, 2 Karagheorgi Servias Street, Syntagma, ✆322 2738 - ☉open daily 8am-2pm, 3.30-6.30; Sat 9am-3pm; Sun 9am-1pm; currency exchange dispenser in operation 24 hours a day.

American Express, 2 Ermou Street, Syntagma, ✆324 4975 - ☉open daily 8.30am-4pm; Sat 8.30am-1pm.

Interbank, 2 Othonos Street, Syntagma, ✆325 4398, 325 4244 - ☉open Mon-Thurs 7.45am-4.45pm; Fri 7.45am-4.15pm; Sat 10am-1pm; currency exchange dispenser in operation 24 hours a day.

Interbank, 12 Skoufa Street, Kolonaki, ℘361 5134, 361 5141, 361 5346 - ⊙open Mon-Thurs 7.45am-4.45pm; Fri 7.45am-4.15pm; Sat 10am-1pm.

Xiosbank, 2-4 Amalias Avenue, Syntagma, ℘331 0529 - ⊙open daily 9am-9pm.

Credit Bank, 2 Stadiou Street, Syntagma, ℘322 0238 - currency exchange dispenser in operation 24 hours a day.

Shops are usually ⊙open daily 8.30am-2pm, and Tues, Thurs and Fri 5pm-8.30pm. Large supermarkets and department stores are ⊙open 8.30am-8.30pm. Many shops are closed on Sundays.

Post Offices are ⊙open Mon-Fri 7.30am-2pm, with four exceptions: those at Syntagma Square, Omonia Square, and the Acropolis are also ⊙open Sun 9am-1.30pm; and the mobile post office in Monastiraki Square is ⊙open Mon-Fri and Sun 8am-6pm.

Credit cards are widely accepted in the major cities.

Telephone

International direct dialling is available and the country code is 30. The city code for Athens is 1 (01 from within Greece). Most phone booths require a phonecard, which can be purchased at kiosks, some hotels and any telephone office. The cards can be used for local and long-distance calls, and costs are ✆1700dr (100 units), 7000dr (500 units) and 11,500dr (1000 units).

Emergency numbers are: Police ℘100 (English not spoken); Tourist Police ℘171 (English spoken); Australian Embassy ℘645 0404; Canadian Embassy ℘725 4011; ℘US Embassy 721 2951; ℘UK Embassy 723 6211.

Driving

Driving in Greece is on the right hand side of the road, and speed limits are as follows.

Built-up areas   - 50kph
Outside built-up areas - 80kph
Motorways   - 100kph

Greece has one of the worst accident rates in Europe, and Greek drivers are not known for their patience, or for that matter, their driving ability. If you decide to drive in the cities, use the utmost care, and don't expect the other drivers to stick to the rules of the road.

Miscellaneous

Local time is GMT + 2, with Daylight Saving operating from the end of March until the end of September.

Electricity is 220 volts AC. It is advisable to carry an adaptor for your appliances.

Health - It is advisable to have private medical insurance, especially if you are travelling from a country that is outside the European Union.

Tap water is safe to drink, but it is so heavily chlorinated that most visitors prefer bottled water. If you are out and about and require a toilet, look for a hotel rather than a restaurant.

Athens has heavy pollution, and this may affect anyone with respiratory problems. It is recommended that these people carry antihistamines, along with the sunscreen that everyone should have.

Tipping - Even though a 15% service charge is included in restaurant bills, it is still expected that patrons will tip a further 10%, plus leave a small tip on the table for the busboy. Hotel concierges expect ✪1000drs, doormen 500drs, barbers and beauticians 10%, and taxi drivers just like to keep the change.

VAT is 18%, and may be reimbursable if 40,000drs is spent per store, the correct form completed and handed with a computerized receipt to the customs office at the airport, along with the goods. Everything will be inspected there, and another form issued which should be mailed to the store where the shopping was done, and the store will mail the refund to you. In other words, unless you have spent megabucks, it is really not worth the bother.

Athens

Athens is a vibrant city that is a strange mixture of the ancient and the modern. The heart of the city is as sophisticated as any other in Europe, but a few streets away it seems as if time has stood still. Here it would not be surprising to see one of the old philosophers on a soap-box with his disciples at his feet. It is not an attractive city by any stretch of the imagination, but it is fascinating and intriguing, and well worth visiting.

History

Around 800BC the famous hero Theseus united many small city-states into the province of Attica. Among them was Athens, and Theseus became its king.

Things went along nicely until around 620BC when a legislator named Draco took centre stage, and introduced laws that were so strict that he has been immortalized by the word 'draconian'. These laws were in force for twenty-five years until another player appeared, Solon, who came to be called the founder of Athenian democracy. He abolished the death penalty for everything but murder, and introduced reforms that set up free elections and brought all classes (except the hapless slaves) into the process of government - democracy.

A century later (490BC) the Persian army arrived at Marathon, but were defeated and a Greek soldier ran the 26 miles back to Athens, announced the victory, then dropped dead. The Persians' second attempt was thwarted by Themistocles, who built a fleet of ships and was victorious at the battle of Salamis, but the Persians came out on top after their attack on land at the pass of Thermopylae.

The middle of the 5th century BC was the beginning of the Golden Age of Athens. The leader at this time was Pericles, the *creme de la creme* of orators in a city brimming with them. He practised democracy at home, and imperialism abroad, and it was he who built the Parthenon, the Propylaea, the long walls to Piraeus, and many of the temples around the city. While he was busy doing this, Aeschylus, Sophocles and Euripides were writing plays, Socrates and Plato were teaching, and former ally Sparta was green with envy.

Then began the Peloponnesian War, which lasted for 27 years. Pericles led Athens for the first two years, but died of a plague that raced through the city in 429BC. The leaders that followed were not up to the job, and Athens was defeated in 404BC. Spartan rule only lasted 30 years, though, and was followed by Macedonian.

Philip of Macedon wanted to unify all of Greece, and to eliminate Persia as a threat. Before he could get started though, he divorced his wife, who in true 'woman scorned' fashion had him assassinated. His heir was his nephew, but the crown went to his first wife's son, Alexander, aged 20.

Well, he isn't known as Alexander The Great for nothing. He conquered Greece, united it against Persia, then conquered Asia Minor, Syria, Egypt, Babylon, Susa, Persepolis, and was on his way to India when his troops cried 'Enough!' and forced him to return to Macedon. Alexander had studied under Aristotle, and was a humane man. He treated the people he conquered with honour, and allowed them to keep their gods and customs. In 323BC, when in his early 30s, he caught a fever and died. His death marked the end of the great classical period of Greece, and the beginning of its decline. There was constant infighting between the city-states, and in 146BC Greece was conquered by the armies of Rome.

For 500 years Greece was subject to Rome. Democracy was abolished, and Greece became merely a Roman province. It was also a stronghold of Christianity - St Paul preached in Greek, and his epistles

Greece

were written to the Greek settlements of Corinth, Thessaloniki and Ephesus.

In 330AD the Roman emperor Constantine chose a village on the Bosphorus to become the eastern capital. He named it Constantinople, and after the decline of the Roman Empire the city became the capital of the Byzantine Empire. For many centuries, Byzantium was the only civilized part of Europe. Then the Eastern and Western churches separated and countries in Western Europe formed their crusades and plundered Constantinople. It eventually fell to the Ottoman Turks, and Greece was reduced to an even less important province, and Athens became a small town. The Parthenon was reborn as a Turkish mosque.

Greece remained under Turkish rule for the next 400 years. In the early 1800s groups of Greek revolutionaries appeared on the scene, and in 1821 they formally began their struggle for independence. On March 25, the Greek flag of independence was raised at the monastery of Agia Lavra, near Patras. This date is now celebrated as Greek Independence Day.

Tourist Information

The Greek National Tourist Offices in Athens are found at:

2 Amerikis Street, Syntagma, ✆327 1300-3 (Head Office).

4 Stadiou Street, Syntagma, ✆322 1459, 322 3111-9 (ext 240).

East Terminal Bureau, ✆969 4500.

Piraeus Office, Marina Zeas, ✆413 5716, 413 5730.

The *Athens News* is a daily English newspaper that lists events and entertainment venues. *Now* is a free bi-monthly publication with lots of local information.

Local Transport

Trolleybus and bus routes crisscross the city, and public transport is very inexpensive and reliable. Tickets must be purchased before boarding, and are available at newspaper kiosks, at special booths or stands found in the main squares, and at several bus stops. The transport information telephone number is ⓒ185, and it operates ⓞdaily 7am-9pm. Buses and trolleys operate 5am-12.30am, and the electric railway operates 5am-12.15am. The railway is the quickest way to travel, but obviously only if you are going to one of the areas it serves (Piraeus to Kifisia by way of Omonia and the centre of Athens).

Commercial Centre

Because of the incredible pollution problems in Athens, motor vehicles have been banned from the commercial centre of the city. The centre is defined as the area surrounded by: Stadiou, Metropoleos and Athenas Streets, and Omonia, Syntagma and Monastiraki Squares. Hotels situated in the commercial centre can be reached via the following streets: Nikis, Karagheorgi Servias, Voulis, N. Nikodemou and back to Nikis.

Three minibus routes cover the centre of the city, and one of them, no.150, allows access to the restricted area.

Bus no. 150: starts from Athenas Street, next to City Hall.

Bus no. 100: starts from Koumoundourou Square.

Bus no. 200: starts from Alexandras Avenue.

These minibuses operate ⓞMon-Fri 6.30am5pm, Tues-Fri until 9pm.

Regular buses serving the area are nos. 025, 026, 027, 209, 210 which go through Metropoleos and Ermou Streets.

Metro

Athens is in the process of building a Metro and only the first stage of this ambitious project has been opened, but even that small amount is expected to reduce traffic congestion by 20%. The project has not been without its problems, though, because every piece of excavation seemed to uncover masses of priceless antiquities. Keramikos station had to be relocated so as not to interfere with a 6th century BC cemetery. Nine layers of civilization, the last dating from the 7th century BC, were excavated at Monastiraki. And digging at Syntagma unearthed a Roman bathhouse whose 200-year-old tiles were as vivid as the day they were taken out of the kiln.

Maps

If you have a good look at two different maps of Athens, you will probably find that some of the street names are spelt differently in each of them. Find another map and chances are you will be presented with an altogether different way of spelling some of the names. If you are looking for a hotel or restaurant, look in the street index of your map and find the street that most closely resembles the name you have been given. Nine times out of ten it will be the right one.

Accommodation

Reasonable accommodation is alas expensive for the anitpodean traveller in Athens. Best to note that the smaller hotels don't accept all varieties of credit cards, or none at all. Check ahead what credit cards they will accept.

Diomia Hotel, 5 Diomias Street, 105 62 Athens, ©01/323 8034, fax 01/322 2412. Located in the heart of Athens near Syntagma Square with views to the Acropolis from rooms to the rear of the hotel. This hotel is a place to sleep in a great location and provides for your basic needs. That said, it is only steps away from a range of cafes and sights, so the location makes up for an otherwise pretty ordinary performance - ✪25,000Drs.

Hotel Achilleas, 21 Lekka Street, 105 62 Athens, ©01/323 3197, fax 01/324 1092. Located in a quiet side street not far from Syntagma Square, this little hotel is drab, but offers reasonably spacious rooms in the heart of Athens. Breakfast is included in the price of the room. It has been recently renovated - ✪25,000Drs.

Acropolis View Hotel, 10 Webster Street, 117 42 Athens, ©01/921 7303, fax 01/923 0705. A beautiful little small hotel that has a bit of character to it. The front rooms do indeed have breathtaking views of the Acropolis. The hotel is located in a quiet residential area at the base of Filopapou Hill. Its 32 rooms are not large, but the whole hotel is very well maintained. A good choice - ✪28,000Drs.

Parthenon

6 Makri Street, 115 27 Athens, ✆01/ 923 4594, fax 01/644 1084. Modern and not especially stylish, but for a hotel so small, the Parthenon has good in-house facilities, including bar, restaurant and a pleasant little garden. Rooms are comfortable, the bathrooms in particular are a pleasing departure from the usual coffin-stood-on-end you find in this price bracket. Located not far south of the Acropolis - ✪18,000Drs.

Marble House Pension, 35 A. Zinni Street, Koukaki, 117 41 Athens, ✆01/923 4058. A quiet, suburban retreat, with a good reputation with travellers on a budget, and staff who are used to English speaking guests. Discount prices are available for guests staying for lengthy stays. Some rooms have share bathrooms, if you want to save some money that way, too. Out of the centre, but a good choice for anyone planning to stay awhile who doesn't want to spend a fortune - ✪14,000Drs.

Amaryllis Hotel, 45 Veranzerou Street & 3rd September, Athens, ✆523 9838, fax 522 5954. A C-class hotel situated on a quiet road in the commercial centre, close to Omonia Square Underground Station, the Main Railway Station and Syntagma Square. 57 rooms, bar/lounge - ✪12,000Drs (including breakfast).

Athenaeum Inter-Continenal, 89-93 Syngrou Avenue, Athens, ✆920 6000, fax 924 3000. Situated in the heart of the business district. 548 rooms, restaurant, lounges, bars, swimming pool - ✪US$259-295.

Andromeda Athens, 22 Timoleontos Vassou Street, Mavili Square, Athens, ℭ643 7302, fax 646 6361. Situated next to the US Embassy and the Concert Hall in the heart of the city. 30 rooms, restaurant, bar/lounge - ✪US$200-300.

Titania Hotel, 52 Panepistimiou Avenue, Athens, ℭ330 0111, fax 330 0700. Situated between Syntagma and Omonia Squares. 400 rooms, 2 restaurants, cafe, bar - ✪16,000-30,000Drs.

Park Hotel, 10 Alexandras Avenue, Athens, ℭ883 2711, fax 823 8420. Opposite Areos Park (Pedionareos) and within easy walking distance of Archaeological Museum. 143 rooms, restaurant, roof garden - standard room ✪40,000drs; superior room 48,000drs; deluxe room 54,000Drs.

President Hotel, 43 Kifissias Avenue, Athens, ℭ648 9000, fax 692 4968. Close to the commercial and business centres. 530 rooms, rooftop pool and restaurant, 2 other restaurants, piano bar - prices on application (but expect ✪more than 45,000Drs).

Food and Drink

It probably won't come as a great surprise, but the first cookbook in History was written by a Greek, Archestratos, in 330BC. What may come as a surprise is that Greek cuisine has a lot more going for it than *mousaka* and *souvlaki*. In fact there is a great variety of dishes for both meat-eaters and vegetarians, many of which date back some 4000 years.

When Greeks gather around a table and enjoy a meal or various appetizers (*mezedes*) with *ouzo*, it is almost a religious experience. The Greek word *symposium* literally means 'drinking with company', and the atmosphere in the local restaurants and *tavernas* is very relaxed, informal and unpretentious.

Following is a selection of eateries in the Plaka, where you are sure to find something that appeals.

Byzantino is found in a small park on Kydatheneon Street. It is a favourite with the locals, and recommended are the Spinach Pie and the chicken dishes. Bottled wine and cold beer are available and prices are moderate.

Domigos is the oldest of three basement restaurants called the Bakaliarzidikas, and is found near the corner of Kydatheneon and Adrianeu Streets, right underneath Brettos Ouzo. The eatery specializes in fried cod fish, and good home-made wines. It is not open in summer because the closeness of the ovens makes it far too hot.

Psaras Fish Taverna is on the corner of Erotocritou and Erehtheos Streets, up the steps that lead from the Plaka to the Acropolis. The tavern dates back to 1898, but has recently reopened after refurbishment. The food and wine are excellent. Next door is *Vasili*, which is run by a former maitre de of Psaras, and offers much the same standard of food.

Spilia Tis Acropolis. Continue walking up Kydathenaon Street, past Adrainou, and you will come to this very nice restaurant, with good food and moderate prices.

Eden Vegetarian Restaurant, on the corner of Mysicleos and Lissrou Streets, is well known for its Eggplant Salads.

Platanos is in Dioghenous Street, next door to the Greek Music Museum, and is a great place to eat at night.

Sightseeing

Ancient Athens - The Acropolis

The obvious place to start a tour of Ancient Athens is **The Acropolis** which has been the symbol of Athens for thousands of years. The word means 'high city', and it was indeed a natural fortress on a rock 156m above sea level.

A view across to the Acropolis

Greece

First inhabited in the Neolithic era, defensive walls were not built until the mid 13th century BC. Around 900BC the city was moved, and the Acropolis became a place of worship, acquiring its first temple. The **Parthenon**, dedicated to Athena, was commenced in the early 5th century BC, only to be completely destroyed by the Persians in 480BC. It was rebuilt in Pericles' reign, and the Propylaia was constructed between 437 and 432BC.

The main problem that the Acropolis has today is pollution, which erodes the marble. Restoration work is being carried out, but the job is taking much longer than was expected, and it seems that the Parthenon is always surrounded by scaffolding. Perhaps they will have it completed in time for the Olympics.

The Acropolis is ⊙open 8am-9pm (summer); 8.30am-3pm (winter), ✆321 0219, 321 4172, 321 0219, 923 8724.

You might want to get transport to the Acropolis, so that you will be full of energy to get yourself up the hill to explore the ancient site. The entrance is in Dionysiou Areopaghitou Street.

The Ancient Theatre of Dionysos

On your left, as you begin the climb, is the oldest known theatre in the world, the theatre of Dionysos. Here, the great Greek poets' plays premiered in the 5th century BC. The cavea and the stage were originally made of wood, but were reconstructed of marble during the 4th century BC. Only parts of the stone have survived. Experts say that the theatre would have been able to accommodate 17,000 people.

The Stoa of Eumenes

The next stop on your ascent is this Stoa, which was built by the King of Pergamon, Eumenes II in the 2nd century BC. Its main purpose was to protect against bad weather or too much sun. As you pass through the Stoa, you can see the ruins of the Asklepieion, built in 429BC after the plague that decimated the population of Athens.

The Odeion of Herodes Atticus

Called the *Herodeion* by modern Greeks, it was built in 161AD by Tiberius Claudius Atticus Herodes, a wealthy teacher and philosopher. It was built in honour of his wife Rigilla, and was used for concerts and recitals. Today it hosts the Athens Festival every summer.

The Propylaea

This is the entrance to the Acropolis and its monuments, and was constructed as part of Pericles' original plan.

The Temple of Athena Nike (Apteros Nike - Wingless Victory)

This is a small temple with eight Ionic columns, in which the Athenians placed a statue of the goddess Nike without wings to ensure that she would not be able to fly away from their city. Today the statue is in the Acropolis Museum.

The Parthenon

This unique masterpiece is 69.1m long, 30.86m wide and was surrounded by 46 columns. The architects had a few problems with design because of the uneven foundation, so one end of the building rests on 12m of marble to bring it level with the rest of the structure. The temple lies east to west, with 17 columns on the north and south walls and 8 columns on the other two sides.

The Parthenon has no straight lines. Horizontal lines curve in the middle, and the 50 columns bulge in the centre then taper off toward the top. Originally the temple had statues and friezes, but over the years they have been removed, some were even souvenired (for example, the Elgin Marbles in the British Museum).

The temple originally contained a ten metre high statue of Athena, made of wood and ivory. She was armed and held a two-metre ivory statue of Nike (Victory) in her right hand. The statue was lost during the first years of the Byzantine period, but knowledge of it comes from ancient sources, and the traveller Pausanias' detailed descriptions from the 2nd century AD.

While you are here, take a good look around you. What you can see, with the exception of the museum, was the extent of Athens in its Golden Age of Pericles.

The Erechtheion

It was built between 420-406BC on the part of the Acropolis that was held to be the most sacred - the place where the goddess Athena caused her most sacred emblem, the olive tree, to sprout. The tree was destroyed in later years by the Persians, but when they were finally driven out, legend says that the tree miraculously grew again.

The figures of maidens that 'support' the roof of the south porch of the temple are called *The Caryatids*. Those you can see here are copies, but four of the original six are in the Acropolis Museum, the fifth is currently being restored at the museum, and the sixth is in the British Museum.

The Areios Pagos

This is the most ancient court of law, and the site of the first aristocratic parliament (or polis) of ancient Athens. The parliament lost power and from the second half of the 5th century BC, it had only judicial responsibility, particularly that of trying murderers.

It was from this spot that St Paul delivered his first sermon to the Athenians in 51AD.

The Acropolis Museum

It is a good idea to visit the museum before you walk around the site, so as to get a better appreciation of what you are going to see. It is ☉open the same times as the Acropolis.

The Pnyx

The Pnyx is situated between the Hill of the Muses, on which is the Monument of Philopappou, and the Hill of the Nymphs, where the observatory stands today. In ancient times Athenians gathered here to listen to the famous orators who spoke from the stone-cut tribune in the middle. It is thought to have been able to accommodate up to 10,000 people. Today it is the venue for the Sound and Light Show.

The Ancient Agora

The ancient Agora is at the foot of the Acropolis near the Theseion metro station and bordering the streets where the Sunday bazaar takes place. It is ☉open Tues-Sun 8am-5pm, ✆321 0185.

Since Agora means 'market' it is a fitting venue for the modern bazaar. In ancient times, however, the Agora was much more. It is where people gathered for dozens of reasons: to buy and sell their goods; to learn the latest news; to criticize the government; to attend a court of law; and visit some of the public offices; or just to have an old-fashioned gossip.

The Theseion-Hephaisteion

Situated at the western edge of the Agora, this was a temple to the god Hephaistos and the goddess Athena. It is now one of the best preserved temple of ancient times. It was built in 449BC.

The Golden Mask of Agamemnon at the National Archaelogical Museum

The Monument of the Eponymous Heroes

The statues of the ten heroes after whom the ten tribes of Attica were named (4th century BC) were here.

The Poikile Stoa

It is thought to have taken its name from the murals that decorated its walls - *poikile* means 'diverse'. It was here that Zenon expounded his Stoic philosophy.

The Roman Agora

This was a single complex that consisted of a courtyard surrounded by colonnades, and arcades that housed shops. To the north of the building was the library built by Hadrian; to the east the Tower of the Winds can be seen. This octagonal structure served as a water-clock and was built in the 1st century BC.

Greece

The Stoa of Attalos

This is a two-storey arcade built from a donation by Attalos III, King of Pergamon (159-138BC). It now serves as a museum for finds discovered in the Agora.

The Basileios Stoa

Built in 460BC, it is situated at the foot of the Theseion, and was the seat of the Archon Vasileus and of the Areios Pagos council.

The Kerameikos

From the Agora, take Adrianou Street, then Ermou Street to no. 148 and you will come to the most important cemetery of the ancient Athenians. It is ☉open Tues-Sun 8am-2.30pm, ✆346 3552.

If you have fitted all that into one day, you are going very well. The next walking tour begins in the area known as Plaka.

Plaka

Nobody really knows where the name came from. Plaka means a stone slab, so some say that the name comes from a slab found in the church of Ayios Georgios of Alexandria, near the ancient theatre of Dionysos. What is known for sure is that this is Athens' oldest and most picturesque neighbourhood, and it has been skilfully restored. A word of warning, though, when you venture into this part of the city make sure you have a map because Plaka is a virtual labyrinth of narrow streets and alleyways. Always remember that uphill is the Acropolis and downhill are Syntagma and Monastiraki.

Philomousou Etairias Square

The name means 'Friends of the Muses', who were the nine patron goddesses of the Arts, and the square is at the crossroads of Kydathenaeon, Farmaki, Olympiou Dios and Anghelou Geronda Streets.

There are cafes, restaurants, bars and night clubs galore, and many shops selling souvenirs - copies of works of ancient art, jewellery of traditional Greek design, worry beads and the ubiquitous T-shirts.

Greece

Children's Museum

In Kydathenaeon Street (no. 14), the museum is a child's paradise. The attic is a reconstructed room with old furniture, radio and heater of an old Athenian house, and here children can play 'dress-ups' in period costumes. The first floor has a reconstruction of the work site of the Athenian metro, and the kids can see what future stations are going to look like, and they can pretend that they are working on the construction. The museum also has a library and a playground - a must if you are travelling with kids. It is ☉open Mon-Wed 9.30am-1.30pm; Fri 9.30am-1.30pm, 5-8pm; Sat-Sun 10am-1pm, ✆331 2995-6.

Tower of the Winds

Outside the eastern side of the Roman Agor, is an octagonal monument, Andronikos Kyristes' clock, built in the 1st century BC. Each of the eight sides was decorated with representations of the eight winds.

The Monument of Lysikrates

In ancient times, the theatrical performances in the theatre of Dionysos were sponsored by wealthy citizens, who were called *choregoi*. The choregos who sponsored the best performance of the year was presented with an award by the city. In 334BC, the prize was won by Lysikrates, and he decided to build a monument to house it, and it has to this day.

The Olympieion

The ancient traveller Pausanias said that the temple of Olympian Zeus was founded by Deucalion, one of the mythical ancestors of the Greeks. In 515BC the ruling dynasty tried to replace the old temple with a more impressive one, but they were ousted before the building was finished. Decimus Cossutius, the Roman architect, was employed by Antiochos IV Epiphanes, King of Syria, to complete the job. When the king died in 163BC, construction was once more abandoned. Then in 131AD the Roman Emperor Hadrian had the temple completed.

The Arch of Hadrian

The Athenians, in gratitude for his work on the Olympieion, honoured Hadrian by building an arched gateway in the north-west corner of the enclosure of the temple. The arch has two inscriptions - the one on the side facing the Acropolis reads: *This is Athens, the ancient city of Theseus*; the other, on the side facing the sanctuary and the extension of the city by Hadrian, reads: *This is the city of Hadrian and not of Theseus*.

Modern Athens

The National Garden

The garden was designed to be part of the Royal Palace of King Otto and Queen Amalia, and was planted between 1838 and 1860. It covers 40 acres, and is open from dawn to dusk.

The Zappeion Megaron

The Zappeion is the small park area between the National Garden and the Olympieion, and in it is the Megaron, a beautiful building built between 1874-1888. It is a Congress and Exhibition Hall, and has witnessed some of the most important moments in this country's modern history. The building also houses art exhibitions, and the occasional concert.

The Panathenaikon Stadium

The horseshoe-shaped stadium, built of white marble, is opposite the National Garden. The first stadium built on this site was constructed from wood in 330BC. The first marble structure, of which the present one is a faithful replica, was built by Herodes Atticus. It was used as a venue for the athletic games held during the feast of Panathenaea, hence its name. The present stadium was built between 1869 and 1870 for the first modern Olympic Games held in 1896.

The Three Temples of Learning

The three buildings were built around the same time in the decades after Independence. They are: The University (1839-1864), The Academy (1859-1887) and The National Library (1887-1902).

Syntagma Square

The Square is really the centre of all the activity in the city. The buildings surrounding it are hotels, banks, ministries and airline offices. Also here are some of the trendiest bars and night clubs, which are only open during the winter.

The House of Parliament

The building overlooks Syntagma Square and was built as a palace for King Otto, the first King of Greece and Queen Amalia. King Georgios, the second king, also lived here, but during his reign two fires destroyed the building to the extent that it was declared unfit for royal occupation. In 1924, it was decided to use the building to house the Greek Parliament and renovation work began in 1934.

The Tomb of the Unknown Soldier in the front of the building, was built in 1929-39 and is guarded day and night by a pair of elite soldiers called *Evzones*, who wear traditional Greek uniforms. The changing of the guard takes place every hour, and is worth seeing.

Omonia Square

Omonia is the oldest central square of the modern city of Athens, and brags that it is ☺open 24 hours a day, 365 days a year. All the major fast food companies have outlets in this square, and the newsstands carry all the foreign newspapers and periodicals. Omonia is the beginning (or the end) of Stadiou, Patision, Panepistimiou, Tritis, Septemvriou, Piraeos, Athenas and Ayiou Konstantinou Streets, and there is an underground station beneath it, appropriately named Omonia.

Avysinias Square (The Flea Market)

Avysinias is the main square in Monastiraki, a district that is a continuation of Plaka, in the heart of the historic centre. Athens' famous flea market is found in the square, and is patronised by locals as well as tourists.

In Monastiraki there are quaint old houses, tavernas, cafes and bars, and Adrianou Street where a bazaar is held every Sunday. There is also a market in and around Ifaistou Street.

Museums

There are literally dozens of museums and archaeological sites in Athens, and it would be possible to write a guide book on them alone. The information offices have lists of them, and it is best to get a copy and choose the ones that would be of interest to you. Always remember to check on the opening hours, though, as they are not all the same.

Places Further Afield

Daphni Monastery

Situated 11km from Athens, the monastery is thought to be the most important Byzantine monument in the area, and its mosaics, which were made in the 11th century AD, are said to be masterpieces. There are conflicting stories about the name of the monastery. Some experts say that it stands on the site of the ancient temple of Daphnios Apollo which had a sacred olive grove (*daphne* = laurel). That seems straightforward enough, but others claim that in ancient times a queen named Daphni was shipwrecked near the bay of Eleusis, and upon being saved built a temple in honour of Apollo. There is yet another myth that says that the nymph Daphne, when fleeing from the amorous Apollo, turned herself into a laurel tree near here.

The mosaics are found on the walls, the dome, the arms of the cross on the roof, and in the sanctuary.

Two city buses (nos. 880 and 860) travel to the monastery from Panepistimiou Street, near Emmanuel Benaki and Harilaou Trikoupi Streets.

Eleusis

Eleusis is one of the most important archaeological sites in Greece. The ancient Eleusinians worshipped Demeter, the goddess of nature, spring and agriculture. A 7th century BC myth tells that the earth once parted and Plouton, the god of the underworld, abducted Persephone, the daughter of Demeter, and took her back to his kingdom. Demeter was beside herself with grief and searched everywhere for nine days and nights, finally arriving in Eleusis and dropping in on the local king Keleos. She stayed at the palace incognito, but when her true identity became known she asked for a temple to be built in her honour, where she went to get away from it all and mourn her loss. The following year not a single seed grew through the world. Zeus realised that he could not let this state of affairs continue, so he sent Hermes to visit Plouton to see if some compromise could be reached. The end result was that Persephone would stay four months of the year in the underworld, and the rest of the time with her mother. This satisfied Demeter, and so she allowed the plants and flowers to grow once more.

The site is open for inspection and there is a museum which displays finds from excavations of the sanctuary of the temple and the west cemetery.

Eleusis is 23km from the centre of Athens on the Athens-Corinth National Road. Bus no. 880 travels to Eleusis from the Athens terminal on Panepistimiou Street, near the Ophthalmiatreio.

Marathon

Marathon is one of Attica's prettiest places, and the road there passes through vegetable gardens, vineyards and olive groves. Nearby there are many lovely beaches, including Schinias beach, where the pine woods almost reach the sand.

It was Herodotus who seemed to know the most about the battle of Marathon. He said that the Persian fleet landed 100,000 men in Marathon in 490BC, and the defending army totalled 11,000 soldiers. Nevertheless, the Greeks were victorious, and Pheidippides, an Athenian soldier, was sent to tell the good news to the city. He ran the

26 miles, delivered the message, 'Nenikikamen' (we have won), and the rest, as they say, is history.

Near the battleground there is a tomb of the 192 Athenian soldiers who died during that famous battle. There is also a small museum with exhibits from all over, not just local artifacts.

The Paralia Marathonos bus leaves from Mavromataion Street, near the Pedion tou Areos, ✆821 8072.

Sounion

The temple of Poseidon stands 60m above the sea at the edge of a cliff on Cape Sounion, and is one of the most breathtaking sights in all Greece. It is about an hour's drive from Athens, and the road runs along the Saronic coast. If you are driving, make sure you stop and investigate some of the coffee shops and fish tavernas along the way.

Two bus routes travel to Sounion from Athens. One takes the coastal road through Varkiza and Legrena. The other goes inland via Ayra Paraskevi, Koropi and Lavrion. The terminal of both lines is in Mavromataion Street, near the Pedion tou Areos, ✆823 0179.

Several private companies run tours to Sounion, and the information offices will have details.

Piraeus

During the 5th century BC, Themistokles realised the importance of Piraeus to the city of Athens, and turned it into the main port, replacing the Gulf of Faliro. The city of Piraeus was planned by the architect Ippodamos, and when the city was replanned in 1834, his ancient plans were used as guidelines.

For movie buffs, the movie *Never on Sunday* was filmed in the city and port of Piraeus.

There is so much to see and do here, that it is best to devote a whole day to a visit. There is the Main Harbour; Zea's marina with its impressive yachts; Mikrolimano, a small harbour; the fashionable suburb of Kastella; the Monastiraki flea market on Dragatsaniou and

Mavromichali Streets (Sunday); the Archaeological Museum; the Maritime Museum; and cruises to all sorts of fascinating places.

Bus no. 40 travels from Syntagma Square; Bus no. 049 travels from Omonia Square; and the metro goes to Akti Kondyli in around 20 minutes.

Greece

The Best of Athens in Brief

The Acropolis. Contains the ancient structures of The Parthenon, the Temple of Athena Nike and The Erechtheion. The Acropolis Archaelogical Museum, also on site, displays recovered sculptures and other relics.

Ancient Greek Agora. Monuments in this area include the Temple of Hephaistos, Temple of Ares, Stoa of Attalos, Beleutrion, Odeon of Agrippa and the Agora Museum,

National Archaelogical Museum. The premier museum in Athens, always crowded and deservedly so. A range of pieces from ancient cups to bronze statues make up this wonderful historical collection. *44 Patission Street*.

National Garden. The former gardens of the royal palace are a popular area to grab a bite to eat during your exploration of Athens. Relax on the grass in the shade of the trees and watch the local Athenians stroll by.

Mount Likavitos. A climb to the top of this mountain is rewarded with sprawling views over Athens and the surrounding region.

Driving Through Greece

Ancient Greece

Itinerary - 6 Days - Distance 780kms

Athens, the Capital of Greece, has a wealth of ancient monuments and sights, and is worthy of many days stay. From Athens drive west to **Corinth**, the site of the Corinth Canal. The archaeological site of **Mycenae** is nearby. Further south is **Nafplion**, the first capital of Greece. From Nafplion head west across the Peloponnese Ranges to **Olympia**, the original site of the Olympic Games. There is a lot to see here, so allow a day. Take the coastal road north of Olympia to Patras, and catch the ferry across to **Nafpaktos**. Drive east to **Delphi**, where you can see ancient monuments and the sanctuary of Apollo. **Arahova**, nearby, is famous for its rugs. Head back south to Athens.

Crete

Itinerary - 8 Days - Distance 635kms

Heraklion is the capital of Crete. The archaeological museum is worth seeing. Drive west from Heraklion to **Rethymnon**. The Venetian port, the museum and the old city are all features of this town. Further along the coast, you reach **Hania**, with its buildings from Venetian and Ottoman times. From Hania, head south over the hills towards **Agia Galini**. This drive is through rural Crete. Near Agia Galini there are several archaeological sites to visit. Travelling east through more small villages, you reach **Ierapetra**. **Vai** beach has a natural palm grove, which you pass through on the way to **Sitia**. From Sitia stop at **Aghios Nikolaos**, a popular tourist town. Drive back along the north coast to Heraklion.

Greece

Ireland

THE LUSH, GREEN ISLAND is off the west coast of Britain and has an area of 68,893 sq km with a population of around 4,000,000. It is joined to Northern Ireland and occupies five-sixths of the entire land mass. Its Irish name is Eire but in 1949 it changed its name to The Republic of Ireland. It became a member of the EEC in 1973. The capital is Dublin. The official languages are English and Irish (Gaeilge), but English is mainly spoken.

Ireland, though an an agricultural country with beautiful scenery, is making a name for itself in the software and information technology industries. It is also noted for the breeding of fine thoroughbred horses.

Climate

Ireland has a moderate climate where the mild south-westerly winds prevail. The Gulf Stream keeps the waters warm. January and February are the coldest months and July and August the warmest. Average temperatures are 39F (4C) -60F (16C). It is advisable to pack a warm jumper and raincoat.

Entry Regulations

A valid passport is necessary. For an extended stay, contact your nearest Irish Embassy.

Duty free allowance is 200 cigarettes or 100 cigarillos or 50 cigars. 1 litre of alcohol over 22% or 2 litres of alcohol not exceeding 22% 2 litres of still wine, 50gm perfume 0.25 litres toilet water. Goods to the value of IR£34. A maximum of 25 litres of beer may be imported as part of the above allowance. Those under 17 years of age may not import alcohol or cigarettes. No vaccinations are required.

Currency

The currency is the Irish Punt (IR£) divided into 100 pence. Approximate exchange rates, which should be used as a guide only, are:

A$	=	0.48IR£
Can$	=	0.57IR£
S$	=	0.50IR£
UK£	=	1.28IR£
US$	=	0.84IR£
Euro	=	0.79IR£

Notes are in denominations of 50, 20, 10 and 5 Punts, and coins are 1 Punt and 50, 20, 10, 5, 2 and 1 Pence. The best rate of exchange is given by Irish banks. Irish currency should be changed back before leaving the country.

Banks ☺open Monday-Friday 10am-12.30pm and 1.30pm-3pm. Most Dublin banks are open until 5pm on Thursdays.

VAT of 15% is added to all goods and services. Cashback is a company that undertakes to refund VAT. Not all stores participate in the scheme. You must have your dockets stamped by customs at your last exit port from the EEC and return the vouchers to Cashback. A fee is charged for this service.

Credit cards are accepted in major stores and hotels.

Ireland

Telephone

There are public telephones all over the country. International direct dialling is available and the International code is 00, the country code is 353.

Driving

Driving is on the left hand side of the road. The speed limits are as follows.

built up areas -   30mph
single roads   -   60mph
highways   -   70mph

Third party insurance is compulsory.

Miscellaneous

Local Time is Summer Central European Time.

Electricity is 220v AC. As plugs vary it is necessary to purchase an adaptor and a small transformer.

Health insurance is essential. Take any necessary medication with you and a copy of your prescriptions.

Tipping. A 15% service charge is added to hotel and restaurant bills, so no tip is required. Taxi drivers expect 10% and porters usually get 50p per bag.

Dublin

Dublin is compact by international standards, with a population of 952,692. It has wide streets, well designed squares and flower beds down the centre of major roads. Main street O'Connell, has most of the banks, shops and theatres. Dublin is situated on the River Liffey which flows into Dublin Bay.

History

Dublin was mentioned by Ptolemy, a geographer, as a place of note in 140AD. The name "Dublin" comes from the gaelic "Dubhlinn" meaning Black Pool, a more modern title than the Irish name in current use "Baile Atha Cliath", the "Town of the Hurdle Ford". The ancient ford was at the site of the present Father Mathew Bridge.

St Patrick visited Dublin in 448 and converted many of the residents to Christianity. Both the settlement and the religion thrived over the next four hundred years. His feast day is celebrated on the 17th March not only in Ireland, but in also in many countries (Australia, New Zealand, USA, Canada) to which the Irish have migrated either by force or free will.

In 840 a fortress was set up by some Norse sailors as a base, then in 852 a Danish force took possession of the town. Battles between the Irish and the Danes continued until 1014, when the Danes were finally beaten at the Battle of Clontarf.

The English appeared on the scene in 1170, and Strongbow, Earl of Pembroke took control of Dublin. On a visit to view his new acquisition in 1171, Henry II granted Dublin its first charter.

The Irish were never happy with English rule, and the following centuries saw wars between the two, culminating in the Rising of 1916, which took place over the Easter week.

The Irish Free State was established in 1922, but the Civil War that followed saw Dublin once again in the centre of the action.

Dublin has become a cultural centre and a large manufacturing industry has developed. Whiskey distilling, brewing, clothing, glass and food processing are its main industries.

Tourist Information

The Irish Tourist Board has developed a computerised information and reservation system called *Gulliver*. It has stored all major queries including theatres, sport, concerts, places to visit and transport. Gulliver is in all Irish Tourist Information Offices.

Tourist offices are found in Suffolk Street, near Grafton Street/Trinity College, ©(01) 669 2082, fax 669 2035; Baggot Street; Dun Laoghaire Ferryport; and The Square Tallaght. 24-hour information is available by phoning ©1-550 11 2233 (58p/min). The website is ✎www.visit.ie/dublin.

Local Transport

Buses are plentiful and reasonably priced with a flat fare. Cruising taxis are not abundant. The best place to find one is at an hotel or bus station.

Accommodation

A city of commerce, Dublin's hotels are often scratching to fill on weekends as the business traffic declines. Consequently, the astute traveller can often get heavily reduced rates if staying over a weekend, especially out of the larger chain hotels. For more information about Dublin, booking hotels online, and so on, see the official website: ☞www.visitdublin.com

Following is a selection of accommodation with prices for a double room per night, which should be used as a guide only.

Jury's Christchurch Inn, Christchurch Place, Dublin 8, ✆01/454 0000, fax 01/454 0012. Families travelling together will find the one price fits all policy very attractive, with each of the 180 rooms sleeping 3 adults or 2 adults and 2 children and costing the same regardless. A big American chain hotel that offers modern conveniences and comfort right across from Christchurch cathedral - ✪£65.

Northumberland Lodge, 68 Northumberland Road, Ballsbridge, Dublin 4, ✆01/660 5270, fax 01/668 8679. Trinity College is a 15 minute walk away from this pleasant old converted mansion. Spacious and elegant rooms - ✪£70.

Aaronmor House, 1b & c Sandymount Avenue, Dublin 4, ✆01/668 7972, fax 01/668 2377. A large, ramshackle turn of the century house converted to a guest house. Rooms vary in size, but the cramped ones are reasonably cheap - ✪from £50.

Waterloo Lodge, 23 Waterloo Road, Ballsbridge, Dublin 4, ✆01/668 5380, fax 01/668 5786. Located just to the south of the city centre, Waterloo Lodge represents good value for the budget traveller. Rooms are bland, but cosy and a small hotel warm welcome awaits every guest. A hearty breakfast is included in room rates which are lower out of season or for lengthy stays - ✪£37.50.

Royal Dublin

40 Upper O'Connell Street, Dublin 1, ✆01/ 873 3666, fax 01/873 3120. Located near Parnell Square in Dublin's north, the Royal Dublin lies in the heart of what might be called the theatre district. A modern lobby, all perfect geometric lines and shapes bleeds off into Georgian sitting rooms complete with frilly cornices, chandeliers and ornate fireplaces. Rooms don't suffer from an identity crisis, however, and are functional, almost chique, modern in design - ✪from £110.

Hotel Conrad Dublin, Earlsfort Terrace 2, Dublin, ✆(01) 676-5555, fax 676-5424. 191 rooms with private bath. Central, opposite National Concert Hall. Restaurant, bars, pub, parking. Standard room £113-179, Deluxe room ✪£140-190.

Jury's Hotel Dublin, Pembroke Road, Ballsbridge, ✆(01) 660 5000, fax 829 0400 ✉(travelweb@hotelbook.com(01206)). Deluxe hotel in Dublin's most exclusive residential area. 400 rooms, restaurant, bar/ lounge, swimming pool - ✪£135-199.

Trinity Capital Hotel, Tara Street, Dublin, ✆(01) 648 1000, fax 648 1010. A new hotel situated between the International Financial Services Centre and the Templar Bar District. 80 rooms, restaurant, bar/lounge - ✪£125-150.

Gresham Hotel, O'Connell Street, Dublin, ✆(01) 874 6881, fax 878 7175 (✉travelweb@hotelbook.com(01529)). A superior 1st class hotel situated in the centre of the city. 288 rooms, restaurant, bar/ lounge, fitness centre - ✪£115-130.

St Stephens Green, Stephens Green, Dublin, ✆(01) 607 3600, fax 661 5663 (✎ travelweb@hotelbook.com(28983)). A deluxe hotel in the city centre. 75 rooms, restaurant, bar/lounge - ✪£110-240.

The Mont Clare, 74 Marrion Square 2, Dublin, ✆(01) 661-6799, fax 661-5663 (✎ travelweb@hotelbook.com(13577)). 80 rooms with private bath. Near sightseeing and station. Restaurants, pub, bar - ✪£85-120.

George Frederic Handel Hotel, 16-18 Fishamble Street, Dublin, ✆(01) 670 9400, fax 670 9410 (✎ travelweb@hotelbook.com(27539)). Situated in the heart of the Temple Bar area. 40 rooms, cafe and bar - ✪£70-140.

Food and Drink

Irish seafood is especially good. Oysters carry the tang of the sea. Brown bread made the way your Grandma made it is the pride of the Irish. Helpings are large.

There is a tourist menu easily recognised by the picture of a chef on the menu cover. These meals are a set price for a three-course meal of simple but good food.

A good selection of wines is available everywhere but it is Guinness and Irish whiskey which are so popular.

The Irish pub is an integral part of Irish lifestyle. It is a gathering place for locals and visitors. Business deals are finalised, family matters discussed, romances conducted and visitors entertained with native wit and song. Every pub has its own charm and clientele. You do not have to drink alcohol to enjoy the lively atmosphere. Many serve coffee and tea and a pub lunch is an economical way to stem the pangs of hunger.

Medieval Banquets are another form of entertainment. Enjoy a wonderful meal and be entertained by musicians, singers and story-tellers. Banquets can be booked prior to departure.

Sightseeing

The city centre has sign-posted walking tours, and this is an excellent way to see the sights. A booklet giving maps and background information is available at the information centre. Fans of James Joyce and his *Ulysses* should make sure they obtain a map that details the positions of the relevant plaques throughout the city.

Take a stroll through **Phoenix Park** which covers 1,760 acres. Within the park stands **Aras an Uachtarain**, the official home of the President. At the entrance to the park is Dublin Zoo founded in 1830.

The **Bank of Ireland** building, in College Green, was constructed between 1729 and 1739 to house the Irish Parliament prior to 1800. The British Government sold the building to the bank in 1802. The showpiece of the building is Pearce's House of Lords with its magnificent Dublin glass chandelier dated 1788. There is also an original masterpiece, the House of Commons Mace.

Trinity College is on the east side of College Green and was built in 1592 on the site of a priory that had been taken over by Henry VIII. The College is the sole constituent college of the university, which was supposed to further the Reformation in Ireland. Covering 40 acres, the College has over 500,000 visitors per year, and the main reason for that is the Library which has the **Book of Kells**, an illustrated manuscript of the Gospels from around the 9th century. Nobody knows where the book was produced, but it is known that in 1007 it was housed at the monastery at Kells, 70km north-west of Dublin. The work is beautifully done, and there are usually two of the four volumes on display at any one time. Although the books are under glass, they are worth seeing. The library is ☉open Mon-Sat 9.30-5pm, Sun 9.30-4.30pm (June-Sept), 12.30-4.30pm (Oct-May).

The **Custom House** on the north bank of the River Liffey is a magnificent building and with the Four Courts is a jewel of Dublin

Two pages from the Book of Kells, Trinity College

architecture. It was commenced in 1781 and completed in 1791. It was burnt down in 1921 but has been reconstructed.

Dublin Castle was the centre of English power. The official residence of the Lords Deputy and Lords Lieutenant, the seat of State Councils and sometimes Parliament and the Law Courts. Between 1680-1780 wholesale reconstruction gave us the essence of the form we have today.

The State apartments are approached from the main entrance by the Grand Staircase. A lobby to the left of the landing leads to St Patrick's Hall. Since 1938 it has been the place of inauguration of the President of Ireland. A small piece of trivia about the castle - Bram Stoker, creator of *Dracula*, was once a clerk employed at the castle.

City Hall, adjoining the castle, was erected as the Royal Exchange between 1769-1799. It is a square building in the Corinthian style with three fronts of Portland stone.

Christ Church Cathedral, the Church of Ireland Cathedral, was first built in 1038, and the crypt, containing the grave of Strongbow, survives today. The crypt was opened in the 1930s, and the Earl of Pembroke was discovered to have been a 5 foot 4 inch redhead with broad shoulders. A large part of the church is Gothic Revival.

St Patrick's Cathedral occupies the site of a pre-Norman parish church. It also belongs to the Church of Ireland. A surprising fact for the first time visitor is that there is no Catholic cathedral in Dublin. St Patrick's contains some interesting monuments, among them the grave of Jonathan Swift, Dean of St Patrick's Cathedral 1713-1745. He was the author of *Gulliver's Travels*.

The **General Post Office** is in O'Connell Street, Dublin's main thoroughfare. It was the headquarters of the Irish Volunteers during the 1916 Rising, and it was here that the Republic was announced. There is a series of monuments in the centre of O'Connell Street including the O'Connell Monument, the Parnell Monument and the statue of Father Theobald Mathew.

Opposite Cathedral Street is the **Anna Livia Millennium Fountain**, which the locals call "The Floozie in the Jacuzzi" because that is exactly what it looks like. Anna Livia represents the River Liffey.

Dublin is noted for its theatres. The **Abbey Theatre** is committed to presenting the works of Irish playwrights. The original building was burnt down in 1951 and a new thesatre opened its doors in 1965.

Guinness Brewery is where Ireland's legendary drink is made and it is open to visitors. Enter by the Hop Store, Crane Street.

The **Irish Whiskey Corner**. The Irish invented whiskey. Monks of the 6th and 7th centuries learned the distillation process that had been used in Asia for perfume. They turned it into what they considered a better use! They called it Uisce Beatha, Gaelic for "The Waters of Life". The first licence was granted to Bushills Distillery in 1608 and they are still turning it out. Visitors are welcome but you must phone ℗(01) 725 566 for an appointment.

The **Dublin Literary Pub Crawl** is a three hour entertainment by two actors performing the works of Dublin's famous writers in authentic settings. It starts at Bailey's and continues on to about ten different pubs. Bookings at any local tourist office.

Dublin has many museums, art galleries and libraries all worth seeing if you can spare the time. The **Dublin Experience**, Trinity College, is a multi-media show which traces the history of the city from its earliest times and introduces the visitor to the modern city and its people. The soundtrack includes narration by several voices and the background music has been specially chosen. For those in a hurry, this is your answer.

The Best of Dublin in Brief

Trinity College. Ireland's most prestigious college is over 400 years old. Tours of the campus are available, but not to be missed is the Old Library which contains the famous *Book of Kells*.

Book of Kells. This breathtaking illustrated copy of the Four Gospels, painstakingly completed at the hands of monks in Scotland (this is the most widely-accepted theory), is preserved from the Dark Ages. Its invaluable pages are constantly illuminated and kept under glass for viewing. *College Green, Dublin 2.*

National Museum. This magnificent museum covers 4,000 years of Ireland's history. Highlights are the Viking artifacts and the Tara Brooch from the 8th century. *Kildare Street.*

Dublin Castle. Some of Dublin's oldest architecture is captured in this structure, which was completed in 1220 and was the seat of British rule in Ireland for over 700 years. *Palace Street, Dublin 2.*

Dublin Writers' Museum. A magnificent tribute to the works of many Irish literary greats including Yeats and Joyce. The Georgian mansion in which the museum is located is itself a work of art. *18-19 Parnell Square North, Dublin 1.*

St Patrick's Cathedral. This Church of Ireland cathedral is the longest and oldest in Dublin. Considering the other churches of Europe, you could quite easily give this one a miss. *Patrick's Close, Patrick Street, Dublin 8.*

Dublinia. An exhibition of medieval Dublin featuring displays and a movie presentation. *St. Michael's Hill, Christ Church, Dublin 8.*

Guinness Brewery. For some a visit to Dublin would be incomplete without stopping in at the Guiness brewery, which has been pumping out the thick liquid for more than 240 years. *James's Gate, Dublin 8.*

The Joyce Tower Museum. This tower, the former residence of the famous writer as captured in the opening of *Ulysses*, is a small but extremely informative museum that should spark the interest of James Joyce fans. *Sandycove, Co. Dublin.*

Kilmainham Gaol Historical Museum. A fascinating shrine to the heroes of Irish Independence, those political patriots who endured atrocities inside its walls. *Kilmainham.*

Dublin's Viking Adventure. A lively and involving recreation of a Viking village with re-enactments of Viking life. *Essex Street.*

Grafton Street. An attractive place to shop among the bustle and buskers.

Temple Bar. Dublin's trendy cultural centre for shopping, dining and drinking.

Ceol Interative Irish Music Encounter. People taken by the distinct melodies of traditional Irish music will appreciate this modern approach to recounting every avenue of its history and development.

Cork

Cork, Irish name Corceigh, is the third largest city in Ireland with a population of around 250,000. It is well inland and lies along the banks of the River Lee which in turn flows into natural harbours. The wide main streets contrast with the narrow alleys of the old part of town. Cork is 254km from Dublin.

History

Cork is one of the earliest communities in Ireland. It grew up around a 6th century monastery. The Vikings established the town of Cork as a trading centre in the 900s. An Irish family by the name of McCarthy ruled over the kingdom of Desmond, the region now known as the counties of Cork and Kerry. After the Anglo-Norman invasion, much of the territory was granted to the Fitzgerald family. As Earls of Desmond, they became increasingly Irish.

Cork city remained a centre of English power. In the late 1500s there was an attempted settlement by English colonists. The most famous person to receive land was Sir Walter Raleigh. The Irish attacked the English but lost the battle of Kinsdale in 1601. During the 1600s, Richard Boyle, Earl of Cork became extremely powerful.

Cork became, and still is, a seat of learning. Among writers from Cork are Frank O'Connor, Sean O'Faolain and Somerville and Ross. Famous people who lived there for some time are Edmund Spenser and philosopher George Berkeley.

Today it exports bacon, dairy produce and livestock. It also has a car assembly plant, a brewery and a distillery.

Tourist Information

The Tourist information office is at Tourist House, Grand Parade, Cork, ©(021) 4271 081, fax 4271 863.

Local Transport

Buses are plentiful but walking is the best way to see this city.

Accommodation

Major credit cards are accepted and prices given are for a double per room per night. Ireland has many bed and breakfasts and so the charge tends is per person per night. All rooms have ensuite, and parking is available. All the places listed are in the city of Cork.

Achill House

Western Road, Cork, ©021-427 9447, fax 021-427 9447, ✆www.achillhouse.com. A recently renovated guesthouse, with a cosy lounge. The hotel has central heating, which is particularly appreciated during cold Cork winters. - ❂£40 per person per night.

Ireland

Acorn House, 14 St Patrick's Hill, Cork , ✆021-450 2474, fax 021-450 2474, ☞www.acornhouse-cork.com. A Georgian guesthouse in the heart of Cork. Highly regarded and comfortable - ✪£20 per person per night.

Crawford House, Western Road, Cork, ✆021-427 9000, fax 021-427 9927, ☞www.cork-guide.ie/corkcity/crawford-house/welcome.html, email ✉crawford@indigo.ie. 25 rooms. An opulent guesthouse with modern decore and lavish room facilities including en-suites with jacuzzis. Centrally located - ✪£40 per person per night.

Fitzpatrick Silver Springs, Dublin Road, Tivoli, ✆(021) 507 533, fax 507 641. 100 rooms. Less than 2km from train, 10 minutes from city centre. In spacious grounds. 2 restaurants, bars, gym, squash. Overlooking the River Lee - ✪£70-94.

Metropole, MacCurtain Street 2, ✆(021) 450 8122, fax 450 6450. 91 rooms most with private facilities. Victorian hotel with new wing added. Very central. Restaurant, bar, parking - ✪£49-79.

Imperial, 14 Pembroke Street, South Mall, ✆/fax (021) 427 4040. 101 rooms with bath. Historical old world hotel that has been renovated. 3km from car ferry, 230m from train. Dining room, bar, 24 hr room service. Closed Christmas-New Year - ✪£52-121.

The **Youth Hostels** in Cork include the following.
Cork International Youth Hostel, 1 Reddyclyffe, Western Road, ✆(021) 454 3289, fax 434 3715 - ✪£3.00-6.50.
Sheilas Hostel, Belgrave Place, Wellington Road, ✆(021) 450 5562, fax 450 0940 - ✪£5.50-10.00.

Many of the pubs in the town and the country have comfortable rooms with breakfast and high tea for a reasonable rate.

Food and Drink
There are plenty of restaurants serving seafood. Try trout, prawns or salmon. There are also excellent steaks, lamb and stews. Don't forget the whiskey and Guinness.

Shopping
There are outstanding bargains available in light tweeds, fine linen, lace, scarves, knitwear, shirts, porcelain and Waterford crystal.

Sightseeing
A trail guide book is available from the information office.

University College was built in 1845 and is part of the National University of Ireland.

St Ann's Shandon Church is famous for its bells. Cork also has Cathedrals, including St Finbar's.

It is the riverside, with its strips of parkland, that makes Cork so attractive. Rest on one of the seats and enjoy the sunset.

Sights Further Afield
The most popular excursion is only five miles from Cork. It is a visit to **Blarney Castle** to attempt to kiss the Blarney stone. The stone is under the battlements and it requires both agility and nerve to attempt this feat. There is nothing between the stone and the ground 26m below. The successful kisser is supposed to be endowed with considerable eloquence. The view from the top of the castle is well worthwhile.

The city of **Waterford**, in the south-east, is where you can see the famous Waterford Crystal being produced, and maybe buy a special souvenir of Ireland.

Driving Through Ireland

A Scenic Tour of Ireland by Road
Itinerary -10 Days - Distance 1610kms

Ireland

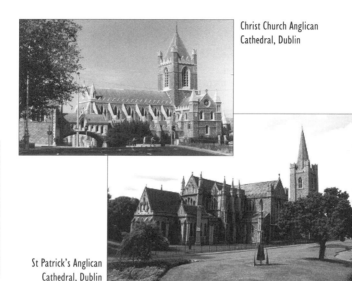

Christ Church Anglican
Cathedral, Dublin

St Patrick's Anglican
Cathedral, Dublin

After exploring **Dublin**, with its historic buildings and atmosphere, head south to **Enniskerry**. The Powerscourt Estate here is well worth a visit. **Glendalough** has ruins of early Christian times. **Arklow** is a popular holiday resort. **Enniscorthy** is the turn-off point to **Rosslare** Ferry terminal, and further south you pass through **New Ross** with its Dutch inspired houses on the way to **Waterford**, of crystal fame.

From Waterford follow the coast through **Youghal**, another popular holiday resort, to **Cork**. Cork is built on the banks of the river Lee. There are many historic buildings to see here. From Cork, head inland to **Blarney Castle**, with its famous stone, and then on to **Glengariff**, a picturesque holiday resort. From here drive north to **Killarney**, where there is much to see and do. Further north of Killarney is **Limerick**, near Shannon Airport. Limerick is a historic place, with many old buildings and castles to see. Driving towards the west coast where you reach **Lahnich**. It is a seaside resort with several golf courses. The road to **Lisdoonvarna** passes along spectacular cliff tops. Lisdoonvarna is well known as a health spa. From here it is a short drive to **Galway**, through **Clarinbridge**, famous for its oysters. Galway is a historic city. Heading northwest from Galway you reach **Clifden** on the coast.

Following the coast you reach **Westport**, which is on Clew Bay. From Westport drive north to **Sligo** with its 13th century church, and **Drumcliffe**, where W.B Yeats is buried. Further north along the coast you come to **Donegal**, with its castle. This area is home of the Donegal tweed. Take the coastal road to **Dunfanaghy**, which is in the centre of the Gaelic speaking region. Letter-Kenny, south from here, is

Ireland

Castletown House

county Donegal's main town. Drive south back through Donegal, to **Carrick-on-Shannon**. This route takes you along the banks of **Lough Allen**. Carrick-on-Shannon is known for its fishing and recreation. From here, head back towards Dublin, passing through **Drogheda**. At Drogheda visit the nearby ancient tombs. **Trim** also has ancient monuments worth seeing. Complete your tour back in Dublin.

Ireland

Italy

THE REPUBLIC OF ITALY encompasses the Apennine Peninsula, Sicily, Sardinia, and to the north, the Alps. The population is around 57,000,000 and the area of the country is 302,225 sq km. The numerous art and architectural treasures, as well as the mediterranean climate along the coast and in the south, make Italy one of the oldest holiday lands of Europe. There is more industry and it is more densely populated in the north, and where the west coast of the peninsula has harbours, the east coast only has flat beaches. The Mezzogiorno area in the south is the least developed and the most disadvantaged.

Italian is the language of most of the country, with French spoken in some of the alpine districts, and German in parts of the Trentino. English is widely spoken in the tourist centres.

Climate

Summer can be very hot, oppressively so, in Rome and places to the south. The capital averages 18-31C in July and 4-12C in January, whereas Milan in the north averages 18-29C in July and -2 - +4C in January.s

Entry Regulations

Visitors must have a valid passport, but visas are not required for a stay of three months or less.

The duty free allowance is 200 cigarettes or 50 cigars or 250 grams of tobacco, 1 litre of alcoholic beverages if alcoholic content is in excess of 22%, 2 litres if alcoholic content is less than 22%. The import of foreign currency is unlimited.

No vaccinations are required for any international traveller.

Currency

The currency of the land is the Lira (plural lire). Approximate exchange rates, which should be used as a guide only, are:

A\$	=	1170.12L
Can\$	=	1,407.96L
NZ\$	=	960.01L
S\$	=	1200.90L
UK£	=	3,144.34L
US\$	=	2,071.81L
Euro	=	1,936.27L

Notes are in denominations of 100,000, 50,000, 20,000, 10,000, 5,000, 1,000 and 500, and coins are 200, 100, 50, 10 and 5.

Banks are generally ☺open Mon-Fri 8.30am-1.20pm, and for one hour in the afternoon, usually between 3pm and 6pm, but this can change from bank to bank, so it is best to check the hours of the bank closest to where you are staying before you are desperately short of money. Exchange counters are found at main railway stations and airports. It is best to exchange money as soon as you arrive in the airport as it is always a hassle trying to change money in the city.

Post Offices in the main cities are ☉open Mon-Fri 8.30am-6.30pm, Sat 8.30am-12.30pm, and those in smaller towns are open Mon-Fri 8.30am-1.30pm, Sat 8.30am-12.30pm. They may also be closed without warning!

Shopping hours are generally ☉8.30am-1pm, 3.30-7.30pm.

Credit cards are widely accepted in shops and restaurants, but not in petrol stations.

Telephone

International direct dialling is available and the international code is 00, the country code 39. Telephone numbers in Rome can be anything from four digits to eight digits, so if you are given a small one to contact, don't think that some of it is missing.

Driving

Italians have the reputation of being amongst the worst drivers in the world, something that does not altogether displease them. Though everyone seems to know what they are doing and the traffic flows, courtesy to other drivers can seem conspicuous by its absence. The best advice for travellers from overseas is to try and stay out of other people's way.

The speed limits are not apparently widely known, but are:

Cars of up to 1100cc

built up area	-	110 kph
open road	-	130 kph

Vehicles over 1100cc

built up area	-	130 kph
open road	-	130 kph

Seat belts are compulsory in the front seat. The locals seem very blase about this law, which seems to be often ignored.

It is possible to hire a car with a driver's licence issued in your home country, but hiring a car is an expensive option. Not only are the rates higher than in most other countries, but there are 25 motorway companies ready to extract toll from drivers, and the toll depends on distance travelled.

Note: If you decide to drive, never leave anything in a parked car as it is almost guaranteed it will not be there when you return. Keep everything out of sight - in the boot at the very least.

Miscellaneous

Local time is GMT + 1, with daylight saving in operation from the end of March to the end of September.

Electricity is 220 volts with round plug pins.

Health - it is absolutely necessary to have adequate medical insurance to guard against a stay in an Italian general hospital.

Siesta is a fact of life in Italy, and you have to learn to live with it. From about 1.30pm to around 3.30pm nothing happens. Everyone goes home, has lunch, and presumably a siesta.

Rome

Rome, 'The Eternal City', sits on the banks of the River Tiber and is the capital of modern Italy. To some it is 'the finest city in the world' but to others its great historical sites, and even St Peter's, do not make up for the dreariness of the place, nor for the fact that a visitor never feels completely safe. When in Rome, do what the Romans do if that makes you happy, but leave all your valuables and your passport in the hotel safe while you're doing it.

History

The origins of Rome go back to around 600BC, and the people who lived there were not Italians but Romans, made up of Latin and Sabine stock. Originally ruled by kings, Rome became a republic in 509BC and was quickly a force to be reckoned with. Using whatever means necessary, usually war or diplomacy, its provinces soon included all the countries of the Mediterranean, including parts of Africa.

Italy

The republic lasted 400 years, then Julius Caesar, the great conqueror, tried to take over as a dictator and was assassinated in 44BC. His adopted son, however, fulfilled his ambitions and ruled as Emperor Augustus Caesar from 30BC to AD14, a period of great peace and prosperity.

Then came Christianity. Its original followers were persecuted, fed to lions, crucified, and generally made to feel unwelcome, especially by the Emperor Nero. But when Constantine became the Emperor he declared Christianity to be the official religion of the Empire.

It has been discovered that during the 2nd century AD, there were more than a million people living in and around Rome, some of them in high-rise apartments - it was truly the capital of the world.

When the capital moved to Constantinople, the Popes became the virtual rulers of Rome. Unfortunately, some of the Popes were not what you could really call "holy men", and in fact they became progressively worse, hitting rock bottom in the eleventh century. In the 14th century they moved to Avignon, and Rome deteriorated to a town of around 20,000 people.

The Renaissance and the return of the Popes to the city saw the birth of the Rome of today. Popes Julius II and Leo X were great patrons of the arts and caused many great buildings to be erected, beginning with the Palazzo Venezia, and St. Peter's.

Tourist Information

The main information office is near the Stazione Termini at 5 Via Parigi, ✆(06) 4889 9255, 4889 9253, fax 481 9316. It is ⊙open Mon-Fri 8.15am-7pm, Sat 8.15am-1.15pm. There is another inside the station, ✆(06) 487 1270, ⊙open daily 8.15am-7.15pm. This is the only branch that is open on a Sunday.

There is also an office in the customs area of the Leonardo da Vinci Airport, ✆(06) 601 1255, which has one desk for Italy and another for Rome. It is ⊙open Mon-Sat 8.30am-7pm.

McDonald's, believe it or not, are in the middle of town near the *Spanish Steps* at the top of the Corso. You can use their toilets for free (you have to pay everywhere else - including in Stazione Termini, the main train station) and they have an excellent free tourist map of Rome with suggested tours.

Local Transport

Metro

Rome has an underground system. Linea A and Linea B intersect at Termini. It is an efficient system but you must have a ticket. These can be purchased from kiosks with the name Tabacci (tobacconists) which sell newspapers and the like. You can use the metro to get just about anywhere, for example, to Ottaviani then walk to St Peter's. There is also a tram and bus service that operates throughout the city. Most of the things that visitors want to see can be reached on foot.

Taxis

The official taxis are yellow and these are the only ones to get. Make sure the driver turns the meter on otherwise you will have an unpleasant scene at the end of your trip as you haggle over money. The locals always win.

Transport from the Airport

When you arrive at *Fumicino (Leonardo da Vinci) Airport* and make your way to the general area after passing through Customs, avoid men soliciting rides to the city. They normally come up to you saying 'Taxi?'. A train now operates from Fumicino to Ostensi (❂L15,000) once every 20 minutes and also another goes to Termini (❂L20,000). A taxi can cost as much as ❂L100,000.

If you have to get an early flight from Rome, it is a good idea to organise a transfer from your hotel to the airport before you leave home. Alternatively, ask the hotel to organise your taxi so that the price is controlled - normally around ❂L60,000.

You have to face the fact that in Rome you are going to end up paying more than you should, whether it is in the cafe, the taxi or the shops. No matter how experienced a traveller you are, the end result will be the same. If the locals don't get you, the gypsies will try. Beware of grubby children bearing carnations.

Accommodation

Following is a selection of accommodation with prices for a double room per night, which should be used as a guide only.

Aldrovandi Palace

Via U. Aldrovandi 15, ©322 3993, fax 322 1435. 125 rooms, solarium, grounds, sauna, restaurant. This hotel was once used as a girl's boarding school. It is opposite Villa Borghese, and a good 20 minute walk from Piazza del Populo. Get the 19 or 30 tram to the Vatican from here - ✪L300,000-L700,000.

Excelsior, Via Veneto 125, ©47 081, fax 492 6205. 320 rooms, sauna, shops, bar, restaurants. Located just up from Palazzio Margherita and not far from the Villa Borghese (park). An old haunt of the movie stars of the 1950s, this place still has some of the charm. Originally built in 1911, it really looks the goods with its grandiose entrance. Ask for an old room - ✪L350,000.

Santa Chiara, Via Santa Chiara 21, ©688 06142, fax 687 3144. 76 rooms, elegant hotel between the Pantheon and Piazza Minerva. You really are in the middle of Centro Storico - ✪L280,000.

Gregoriana, Via Gregoriana 18, ©679 4269, fax 678 4258. A 3-star hotel with 19 rooms that represents good value. This is a former convent near the Spanish Steps - ✪L250,000 including breakfast served in the room.

Abruzzi, Piazza della Rotonda 69, ✆679 2021. 25 rooms. It is a little loud here, compensated by a view of the Pantheon and one of the most exciting piazzas in Rome - ✪L100,000.

Hotel Mediterraneo, Via Cavour, 15, Rome, ✆(06) 488 4051, fax 474 4105 (✎hb@bettojahotels.it). A central 4-star hotel. 266 rooms, restaurant, bar/lounge, rooftop views of the city - ✪L525,000.

Hotel Cicerone, Via Cicerone, 55, Rome, ✆(06) 35 76, fax 6880 1383 (✎cicerone@travel.it). A 4-star hotel near the Palace of Justice. 250 rooms, restaurant, bar/lounge - ✪L520,000.

Barocco Hotel, 4 Via della Purificazione, ✆(06) 487 2001, fax 485 994. A 4-star hotel in the centre of the city. 28 rooms, restaurant, bar/lounge - ✪L460,000-499,000.

Tulip Inn, Viale Ippocrate, 119, Rome, ✆(06) 445 7001, fax 494 1062 (✎globus@flashnet.it). Located in the university area. 100 rooms, restaurant, bar/lounge - ✪L300,000 including breakfast.

Hotel Rimini, Via Marghera, 17, Rome, ✆(06) 446 1991, fax 491 289 (✎rimini@travel.it). Situated between the archaeological area and the university. 35 rooms, restaurant, bar/lounge - ✪L140,000-210,000 including breakfast.

Rome's **Youth Hostel** is *Foro Italico*, AF Pessina, viale delle Olimpiadi 61, ✆(06) 323 6267, ✆(06) 324 2613.

As this is the Eternal City there are quite a few places run by religious orders that provide accommodation for visitors. You do not have to be a Roman Catholic to take advantage of these places. The cost is very reasonable, and the lodgings are, of course, safe. You do have to obey the rules though. Ask at the Information Office at the airport. If you have no luck there or at Termini go to the Vatican and ask at the information centre on the left-hand side of the square as you face the main entrance.

Italy

Food and Drink

A dish on any menu that has the word *'Romana'* in its name is supposed to have originated in Rome, and lovers of Italian food probably include several of these among their favourites. The specialties of Rome, however, are supposedly tripe, brains and other forms of offal.

One thing visitors do notice is that dishes cooked in the old country tend to have a lot more oil in them than their counterparts in foreign countries.

You won't have to go far to get a cappuccino, but getting a hot one is not so easy. When ordering, try asking for it to be *bollente*.

The oldest restaurant in Rome is the **Campana** at 18 Vicolo della Campana, off Via della Scrofa, ✆656 7820. It has apparently been operating since 1518, but the atmosphere is a bit heavy, and so is the food - closed Monday.

One of the 'in' places to eat is **Ristorante '34**, 34 Via Mario Fiori, ✆679 5091. It specialises in modern Italian cuisine, and has some pretty amazing dishes - closed Monday.

Another 'in' place, especially with the young, is **Trattoria all'Arancio** at 51 Via dell'Arancio, ✆6847 0095.

An important tip is to eat out at a *trattoria*, rather than a *ristorante*, which is usually much more expensive. Another is to try the local house wine. It is often surprisingly good, and not the more expensive bottled variety.

Shopping

The fashion shopping district is along *Via dei Condotti* and the streets on either side of it and intersecting it. There are famous labels from France and Switzerland as well as local designers. This is not the place for bargain shopping, but if you appreciate fine material and workmanship, it is worth a visit. *Via Frattina* has shops with probably the most reasonable prices in the area.

Along the *Corso* are the more down to earth outlets, and amongst the shops you may find a few offering quality leather and silver goods.

Down from *Piazza Barberini* there are some quality men's clothing stores, and between *Piazza del Popolo* and *Piazza de Spagna* there are a lot of boutiques.

Sightseeing

Centre of the City

The centre of the city is generally agreed to be *Piazza Venezia*, and it can't be missed because it is home to the **Monument to Victor Emmanuel II**. Locals call the monument "the typewriter", and it does resemble one from the front, but whatever you call it, it really is different. There have been suggestions that it be demolished, but such a project would probably cost more than the monument is worth. The square is named after another of its buildings, **Palazzo Venezia**, built in 1455 by Cardinal Pietro Barbo, who later became Pope Paul II. The Museo del Palazzo Venezia has its entrance in Via del Plebiscito, and is ⊙open Tuesday to Saturday 9am-1.30pm, Sunday 9am-1.00pm. Cost is ✪L10,000. Mussolini used this as his offices when in power. It is one of the first Renaissance Palazzi, built in the 1450s. It is known for its collection of decorative arts and baroque pieces.

Some of the most important Roman streets radiate from Piazza Venezia: *Via IV Novembre,* which leads to the Via Nazionale, then on to Piazza Esedra and the Railway Station - Stazione Termini; *Via del Plebiscito,* which runs into Corso Vittorio Emmanuele and leads to St Peter's; *Via del Corso,* which leads to Piazza Colonna and Piazza del Popolo; and *Via dei Fori Imperiali,* which passes through the centre of ancient Rome.

Italy

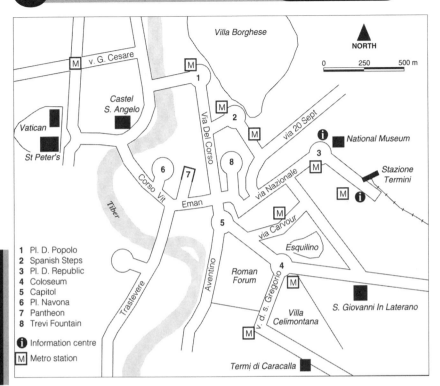

1 Pl. D. Popolo
2 Spanish Steps
3 Pl. D. Republic
4 Coloseum
5 Capitol
6 Pl. Navona
7 Pantheon
8 Trevi Fountain

ℹ Information centre

Ⓜ Metro station

Walking Tour of Old Rome

Almost behind the Victor Emmanuel Monument is the **Capitoline Hill**, one of the seven hills on which the city is built. Formerly home to ancient temples, most notably Jupiter, it has undergone many changes over the centuries. Michelangelo designed and supervised the construction of the **Piazza del Campidoglio** (or Capital Square), along with the buildings surrounding it and the staircase leading to it, for Pope Paul III who wanted to impress Charles V (or so it is claimed). Of course, Michelangelo was never noted for the speed of his execution, and the buildings were not ready in time for Charlie's visit.

The central bronze statue of Marcus Aurelius on a horse, positioned upon the Michelangelo-designed base, has now been restored and placed in the Palazzo dei Conservatori museum. Today a replica, also cast in bronze, graces the centre of the square.

As you stand on the top of the steps before Marcus, on three sides of you are: the **Senator's Palace** (Palazzo dei Senatori), which stands in the centre and is now Rome's official Town Hall; the **Palazzo dei Conservatori** on your right; and the **Palazzo dei Musei** (Palazzo Nuovo) on your left. The last two places have incredible displays of priceless works of art. They contain the largest collection of ancient sculptures in the world - busts of emperors and philosophers abound. The famous *Etruscan She Wolf* that suckled Romulus and Remus (added to the museum in the sixteenth century) is here. It is ⏰open Tuesday to Sunday 9am to 1pm, Holidays 9am to 1.15pm. Admission is ⊙L15,000, ✆(06) 671 02071. The last Sunday in the month is free, and people over 60 years of age enter free.

The long staircase behind the Victor Emmanuel Monument is called the **Aracoeli Stairs**. They sit to the left of the stairs that lead to the Piazza di Campidoglio on the Capitoline Hill, and will take you instead to the Church of **St Maria in Aracoeli**. It seems they have just managed to squeeze Victor's monument in between. The foot of these stairs hosted famous assasinations - including Tiberius Gracchus in 121 BC. The Church dates from the 6th century and served as a seat of Government at one stage in the 1300s. It has several chapels, and tombs with headstones sculptured by artists such as Donatello, but the *piece de resistance* is the **Bambino d'Aracoeli**, a wooden statue of the Child Jesus, carved out of olive wood taken from the Garden of Gethsemane. It is kept in the **Sacristy Chapel**, except during the Christmas season when it forms the centrepiece of the Crib. ⏰Open daily 9am to 6pm.

The Roman Forum

The **Roman Forum** can be reached by taking the path to the left of the Senator's Palace. If you walk down to the right of the Senator's Palace, past the main entrance to the Museum, on your right up a flight of stairs you have an excellent view of the Forum defined by the **Via dei Fori Imperiali** to the left, the **Palatine** to the right, and in the distance the **Arch of Titus** silhouetted against the great Colosseum behind it.

Having now gone to the left of the Senators Palace, there is a delightful little space covered with trees and seats where you can have a rest and admire the vista looking out over the **Forum of Caesar** to urban Rome, with the copulas of Churches dotting the skyline. Around here municipal police, with their plumed hats and other flourishes, chat to all and sundry and do not even pretend to be busy.

Continuing down the hill you pass on your left the **Museo Centrale del Risorgimento**, which had an exhibition of Chagall on the day I passed. You have to pay a fee before entering. While walking down the road towards the Via dei Fori Imperiali, you enjoy an excellent view of the reliefs on the **Arch of Septimus Severus**. Without stopping, the walk from the Capitoline Hill is only about five minutes.

The entrance to the **Roman Forum** is directly opposite the end of Via Cavour, some 50 metres from where you entered the Via dei Fori Imperiali as you walked down the hill. The Forum was the cradle of Roman civilisation, the city's most important social and political site. This is the original Forum, but as Rome grew and developed it became too small and other Fora, or meeting places, were developed. Consequently there is the Imperial Fora, Trajan's Forum, the Forum of Augustus, the Fora of Caesar, the Vespasian and the Domitian.

Unless you are well-versed in Roman history, it is suggested that you either visit the Roman Forum as part of a guided tour, or pick up a book about it at your hotel desk or at any of the numerous souvenir stalls. Without someone or something to explain what the various columns, arches, and parts of buildings are (or were connected to), the whole thing can look like a demolition site where the workers are at lunch. We will attempt to shed some light here.

The original Forum suffered considerable damage from invasions over the years, at the hands of both armies and antique collectors. It was totally neglected for centuries, and at one stage was even used to corral cattle. Excavations began in the 18th century, and archaeologists soon uncovered the extent of dilapidation.

After entering the Forum and descending the ramp you will encounter the remnants of a number of buildings. The **Temple of Antoninus Pius and Faustina** (141 AD) was converted to a church in the Middle Ages, and is now **St Lorenzo in Miranda**. To its right is the **Basilica Aemilia**, facing the Via Sacra which was basically the Bank of Ancient Rome. The financial transactions were done here. You should even be able to see some signs of coins in the pavement. On a historical note, when the Goths invaded around 410 AD, Roman money-changers were convinced that their enemies would want to do a deal, and tried to rip them off - instead they got torched themselves.

Via Sacra
In front of the right hand side of the Basilica, as you look towards the Forum, the **Temple of Janus** once abutted the Via Sacra (incidentally, regarded as Rome's oldest road). There is no trace of this Temple now. On the right of the building - to the north west - is the **Argiletum**, a road that was said to have been full of bookshops! Further still to the north-west is the **Curia**, or Senate house, facing the right hand side of the Basilica Aemilia.

The Curia
The Curia was built by Julius Caesar for the Senators who represented the 30 electorates of Rome. It was destroyed by fire several times and rebuilt by Diocletian in 283AD so that the

The Arch of Septimus Severus

Italy

ineffectual senators could continue their discussions. The statue of Victory, deity of the Senate, stood at one end of the building and with the passing of the centuries and the rise of Christianity, shifted with the fluctuations of power; this 'god' was removed and replaced according to whether a Christian or a pagan was ruling at a particular time. In the end St Ambrose, and later St Augustine in his famous *City of God* text, put the issue beyond doubt, and the statue was gone for goods.

To the south of the Curia is the **Comitium**, a public square where the gossip of Ancient Rome was given full vent, and a little further on (in the Via Sacra) is the **Lapis Niger**.

Lapis Niger

This is the most important relic in the Forum. The black piece of marble marks the tomb of Romulus. It is covered by what looks like a corrugated piece of iron roofing supported by some rough pipes - something you might rig up to house chooks, not drape across a memorial to the mythological founder of an ancient city. It has not changed in the many times I have visited the Forum, so I suppose this is inexplicably the way they do things in Rome. If you stop here and look up, you will see that we have been heading into the centre of the Forum, and to the far western side of the Forum back towards the Capitoline Hill from which we came.

Arch of Septimus Severus

Directly to the west of the Lapis Niger is the Arch of Septimus Severus, erected in 203AD to celebrate the African's 10 years in power. This arch does not match the superior quality of the Arch of Titus. Septimus' son Greta was murdered by his brother Caracalla, and after the deed the evil brother scraped Greta's name from the Arch; perhaps creating a greater reminder than if he had chosen to leave the stone alone.

Next to the Arch is the **Imperial Rostra**. Its brick wall and curved steps were moved by Julius Caesar from the Comitium. Behind this wall to the west is the **Umbilicus Romae**, marking the centre of Rome, and next to it is the **Vulcanal** - an altar cut into the rock and venerated in Ancient Rome. Still behind the Imperial Rostra, but further across, is the **Golden Milestone**, used to measure distances from Rome to other points in the empire. This bronze column was erected by Augustus.

Behind these three monuments and into the Capitoline Hill is the **Temple of Concord**, built to celebrate the peace between the patricians and the plebeians. It was rebuilt by Tiberius, and today only the base exists as a reminder of the work. To the south stood the **Temple of Vespasian** (79AD), of which a few columns still remain. Apparently Vespasian was placated while on his deathbed by the thought that the empire would honour him as a God when he died.

Continuing to the southwest against the hill, we come to the **Portico deorum Consentium**, dedicated to the 12 Olympian Gods and restored by Julian the Apostate in 367AD.

Temple of Saturn

Now we head south east, or back down the Forum from the Capitoline Hill. Crossing the Clivus Capitolinus, which is an extension of the Via Sacra, we come to the Temple of Saturn, built in 497BC and restored in 42BC. In the basement of the temple was the Treasury of the State, to which various emperors helped themselves at times. The eight colums of the Portico survive. Saturn was an Etruscan god who came to be associated with farming and agriculture.

Basilica Julia

The Basilica Julia marks the southwest side of the Forum and stands south east of the Temple of Saturn. It was built by Julius Caesar in 54BC and completed by Augustus. Burnt out later, it was restored by

Diocletian in 284AD. The Basilica Julia was the court for civil cases and consisted of a large central hall surrounded by a colonnade of pillars, completed with a portico. All that is left are the foundations of the 284AD building.

The **Column of Phocas** faces the Basilica Julia and is in front (southwest) of the Imperial Rostra. Erected in 608AD to honour Phocas the Eastern, a Byzantine emperor, it was in fact the last monument to be erected in the Forum. Other columns facing Basilica Julia can be seen in various states of height and disrepair, memorials to various entities, but the Column of Phocas is the white construction towering above the rest.

East of the column of Phocas (very close), the *fig tree, olive tree and grape vine* symbols of Italian Agriculture were planted and venerated on this spot in the Ancient Forum. Beside this - still in front of Basilica Julia - is the **Lacus Curtius** that illustrates just how superstitious pagan Romans were. Lightning struck this spot in 445BC, so the irregular pavement was declared 'holy'. It used to be a little pond before the area was drained to make way for the Forum. Considering how crowded-in all these buildings and monuments were, the place must have been chaos on a busy day.

Temple of Castor

To the east of Basilica Julia, across the laneway from *Vicus Tuscus*, is the Temple of Castor (and Pollux), or the Temple of the Dioscuri, patron of the Cavalry. It was the club of Roman knights and businessmen. Three lonely columns are all that is left of this building. Behind the temple is the **Pool of Juturna** (fenced off) where the gods, Castor and Pollux, appeared and announced the Roman victory at the Battle of Regillus while watering their horses at the pool.

Julius Caesar

To the north east of this Temple, the Arch of Augustus (19BC) once straddled the Via Sacra. Also adjoining it was the Temple of the 'divine' Julius Caesar, built by Octavianus in 42BC. After Julius Caesar was assassinated, Mark Anthony and others brought the body here for cremation.

Oratory of the 40 Martyrs

It seems appropriate for this Church to be located at the head of the Via Nova, where it fits in with the military theme of its surrounds. The Oratory celebrates the 40 martyrs of Sebaste. These men were soldiers of the Imperial Army, stationed in what is present day Armenia, who were condemned to death by the Imperial Command for being Christian and were tossed into an icy lake. Their chant as they froze to death was '40 we are, 40 crowns we ask'. One of the soldiers apostatized and withdrew, at which point a member of the executing squad jumped in to take his place. They got their wish and were later venerated by the Catholic Church. The Oratory was built in the 8th century.

Santa Maria Antique

Further south is the Santa Maria Antique, which is normally shut. You can ask at the entrance to the Forum. It has some well preserved Byzantine frescos from the early 8th century. This is the most important Christian Church in the Forum, and one of the oldest in Rome (6th century). Transformed from a pagan structure - probably Augustus' library - the frescos contain stories of the saints - the adoration of the cross is in the apse, with scenes of the crucifixion in the left chapel.

Regia

This was the residence of the *pontifex maximus*, who presided over of the ancient pagan rites which covered everything, including those dedicated to Jupiter or Mars. The position was venerated by society and held by a male who was the only person permitted to enter the temple of Vesta. The rites and procedures of pagan society were based on superstition and order, and they tended to be pretty bloody in practice. For example, the race winner of the October Festival of the Horse was cut into pieces, and parts of his body from the genitals to the head were offered to various gods. As you can imagine, plenty of blood was splashed around in the process.

The Temple of Vesta

This temple housed the flame brought by Aeneas from Vesta's temple in Troy, which was then tended by the Vestal Virgins. For over a century they protected other signs of divine providence, but knowledge of the fate of these signs disappeared with the last vestal. Mystique surrounded the Vestal Virgins - a position carrying much prestige and held only by women of noble birth. They were entrusted with the soul of the State, which the flame symbolised. The Vestal Virgins were required to remain virgins for at least 30 years, and were buried alive if caught breaking their oath. They could stay the execution of a criminal, have an audience with the emperor without appointment, occupy the best seats in the house, and were treated generously by the State when they retired. All that remains of the two-storey cloistered building which housed the Vestals is a rose garden and the smashed remains of portrait statues. The statue that still has a head is reputed to be the likeness of a Vestal who became a christian.

The Temple of Romulus

This was built by Maxentius in 309AD to honour his son. It was later used (6th century) as the portico of the **Church of St Cosmas and Damian**, two eastern church martyrs from the time of Diocletian. Part of this building also housed the **Temple of Peace**. It is famous for the quality of its preservation and its bronze doors, still on their original hinges and possessing the same lock.

Next to it, to the east, is the mammoth **Basilica of Maxentius**. Maxentius commenced the project only to have his nemesis Constantine complete it. It is 300 feet long (more than 100 metres) with a nave and 2 aisles of which only the one on the north east side still stands.

In the east corner is the **Basilica of St Francesca Romana**, built into the Temple of Venus and Rome, whose massive ruins are entered from the Fore Imperiali. The Basilica contains the Forum Antiquarium - housing artifacts and relics taken from the Forum, including the churches. This building must be entered from outside the Forum.

That brings us to the far end of the Forum, to the Arch of Titus and the final chapter of our tour.

Arch of Titus
Built by Domitian (81AD) to commemorate the victories of Vespasian and his son Titus in Jerusalem, this monument is very interesting because on the inside there are reliefs showing a victory parade through Rome. The loot seized from the Temple, including silver trumpets and a menorah (seven-branched candelabrum), is clearly featured. Understandably, Jews do not walk through this Arch. This is more or less the exit of the Forum.

This excursion will take a good three to four hours of roaming, reclining and viewing.

Palatine
As you face the Arch of Titus before leaving the Forum, to your right a path leads up to the Palatine - Rome's oldest hill and the place where Romulus is supposed to have founded the city in 754BC.

During the republican period this was "nob hill", home to the noble families. When Augustus became Emperor he built his palace on the site. Over time other Emperors added to the buildings, then in the Middle Ages it was converted into a fortress, and in the 16th century it became a vast garden. Archaeological excavations in this area have proven that the hill was actually inhabited as early as the Iron Age, making this historical dig arguably the most important in Rome.

Among the ruins of various buildings, to the east of the hill, is the Palatine Stadium, or Racecourse. Historians are not entirely sure if this 160m x 80m showground was used exclusively as a stadium or as a racecourse - or perhaps both - and also have not been able to ascertain whether it was open for public as well as private functions. Moreover, it may have been just a large garden.

The area is truly amazing, harbouring sunken treasures of masonry and the remnants of buried palace upon palace - Caligula, Augusta, Nero, Domitian and others, all built their regal homes here. Areas may be cordoned off as archaeological work continues on this precious site.

The Palatine is ☺open October to April 9am-4pm daily, and the price is included in the entrance to the Forum.

Make your way beyond the stadium to the Belvedere Terrace, where you can get a great view of the Circus Maximus. The Terrace was built by Septimus Severus from 193-211AD.

Circus Maximus

The Circus Maximus was built by Tarquinis Priscus, and additions were made by Julius Caesar. It was thought to have held as many as 100,000 spectators. It was to this venue, not to the Colosseum, that the Romans flocked to see the persecution of the Christians ordered by Emperors Nero, Domitian, Trajan, Septimus Severus, Decius, Valerian and Diocletian. The latter was responsible for the 'Great Persecution', by which he sought to systematically eradicate Christianity.

Return to the **Arch of Titus**. As you leave the Forum you will notice you are heading towards the **Colosseum** in front of you. While walking in the direction of Via di San Gregorio and the Colosseum, look right and you will see the **Arch of Constantine**, all on its lonesome and completely overshadowed by the Colosseum.

Italy

Arch of Constantine

Built to commemorate the Emperor's victory at the bridge of Milvio in 312AD, this arch is the best-preserved in Rome. The reliefs on the arch, facing you, feature some of the battles of Constantine. The rest relate to the exploits of other emperors, including Trajan, Hadrian and Marcus Aurelius, and have been taken from other monuments. Near the arch is a cone-shaped fountain, the **Meta Sudans**, where gladiators washed themselves after leaving the Colosseum.

Colosseum

Next stop is the Colosseum, or the *Amphitheatrum Flavium* as it was known in its heyday. Construction began in 72AD, under Emperor Vespasian, on the site of a stagnant lake. It was inaugurated by Titus in 80AD, with a celebration that lasted more than three months and saw the killing of 500 wild animals and more than a few gladiators. It was an incredible structure. The highlights of its ingenious design were: underground passages and tunnels from which people and animals could be brought into the arena, facilities for transforming the arena into a lake to stage naval battles, and devices for covering the whole stadium with a large awning during times of bad weather. Considering the ravages of time, including an earthquake in the 5th century, what is left standing today is impressive - but try to imagine the whole of the building covered in marble, with a marble statue of a god or honoured individual in each of the arches on the second and third floors. Pretty amazing! It is ☉open (when they are not on strike): Summer (June to end of August) Mon, Tues & Thurs to Sat 9.00am to

7.00pm, Wed and Sun 9.00am to 1.00pm; rest of the year, 9.00am to 3-4pm. Cost ✪L15,000. Over 60 years free.

You can then retrace your steps along the Via dei Fori Imperiali to the Piazza Venezia, and see the rest of the buildings associated with the Forum whose entrances or exteriors have frontage on this street.

The Via dei Fori Imperiali leads from the Colosseum back to the Piazza Venezia, passing some interesting ruins and buildings on its way. The first thing you will probably notice is the multiplicity of statues of Julius Caesar evenly spaced along the length of the Fori Imperiali.

As you return along the Fori Imperiali from the Colosseum you will first encounter the **Temple of Venus and Rome**, built by Emperor Hadrian in 135AD. It faces the Colosseum and backs onto the Forum. Its ruins are immense. Adjoined to this is the **Church of Santa Francesca Romana**, first built in the 10th century but restored so often that none of the original buildings survive. Inside, however, there are some pieces dating from the 12th and 13th centuries, including the original Campanile, and the tomb of Pope Gregory XI. The church is part of a monastery that houses the Museum of the Forum.

Next is the one remaining nave of the **Basilica of Maxentius**, completed by Constantine in 312AD, with a fine coffered ceiling and vaults reaching as high as 25 metres. The Basilica had two entrances, one onto the Via Sacra of the Forum, the other towards the Colosseum. Today it is used for concerts in the summer.

You can then visit the **Church of Saints Cosma and Damian**. It was founded by Pope Felix IV in 527AD on the site of the Templum Sacrae Urbis, and was restored in the 17th century. There are some very interesting 6th century mosaics in the apse.

Also along the walls of the Basilica of Maxentius are a series of reliefs showing the development and growth of the Roman Empire. In addition, a very informative diagram of the excavations of the Roman Forum has been set up on the Fori Imperiali.

St Pietro in Vincoli

Moving from the Colosseum up to the beginning of Via Labicana (behind the taxi stand), you can head around the Esquiline Hill, Via N. Salvi, then onto Terme d Tito Lgo Polveriera and into Via Eudossiana. You have basically retraced your steps parallel to the Fori Imperiali to get to this Church. It was built by Sixtus III in 432AD to house the chains that bound St Peter both in Jerusalem and in Rome. They are now placed beneath the altar so as to be seen and venerated. The *Moses* by Michelangelo is also in this Church.

Imperial Forums

Now we come to what are known as the **Fori Imperiali** (Imperial Forums). They were built in the last days of the Republic to accommodate the larger population. The first was built by Julius Caesar on the corner of Via di Tulliano and the Via di Fori Imperiali. Other Fori - of Augustus, Vespasian, Domitian, Trajan and Hadrian - are on the right in the same vicinity. During the Middle Ages this important area was buried under tons of soil, and it was not until 1924 that excavations began.

The **Forum of Nerva** has only a few columns left, which are known as the *'colonnacce'* and have a fine frieze.

The **Forum of Augustus** is entered from the Piazza del Grillo, to the left of the Via dei Fori Imperiali. It commemorated the Battle of Philippi when Augustus defeated Brutus and Cassius, the murderers of Caesar. This was the beginning of Augustus's climb to fame. The forum was built on the site of the Temple of Mars Ultor, and some remains of this can be seen today.

The **Basilica Argentaria**, used for commerical meetings in the later years of the Empire, is nearby.

The **Forum of Caesar** is to the left of the Via dei Fori Imperiali as you come from the Colosseum, and was built in 54BC to commemorate the Battle of Pharsalus. The Temple of Venus Genetrix once stood here and three of its columns still remain. The statue of Julius Caesar is a copy. The original is in the Campidoglio.

The **Forum of Trajan** is below street-level. It was built to celebrate victories over the Dacians. Designed by Apollodorous of Damascus, it consisted of a piazza, two libraries, temples, basilicas and monuments, and the Basilica Ulpia. The most outstanding feature now is Trajan's Column, which stands 42m high. It has a series of reliefs depicting the victories of the Emperor in the 1st century AD, and his vault is under the column. The statue on the top, however, is St Peter, placed there by order of Pope Sixtus V in the 17th century.

Trajan's Market was a group of buildings next to Trajan's Forum where merchants and markets operated. The Palace of the Knights of Rhodes from the 15th century is now on the site.

Vatican City

The Vatican is the spiritual centre of the Roman Catholic religion and the smallest country in the world. The Vatican's political situation became clearer in 1929, with the Lateran Treaty, by which the Vatican recognised the Italian State and the Vatican was recognised as an independent state with the rights of a nation.

Its history began with the Emperor Constantine, who wanted the first great Christian church to be built on the spot where St Peter was martyred. The present St Peter's Basilica was commenced in 1506 on the site of Constantine's church. The original architect was Bramante, but his plan was modified in 1547 by Michelangelo, whose apse and dome remain. Maderno took over and changed the ground plan from a Greek cross to a Latin cross. Then, in 1657, Bernini completed the building with the Colonnade of St Peter's Square and its statues of 140 saints.

By Metro

The best way to the Vatican is by using the Metro. You take *Linea A* and get off at the last stop, which is **Ottaviano**. When you get out of the station you will find yourself on *Via Giulio Cesare (Julius Caesar)*. Head down the first cross steet, on which are are almost standing - *Via Ottaviano*. This will bring you to *Piazza di Risorgimento*. It is about a 10 minute walk (6 minutes for the young). You will see the walls of the Vatican State off to the right - if you want to go to the Sistine Chapel and the Vatican Museum, head across the Piazza to the right, dodging the traffic coming down the hill from left and right. Head up the hill once you have negotiated this mayhem. You have another 15 minute walk from here. If you are already tired, there are taxis in the Piazza.

If you are going to St Peter's, follow the wall straight ahead which runs along the *Via Porta Angelica* street. On the way you will pass the gate of Sant Anne, manned by the Swiss Guard in work dress. Keep walking and soon you will come upon a small Piazza *Citta Leonina*. This is where the buses stop.

You go through an opening in the Wall, or *Borgo*, that links the Vatican to Castel Sant Angelo. Going through this opening (big enough for cars and buses) you will find a kiosk on the right that sells all sorts of newspapers and magazines, and further left, a fountain which is used by locals for many things - from water for the flower seller to a basin for backpackers on their way to St Peters, who are in need of a surface wash after camping out.

You will then encounter the vast columns of St Peter's Square, and between them you will see the obelisk in the centre and the elegant fountains that surround it. So here you are. Wow! Take a moment to find your breath, and proceed.

St Peter's Square

The **obelisk** in the centre of the square was brought from Egypt by Caligula to stand in nearby Nero's Circus, where many Christians (perhaps including St Peter) met their maker. The cross on top was not, of course, part of the original obelisk.

Two beautiful fountains flank the structure. As you face St Peter's, the one on the right was designed and constructed under the supervision of Carlo Maderno in 1614, and the other on the left, built later in the century, was a copy of the former. Given that Bernini had it built, he may disagree with this opinion of its originality. On the ground between the fountain and the obelisk is a round stone that indicates the point of the ellipse where all the columns of the colonnade line up on that side. Another stone marks the spot on the other side of the obelisk. You constantly see people standing on either spot and marvelling at the effect.

The Pope and Our Lady

Behind and to the right of the colonnade that surrounds the Square is the Apostolic Palace where the Pope lives. Part of it seems to jut out and overlook the Square. The third window along on the top floor is the apartment of the Pope. At midday every Wednesday and Sunday he makes a short speech from here, gives his blessing and leads the Angelus - a devotional prayer to the Virgin Mary. At the apex of this building are three windows positioned above each other. The top one has been filled in and replaced by a mosaic of Our Lady which presides over the Square. Its appelation is *Mater Ecclesia* (Mother of the Church). It is rumoured that in the early 1980s a university student told the Holy Father Pope John Paul II, during an audience, that the Square was not finished. When asked what he meant, the student replied that there was no image of Our Lady to be found there. So the Pope did something about it immediately. In fact, throughout Rome you will notice signs of John Paul II's incredible activity. During his Pontificate, places all over the city have been built, rebuilt or repaired, and these bear the image of his shield, distinguished by a large 'M' for Mary.

Information Centre

On the far left hand side, near where the steps start to rise to the basilica of St Peters, is the Information Centre. The staff here are most helpful. The hours are: ☉daily 8.30am-7.00pm, although sometimes it may close early, ✆ 6988 4466. The web site to visit is ✇www.vatican.com.va

As you look up at St Peter's you see at the base of the steps two imposing statutes. St Peter is on the left, holding the keys, and St Paul is on the right, holding the sword. Then as you mount the stairs (always from the side - only on ceremonial occasions, such as a Mass in the Square, are the front gates opened) you realise just how enormous this place is.

St Peter's Basilica

St Peter's is the second largest church in the world. The facade is 114.69m long and 45.44m high. The balustrade is supported by eight Corinthian columns and has two enormous statues of **Christ** and **John the Baptist** in the centre, and all the apostles, except St Peter, at the sides. There are nine **balconies**, and the Pope gives his address to the world *Ubi et Orbi* on New Year's Day from the one in the centre. (His Wednesday address and the praying of the Angelus is given from his office window to the right of St Peter's, the third window from the end.) The facade was designed by Maderno and was restored to its original pink/light ochre colour in time for the Great Jubilee of 2000.

Five open entrances lead into the vestibule or Loggia, which is 71m long, 13.5m wide and 20m high. Opposite the main door of the basilica, over the central entrance, is the mosaic of the **Navicella** (St Peter walking on the sea) which was originally in the old Basilica of Constantine. To the far left is a statue of **Charlemagne** on a horse; and to the right, one of Constantine in a similar pose behind glass doors. There are five entrances to the church. The last door on the right, the **Porta Santa**, is only opened every 50 to 100 years for the Jubilee. The 25th December saw the opening of the Sancta Porta for the commencement of the Jubilee Year at the eve of the new millennium. Going through the Holy Door symbolises a personal desire to start again in one's quest to achieve happiness in eternity; the desire to start anew, to forgive others, and to seek forgiveness. The Holy Father has asked that the especially wide door symbolise an opening that embraces all people.

The interior of the church has an area of 16,160 sq km and is 211.5m long. The central arm is 186.36m long, 27.5m wide and 46m high. The transept is 137.5m long and the cupola from the lantern measures 132.5m. There are 229 marble, 533 travertine, 16 bronze, and 90 stucco columns. No less than 44 altars grace the floor.

Italy

The place is unquestionably huge, and there are even marks on the floor showing where other churches would fit, such as St Paul's in London. However, as a young sculptor once said, this is a house of prayer - there has to be a God, otherwise you would not build it.

So let's begin a tour of St Peter's.

First of all, make sure you are appropriately dressed - shoulders for both men and women are to be covered, so no tank tops, and no mini-skirts either. It is better to overdress for St Peter's.

In the centre near the entrance there is a porphory-coloured disk that indicates the place where **Charlemagne** was crowned Holy Roman Emperor around 800AD. Enter through the Portico.

The Pieta

To the right of the Porta Sancta is **Michelangelo's Pieta**, in the first chapel to the right of the entrance. The piece is now behind bullet-proof glass because some nutcase actually attacked it. Sculpted when he was only twenty-five years old, the Pieta is one of the very few sculptures that the great artist actually signed - on the Virgin's sash - and many consider it to be his best work.

As you move further down the right aisle you come across an altar and chapel dedicated to **St Sebastian**. To its left is a statue of **Pope Pius XII**.

Walking on further you come to the **Chapel of the Blessed Sacrament**, open for those who wish to pray. The Sacred Host is kept here - which Catholics believe is the body of Christ present in the form of bread - and is often exposed in a Monstrance - which is an ornate, richly-decorated artifact normally encrusted with jewels. The Host is circular and placed behind crystal in the centre of the monstrance. Normally when entering a chapel where the Host is exposed in such a fashion, one genuflects - that is, drops to one knee out of respect. But on this occasion you are in one of the most

Italy

spiritually symbolic places on earth, so dropping to both knees for a moment of adoration may be more appropriate. The entrance is normally manned by an official as photographs are not permitted here. It is a place to pray. You will see in front of the monstrance, or tabernacle, that there is a large central piece on the altar in which the host is normally housed. Two nuns, one on either side of the aisle, kneel in prayer; this religious order dedicates itself to attending in perpetual adoration.

Leaving the chapel and turning right, you come to a monument to Gregory XIII just across the way. This pope is famous for the reform of the calendar (Gregorian, October 1582) presently in use - so he is responsible for the Year 2000 celebrations.

Here you get a sense of how big things are - if you try to use a flash to take a picture, your photos end up blurred and dark. Details are okay, but the general scene (unless lit by the arc lights for a ceremony) is difficult to photograph.

From here on the design and construction of this part of St Peter's is normally attributed to Bramante and Michelangelo. You now enter the **Gregorian Chapel** built in the time of Gregory XIII. The twelfth century fresco above the altar is that of Our Lady of Succor. If you continue on, you enter into the right arm of the transept of St Peter's. The first Vatican Council was held here in 1869, and the dogma on *Papal Infallibility* was defined and declared. The Altar to the right is dedicated to St Processus and St Martianus.

However, it is time we entered the nave. To the left, beside one of the giant pillars that support the dome, is the **bronze statue of St Peter** that predates the basilica. The right foot is worn where it has been constantly kissed and touched.

We now approach the main altar with its baldicino, designed by Bernini with copper from the Pantheon. The **Confessions**, which is

Italy

the sunken area in front of the main altar, is surrounded by candles that burn continuously. Looking down into the richly decorated vault of the main altar, there is a small recessed sanctuary. It is the site of the 2nd century aedicula that was built on St Peter's tomb, regarded as being in the left hand column of this construction. Here catholics normally pray a creed while attending the site of the tomb of St Peter.

An ornate box in the centre, behind the gilded gates, contains the *pallia* - a thin woven garment of lambs' wool with black crosses. These are bestowed on Metropolitans (that is, certain Archbishops with 'territorial sees' of consequence - such as the Archbishops of Sydney and New York). Such garments are placed on the shoulders of the Archbishop by the Pope after consecration.

Above us the copula rises to the heavens, with magnificent frescos, statues and a high relief stucco. The four pillars surrounding the main altar each have a niche complete with a facing statue. From the Confessions, where we have been standing, the statue attached to the column on the right is one of **St Longinus**. He was the Roman soldier who pierced Christ's side with a lance while He was still on the cross. After the event, he became a christian and a martyr for the faith. *(Behind this statue are the stairs to the crypt beneath St Peter's)*. The statue on the left hand side is that of **St Andrew**, brother of St Peter and the man who introduced him to Christ. The statue on the far left hand side is of **St Veronica**, who wiped Our Lord's face with a cloth during the passion. The statue on the fourth column to the far right is that of **St Helena**, the mother of Constantine who discovered the true cross. Each statue once bore the holy relic that signified their association to the faith - the tip of the spear, at head of St Andrew, since given to the Greek Orthodox Church; part of the fragment that cleaned the face of Christ; part of the true cross.

Moving behind the main altar we face the magnificent alabaster window of the Holy Spirit, in the form of a dove that gives light to St

Peter's. It marks the end of the Basilica. Below this amazing piece of art is the *Chair of Peter* by Bernini, dominating the apse. It is designed in the best baroque style - surrounded by gilded bronze clouds and swails of stucco, flanked by the statues of four fathers of the Church: St Augustine and St Ambrose from the Latin Church (that is the Roman Catholic tradition), and St Athanasius and St John Chrysostom from the Greek Tradition, which the Roman Catholics also embrace. The whole structure symbolises the supreme authority of the Pope and is cast in bronze. Monuments to Paul III and Urban VIII flank the stunning chair. Below is an altar upon which Mass is normally celebrated at 5.30pm every afternoon for those who wish to attend. Of course, at this time you cannot walk around this part of St Peter's.

As we walk over to the left side we come upon a feature of a column which has a mosaic of Our Lady inlaid in the shaft above an Altar dedicated to Popes Leo II, III and IV. This is an ancient image that is entitled *Mater Ecclesia*, the same appelation as the image that presides over the Square. To the right is a marble relief of Pope Leo the Great dissuading Attila the Hun from invading Italy.

As we move away from the apse we come to the statue of Pope Alexander VII (1655-1667) in a prayerful pose, facing death while a skeletal hand clutching an hourglass comes up from below. This striking relief engulfs the door underneath, which is an exit from St Peter's. It was Bernini's last work of art before his death.

We now cross the transept and pass the one altar dedicated to St Joseph, foster father of Jesus Christ. It takes up the whole of this area, which has many pews for people to pray. Masses are held here throughout the day. It is more open than the Chapel of the Blessed Sacrament, as they normally do not have Exposition. There is a tabernacle and a red vigil light which if burning indicates the presence of the Blessed Sacrament. Around the columns are confessionals normally manned by priests who can speak different languages (the languages are usually indicated). If you are not a Catholic, do not be surprised if suddenly someone next to you bobs down on one knee as they are going past.

We then pass a monument to Pius VIII, the sacristy of St Peter's and the Treasury. The price is ✪L8000 to go into this area.

The way narrows a little further along as we pass a monument to Leo XI, created in a rather austere style compared to the 'Bernini extravaganza' we have recently witnessed. Leo, although a Medici, was another of the steady, talented and sober Popes after the Protestant upheavals and the subsequent Council of Trent. However, he was only Pope for four months. The base relief shows Henry IV, King of France, renouncing protestantism in front of Leo when the latter was a Cardinal in 1593.

We then pass the chapel of the Choir that is perpetually behind grills - so no entry. After that we come to the Chapel of the Presentation on the right hand side and the body of St Pope Pius X (1835-1914) beneath the altar. It is not a particularly striking chapel, only a side altar really, but what makes it special is the saint's body lying beneath. A real father to his flock - the Church in the twentieth century - Pope Pius X was a reputed saint in his own lifetime. You will often see even young people kneeling here at the altar in prayer. To the right, cast in bronze, is a sculpture to the memory of Pope John XIII and the Second Vatican Council. Note that only saints are buried under the Altar whereas those not yet canonised or beatified (which means much the same thing, except the individual is not yet automatically celebrated by the universal church) may have a memorial or statue to their memory somewhere else. Thus Pius X gets a guernsey whereas the monument to Pope John XIII is on the side.

Entrances to Other Parts of St Peter's

We now come to the lift to the **copula**. The cost is ☉L8000. It ☉opens from 8.30am to 5.00pm and the last lift is at 4.45pm sharp. As you enter St Peter's it is on your left, but ask any of the attendants if you are unable to find it. Once you step out of the lift you are on the roof of St Peter's, at the same height as the giant statues that peer down at the Square. There are toilets, and you will find a drinking fountain and gift shop. From this point you have 300 or more steps to climb in order to reach the top. It is not a venture to be feared, although be aware that it becomes a little narrow. At one point you find yourself leaning over as you follow the path between two walls - obviously you are in the cavity of the copula high above the main altar. Anyone in reasonable health can make it to the top with relative ease. Once you come out at the top you have a marvellous view of Rome - The Tiber, the Pantheon and beyond, the multiple domes of baroque churches in the distance, the Victor Emmanuel Monument, Capitoline Hill, and behind, a wonderful view of the Papal gardens with their manicured lawns and fountains. This is a real retreat in the swirl of Rome. The climb is an absolute must! On the way down you simply retrace your steps.

Entrance to the Interior of the Dome

As you leave St Peter's, go to your left along the forecourt and then down the stairs. Turn left again and you find yourself in a small courtyard. Besides toilets and a gift shop, there is a lift to the terrace above the aisles of the basilica. From there you can walk to either one of two **walkways**. The lower one is 53 metres (160 feet) above the floor, and the higher one about 73 metres (220 feet) above the floor of the interior. Within the building, it affords a wonderful view of the Basilica, but the area may be closed at the time of your visit. It is definitely closed when there is a ceremony being held. There is a charge.

Entrance to the Vatican Grottoes

These can be reached through a passage just behind (or really inside) the pillar behind St Longinus, up on the right hand side of the baldachino as you face the altar in front of the Confessions. It is one of the four major pillars of the dome over the main altar. When you come down the stairs you will notice each of the four saints upstairs (St Longinus, St Helena, St Veronica and St Andrew) has a chapel dedicated to them downstairs, underneath the place where they stand above in the 4 main pillars. Other chapels surround the **Chapel of St Peter** in a semicircle. Among them are Polish and Irish Chapels. The striking thing about the Polish chapel is the image of Our Lady of Chestacowa that presides. At the head of the semicircle around the tomb of St Peter is a small chapel that houses the tomb of Pope Pius XII.

These chapels are small, and the tomb of St Peter is in the pillar which you can see as part of the crypt to the right of the Chapel of St Peter - you get a better view if you move further along the crypt. You will have to accept this on faith as their is no sign or anything. As you move forward under the main nave of St Peter's you come across **tombs of the Stuarts** on the left hand side. The royal house of Scotland were exiled to Rome in 1689. James III is buried here as are his two sons, one of whom (Henry) became a Cardinal. Opposite, and a short distance further down, is the tomb of **Pope John Paul I** - the smiling pope - who was pope for 34 days. Nearby is a small inset on the far left hand side - the tomb of **Pope Paul VI**. You can exit into the Square at this point, coming out at the far right hand side near the stairs.

Below this level are what is called the **Scarvi** which in essence are catacombs. You have to have prebooked to enter here. Enquire at the Vatican Information Office.

Back in the Central Nave of St Peter's

Positioned on the pillars along the central nave are statues of the founders of institutions within the Catholic Church who have been canonised.

The Vatican 'Palace'

The Vatican Palace is a large group of buildings, mostly museums, galleries, libraries and archives, but a few floors house the Pope and the Pontifical Court and are, of course, off-limits to visitors. However, the Pope's office can be seen from the Square.

Vatican Museums

The Vatican Museums can be reached by a shuttle bus from the Information Office on the left of the piazza (daily except Wed and Sun), otherwise it involves quite a hike from St Peter's around the Vatican walls, by way of Via di Porta Angelica, Via Leone IV and Viale del Vaticano.

It would be impossible to see all the treasures of the museums in one visit, or even a few, so it is best to follow one of the four sign-posted tours which take from ninety minutes to five hours to complete. The most popular is *Tour A*, for which you can hire an audio guide. If you are a fan of the work of Raphael, note that the four rooms devoted to his pieces are part of *Tour C*.

Sistine Chapel

All the tours lead eventually to the Sistine Chapel. Named after Pope Sixtus IV for whom it was built, the Chapel is now used only for Conclaves (meetings held by Cardinals to elect a new Pope) and certain solemn ceremonies.

For those who are not really into the history of art, the first thing to know is that Michelangelo did not paint the entire chapel. The six panels on each side wall were the work of others, and they are

Italy

extremely well executed. The rest, the work of Michelangelo, is simply breathtaking.

The chapel paintings have been restored, and there was a great deal of controversy about the end result. Some claim that the top layer of Michelangelo's works has been removed, leaving much brighter colours than he envisaged, but the Vatican is quite content with the restoration, saying that the colours now on show are precisely what the artist intended. The restoration project was financed by a Japanese company in return for exclusive rights to all pictures. Consequently, it is not permitted to take photographs of any kind in the chapel. This fact does not seem to have got through to tourists though.

Back to Rome

One other tour that can be made from Piazza Venezia is to the Trevi Fountain. Take Via Cesare Battisti to Piazza dei SS Apostoli (named after the Basilica of SS Apostoli). Built in the 6th century, the church has been restored many times, and completely rebuilt once. It houses some valuable works of art. Continue on to Piazza Navona, and from there to Piazza Colonna. Cross Via del Corso and follow the signs.

Trevi Fountain

The famous Trevi Fountain is one of the most beautiful fountains in Rome, and indeed the world. It was built for Pope Clement XII and finished in 1762. The central figure is Neptune in his chariot, drawn by two sea-horses preceded by two tritons (mermen). When I first saw Trevi, I was amazed that it was actually attached to a building: the facade of the Palace of the Dukes of Poli. The fact that it is not a free-standing construction, but instead merges faultlessly with its neighbour, only adds to the appeal.

The name Trevi comes from the word 'trivio', meaining crossroads, or more precisley: where three roads meet. It is rather aptly named. There was a bath-house complex on the site as early as 20BC, and the reliefs

Italy

on the sides of the arch tell the story of soldiers returning from battle and being told of a natural spring by a young girl. The water was called Virgin Water in her honour. The custom of throwing a coin into the water to ensure a return to Rome seems to have no established beginning. It used to be that one had to drink the fountain's water, but maybe it was a bit murky at times. The Fountain was restored a few years ago, and it really is a sight to behold.

From here you can walk to **Piazza Barberini** and along Via Barberini, where there are some really good boutiques for men and women, as well as a few travel agents. Or you can walk the other way, to Via Del Corso, really the main street of Rome. It runs in a straight line from Piazza Venezia to the Piazza del Popolo, becoming Via Flaminia and continuing to the Milvio Bridge. There are palaces on both sides of the street, and in the Middle Ages this was the scene of the famous Berber horse races of the Carnival.

Catacombs

No trip to Rome would be complete without a visit to a catacomb, and we suggest the **Catacombs of Priscilla** at Via Salaria 430. Take Trolley Bus 35 from Stazione Termini, get out at Piazza Crati and walk a short distance. Ring the bell at the convent door and a Benedictine nun will be only too happy to guide you through the catacombs. Two attractions not to miss are: the oldest known painting of the Virgin and Child with Isaiah, produced in the 2nd century and found in a small chapel; and a fresco with the earliest known depiction of The Breaking of the Bread at the Last Supper. The catacombs are ☉open Tues-Sun 8.30am-noon, 2.30-5pm, and an admission fee is charged.

Other Churches

Rome is littered with Churches, both ancient and more recent. Each has a history, from **St John Lateran Basilica**, the church of Rome, to

Italy

St Mary Major near Termini, with its magnificient ceiling leafed with gold from the 'new world', a gift of Phillip II of Spain.
Additional information for interested travellers:

Gesu Church of St Ignatius of Loyola, Piazza de Gesu, ☎678 6341.
St Paul Outside the Walls, Porta San Paolo (Via Linea B), ☎541 0341.
Our Lady of Peace, tomb of Blessed Josemaria Escriva, founder of Opus Dei, viale Bruno Buozzi 73, Parioli district, ☎808 961.

Before coming to Rome determine what your priorities are and stick to them.

Best of Rome in Brief

St. Peter's Basilica (Basilica di San Pietro). The world's grandest Church. Quite simply, a walk within its majestic walls should be the top item on your sightseeing itinerary. The inspired works of Michelangelo and Bernini astonish visitors into a respectful muse. The best views of Rome are from the roof. *Piazza San Pietro*.

Vatican Museum. The collection in this enormous museum covers just about every era imaginable. The roof of the Sistine Chapel is the most famous drawcard, completed by Michelangelo after he spent 4 years with a brush in his hand. Young Raphael's fine contributions to nearby rooms should also be appreciated. *Viale Vaticano, Vatican City*.

Roman Forum (Foro Romano). The "town square" of Ancient Rome, this area was a bubbling centre of activity, primarily for the administration of law and religion. Its ruins mark out the most important point in the ancient civilised world. *Via dei Fori Imperiali*.

Italy

Colosseum (Colosseo). A marvel of anicent architecture, this stadium was built just under 2,000 years ago and accomodated 50,000 spectators - an amazing feat of engineering. *Piazzale del Colosseo, Via dei Fori Imperiali.*

Palatine Hill. Although submerged in history, this area is mostly a collection of non-descript ruins. It contains places that were once used for banquets, gardens, stadiums, courtyards, temples, and the Circus Maximus, but you have to stretch your imagination to bring these stones into order and fill in the gaps. *Via dei Cerchi.*

Arch of Constantine. This monument was established to commemorate Constantine's defeat of Emperor Maxentius in 312 AD, and so also marks the point in time that Christianity was no longer persecuted in Rome. *Piazzale del Colosseo.*

Palazzo Nuovo. In the courtyard of the museum and kept behind glass is the original bronze statue of Marcus Aurelius upon his horse; the statue in Piazza del Campidoglio is Michelangelo's Renaissance copy. *Piazza del Campidoglio.*

Catacombs. These are the burial grounds of early Christians, a network of tunnels and grottoes circling Rome's centre. The Catacombs of San Callisto and the Catacombs of San Sebastian are the two most popular. *Via Appia Antica.*

Trajan's Column. Standing 40-metres high, this victory column records the successful military campaigns led by Trajan. Over 2,500 figures on the column tell the story. *Piazza Venezia.*

Capitoline Hill (Campidoglio). Michelangelo designed the Renaissance steps and the square, paying particular attention to the aesthetic harmony of its architecture. *Piazza del Campidoglio*.

Palazzo dei Conservatori. The bronze statues are the main attraction, but the classical paintings also hold your attention - a superb collection. *Piazza del Campidoglio*.

Trevi Fountain. This unique artwork flows from the adjacent building in a wonderful surge of water and stone.

Pantheon ("All the Gods"). This temple is most famous for its domed roof, which inspired Michelangelo when he was designing the dome of St. Peter's Basilica. It is the crown jewel of ancient Roman architecture, and in wonderful condition. *Piazza della Rotunda*.

National Museum of Rome (Museo Nazionale Romano). A must for Roman statues and portraits immortalising famous leaders, and for rare mosaics, frescoes, coins and more. There are also great Greek statues preserved from "borrowed" Greek culture. Houses the best ancient Roman art in the world. *Palazzo Massimo alla Terme*.

Villa Borghese. A park and garden setting known for its musems and zoo.

Borghese Gallery. Some of the world's most valuable paintings and sculptures are on display in this remarkable and recently-restored gallery. Bernini's *David* should not be missed. *Piazza Scipione Borghese*.

Italy

Castel Sant'Angelo. This castle has served many functions since it was built 1800 years ago, from mausoleum to medieval fortress to papal residence to the art museum it is today. *Lungotevere Castello 50.*

St Peter-in-Chains Church (San Pietro in Vincoli). Michelangelo's statue of Moses is in this church, and the chains that held St. Peter are kept beneath the altar. *Off Via Cavour.*

Nero's Golden House (Domus   Aurea). What is left of Emperor Nero's colossal estate, or Golden House, is now open for public viewing. *Viale d. Domus Aurea.*

Mammertime Prison. This interesting prison found its way into history when both St Peter and St Paul were incacerated here. Near *Capitoline Hill.*

Piazza Venezia. This historical square is the hub of the city.

Victor Emmanuel Monument (Vittorio Emanuele Monument). Quite possibly the most unpopular chunk of marble to be found on Rome's streets - particularly with the locals. This monument to an Italian king has been scathingly dubbed "the typewriter"or "the wedding cake". *Piazza Venezia.*

Church of San Luigi dei Francesci. Caravaggio painted the marvellous chapel interior. *Near the Pantheon.*

Santa Maria sopra Minerva. This church was built in the Gothic style - and is Rome's only structural example of this style. *Christ Bearing the Cross* by Michelangelo is here. *Near the Pantheon.*

Baths of Diocletian. These were the largest baths in Rome, built in 300AD. Highlights of a tour of these ruins are the Octagonal Hall and the Church of Santa Maria degli Angeli. *Piazza Repubblica.*

Santa Maria della Vittoria. Home of Bernini's intruiging statue of *St. Teresa in Ecstacy. Largo Susanna.*

Cappuccin Crypt. For something different, in the basement of this crypt you will find an "exhibition" comprising the neatly-placed bones of about 4,000 monks. *Beneath Santa Maria della Imaculata Concezione Church, Via Veneto.*

Etruscan Museum (Villa Giulia Museo Nazionale Etrusco). An important museum for Etruscan art, with many coveted works from the B.C. era on display. *Piazzale di Villa Guilia 9.*

Spanish Steps (Piazza de Spagna). A famous location with a knack for attracting a few of literature's well-known wordsmiths to its steps, such as Geothe and Keats. It is a popular night spot.

Florence

Florence lies in the heartland of Tuscany, on the banks of the River Arno. To say that it is a beautiful city, is not doing it justice, it is simply like no other.

History

Florence was originally a Roman camp, and has been the seat of a bishop since the 4th century.

In the 13th century Florence was probably the richest city in Europe. Her currency, the florin, was international tender. Her people were, in the main, moneylenders and cloth and woollen merchants. There was no shortage of gold and rich families, but the richest of all were the Medici and they became the ruling dynasty. Fortunately for Florence the Medici were patrons of the arts, in fact the greatest patrons in Europe. They almost single-handedly financed the Renaissance. Cosimo the Elder was the patron of Donatello and during his time the first Renaissance buildings appeared in the city.

His grandson, Lorenzo the Magnificent, was a good friend of Botticelli, and took Michelangelo into his home as a 15-year-old and treated him as a son.

Other great masters who spent at least some, if not all, of their lives in Florence include: Giotto, Brunelleschi, Masaccio, Botticelli, Leonardo da Vinci, Raphael and Vasari.

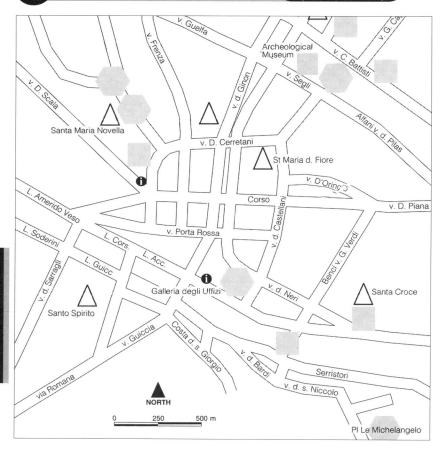

Tourist Information

The Tourist Information Office are at: 1R Via Cavour, ℘(055) 290 832, fax 276 0383, next to the Palazzo Medici, ☼open Mon-Sat 8.30am-7.15pm, Sun 8.30am-1.45pm; 16R Via A. Manzoni, ℘(055) 234 6284, fax 234 6286, ☼open Mon-Sat 8.30am-1.30pm; Commune de Firenze, exit SMN rail station near track 16, ℘(055) 212 245, fax 238 1226, ☼open daily 8.15am-7.15pm.

Local Transport

There is a bus service, but in Florence you can conveniently walk to everything that is worth seeing.

Accommodation

No one will be surprised to learn that discounts can be had for cash in many of the smaller hotels and pensiones in Florence. Discounts can also sometimes be acquired if you stay for several days. It is generally cheaper to book with the hotel direct rather than use a tourist information service. In season, people flock to Florence, so prices fluctuate wildly, as does room availability. The summer and winter months are generally fairly empty while spring and autumn are generally busy. During summer, pay the extra for air conditioning. In smaller places you can save money off the rates listed below if you don't mind sharing a bathroom.

Annalena, Via Romana 34, Firenze, ©055/222 402, fax 055/222 402. Typical Florentine accommodation in a small hotel dating from the 15th century. The 20 rooms available are reasonably comfortable, the building is not without charm, and the owner offers small hotel service and attentiveness, but don't expect luxury - from ✪250,000L.

Italy

Hotel Casci

Via Cavour 13, Firenze, ©055/211 686, 055/ 239 6461. With both railway station and Duomo nearby, this neat little 25 room hotel is sure to please. The building itself is 14th century and still has some of the original frescoes in the public spaces. The staff are used to English-speaking guests - ✪L170,000.

Mirandi alla Crocetta, Via Laura 50, Firenze, ©055/234 4747, fax 055/248 0954. Set in a building which was originally a 17th century convent, this pensione is found on the first floor in a quiet street some minutes walk north to the Duomo. Polished wooden floors, oriental rugs, white walls and high ceilings give the apartment a clean, fresh feel. A pleasant, quiet retreat from Florence's bustle - from ✪150,000L.

Regency, Piazza Massimo d'Azeglio 3, Firenze, ✆055/234 2936, fax 055/234 6935. Opulence Florentine-style with richly patterned carpets and heavy wooden furniture. At the rear of the main building is a glassed-in breakfast room which overlooks a large, shady garden that makes for a very pleasant retreat after a hot day in the city. For a special treat only - ✪L470,000.

Hotel Academia, Via Faenza 7, Firenze, ✆055/293 451, fax 055/219 771. An elegant little hotel about equidistant between the railway station and the Duomo. A comfortable stay right in the middle of the action - ✪L220,000.

Hotel Loggiato dei Serviti, Piazza S.S. Annunziata 3, ✆055/289 592, fax 055/ 289 595. Built in the 16th century as a monastery, the building gives an impression of simple solidity. The rooms are fully equipped with all the modern conveniences - ✪L350,000.

Albergo Losanna, Via Vittorio Alfieri 9, Firenze, ✆055/245 840, fax 055/245 840. Clean, simple accommodation in a small homey pensione. Cheaper rooms with share bathroom available. Breakfast is included in the price of the room - ✪L150,000.

Hotel Vasari, Via B. Cennini 9-11, Firenze, ✆055/212 753, 055/294 246. Renovated in the early nineties this neat little 30 room family run hotel is pleasant, comfortable and clean. Value for money - ✪L200,000.

Hotel J & J, Via di Mezzo 20, 50121 Firenze, ✆055/234 5005, fax 055/240 282. This 20 room hotel is considered one of Florence's hippest. The architect owner took a 16th century monastery and totally reformed it in the early nineties. Lots of nooks and crannies throughout the building have been turned into pleasant places to sit and chat after a heavy days sightseeing. Some of the rooms feature rooftop balconies with views to die for - ✪L400,000.

Westin Excelsior is the top of the range in Florence. It is situated on the banks of the Arno at 3 Piazza Ognissanti, ©(055) 264 201, fax 210 278. It is close to Ponte Vecchio, Uffizi, and Pitti Palace. 168 rooms, award winning restaurant, bars, lounges - standard room ✪L864,500-1000,000, Deluxe room L865,500-1135,000.

Lungarno Hotel, 14 Borgo San Iacopo, ©(055) 27 261 fax (055) 268 437 (✉travelweb@hotelbook.com(19420)) is also on the banks of the river, 100m from the Ponte Vecchio. 66 rooms, restaurant, bar/lounge - ✪L280,000-560,000

Bettoja Relais Certosa Hotel, 2 Via Di Colle Ramole, ©(055) 204 7171, fax 268 575 (✉travelweb@hotelbook.com(10750)). 15 minutes from Ponte Vecchio by hotel courtesy bus. 70 rooms, restaurant, bar/lounge, tennis court - standard room ✪L240,000-400,000.

Pitti Palace Hotel, 2 Via Barbadori, ©(055) 239 871, fax 239 8867 (✉travelweb@hotelbook.com(17929)). A 3-star hotel in the centre of the city with great views from the 6th floor Breakfast Room. 72 rooms, bar/lounge - ✪L140,000-330,000.

Fleming Hotel, 87 Viale Guidoni, ©(055) 437 6773, fax 435 894 (✉travelweb@hotelbook.com(02390)). In the commercial centre, 4 minutes from the airport, and within easy reach of the historical centre by public transport every 6 minutes. 118 rooms, restaurant, bar/lounge - ✪L125,000-310,000.

Florence's **Youth Hostel** is **Villa Camerata**, Viale Augusto Righi 2-4, ©(055) 601 451, fax (055) 610 300.

Food and Drink

Although there are a large number of restaurants in Florence, it is really a place where you only eat if you are hungry. That is not to say that the food is not good, it is just that there is nothing special about it. Florence has many other great things to offer.

If you want to try a typical Florentine eatery, one where the locals go, then head for **Il Latini**, 6R Via dei Palchetti, ✆(055) 210 916. It is near the Piazza Goldoni, and is ☉open Wed-Sun for lunch and Tues-Sun for dinner.

If you in Florence on a Monday when Il Latini is closed, try **Pane e Vino**, 70R Via San Niccolo, ✆(055) 247 6956, which is small and informal, but has good food and an excellent wine list.

Shopping

There is no doubt that the quality of goods bought in Florence is first class, but you have to pay for it. Gone are the days when you could pick up a leather bargain, but even so window shopping is a delight because of what is on offer.

There are more shoes for sale in Florence than in any other city in Italy, and a walk down the Via dei Tornabuoni will have dedicated shoppers drooling. This street is the continuation of the bridge next to the Ponte Vecchio when heading away from the Uffizi.

There are a couple of quite good markets that sell fake 'designer' gear with fake 'authentic' labels, and some of it is worth a close look. Enquire at the information centre.

Sightseeing

A walking tour can start at those two symbols of Florence - the **River Arno** and the **Ponte Vecchio**, the quaint old bridge that crosses it. Originally the little shops on the bridge were owned by butchers, but the Medici replaced them with jewellery shops and they are still there.

Walk down Via Por Santa Maria to the **Piazzo della Signoria**, a slightly odd-shaped square, and the **Palazzo Vecchio**, which was built in the 14th century for the city's Priors. It is now the Town Hall, and can be visited to see the Hall of the Five Hundred and the Hall of Justice. Incidentally, the copy of Michelangelo's David in this square is where the real one originally stood before it was taken under cover to help preserve it. The **Loggia dei Lanzi** is in front of the Palazzo. It was built in the late 14th century for public government ceremonies, but it is now an open-air museum containing some famous sculptures such as Cellini's *Perseus*,

Next stop is **Galleria degli Uffizi**, more commonly known as 'The Uffizi', one of the great galleries of the world, and the biggest in Italy. It has forty-five rooms containing what can only be described as art 'treasures'. Over a million people visit the Uffizi each year, and often it is necessary to join a long queue to gain admission, but it is well worth it. The ground floor has the restored Church of San Pier Scheraggio with its frescoes, Andrea del Castagno's *Famous Men* and Botticelli's *Annunciation*. The first floor has the prints and drawings section, but only the room at the top of the stairs on the left is open to the general public. The second floor has the major collection, and has three corridors of mainly sculpture surrounded by rooms containing the paintings. The ceiling in the third corridor should not be overlooked. The rooms with the paintings are set out two ways: chronologically for the Florentine; and geographically for the rest. Each room is numbered for easy identification.

It is possible to by-pass the very long queues that often develop for entry to the Uffizi. You can arrange to pay for your entry by credit card before your leave home using the Italy Tourist Offices' website: ☞www.enit.it.com/, or by asking your hotel desk to arrange it if you are staying in Florence for a few days.

Museums are normally ☉open Tues-Sat 9am-1pm (or 2pm), 3pm (or 4pm)-7pm, Sun 9am-2pm. Smaller museums may, however, vary their hours. Entry fees are quite high for some of the galleries, though not when you consider what you will be seeing, but be prepared. All

Italy

European citizens over the age of 5 years are admitted free to all national museums and galleries, on production of their passport.

It is necessary to backtrack now to get to the **Cathedral** complex. The church is one of the longest in the world. Longer are the Cathedral in the Ivory Coast, St Peter's in Rome and St Paul's in London. Most churches exude an air of holiness, this one doesn't. The most famous thing about it is *Brunelleschi's dome*, an architectural masterpiece. It consists of two domes with a space between (that can be climbed by anybody fit enough) which give the appearance of a cupola without any supports. It took Brunelleschi over fifteen years to complete the dome, and it has recently been discovered that he is buried in the cathedral, probably as a reward for his labours.

The cathedral has another famous attraction, the East Gate of the **Baptistry**. Here are found the ten panels by Lorenzo Ghiberti that are known as the *Doors of Paradise*. They begin with Adam and Eve in the top left and continue horizontally. Experts have stated that the sculpture is 'a painting in bronze', and it really is quite breath-taking. It is very difficult to take a photo of the doors because there is always someone closely examining them. (Unfortunately, some of the panels will probably be replaced by copies when you are there. The originals are being restored in what is turning out to be a lengthy job.)

The **Museo dell'Opera del Duomo** is a museum containing the works of art that were once in the cathedral, and it is at 9 Piazza del Duomo. It has some interesting exhibits such as Donatello's choir loft, the gear that Brunelleschi used for the dome, and a *Pieta* that Michelangelo smashed because it wasn't good enough and someone reassembled 300 years later.

From the left side of the cathedral walk up Via Ricasoli to no. 60 and you have found the **Galleria dell'Accademia**, the home of Michelangelo's *David*. It would be worth the price of admission if that was the only work on display, but not so. There are also Michelangelo's unfinished *Captives* that he worked on for the tomb of Pope Julius II; and paintings by such artists as Fra Filippo and Ghirlandaio. It is a nice, bright and airy gallery.

A block or so behind, and forming one side of the Piazza Santissima Annunziata, is the **Ospedale degli Innocenti** (Gallery of the Hospital of the Innocents). Originally an orphanage, it is now a gallery, that has some fine Renaissance paintings, including Ghirlandaio's *Adoration of the Magi*.

The Piazza San Marco, off Via Cavour, almost opposite the Galleria dell' Accademia, has the Dominican **Monastery of San Marco**, where Fra Angelico lived and painted. It has now become a gallery dedicated solely to his work. His paintings are not as worldly as the others of the Renaissance, but his genius cannot be denied.

Back almost where we began, east of the Palazzo Vecchio, is the old **Santa Croce**, the biggest Franciscan church in Italy. The first thing you see when you walk in is the absolutely awful tomb of Michelangelo, the work of Vasari. Others buried here include Machiavelli and Galileo. Worth looking at now are Giotto's *The Death of St Francis* and other frescoes by his pupil Taddeo Gaddi. In the cloisters is the portico of the Pazzi Chapel, which some say is the greatest achievement of Brunelleschi.

In the Piazza Santa Croce is a new attraction, **Museo del Rinascimento** (Museum of the Renaissance). It features wax tableaux of the Masters of the Renaissance creating their works of art. For example one display has Michelangelo on his scaffold in the Sistine Chapel, and another has Leonardo da Vinci painting his mysterious model, *La Giaconda*.

It may not be for the serious art student, but it might be good for those whose knowledge of art is not really up to scratch. Anyway, it is ☉open daily 10am-7pm.

The Best of Florence in Brief

Uffizi Gallery (Galleria degli Uffizi). Without question the best collection of Italian art anywhere, represented by Raphael, Michelangelo, Botticelli, da Vinci, Giotto and more. Its contents are bursting with genius. *Piazzale degli Uffizi 6*.

Galleria dell'Accademia. Come here to see Michelangelo's Renaissance masterpiece, the statue of *David*, an image of which there are so many duplications around the world. *Via Ricasoll 60*.

Duomo (Cattedrale di Santa Maria del Fiore). Brunelleschi's ground-breaking dome, a marble exterior and the enormous *Last Judgment* painting are worth a look here. *Piazza del Duomo*.

Giotto's Bell Tower (Campanile). Over 80 metres tall, this tower was created by Giotto in a revised Gothic design. A climb to the top affords a magnificent outlook over Florence and its hills. *Piazza del Duomo*.

Italy

Museo dell'Opera del Duomo. Fans of sculpture should come here to examine the creations of Brunelleschi, Ghiberti, Donatello and Michelangelo. *Piazza del Duomo 9*.

Palazzo Pitti. This palace has seven museums on its grounds, the most important of which is Galleria Palatina, where Raphael features most prominently. The expansive and picturesque Boboli Gardens (Giardini di Boboli) fill the background. *Piazza de'Pitti*.

Medici Chapels (Cappelle dei Medici). Michelangelo laboured intensely to decorate these Medici tombs, located inside a chapel, with Renaissance extravagence. *Piazza Madonna degli Aldobrandini 6*.

Palazzo Vecchio. Former palace of the Medici, Vecchio has a good collection of art and its exterior, particularly its tower, also justifies a visit. *Piazza della Signoria*.

Museum of San Marco (Museo di San Marco). This museum focuses on medieval and Renaissance art. The highlight piece is *The Annunciation* by Fra Angelico. *Piazza San Marco 1*.

Bargello (Museo Nazionale del Bargello). Donatello and Michelangelo are the stars of this sculpture museum. *Via del Proconsolo*.

Baptistry (Battistero San Giovanni). This is Florence's oldest building, featuring architectural flourishes in marble and bronze. The finely-crafted doors are the main attraction. *Piazza S. Giovanni*.

Church of Santa Maria Novella (Basilica di Santa Maria Novella). This thirteenth century church contains two prized possessions worth seeing, Brunelleschi's crucifix and Masaccio's *The Holy Trinity*. *Piazza Santa Maria Novella*.

Palazzo Medici-Riccardi. Gozzoli's *Journey of the Magi* series graces these walls. *Via Camillo Cavour 1*.

Ponte Vecchio. Stroll across this famous Florentine bridge, browsing through the shops along its edges.

Orsanmichele. A church with some interesting sculptures on its external facade and even more artwork tucked away in a little museum at the top of the church. *Via dei Calzaioli*.

Brancacci Chapel. The work of Masaccio, responsible for *The Holy Trinity* in Basilica di Santa Maria Novella, is the emphasis of this Renaissance collection. *Piazza del Carmine*.

Archaelogical Museum (Museo Archeologico). Egyptian and Etruscan art in a collection that ranks very highly. *Via della Colonna 38*.

Michelangelo's House (Casa Buonarroti). Preserves a select variety of the master's early works. *Via Ghibellina 70*.

Science Museum (Museo di Storia dells Scienza). A fascinating look at technology from the Renaissance period onwards, in the form of old telescopes, clocks and more. *Piazza dei Giudici 1*.

Santa Croce Church (Basilica di Santa Croce). There is a famous Florentine name at every turn in this church, whether it be the tomb of Michelangelo and Galileo or the surrounding artwork of Donatello and Giotto. *Piazza Santa Croce 16*.

Venice

When one thinks of Venice, one can only imagine the gondolas swishing through the lagoon and down the canals under the Bridge of Sighs. Sleek water vessels guided by gondoliers festooned in bright colourful outfits make Venice, as does St
Mark's Basilica and the Doges Palace with its works by Titian and Tintoretto. The birds in St Mark's Square welcome the romanticist, and Harry's Bar - *the* Harry's Bar - lets visitors from the USA and others know they are now in the precincts of the once rich and famous.

History

Venice is situated on a lagoon facing the Adriatic sea. Many many islands are linked by bridges and boats. The centre of the city on the lagoon is a car free zone.

During the Middle Ages Venice became an important trading centre between east and west and amassed a colossal wealth. The Republic lasted a thousand years with the Aristocracy electing from its members the Doges who would run the state. Responsible for the sacking of Constantinople, Venice went on to take over strategic trading positions, acquiring Cyprus and Crete and other relevant positions on trading routes. This ensured a wealthy legacy for what had become the most important trading centre in Europe.

With the dawn of the sixteenth century and the discoveries and occupation of the Americas, especially by Spain, Portugal, France and England, other trade routes became more important. The decline in importance of this great city had started. Once Napoleon conquered this part of the world, divesting Venice of many of its treasures and leaving the 'drawing room of Europe' somewhat scant of delightful furniture, the gradual decline of Venice as a trading power became a sudden torrent.

However, tourism has become the great source of income for this once formidable centre of power. The focal point is St Mark's Square where since 830AD, the bones of St Mark the evangelist, and biographer of sorts of St. Peter, have been buried. Popes have come from the Patriarch of Venice - including in the twentieth century St Pius X, a local boy from the district of Mantua, John XXIII and John Paul I.

Climate

Most rain falls in Spring (March-April) and Autumn (September-October). The hottest months are July and August, and the coldest late December and January. It is not unusual to see the gondolas tied up and romantically covered in snow. It rains about 100 days a year.

Tourist Information

There is a Tourist Information centre at the Train Station Santa Lucia ☉open from 8.30am - 6.30pm at night. Some travel writers have been critical of the assistance, or lack of it, given here. One describes the staff as 'surly and unhelpful'. They are certainly very busy. (You may find it preferable to take vaporetto (water bus) number 82 to San Marco Piazza and visit the tourist information centre there.) Be that as it may, you can pick up a free map of the city, though you can buy a relatively cheap and more detailed map at kiosks. Also it is suggested you collect the latest *Un Ospite de Venezia* which covers all the tourist information you need to know - public transport timetables, opening hours, emergency telephone numbers, and so on. It is useful for planning your stay if you have not already done so. You should also be able to get a copy of this at your hotel, particularly if you are staying at one of the better ones.

Italy

There is also a tourist information centre in St Mark's Square - Azienda de Promozione Turistica - San Marco, ©041-522 6356. ©In Summer - June to August - 9.30am to 6.30pm - Monday to Saturday. In other months - 9.30am to 3.30pm. Monday to Saturday.

Other numbers you can phone for assistance with tourist information is Azienda di Promozione, Turistica di Venezia Castello 4421 ©(041) 529 8701 or 529 8711.

Local Transport

The causeway that caters for both rail and road is almost three kilometres long and links Mestre with Venice.

Car

If you are travelling to Venice by car the best place to leave the car is at the parking station near the railway station in Mestre. The cost is about ⊙L10,000 - L15,000 (under cover parking) for the day. Driving across the causeway the highway comes to an end and parking must be found. Simply follow the directions. The cost is about ⊙L35,000 for the day there at Tronchetto. From there to St Mark's Square by vaporetti, (number 1(slow) or 82(quicker)) will cost about ⊙L6,000.

Plane

The main airport for Venice is **Venice Marco Polo** some 8 kilometres north east of Mestre on the mainland. From the airport you can get an ATVO bus to the Tronchetto vaporetto stop. The cost will be about ⊙L6,000. There is another local bus that takes longer and is cheaper but you will have to ask directions as to where it stops. It is not a good idea to get this bus if you have anything other than hand luggage or a simple backpack. You can also get to the centre of Venice by Water Taxi. Enquire at the tourism desk when you arrive. It operates from early morning to late at night and is a great way to be introduced to Venice.

Italy

Vaporetto

This is a 'water bus' and is the best way to get around Venice. The cost is reasonable: some ❂L6000 from St Lucia Station to St Mark's Square. Check the information desk for schedules which will give you an idea of which ones to catch, how much to pay, and exactly what a ticket covers - round trip, one way, and so on. As with popular tourist destinations in Italy there are thieves and cheats, including individuals masquerading as bona fide water taxi drivers.

The main numbers to remember for the vaporette are as follows. Number 1 stops at every dock imaginable along the Grand Canal and is for those after a slow ride. The 82 is the quicker one stopping at the main centres - Tronchetto where you have parked your car, and a number of other stops including the Train Station, Rialto and San Marco. This is the 'Metro' equivalent for Venice.

Rail

The main station of Venice - San Lucia Stazione - is situated to the west of the island. It is about a 50 minute walk from San Marco and has all the necessary information kiosks for the traveller, as well as booking agencies. Since rail is the main method used by visitors to Venice, the station is very busy and it is often better to seek out a travel agent - the ubiquitous American Express near St Mark's Square, ✆041 520-0844 is ☉open from 9-5.30pm, and if it is a Saturday, get there before 1.00pm.

Currency Exchange

American Express near St Mark's Square in San Moise 1471, ✆041-520 0844. They will cash American Express travellers cheque and provide the other services that come with one of their outlets. Thomas Cook have two locations - 5126 Riva del Ferro 3/124, and closer to where the action is at Piazza San Marco (St Mark's Square) 142, 30124. They, like American Express, do not charge a fee on cashing their own travellers cheques but will charge something for others - normally about ☉L5,000.

Accommodation

A website for accommodation that is useful is ☞www.itwg.com Prices listed here are for a double. All rooms have a phone, ensuite of some description, TV, and airconditioning. All those listed take major credit cards. These hotels do not close during the year unless mentioned in the description, and rates vary depending on the canal view, and time of year. Rooms with a view cost more.

Accademia (Pensione), Fondamenta Bollani, Dorsoduro 1058, ☏041 521 0188, 523 7846, fax 041 523 9152 , (✎pensione.accademia@ sflashnet.it). A a pleasant pensione with breakfast included, open terrace and comfortable rooms with the obligatory touch of Venetian opulence exhibited in the chandeliers and some furnishings. 22 rooms, breakfast room and bar. Near the Grand Canal and the Accademia museum. Vaporetti - Accademia - ☉L150,000-L300,000.

Agli Alboretti, Accademia 884, Dorsoduro, ☏041-523 0058, fax 041-521 058 (✎alborett@gpnet.it). A small yet fashionably furnished family hotel, 20 rooms, sitting room. The restaurant next door is noted for its wine list. Opposite the Accademia Museum. Vaporetti - Accademia - ☉L150,000-250,000.

American, Rio di San Vio, 628 Accademia, 30123, ☏041-520 4733, fax 041-520 4048, ☞www.hotelamerican.com, ✎reception@ hotelamerican.com. 25 rooms, rather old world on the canal. Vaporetti - Accademia. A restored comfortable hotel with a breakast room and a terrace in a quiet residential area close to the Accademia and just off the Grand Canal. A shot water taxi or Vaporetti ride to Piazza San Marco, or you can walk and visit the Peggy Guggenheim Museum of Modern Art and the Palazzo Grassi on the way - ☉L200,000 - 370,000.

Hotel Messner, Dorsodero 216/237, Venzia, ©041 522 7443, fax 041 522 7266. Housed in an old palace it is 100 metres from Sancta Maria di Salute. Restaurant and bar. Vaporetti - Zattere - ☺L220,000-250,000.

Calcina, Fundamenta Zattere ai Gesuati, Dorsoduro 780, 30123, ©041-520 6466, fax 041-522 7045. 28 rooms, recently refurbished, breakfast room and terrace. Vaporetti - Zattere - ☺L200,000-L300,000.

Des Bainsi, Lungomare Marconi 17, Lido 30126, ©041-526 5921, fax 041 526 0113. 200 rooms, restaurants, bar, terrace, swimming pool, tennis court, park, classical furniture with most bathrooms featuring marble. Part of the Sheraton Chain. Closed during winter - so check. Vaporetti - Lido - ☺L250,000-400,000.

Bel Sito & Berlino, Campo Santa Maria del Giglio 2517, ©041-522 3365, fax 041-520 4083, 40 rooms, small bar, good location though rooms vary with some a little small. Vaporetti - Santa Maria del Giglio - ☺L190,000-L350,000.

Do Pozzi, Calle Larga XXII Marzo 2373, ©041-520 7855, fax 041-522 9413. 32 rooms, De Raffale Restaurant, terrace. Icons and Ottoman weaponry adorn the public areas. Rooms are small but comfortable. Vaporetti - Santa Maria del Giglio - ☺L150,000-L250,000.

The Westin Excelsior, Lungomare Marconi 41, 30125, Venice Lido, ©041-526 0201, fax (041) 526 7276. 196 rooms, restaurants, lounges, tennis courts, golf course, water sport facilities (your typical US-based outfit). The furnishings in the recently renovated rooms have been decorated in Iberian-Mauresque style. Many rooms have views of the sea, lagoon or the city. These are more expensive than others. Vaporetti - Lido - ☺L455,000-700,000.

Campo Santa Maria Del Giglio, 2467, 30124, ✆041-794 611, fax 041-520 0942, ➳www.sheraton.com. 93 rooms, bar, restaurant, terrace, on Grand Canal. Vaporetti - Santa Maria del Giglio. This former palace of the Doge Andrea Gritti is all class. If you feel uncomfortable being waited on hand and foot, and using the fine furnishings in your surrounds then find another hotel. The service is superb and the rooms are both elegant and spacious, with different themes enhancing the quality of the hotel. This is a Venetian experience, and it is never closed. Vaporetti - Santa Maria del Giglio - ✪L750,000+.

Hotel Villa Edera, Via Negroponte 13, Lido Di Venezia, ✆041-731 575, fax 041 770 263. 23 rooms, bar, parking provided, 2-3 star hotel, nothing special but serviceable and comfortable. Vaporetti - Lido - L280,000-350,000.

Flora, San Marco, Calle Larga XXII Marzo 2283a, 30124, ✆041 520 5844, fax 041 522 8217, ➳www.hotelflora.it, email✎info@ hotelflora.it. 44 rooms, restaurant, bar and garden. A delightful family run hotel with its own garden and very close to San Marco. Vaporetti - San Marco - ✪L280,000- 360,000

Kette, Piscina San Moise, San Marco, 2053, 30124, ✆041 520 7766, fax 041-522 8964, ➳www.hotelkette.com, ✎info@hotelkette.com. 60 rooms, restaurant. A sixteenth century building housing a tourist hotel that, though rather bland, is very close to Piazza San Marco. Vaporetti - San Marco - ✪L360,000-500,000.

Italy

Marconi, Riva dek Vin, San Polo 729, 30125, ✆041 522 2068, fax 04 1-522 9700. 28 rooms, dining room, terrace. Situated next to the Rialto Bridge on the Grand Canal. Unexceptional. Vaporetti - Rialto - L415,000-L550,000.

Hotel Locanda Ovidius, calle del Sturion, San Polo 677A, ✆041 523 7970, fax 041 520 4101, ✎www.hotelolvidius.com. On the first floor of the palace. There are only 9 rooms here, so it is very small. Breakfast included. Vaporetti - Rialto - L350,000-400,000.

Food and Drink

You can eat while standing up at bars purchasing a sandwich, roll or pizza with your house wine or cafe. The best places are off the main tourist track. You can always eat in your hotel and it is always a good idea to ask the staff thereif they could recommend a restaurant for an enjoyable dinner or a cafe for a quick bite. *Do Leoni*, ✎www. hotelondra.it

The Best of Venice in Brief

St Mark's Square (Piazza San Marco). The centre of Venice's land based appeal, this huge square is bounded by the city's best sights and filled with the people who flock to see them, along with plenty of pigeons doing some flocking of their own.

St Mark's Basilica (Basilica di San Marco). This rich and elegant church contains the tomb of St. Mark along with considerable treasures of art and other preserved relics. The architecture is a mixture of styles, but the Byzantine style overshadows the competition. *Piazza San Marco*.

St Mark's Bell Tower (Campanile di San Marco). An elevator will assist in your ascension to an outlook over Venice like no other in the city. *Piazza San Marco*.

Doge's Palace (Palazzo Ducale). Once home of the ruling doge and of the Venetian Government, the Palace represents the pinnacle of the city's power across Europe. Enjoy the art and architecture, of which there are several highlights, then cross the Bridge of Sighs and enter the old prison, retracing the steps of many unfortunate victims whose lives were on the path to a torturous end in the Palazzo delle Prigioni. *Piazza San Marco*.

Grand Canal (Canal Grande). A leisurely serenaded gondala ride through the Grand Canal of Venice is one of the world's most famous activities and an unforgettable event. It is the best way to take in the medieval architecture of palaces and mansions built on the shoreline, whose continued existence (at least until the whole place sinks completely) is protected by law.

Galleria dell'Accademia. An important collection of gothic and Byzantine art drawn from five centuries. *Campo della Carita, Dorsoduro.*

Glassblowing. This is a fascinating practice but its novelty does wear off fairly rapidly, so make sure you don't go out of your way to see this at the expense of another of Venice's attractions. There are places adjoining St Mark's Square that have short shows.

Museo Civico Correr. For a whisk through Venetian history, this city museum displays some noteworthy pieces from the Venetian Republic and offers insights into the city's most prolific artistic era (1400-1600). *Piazza San Marco.*

Chiesa dei Frari. This Gothic church is a gem of artistic endeasvour, marvellously decorated by Bellini, Titian and Donatello. *Campo dei Frari.*

Ca'Rezzonico. Occupied by some famous figures over the years, this well-furnished palace has some internal drawcards, particularly some works by the distinguished artist Longhi. *Fondamenta Rezzonico, Dorsoduro 3136.*

Scuola di San Rocco. Tintoretto put his touch permanently on this building, covering its walls with more than 50 of his canvas paintings. The greatest is the *Crucifixion* upstairs. *Campo San Rocco, San Polo.*

Scuola di San Giorgio degli Schiavoni. Carpaccio is responsible for the works in this building, which is worth visiting if you have the time and inclination. *Calle Furiani, Castello.*

Ca' d'Oro. Another palace worth seeing for its museum and overall lavish design.

Peggy Guggenheim Collection (Collezione Peggy Guggenheim). The modern art of Picasso and some of his contemporaries is on show in this remarkable museum. *Ca' Venier dei Leoni, Dorsoduro 701.*

Driving Through Italy

Florence

Itinerary - 6 Days - Distance 766kms

Florence (Firenze) is famous for its history, art and culture. There is much to see and do here, a week could be spent in the city alone. From Florence drive north to **Pistoiaz**, a medieval town situated at the base of the Appenines. There are many historic buildings here. Further on you reach the town of **Lucca**, which is well known as an olive oil production centre. The town dates from Roman times.

Head south to **Pisa**, famous for its leaning tower, but there are many other scenic buildings. From Pisa, drive south along the coast. From **San Vincenzo** you can see across to the island of Elba. The towns of **Grosseto**, **Orbetello** and **Tarquinia** are old towns dating from medieval times. Tarquinia hosts the National Museum.

Head away from the coast towards **Vetralla**. Many tombs dating from Estruscan times are located nearby. **Viterbo** and **Orvieto** are picturesque old towns with cobbled streets and historic buildings. **Todi** has remains dating from Roman times. Drive further north to **Assisi**, the birthplace of St Francis. From here, travel to **Perugia**. This walled town is situated on a hill and looks down on the Tiber Valley. The National Gallery of Umbria has many fine works. On the way back to Florence, you pass the **Arezzo** and **Siena**, with many historic buildings. Siena is also famous for the Palio horse race, held each summer. From Siena it is a short drive back to Florence.

Rome and Naples

Itinerary - 6 Days - Distance 719kms

From Rome, drive to the coast and start your journey heading down the coastal road. **Anzio** and **Terracina** are well known holiday places, and also have fine examples of ruins dating from Roman times. Further along the coast you reach **Pozzuoli**, a port established in Roman times. Pozzuoli is just outside **Naples**, the third largest city in Italy. Naples is situated below Mt Vesuvius. There are many historic churches and museums here, as well as all the attractions of a large city. Just out of Naples, you find the remains of the eruption of Mt Vesuvius at **Ercolano** and **Pompei**. These towns are now excavated and the ruins may be visited. At the southern end of the Bay of Naples you reach the town of **Sorrento**. This is a popular holiday resort.

Drive along the coast through **Positano** to **Amalfi** and **Salerno**, a pretty town notable for being the site of the U.S. landing in World War II. Head north to **Avelino**. This town has been completely rebuilt after an earthquake earlier this century. North of Avelino lies **Benevento**, which has many buildings dating from Roman times. From here, drive towards **Cassino**, through **Isernia**. The abbey at Cassino was destroyed in World War II but has been replicated. Heading back towards Rome you pass through **Ferentino**, overlooking the Sacco Valley. From here, it is a short drive back to **Rome**, with its many things to see and do, as well being noted for world class shopping.

Italy

The Netherlands

THE KINGDOM OF THE NETHERLANDS (Holland) is a constitutional monarchy with a parliamentary system and is one of the most densely populated countries in Europe. The 15,010,500 people live in 40,844 sq km.

Once famous for dykes, windmills, wooden clogs and tulips, it is now probably as well known for its legalisation of soft drugs and its condoning of euthanasia.

The Netherlands is a very flat country, with more than one-fifth of its land under sea level. The language of the people is Dutch. Most people in the towns and cities can speak English.

Climate

The continental influence ensures that there are seasonal extremes of temperature, with the coldest month being January, and the hottest July. The absence of mountains allows the winds from the west to

pass straight over the country, bringing some damp weather but not excessive rain.

April and early May is the best time to visit to see the tulips in full bloom.

Entry Regulations

Visitors must have a valid passport, but visas are not required for visits up to three months. It is necessary to check with the Embassy or Consulate in your home country about the duty free allowances current at the time of your visit. There is no restriction on the import or export of currency.

Currency

The currency of the land is the Guilder (Gulden), alternatively known as the Florin, and always abbreviated as Fl or F. It is divided into 100 cents. Approximate exchange rates, which should be used as a guide only, are:

$$
\begin{array}{lll}
A\$ & = & 1.35Fl \\
Can\$ & = & 1.60Fl \\
NZ\$ & = & 1.09Fl \\
S\$ & = & 1.40sFl \\
UK£ & = & 3.58Fl \\
US\$ & = & 2.36Fl \\
Euro & = & 2.20Fl
\end{array}
$$

Notes are in denominations of 1000, 100, 50, 25, 10 and 5 Guilders, and coins are 2 1/2 and 1 Guilder, 25, 10 and 5 cents.

Banks and Post Offices are normally ☺open Mon-Fri 9am-5pm, although some larger post offices also open on Saturday morning.

Most *shops* are ☺open Mon-Fri 9am-6pm, Sat 9am-5pm. Late night shopping until 9pm is either Thurs or Fri depending on the city.

Credit cards are widely accepted in the cities.

Telephone

International direct dialling is available and the International code is 89, the Country code 31. It is expensive to make overseas calls from hotels.

Driving

The Netherlands has a well-maintained road system, and the speed limits are:

built-up areas -   50km/h
open road   -   100km/h

Driving is on the right, overtaking on the left, and traffic from the right has right of way.

Miscellaneous

Local time is GMT + I (Central European Time), and clocks are put forward one hour in summer.

Electricity supply is 220v AC with round 2-pin plugs.

Health - The Netherlands has a very good health system but it is very expensive for visitors who are not citizens of the European Community (EC).

Amsterdam

Amsterdam, known as the 'Venice of the North', is situated on the River Amstel, and is named after the dam that was built across the mouth of the river in the 13th century. Two series of canals form islands on which the city centre is built, but it appears that the canals actually run down the middle of tree-lined avenues. It creates a very pretty picture, unless you happen to be in the "red light" district, where the windows of the houses are showcases for young ladies displaying their "wares".

History

The Dutch have always had to wage war, not against would-be conquerors, but against the relentless sea whose levels rose to invade the land. Then they had to contend with trying to stop mighty rivers from flooding rich farmland.

For about a thousand years after Roman rule, they seemed to be fighting a losing battle as the sea level rose, piercing the dune belt and forming the Zuider Zee.

In the Middle Ages the tide began to turn. The sea level began to fall slightly, and the windmill was introduced. With these breaks the northern Dutch could relax a little and turn their attention to international trading. The end result was increased prosperity and the rising importance of Amsterdam.

At this stage, The Netherlands was ruled by Spain, but the wealthy merchants rebelled against the feudal system and the interference of the Church. In 1555, the Revolt of The Netherlands broke out against Philip II, and was successful in the northern provinces. Amsterdam continued to flourish while Antwerp, still ruled by Spain, declined. It was not until 1648 that Spain acknowledged the independence of the Dutch.

The modern kingdom began when William I of Orange-Nassau was crowned in 1815. It was in 1848, during the reign of his son, William II, that the Dutch peacefully gained a democratic constitution. The present monarch is Queen Beatrix.

Tourist Information

Tourist information offices in Holland are known as VVV (pronounced "Fay-Fay-Fay"), a contraction of Vereniging Voor Vreemdelingsverkeer. They can provide information on all local attractions, public transport, and can arrange accommodation.

The Amsterdam Tourist Board (formerly VVV Amsterdam) is at Stationsplein 10, in front of Central Station, ℰ0900 400 4040 (1 Guilder/minute), fax (020) 625 2869.

In major towns you can also look out for the sign "i-Nederland".

Local Transport

Amsterdam has an efficient local transport system, made up of trams, buses, trains and the Metro. For information on all city transport, ℰ(020) 627 2727.

Accommodation

Following is a selection of accommodation with prices for a double room night, which should be used as a guide only. The area code is 020.

The Netherlands

Amstel Botel, Oosterdokskade 2-4, 1011 AE Amsterdam, ©020/ 626 4247, fax 020/639 1952. For something a bit different, try this giant boat house moored a short walk from the Centraal Station. 176 rooms which are modern and offer reasonable comfort in a very central location at good rates for the area - ✪150Fl.

Hotel de Filosoof

Anna van den Vondelstraat 6, 1054 GZ Amsterdam, ©020/683 3013, fax 020/685 3750. The philosophy professor owner wanted to give her hotel a unique character, and that she has certainly done. The hotel is decorated throughout with all manner of object d'art designed to provoke the onlooker with philosophic thoughts. The rooms are small, but comfortable, and the unique ambience and themed rooms are an experience - ✪185Fl.

Toro Hotel, Koningslaan 64, 1075 AG Amsterdam, ©020/673 7223, 020/675 0031. A beautiful late 19th century mansion on the edge of Vondelpark, this 22 room hotel offers a peaceful and classy retreat which is still very close to the action. Rooms are well appointed and those to the rear overlook the park - ✪250Fl.

Piet Hein, Vossiusstraat 52-53, 1071 AK Amsterdam, ©020/662 7205, fax 020//662 1526. A converted mansion opposite Vondelpark in the museum quarter, it is elegant and classy. The 36 rooms are spacious and comfortable. The more expensive front rooms overlook the park and two have beautiful balconies - from ✪135Fl.

Van de Kasteelen, Frans van Mierisstraat 34, ©020/679 8995, fax 020/679 8995. Simple and cheap accommodation. Good for travellers on a budget - ✪110Fls.

Golden Tulip Grand Hotel Krasnapolsky, Warmoesstraat 171, Amsterdam, ©(020) 554 9111, fax 622 8607 (✉travelweb@

hotelbook.com(28583)). Superior first class hotel located on Dam Square opposite the Royal Palace. 138 rooms, restaurant, bar/lounge - ✪405-1000Fl.

Hotel Pulitzer, Prinsengracht 315-331, Amsterdam, ©(020) 523 5235, fax 627 6753. 5-star hotel in 24 seventh century canal houses. 224 rooms, restaurant, lounge/bar - standard room ✪350-580Fl, deluxe room ✪390-695Fl.

Amsterdam Hotel, Damrak 93-94, Amsterdam, ©(020) 555 0666, fax 620 4716 (✎travelweb@hotelbook.com(20410). Situated in the heart of business and entertainment centre, opposite De Bijenkorf department store. 80 rooms, restaurant, coffee shop, bar/lounge - ✪240-350Fl.

Mercure Amsterdam Airport, Oude Haagseweg, Amsterdam, ©(020) 617 9005, fax 615 9027 (✎travelweb@hotelbook.com(09189)). Superior first class hotel with 151 rooms, a restaurant and bar/lounge - ✪200-465Fl.

AMS Hotel Holland, 162 PC Hooftstraat, Amsterdam, ©(020) 676 4253, fax 676 5956 (✎info@ams.nl). Within walking distance of Vondel Park and historical city centre. Has 62 rooms and facilities including breakfast room and bar/lounge - ✪140-200Fl.

Best Western AMS Hotel Beethoven, Beethovenstraat 43, Amsterdam, ©(020) 664 4816, fax 662 1240 (✎beethoven@ bestwestern.nl). 4-star hotel 10 minutes by tram from city centre. 55 rooms, restaurant, bar/lounge - ✪190-290Fl.

Food and Drink

Dutch food is normally of a very high standard, and restaurant prices are not quite as high as in other European countries.

Many restaurants are members of the "tourist menu" plan - a three course set menu, organised individually by each place, for a reasonable price. Look for a blue sign outside the cafe.

Another chain of restaurants that is worth trying is **Neerlands Dis**. Members of this display a sign with a red, white and blue soup tureen, and they serve traditional Dutch cuisine.

Dutch soup is in a class of its own, and is highly recommended.

A sign outside an establishment with the word 'Pannekoekhuis' means that they specialise in pancakes, both sweet and savoury. These are usually a meal in themselves, and are delicious.

There are many Chinese and Indonesian restaurants in Amsterdam, but they are not only for the locals. Indonesia, having been a colony of the Netherlands, has certainly had a culinary influence.

Shopping

The shopping streets, many of them pedestrian traffic only, begin at Dom Square. The Magna Plaza is a super deluxe department store housed in the former GPO in Dom Square. It offers a wide range of shops under one roof. The shopping streets, many of them pedestrian traffic only, begin at the Square, and one of the busiest is Nieuwendijk. Anything you wish to buy, from cheap, tacky souvenirs to works of art can be found in this area.

Sightseeing

A good place to begin a walking tour of Amsterdam is at the Central Station.

Walk straight ahead along the Damrak to **Dam Square**, where there are always plenty of people standing around the War Memorial in the centre. Some are obviously waiting for other people to meet them, others look as if they are trying to work out where they are, and this loitering is possibly the result of Holland's relaxed drug laws. It all looks very peaceful, but beware of pickpockets.

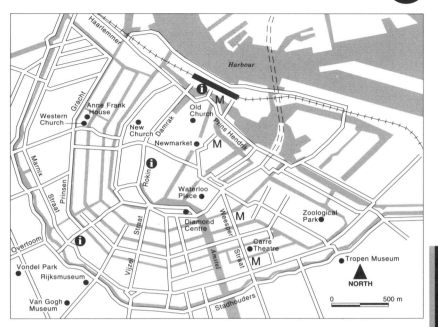

On one side of the Dam is the **Royal Palace**, which was built in the 17th century as a town hall. It is ☉open to the public during Easter, and the summer and autumn school holidays, Mon-Sat 12.30-4pm.

Nearby is the **Nieuwe Kerk** (church) which has been the venue for coronations since 1815, and further on are the tear-drop shaped towers of the **Old Post Office**, which now houses a department store.

At Dam 12 is **Madame Tussaud's**, ✆(020) 622 9949. It is ☉open daily 10am-5.30pm (July-August 9.30am-7.30pm and admission is ✪18.50Fl adult, 15Fl child up to 14 years.

From the Dam take Kalverstraat, a pedestrian shopping street, and at no. 92 there is a narrow alley leading to a beautiful 16th century

The Netherlands

arched gateway with the city coat of arms. This is the entry to the **Amsterdam Historical Museum**, which is ☉open Mon-Fri 10am-5pm, Sat-Sun 11am-5pm, and has a very good restaurant. Almost opposite the restaurant is the **Schuttersgalerij** (Shooters' Gallery), with large paintings of 17th century crack shots, and that leads to a beautiful, secluded area with gardens surrounded by 14th and 15th century houses that have been restored and are occupied. For hundreds of years from 1346 this was a home for Lay Sisters, called the Begijnhof. There is a 17th century Presbyterian church at the far end, a tiny Roman Catholic church, and the oldest surviving house in Amsterdam, built of wood and dating back to 1475.

An exit from the Begijnhof leads to a street simply called Spui, then take Kalverstraat to Muntplain, then take Vijzelstraat, or catch bus 49, to Stadhouderskade then turn right (or stay on the bus) and continue on to the famous **Rijksmuseum**, ✆(020) 673 2121, fax 679 8146, which is ☉open daily 10am-5pm. A world-renowned gallery, maybe not equal to the Prado in Madrid or the Louvre in Paris, but nevertheless not to be missed. As would be expected there is a very good collection of the works of Rembrandt, including the famous *The Night Watch*, but there is much more to see and it is advisable to pick up a guide to the gallery and allow yourself plenty of time.

From the rear of the Rijksmuseum, walk along Museumstraat, turn right into Honthorststraat, then left into Paulus Potterstraat and at no. 7 is the **Rijksmuseum Van Gogh**. This gallery not only has an outstanding collection of Van Gogh's paintings and drawings, it also has his personal collection of works by contemporary artists. It is ☉open Tues-Sat 10am-5pm, Sun and public holidays 1-5pm, and again you should allow plenty of time to study and appreciate the collection.

In the same street, at no. 13, is the **Stedelijk** (Municipal Museum), which is ☉open daily 11am-5pm, and has mostly modern art. Nearby is the **Concertgebouw**, well-known by music lovers. From the concert hall the return trip to the station can be made by tram or bus, or by boat along the canal.

The attractions below do not fit so easily into a walking tour, but the use of public transport will make them easily accessible.

Anne Frank's House, Prinsengracht 263, ✆(020) 556 7100, is to the west of Dam Square. The building is maintained by the Anne Frank Foundation and is ☉open daily 9am-5pm, (April 1-Sept 1 9am-9pm). For those of us who are old enough to have read the book and seen the movie, this is a very moving museum, those who are younger should visit to learn and remember.

Rembrandt House is to the south-east of Dam Square, on Jodenbreestraat 4-6, near Waterlooplein. The artist lived here for 20 years and there is a collection of his drawings and etchings. ☉Open Mon-Sat 10am-5pm, Sun 1-5pm, ✆(020) 624 9486.

A few streets away, in J.D. Meyeplain, is the **Jewish Historical Museum** housed in a restored 17th century synagogue. It is ☉open daily 11am-5pm, ℰ(020) 626 9945.

The international airport is at **Schipol**, about 16km from the city centre, and just south of that is the town of **Aalsmeer**, the centre of the flower-growing industry. This is where the famous flower auctions take place ☉daily 7.30-11am, and visitors are welcome.

There are two things left to organise, and Amsterdam is famous for both.

The first thing is a trip on the **canals**. These can be organised through any VVV or information centre.

The second is a visit to a **diamond cutting centre**, many of which have tours (although none of them give away free samples). Here are a few:

Amsterdam Diamond Centre, Rokin 1 - ☉open daily except Thurs 10am-5.30pm, Thurs 10am-6pm, 7-8.30pm.

Coster Diamonds, Paulus Potterstraat 2-4 - ☉open daily 9am-5pm.

A. van Moppes and Zoon (Diamond Centre), Albert Cuypstraat 2-6 - ☉open daily 9am-5pm.

The Best of Amsterdam in Brief

Rijksmuseum. The largest collection of works by accomplished Dutch painters such as Rebrandt, Rubens and Angelico, in this 200-room museum. There are other items of interest reflecting different cultures around the world. *Stadhouderskade 42.*

Anne Frank House (Anne Frankhuis). Contains documents and records tracing the story of the Anne Frank and her family, who cowered in this house for 2 years during the Nazi occupation. It has been kept exactly the same way since this time and as such is a moving experience for its many visitors. *Prinsengracht 263*.

Van Gogh Museum. Those interested in Van Gogh's work can visit no better place for an insight into the artist's career. This museum displays the collection owned by Van Gogh's brother, which consists of about 200 paintings by Vincent and also some by his predecessors and contemporaries to illustrate his influences. *Paulis Potterstraat 7-11*.

Amsterdam Historical Museum (Amsterdams Historisch Museum). A painstaking journey through practically every element of Amsterdam's fascinating history and rich culture since is humble beginnings. *Kalverstraat 92*.

Stedelijk Museum of Modern Art. A few names which might spark your interest in this popular museum are Warhol, Picasso, Monet, Cezzane, van Gogh and Renoir. *Paulus Potterstraat 13*.

Dutch Theatre (Hollandsche Schouwburg). Linked to the Nazi deportation of Jews in this area, the Dutch Theatre now acts as a memorial to the thousands and thousands of deaths which ensued as part of the Holocaust. *Plantage Middenlaan 24*.

Tropenmuseum (Tropical Museum). Dedicated to the culture and plight of the Third World and attempts, quite successfully, to duplicate the appearance and lifestyle of selected tropical areas using large models. If you happen to be visiting Amsertdam in the cold month of January, escaping into this museum might temporarily fool your mind into believing you're in a warmer place. *Linnaeusstraat 2*.

Dam Square. Amsterdam's hub, with a number of attractions and a general atmosphere of lively activity.

Canal Boat Cruise. There are many tours providing this popular service, which is a good way to see some of the city's architecture without relying on your feet.

Rembrandt's House (Museum Het Rembrandthuis). A faithfully-recreated snapshot of Rembrandt's house as it would have looked to the famous artist when he was in residence there, replete with old wall-mounted sketches. *Joldenbreestraat 4-6*.

Royal Palace (Koninklijk Paleis). Built at the peak of the city's wealth during the seventeenth century, the interior of this palace is lavish and worth a look, though access is only granted during the summer. *Dam Square*.

Westerkerk. The highlight of this church is not the resting place of Rembrandt but the view from the steeple.

Begijnhof. A little gem of Amsterdam's past is trapped here in a quaint courtyard. Some of the archiecture stretches back five centuries. *Begijnensteeg Lane*.

Waterlooplein Flea Market. Since its inception over a century ago, merchants have plied their diverse wares every day in Amsterdam's busiest market. *Waterlooplein*.

Dutch Resistance Museum (Verzetsmuseum). Recounts some daring and cunning exploits of the Dutch during the Nazi occupation using primary memorabilia to explain the story. *Plantage Kerklaan 61*.

Jewish History Museum (Joods Historisch Museum). Provides a very good history of Jewish religion and culture in the city. Jonas Daniel *Meijerplein 2-4*.

Herengracht Canal Mansion. The pause button has been hit here on Amsterdam in the seventeenth century. Contains a museum focusing on this rich era. *Herengracht 605*.

Maritime Museum (Scheepvaartmuseum). With an enormous collection of vessels, this musem pays tribute to Amsterdam's port history and its close affiliation with the sea. There are full models and other shipping bits and pieces. The Maritime Museum gets mixed reactions, so unless you have a firm appreciation and interest in nautical history, there may be better places for you to spend your limited time in this city. *Kattenburerplein 1*.

Artis Zoo. A old and large zoo with many exhibits and thousands of animals. *Plantage Kerklaan 38-40*.

Driving Through Netherlands

The West Country

Itinerary - 3 Days - Distance 28kms

From Amsterdam, drive west to the coast and **Harlem**, with buildings dating from the 17th century. Driving down the coast you reach the **Keukenhof**, the largest flower garden in the world. (This is open from April - mid May).

From here, head towards **Leiden**, an ancient university town, with much to see and do. Further south you reach **The Hague**, the seat of government, and the home of the Queen. **Delft**, nearby is famous for its porcelain, as well as being very picturesque. **Rotterdam** is the largest port in the world. You can take a cruise through the harbour area, as well as visit museums, shop and wander through the old city. From Rotterdam drive out to the delta. **Haringvlietdam** has the first dam in the Delta works, while at **Stellendam** you can visit a display of the area prior to the flood protection scheme. **Neeltje Jans** has an exhibition explaining the Delta Works. Head down the coast to **Veere** and **Middelburg**, historic towns with old buildings.

North Holland

Itinerary - 3 Days - Distance 363kms

Amsterdam, the capital of The Netherlands, is a busy city with its canal systems, unique buildings and many galleries and museums. From Amsterdam, drive towards **Marken**. This is a traditional village joined to the mainland by a dyke. Head north to **Volendam** and **Edam**. Volendam is a fishing village built on piles to combat floods, while Edam is well known for its cheese. There is a museum dedicated to cheese making here. **Hoorn**, nearby, has a town in minature showing the way of life in the 17th century.

At **Enkhuizen** you can see an outdoor museum village, which shows the way of life in flood prone areas. Drive to the coast to **Den Oever**. Here you cross the dyke built to control the inland waterways. Across the dyke is **Harlingen**, parts of which have been restored. Make your way through **Bolswood** to **Sneek**. These are picturesque towns built on the canal system. From here, head south to **Zwolle**. Zwolle is an old town dating from the 13th century, with interesting buildings.

Further south again you reach **Apeldoorn**, which has a restored palace open for visitors. **Arnhem**, the last stop, was the scene of a famous battle in World War II, and has a commemorative museum.

Portugal

PORTUGAL HAS A MAINLAND AREA of 89,000 sq km, and is bordered by Spain to the north and east, and the Atlantic to the west and south. By land it is necessary to travel through Spain to get to the rest of Europe, and this has made Portugal seem quite remote from the rest of the continent. An example of this is that Portugal remained neutral during World War II.

The population of mainland Portugal is 10,800,000, almost 2,000,000 of whom live in Lisbon, the capital. The language of the people is Portuguese, but people in the hospitality industry speak English.

Climate

January averages in Lisbon are 8-15C, and those in June are 10-25C. July and August are the main tourist months, and the average highs are around 28C, which is a bit warm for serious sightseeing. June and

September are probably the best months to visit, although the days in September can have up to four hours less sunshine than June days.

Spires of Jeronimos Monastery, Lisbon

Entry Regulations

Visitors must have a valid passport and on-going travel documents for a stay of up to three months. Visas are not necessary, but it is best to check with your travel agent when making your reservations.

The duty free allowance is 200 cigarettes or 100 cigarillos or 50 cigars or 250gm of tobacco, 1 litre of spirits and 2 litres of wine. There is no restriction on the import or export of foreign or local currencies.

No vaccinations are required by any international traveller.

Currency

The local currency is the Escudo (ESC). Approximate exchange rates, which should be used as a guide only, are:

A$	=	125.81ESC
Can$	=	145.78ESC
NZ$	=	99.41ESC
S$	=	122.79ESC
UK£	=	325.57ESC
US$	=	214.52ESC
EUR	=	200.48ESC

Banks are ☺open Mon-Fri 8.30am-3pm.

Shops are usually ☺open Mon-Fri 9am-1pm and 3-7pm, although those in the tourist areas will often be open longer. Most shops are only open in the morning on Saturdays, and are closed on Sundays.

Portugal

Telephone

International direct dialling is available, and the country code is 351, the access code 00. Coin operated public phones are easily found in Lisbon. The number for emergencies is ⓒ115.

All phone numbers have nine digits and no area codes.

Driving

Driving in Portugal is on the right hand side of the road, and speed limits are:

built-up areas   -50kph
outside built-up areas -80kph

Theft from cars is very common, so if you are driving a hatchback, remove the cover so that everyone can see that you have left nothing to steal. Otherwise hopeful crims will break the rear window.

Miscellaneous

Local time is GMT + 1, but Portugal does not have daylight saving, so from April to October it is one hour behind the rest of continental Europe, and the same as Great Britain.

Electricity is 220 volts AC. It is advisable to carry an adaptor for your appliances.

Health - It is advisable to have private medical insurance, especially if you are travelling from a country that is outside the European Union.

Tipping - The tip is included in the every bill, be it from a hotel, restaurant or taxi, but an extra 5-10% is always appreciated, if it has been earned.

Lisbon

Home to almost 2 million people, Lisbon is situated at the mouth of the Tagus River, and hosted EXPO '98.

Most visitors spend their time in the three neighbourhoods that line the harbour front: Baixa, the Bairro Alto, and the medieval Alfama, which has the castle on a hill to the east.

Although the unification of Europe is bringing with it changes to Portugal, Lisbon still has a lot to offer the visitor, and at prices that will come as a nice surprise after other places on the Continent.

History

Lisbon is older than any other western European capital. As far back as the 12th century BC, Phoenician sailors, attracted by the protected harbour, built the first settlement on top of Sao Jorge, and called their town Alis Ubbo (Serene Harbour), from which the present name originates.

After the Second Punic War in 201BC, the victorious Romans established Lisbon as the capital of their province of Lusitania. The Romans were followed by various Germanic tribes, then came the Moors, who conquered Lisbon in 714 and held it until the early 12th century.

Afonso Henriques, the first king of Portugal was determined to recapture Lisbon, and in 1147, when the city was the second largest in western Europe, he laid siege along with knights who were returning from the Second Holy Land Crusade. After four months, the starving

Moors called for a truce, which Henriques accepted, but overran the city when the guards were removed. Lisbon became Portugal's capital a century later under the rule of King Afonso III.

During the 16th century a period of great wealth for the Portuguese began. Vasco da Gama had sailed to India in 1497, and had given Portugal a monopoly on eastern spices. For the next two centuries, Lisbon had greater revenues than any other city in Europe.

Then Nature struck. In 1531 and 1597, severe tremors shook Lisbon, and on November 1, 1755 the worst earthquake to hit a European city occurred. From a population of 270,000, 30,000 were killed in a few hours. The buildings that remained were torn down, and the first urban renewal in Europe began. Prime Minister Marques de Pombal had the new city planned within weeks of the earthquake, with wide boulevards and squares.

The twentieth century has not been without its trauma. In 1908, both the king and his heir were murdered, and two years later, the monarchy was over. The city was the scene of revolts and much violence until the establishment in 1933 of the Salazar regime. There followed a long period of dictatorship until the Flower Revolution of 1974. The first act of the new government was to give independence to the Portuguese colonies of Angola, Mozambique, Guinea and Cape Verde, which had as much impact on Lisbon as the 1755 earthquake. East Timor was simply abandoned. The country was forced to accept the return of 750,000 of its nationals, and the population swelled by ten percent in a matter of months. Despite this influx, Lisbon is still the smallest capital in western Europe.

Tourist Information

The Tourist Information Office, Palazio Foz, Praca dos Restauradores, is ☉open Mon-Sat 9am-8pm, Sun 10am-6pm, ✆21 346 3314.

There is also an information office at the Portela de Sacavem Airport, near the exit.

Portugal

Local Transport

The Metro is easy to use and is the best way to go to the Gulbenkian Museum, the fairgrounds, bullfights, the Colombo Mall and the Expo Site.

Other means of transport are Trolleys, Buses and Elevadores (which can either be lifts or funiculars). There are four Elevadores:

The *Elevador de Santa Justa* links Rua de Santa Justa to Largo do Carmo - ☉every day 7am-11.45pm.

The *Elevador da Gloria* (funicular) links Praca dos Restauradores to the Miradouro de Sao Pedro de Alcantara - ☉every day 7am-12.55am.

The *Elevador da Lavra* (funicular) links Largo de Anunciacao to Rua Camara Pestana - ☉Mon-Sat 7am-10.45pm, Sun 9am-10.45pm.

The *Elevador da Bica* (funicular) links Rua da Sao Paulo to Largo Calhariz - ☉Mon-Sat 7am-10.45pm, Sun 9am-10.45pm.

If you are going to be in Lisbon for an extended period you might be interested in purchasing the **Lisbon Card**. It offers unrestricted access to all public transport (Carris) and entry to 26 museums, monuments, etc. It is available at several points in the city, ✆21 361 0350, fax 21 361 0359, and costs are:

24 Hour Card - ○adult 1900ESC, child (5-11) 750 ESC

48 Hour Card - ○adult 3100ESC, child 1100 ESC

72 Hour Card - ○adult 4000ESC, child 1550 ESC

Accommodation

Following is a selection of accommodation with prices for a double room per night with an ensuite, which should be used as a guide only. Credit cards are accepted, and both heating and air-conditioning are part of the scene.

Novotel Lisboa, Avenida Joe Malhoa, Lote 1642, 1099-051 Lisboa, ✆21-724 4800, fax 21-724 4801, email ✒H0784@accor-hotel.com. 246 rooms, bar, restaurant, 2 swimming pools, not exactly in the city centre. A mammoth building. Just a place to sleep is basically what you are getting here - very little charm. Metro: Linha de Gaivota (Blue), Pontin la-Baixa Chiado - ✪13800ESC.

Ibis Hotel, Lisboa-Centro, next to the Novotel Lisboa, Avenida Joe Malhoa, ✆21-727 3181, fax 21-727 3287. Over 200 rooms. A large hotel that gives you a bed and is next to the Metro, like the Novotel - ✪10,500ESC.

Sofitel Lisboa, Avenida de Libertade 127, 1269-038 Lisboa, ✆21-322 8300, fax 21-322 8310, email ✎ sofitel-lisboa@mail.telepac.pt. 170 rooms, bar, restaurant, valet parking. Located on the main Avenida in Lisboa that on the outside has a Portuguese colonial feel but inside is a sleek modern hotel. Old world charm is absent here - ✪41,000ESC.

Hotel Lisboa Plaza

Avenida Travessa do Salitre 7, 1250 Lisboa, ✆21-346 3922, fax 21-347 1630, email ✎ plaza.hotels @mail. telepac.pt. Restaurant, bar, valet parking. A delightful, smallish 4 star hotel just off the Avenida da Libertade. The concierge will give you directions to the Metro nearby - ✪34,000ESC.

Florescente, Portas de So Anto 99, 1100 Lisboa, ✆21-342 6609, fax 21-21 342 7733. 60 units with ensuite. No lift but rooms are clean though a little small. Situated in a busy area where restaurants and coffee shops abound. In essence it encourages you to get out and about. Staff are pleasant - ✪9,000ESC.

Residencial Geris, Calcade do Garcia 6, 1150 Lisboa, ✆21-881 0497, fax 21-999 2006. 16 rooms. Clean rooms with some old quaint touches. No lift. A good deasl for the price which includes breakfast - ✪16,000ESC.

Portugal

Tivoli Hotel, Avenida Da Liberdade 185, Lisbon, ©21 319 8900, fax 21 319 8950 (✔travelweb@hotelbook.com(00531)). A deluxe hotel in the city centre with 327 rooms, three bars and two restaurants - ✪29,500-49,000ESC.

Lisboa Hotel, Rua Barata Salgueiro 5, Lisbon, ©21 355 4131, fax 21 355 4139 (✔travelweb@hotelbook.com(17942)). Only 150m from Rossio Square. Has 61 rooms and the Oasis Piano Bar for snacks - ✪20,000-25,000ESC.

Madrid Hotel, Rua Do Conde De Redondo 24, Lisbon, ©21 319 1760, fax 21 315 7575 (✔travelweb@hotelbook.com(28510)). Situated in the heart of the city. 86 rooms, restaurant, bar/lounge - ✪17,000-30,000ESC.

Lutecia Hotel, Avenida Frei Miguel Contreiras 52, Lisbon, ©21 840 3121, fax 21 840 7818 (✔travelweb@hotelbook.com(19507)). Situated 3km from Lisbon Airport. 151 rooms with facilities including a restaurant, 2 bars, and a cinema and theatre in the building - ✪12,000-24,000ESC.

Capitol Hotel, Rua Ecq De Queiroz 24, Lisbon, ©21 353 6811, fax 21 352 6165 (✔travelweb@hotelbook.com(21410)). Situated in a quiet side street off the city centre, a short walk to the Marques Pombal Square Park. 57 rooms, restaurant, bar, coffee shop - ✪11,000-23,000ESC.

Executive Inn Hotel, Avenida Conde Valbom 56-62, Lisbon, ©21 795 1157, fax 21 795 1166 (✔travelweb@hotelbook.com(25624)). A first class hotel in the New Quarters. Half a kilometre from Rossio Train Station. 72 rooms, restaurant, bar - ✪9000-20,000ESC.

Food and Drink

Although there are hundreds of restaurants in Lisbon, there is not a great deal of variety in the menus. Don't except to be able to pop down to the corner Chinese caff.

There are a couple of things to watch out for when dining in a Portuguese restaurant. One is that it is quite common for unordered appetizers to be served at the beginning of a meal, but bear in mind that these are not free, and will be added to your bill. The other is that the prices on your bill might vary from those on the menu. The reason is that the menu prices are for meals served in the dining room (*salao*), but if you are seated on the *esplanada* or *balcao* (terrace), the meals will be more expensive.

A good thing to watch out for is that some restaurants offer half-serves for about a third less than a full serve. As meals are usually on the large side, half-serves are enough for most people.

Following is a selection of restaurants, with approximate prices for a three course meal, excluding drinks.

Adega do Ribatejo, Rua Diario de Noticias 23, Bairro Alto, Lisbon, ©21 346 8343 (2500-4000ESC). This tavern offers reasonably good food from a changing menu. Professional singers entertain with very loud traditional songs, but even so, you have to get there before 8pm or join the queue. It is ☺open for lunch and dinner Mon-Sat and there is a minimum charge of ✪2000ESC.

Alcantara Cafe, Rua Maria Luisa Honstein 15, Alcantara, Lisbon, ©21 363 7176 (✪4000-65000ESC). Set outside the city centre near 25 of April Bridge, the cafe offers excellent seafood and a large wine list. The kitchen stays ☺open until 1am, and drinks are served until 2am - open daily for dinner only.

Bonjardim, Travessa de S. Antao 11, Baixa, Lisbon, ©21 342 4389 (✪2500-4000ESC). Found in an alley between Praca des Restauradores and Rue Portas de Santo Antao. It is known locally as *Rei dos Frangos* (King of Chickens), which will give you some idea of the specialty. Gets very crowded at peak time (☺8-10pm).

Casa Faz Frio, Rua de Dom Pedro V 96-98, Bairro Alto, Lisbon, ©21 346 1860 (✪under 2000ESC). An old wine cellar that has been refurbished now offers a changing menu of traditional Portuguese dishes. This is worth trying, but they do not take credit cards.

Gambrinus, Rua Portas de S. Antao 23-25, Baixa, Lisbon, ©21 346 8974 (❂4000-6500ESC). This restaurant has been operating for 70 years, so they must be getting something right. The specialty is seafood, but there are some meat dishes.

Tavares Rico, Rua Misericordia 35-37, Chiado, Lisbon, ©21 342 1112 (❂4000-6500ESC). It has a French-inspired menu, but with enough Portuguese dishes to stop the guilts. Food is great, but it is ☉closed on Saturday and lunch Sunday. Jackets and ties are necessary for the gentlemen.

Shopping

Lisbon is not the place to shop for a stylish new outfit, but it is good for silver and gold jewellery and handicrafts, particularly carpets and needlework from the Azores and Madeira. Probably the best places to look for needlework are **Madeira House** in the Baixa, and **Principe Real** in the Barrio Alto.

Most of the antique stores are found along Rua Dom Pedro V and its continuation Rua da Escola Politecnica in the Bairro Alto.

Lisbon's biggest shopping mall, **Amoreiras**, has almost 250 stores, a supermarket, 10 cinemas, a chapel and 50 restaurants.

Lisbon flea market, the **Feira da Ladra**, is held Tuesday and Saturday from early morning until sunset. The open-air stalls fill the Campo de Santa Clara, three blocks east of Sao Jorge's Castle. Trolly no. 28 and bus no. 12 will get you there. Practise your bargaining skills beforehand.

Portugal

Sightseeing

The Baixa Tour

The tour begins in the middle of the city at the **Rossio**, which is also known as Praca de Dom Pedro IV, after the first king of Brazil whose statue is in the centre of the square. Rossio was designed by the aforementioned Marques de Pombal, and is filled with stores, banks, cafes and hotels. It is a very busy place, with people continually coming and going, and it has some very pretty Art Nouveau buildings for you to inspect. One of these, the **Cinematografo**, we suggest you only appreciate from the outside because it is a pornographic theatre.

The neoclassical **Teatro Nacional Dona Maria II** (✆347 2246 for current program) is on the north side of the square. It was built in the first half of the 19th century and has a statue of Gil Vincente, the father of Portuguese theatre, at the top of the pediment.

To the left of the Teatro is the **Estacao do Rossio**, which you could be forgiven for thinking is a palace. It is actually a train station that was built in 1887 in neo-Manueline style. On its other side is the **Praca da Figueira**, another lively square with its share of outdoor cafes that offer good views of the castle. The statue in the centre is of King Joao I, the founder of Portugal's second dynasty, the Aviz line.

Next we come to the **Baixa** (lower town), which is between the Rossio and the Praca do Comercio, and is a shopper's paradise with several pedestrian streets. Before you start serious shopping, walk to Rua de Santa Justa to see the **Elevador de Santa Justa**, a vertical elevator that offers easy access to the Largo do Carmo. The trip only takes a few minutes and costs ✪150ESC, but it offers great views of the city and the river.

The **Praca do Comercio** is another pretty square, where many historic events have occurred. The statue in the centre of this square is of Dom Jose I, who was ruling when the buildings were reconstructed by the Marques de Pombal.

Alfama Tour

The Alfama was one of the few parts of Lisbon that survived the 1755 earthquake, so is presented in all its Olde Worlde glory of winding cobbled streets. To start this tour it is best to get bus no. 37 from Praca Figueira to the Castle, and walk down to the Alfama.

Castle Sao Jorge is the birthplace of the city and it is ⏲open daily until sunset with no entry fee. Inside the castle is a multimedia video presentation called the *Olisiponia*, which offers an overview of Lisbon's history in English for ✪600ESC, ⏲daily 10am-5.30pm.

After exploring the castle, which won't take long, walk to **Largo Santa Luzia** and the Miradouro de Santa Luzia, a terrace from which there are panoramic views. You might want to stop for a coffee at the *Cerca Moura* bar/cafe, or visit the **Museum of Decorative Arts** next door, although the museum gives all the information only in Portuguese. From near here stairs lead down into the Alfama.

The Chiado and Bairro Alto Tour

The tour begins on the Rua do Carmo, which was home to the most elegant shops in the city before all the buildings were destroyed in a fire in August 1988. Many have been reconstructed, and have retained the spirit of the district. Turn right onto Calcada do Sacremento and you will come to **Largo do Carmo**, a square that has the ruins of the **Convento do Carmo**. You can wander through the earthquake-ruined Gothic arches at will, but it will cost ✪300ESC to visit the museum, which is ⏲open Mon-Sat 10am-5.30pm, ✆346 0473.

Return to Rua Garrett and walk along it to **Largo do Chiado**, the best-known square in the area, stopping at a few of the interesting little shops along the way. The square is home to the well-known cafe *A Brasileira*, which doesn't quite live up to its reputation, or maybe the service was better when it was the haunt of the literary crowd. On the patio there is a statue of Fernando Pessoa, and that of Antonio Ribeiro stands in the middle of the square.

The square also has two churches, **Nossa Senhora de l'Encarnacao** and the Italian community's **Nossa Senhora do Loreto**.

In nearby **Praca Luis de Camoes**, there is a statue of Portugal's most celebrated poet, Luis de Camoes. You can also get a good view from here of the two churches at Largo do Chiado. Walk down Rua Serpa Pinto and see the **Teatro Nacional de Sao Carlos** (program ✆346 8408, tickets ✆346 5914), an Italian-style building whose interior was modelled on La Scala in Milan.

Also in Rua Serpa Pinto is the **Galeria Nacional do Chiado**, which has displays of paintings and sculptures by major Portuguese artists like Columbano, Silvo Porto, Joao Voz, and others. But don't be misled by the name of the gallery, it is really devoted to works from the 19th and early 20th centuries. It is ☉open Tues 2-6pm, Wed-Sun 10am-6pm, and entry is ✪400ESC.

In the 16th and 17th centuries the **Bairro Alto** consisted of palatial residences and small public parks and squares. Later these were replaced by working-class houses and shops, and the area became the 'red light district'. It is currently undergoing another metamorphosis as a boutique and family restaurant area.

At the edge of the Chiado is the **Igreja Sao Roque**, which was built by the Jesuits in the 16th century, partially destroyed in the 1755 earthquake, and reconstructed soon after. It doesn't look much on the outside, but inside it is one of the most richly decorated churches in Lisbon. The **Chapel de Sao Joao Baptista** (from the chancel it is the first chapel on the left) is a sight to behold. It was constructed in Rome and transported piece by piece by boat. A mixture of metals and gems it is a wonderful example of Italian baroque art. Adjoining the church is the **Museu de Arte Sacra de Sae Roque**, which has an interesting collection of sacred objects. It is ☉open Tues-Sun 10am-5pm, and entry is ✪150ESC, except on Sunday when it is free, ©346 03 61.

On Rua de Sao Pedro de Alcantara, there is a lookout and garden called the **Miradouro de Sao Pedro de Alcantara**. From here there is a good view of downtown Lisbon with the Tagus in the distance.

Returning along Rua de Sao Pedro de Alcantara towards Rua da Escola Politecnica takes you to **Praca do Principa Real**, a pretty square with a park that is a great place to have a rest, or perhaps you would rather visit the *Cafe o Paco do Principe* for a bite to eat.

Further along the street is the **Jardim Botanico**, which is ☉open Mon-Fri 9am-6pm, Sat-Sun 10am-6pm (summer until 8pm), and entry is ✪200ESC. The garden is quite high and offers good views of the city. Near here is the **Museu de Ciencia**, which is really only for those with a particular interest in science and who can speak Portuguese, as all the exhibits have text in that language only.

The remaining attractions in Lisbon don't fit well into walking tours, so perhaps you might consider taking a hop on/hop off double-decker Tagus Tour which costs ✪2000ESC and operates ☉hourly from 11am May-September.

Gulbenkian Museum

Situated in the north of Lisbon at Avenida de Berna 45, this is the best of the city's museums and should not be missed. Calouste Sarkis Gulbenkian was an Armenian businessman who made his fortune in the oil industry. During World War II Portugal granted him asylum, and in gratitude he left the city of Lisbon his art collection, which spans 2000 years. It is impossible to exaggerate how priceless this collection is, so make sure you allow enough time to take in as much as possible. The exhibits are arranged chronologically, from ancient Egyptian right up to Art Nouveau, and include masterpieces by artists such as Rembrandt and Renoir, and a collection of jewellery designed by Rene Lalique. The museum is ☺open Tues 2-6pm, Wed-Sun 10am-6pm (closed Monday) and entry is ✆500ESC, free on Sundays.

Se Patriarcal (Cathedral)

Built around 1147, this is one of the oldest monuments in Lisbon. Of course, it has been damaged by several earthquakes and has undergone many modifications, but its exterior remains an excellent example of Romanesque architecture. In short, it looks like a fortress.

Buried in the church is St Anthony, the patron saint of Portugal, whose remains were brought here in the 12th century. The cathedral is a few blocks east of Praca do Comercio.

Expo 98

Lisbon hosted Expo 98 during the 500th anniversary of Vasco da Gama's voyage to India. The riverside Expo grounds are east of the Santa Apolonia train station in an area of luxury housing and restaurants. To visit Europe's largest aquarium, take the Metro to the last stop (Oriente) and join the riverside promenade.

Vasco da Gama Bridge

Erected to connect the Expo grounds with the south side of the Tagus, this bridge was opened in 1998. At 14km it is the second-longest bridge in Europe.

25th of April Bridge

Built in 1966, this is one of the longest suspension bridges in the world at one mile. It was originally named after the dictator Salazar, but the name was changed to recognise the revolution of 1974. The bridge was modelled on the Golden Gate Bridge in San Francisco, and was built by the same company.

Cristo Rei

Across the Tagus River from Lisbon there is a huge statue of Christ, with outstretched arms, seemingly blessing the city. It was built by the generosity of grateful Lisboetas who wanted to thank God for keeping their country out of World War II.

To get up close and personal with the statue take a ferry from Praca do Comercio to Cacilhas, then a bus marked 'Cristo Rei'. There is a lift inside the statue, which operates ⊙daily 9am-6pm and costs ✪250ESC. Needless to say there are great views from the top.

Places Further Afield

Beaches closest to Lisbon are at **Cascais** and **Estoril**, which are only 16km to the west, or if you prefer a secluded swim the long beaches of **Setubal** are 88km to the south.

The forest of **Sintra**, with its three fascinating palaces, is 11km inland from the coast, and the train trip takes 45 minutes.

The huge baroque palace complex at **Mafra** is 90 minutes by train from Lisbon, or if you are travelling by car a trip can be combined with a stop at **Queluz** where there is another palace to explore.

The Best of Lisbon in Brief

Alfama. A culturally rich and charming part of Lisbon which through its architecture reminds visitors of its Visigothic roots, Arabic influence and fishing port heritage. Wonderful little details delight walkers at every turn.

National Coach Museum (Museu Nacional dos Coches). This museum is filled with many royal carriages, from rustic examples dating back to the seventeenth century to others bearing exquisite decorations (greater attention was paid to

Portugal

aesthetic appeal than improving suspension). More people pass through the doors of this museum than through any other attraction in the city. *Praca Afonso de Albuquerque.*

Jeronimos Monastery (Monsteiro dos Jeronimos). This huge church, built in 1502, boasts a fine combination of Gothic and Renaissance architecture. The interior and the cloisters are magnificent. A visit here is imperative for visitors to Lisbon. *Praca do Imperio.*

Bairro Alto. Wander past parks and gardens, Sao Roque Church, restaurants and cafes, a good shopping district, and the ruins of Convento do Carmo.

Gulbenkian Museum (Meseu de Fundacao Calouste Gulbenkian). A superb collection which pulls together precious art from the Ancient Civilisations, Europe and Asia over two millenia. It is Lisbon's premier museum in every way and should be on your must-see list. *Av. de Berna 45.*

National Museum of Ancient Art (Museu Nacional de Arte Antiga). The country's best collection of Portugese and European art featuring several drawcards. On show are some pieces by Gonclaves, Bosch, Raphael and more. *Rua das Janelas Verdes 9.*

Sao Roque Church. Inside is the remarkable Chapel of St. John the Baptist, constructed in the Vatican and transported by ship to Lisbon. Its mosaics are designed with amazing attention to detail. *Largo Trindade Coelho.*

Cathedral (Se). Most agree that the interior of this church, consisting of the cloister, sacristy and treasury, is no match for its exterior, which is a daunting combination and Gothic and Romanesque styles. *Largo da Se.*

St George's Castle (Castelo Sao Jorge). Once a fortress of the Visigoths and dating back to the fifth century A.D., this castle endured a tumultuous history of defeat and defence. It is worth a visit to appreciate a leisurely walk through its gardens and the views from its walls. *Rua Costado Castelo.*

Memorial to the Discoveries (Padrao dos Descobrimentos). Magellen and de Gama can be found here among other famous Portugese voyagers and adventurers, carved in stone as part of this large monument by the Tagus River. *Praca de Boa Esperanca.*

25th of April Bridge. This suspension bridge crosses the Tagus and is one of the longest of its kind in the world.

Museum of Decorative Arts (Museo de Artes Decorativas). A chance to peek in at the houses occupied by the upper class and decorated by them in various styles. *Rua Limoeiro*.

Cristo Rei. On the other side of the Targus River is a giant statue of Christ on a vantage point overlooking Lisbon with good views.

National Tile Museum (Museo Nacional do Azulejo). The Portugese use tiles frequently in their art and architecture, producing elegant designs. This museum displays a broad cross section. *Inside the Convento da Madre de Deus, Rua da Madre de deus 4*.

Belem Tower (Torre de Belem). Once an important landmark in Lisbon, this beautiful tower is very photegenic and offers wonderful views from its top level.

Maritime Museum (Museu de Marinha). Those interested in models of old warships and the history of Portugal's exploits on the world's oceans should head down to the Museu de Marinha. *Praca do Imperio*.

Trolley Ride. Take the opportunity to experience a ride on these trolleys. Chances are you will board one built in the early part of the twentieth centry that is still in safe operation.

Bullfight. A Portugese bullfight differs dramatically from the kind you will see in Spain. It is a chance for the bull to get some of its own back, since its group of targets deliberately stand their ground when the animal charges, then attempt to bring it down with their bare hands. An added bonus is that you don't have to watch the bull being killed right before your eyes at the conclusion of the fight.

Driving Through Portugal

A Scenic Tour of Portugal by Road

Itinerary - 8 Days - Distance 820kms

From Spain, cross into Portugal at the south coast, and travel along the coastal road to **Faro**. From here you can enjoy the **Algarve**, with its many fine beaches, hotels and restaurants.

Turn north and head towards **Lisbon**, along the coast, passing towns such as **Odemira** and **Sines**. **Setubal** is well known as a wine producing region. From here drive into Lisbon, the capital with its gracious atmosphere. There is much to see and do in this cosmopolitan city, so allow yourself time to enjoy it.

Head north from Lisbon by the little coast roads to **Sao Martinho Do Porto** and **Nazare**, picturesque seaside towns. At Nazare, make your way inland to **Alocobaca**, with its monastery. Further inland is

Fatima, a place of pilgrimage for people from all over the world. From here, drive northwards to **Leiria**. Around this region are stands of pine forest, and overlooking the town is a medieval castle. North of Leira is **Combra**, a former capital of Portugal. It houses one of the oldest universities in the world.

At the coast west of Coimbra is **Figuera da Foz**, a busy tourist town. Between these two towns you pass through **Montemor-o-Velho**, a medieval town with many historic buildings.

Take the road north from Coimbra, through **Curia** and **Lusa**, (both spa towns) to **Aveiro**. This is another very old town set on a canal system. There are many historic churches to visit, and the beaches and lagoon are ideal for water sports.

A view of the Praca Do square with the Rio Tegu in the background.

Further north, through picturesque little towns, you reach **Porto**, Portugal's second city. Porto again, has many historic buildings and churches, but is probably most famous for its fortified wine industry. The port wine cellars can be found in **Vila Nova de Gaia**, on the south side of the Douro River. Many of the cellars are open for tours. North of Porto along the coast are more beachside resorts, notably **Povoa de Varzim** and **Viana do Castelo**.

Spain

SPAIN IS A CONSTITUTIONAL MONARCHY, with a total area of 504,782 sq km, of which the mainland takes up 492,463 sq km. It has a total coastline of 3144 km. The population is around 39,500,000, and the main cities are Madrid, Barcelona, Valencia, Seville, Malaga and Saragossa. The official language is Castilian (otherwise known as Spanish), which is derived from Latin but includes many Arabic words. Catalan is spoken in the north-east and is more like Provencal. The Basques, who come from the Bay of Biscay area, have a completely different language of unknown origin. As a visitor the majority of people you come into contact with will be able to speak some English.

Climate

Even in summer the north coast is frequently rainy and misty. The central plateau has extremes of temperature from -12C in winter to 35C in summer, and the wettest months are March and April. The

Spain

provinces on the Mediterranean have high humidity in summer, while Andalusia has no real winter except in the very high places.

Entry Regulations

Visitors must have a valid passport, and Australians must have a visa for visits up to 30 days.

People from the UK, the US and New Zealand do not require visas, and other nationalities should enquire at the Spanish Consulate in their home city.

The duty free allowance is 200 cigarettes or 50 cigars or 2500 gm of tobacco; 1 litre of alcoholic beverage (over 22 degree strength) or 2 litres of alcoholic beverages (under 22 degree strength) or 2 litres of wine; 500 gm of perfume.

No vaccinations are required for any international traveller.

Currency

The currency of the land is the Peseta (Ptas). which is divided into 100 centimos. Approximate exchange rates, which should be used as a guide only, are:

A$	=	100.42Ptas
Can$	=	120.98Ptas
NZ$	=	82.50Ptas
S$	=	105.91Ptas
UK£	=	270.20Ptas
US$	=	178.03Ptas
Euro	=	166.39Ptas

Notes are in denominations of 10,000, 5000, 2000 and 1000 Pesetas, and coins are 500, 200, 100, 50, 25, 10, 5 and 1 Pesetas.

Banks are ☼open Mon-Fri 8.30am-2pm, although some big city banks remain open until 4.30pm and also open on Sat 8.30am-1pm. Outside banking hours, money changing facilities will be found at airports, train stations and booths near the main tourist areas.

Post offices are ☼open Mon-Fri 9am-2pm, although again the Head Post Office in each city normally remains open until 8pm.

Shops are normally ☼open Mon-Sat 9am-1pm, 4.30-8pm. Supermarkets are usually closed on Sat afternoon. On fiesta days, which are plentiful,

Plaza de Cibeles, Madrid

Spain

Spain

it is possible that all shops and services will cease to operate, but not in the main cities.

Credit cards are widely accepted, and there are plenty of ATMs in the large cities.

Telephone

International direct dialling is available and the International code is 07, the country code 34. All phone numbers throughout the country have nine digits, and there are no area codes.

Driving

An International Driving Licence is necessary to hire a car, but in practice an overseas licence is often accepted.

'A' roads are toll motorways with a speed limit of 120km/h; 'N' roads are main roads with a speed limit of 90km/h; and 'C' roads are local roads where nobody is in a hurry. Traffic drives on the right.

Miscellaneous

Local time is GMT + 1, with daylight saving in force from the beginning of April to the end of September.

Electricity is 220 volt AC, 50 cycles, with round two-pin plugs.

Health - Good health facilities are available, but it is advisable to have health insurance. Milk should be boiled, and water away from the city areas should be avoided. Bottled water is available.

Torro del Oro, Madrid

Madrid

Madrid, the capital and largest city of Spain, is situated in the geographical centre of the country at 700m above sea level, making it the highest capital in Europe.

It is a pretty city with wide streets and spacious, green parks.

History

Spain came under Roman rule in 206BC as a result of the Punic wars between Carthage and Rome. When the Western Empire collapsed, Madrid, Toledo, Segovia, Soria and Guadalajara were taken over by the Visigoths, a Germanic people, who took the language and religion of their captives. This kingdom was overthrown by the Arabs in 711, although a small band of nobles held out for 300 years.

The 10th century saw the Christians of the north-west begin a revival that, over the next three hundred years, reduced the size of the Moslem holdings. Then in 1212, the Moors were defeated by Alfonso VIII, and came away with Granada as the only area over which they had any influence. This too came to an end, but not until 1492.

Christian Spain was made up of several independent kingdoms, but the wedding of Isabella of Castile and Ferdinand of Aragon in 1479 united the two main royal houses and formed the basis of the modern country.

In 1522, the Habsburg Charles I of Spain, who was also the Holy Roman Emperor, granted Madrid the title of "Imperial and Crowned City", after the unsuccessful Revolt of the Comuneros. In 1651, Philip II made Madrid the capital of the great Spanish colonial empire.

Tourist Information

Information offices are found at:

Barajas Airport, ✆(91) 305 8656.

Charmartin Station: Vestibulo, Puerta 14, ✆(91) 315 9976.

Plaza Mayor, 3, ✆(91) 588 1636.

Near Prado Museum (opposite Palace Hotel), ✆(91) 429 4951.

Local Transport

The best form of transport is the Metro, which is fairly cheap and goes to all the important parts of town. There are ten lines that are marked on a handy pocket map that is obtainable from the information office or at a Metro station.

The thick red lines of the city bus routes are almost impossible to work out unless you are a native of the city, but the yellow lines showing the minibus routes are much easier to see and to follow.

Taxis are everywhere and can be hailed in the street, but as usual they are an expensive option.

Accommodation

You can normally obtain accommodation and assistance at the aeropuerto when you arrive, but most people visiting a major city like Madrid perfer to have everything organised beforehand. Below is range of accommodation that will give you some idea of what it costs to stay in Madrid, and what level of service you should expect to receive.

Here the prices are for a double with an ensuite. Credit cards are accepted, and both heating and air-conditioning are part of the scene.

Hotel Europa, Carmen 4, 28013 Madrid, ✆91-521 2900, fax 91-521 4696, email ✉ hoteleuropa@genio.infor.es. 75 units, very clean, cafeteria next door. The food at the hotel is sold at a reasonable price. It is a good to bring ear plugs with you if you plan to stay at the Europa - this is a busy part of town whether your room faces the street or the courtyard. Metro: Sol - ✪9,000Ptas.

Spain

Arosa, Salud 21, 28013 Madrid, ☏91-532 1600, fax 91-531 3127, ☞www.bestwestern.com. 135 units, situated in the Gran Via area. Restaurant, bar, lounge, concierge. Rooms are large and you will be well looked after here. There is a shuttle service from the airport during daylight hours. Metro: Gran Via - ✪22,000Ptas.

Novotel Madrid Puente de la Paz, Albacete 1, Esquina Avenida de badajoz, 28027 Madrid, ☏91-724 7600, fax 91-724 7610, email ✉H0843@accor-hotels.com. 236 rooms, bar, restaurant, pool, parking. Metro: Las Musas/Canal - ✪19,800Ptas.

Melia Castilla, Capitan Haya 43, Madrid, ☏(91) 567 5000, fax 567 5051 (✉melia.castilla@solmelia.es). Has 910 rooms, a restaurant and a combined bar/lounge. There is also a casino and a disco - standard room ✪11,800-29,900Ptas, deluxe room 22,500-41,000Ptas.

Gaudi

Gran Via 9, 28013 Madrid, ☏91-531 2222, fax 91-531 5469, ☞www.hoteles-catalonia. es. A wood-paneled delight with 85 units. The staff here know how to look after their guests. Restaurant, bar. This four star hotel is positioned near Plaza Mayor and the Prado. Metro: Gran Via - ✪26,500Ptas.

Sofitel Madrid Plaza de Espana, calle Tutor 1, esquina Ventura Rodriguez, 28008 Madrid, ☏91-541 9880, fax 91-542 5736, email ✉H1320@accor-hotels.com. 97 rooms, restaurant. The welcoming architecture of the entrance and a helpful staff make this a pleasant and comfortable hotel in which to stay. They have a shuttle bus service to the airport and railway. Metro: Legazpi Moncloa - ✪42,000Ptas.

Chamartin Hotel, Agustin De Foxa S/N, Madrid, ℂ(19) 334 4900, fax 733 0214 (✎travelweb@hotelbook.com(08599)). First class hotel situated 1km from city centre. 378 rooms, restaurant, bar/lounge, gym - ✪14,500-21,900Ptas.

Florida Norte, Paseo De La Florida 5, Madrid, ℂ(91) 542 8300, fax 547 7833 (✎travelweb@hotelbook.com(25296). Only 1km from city centre, 30m from North Train Station. Has 399 rooms, restaurant, bar/lounge - ✪13000-18500Ptas.

Best Western Hotel Arosa, Salud 12, Madrid ℂ(91) 532 1600, fax 531 3127. Central location. 140 rooms, restaurant, bar/lounge - ✪10,574-22,739Ptas.

Arosa Hotel, Salud 21, Madrid, ℂ(91) 532 1600, fax 531 3127 (✎travelweb@hotelbook.com(13374)). Close to subway and the Prado Museum. 139 rooms with facilities including a restaurant and bar/lounge - ✪9440-27364Ptas.

Madrid has two **Youth Hostels**:
Marcenado, Calle Sta Cruz de Marcenado 28, ℂ(91) 547 4532.
Richard Schirrman, Casa de Campo, ℂ(91) 463 5699.

Food and Drink

Madrid is famous for its cafes and bars (*tabernas* and *tascas*) and there are many around the Cortes, the Puerta del Sol, the Plaza Mayor and the Plaza de Santa Ana.

Drinks are usually served with *tapas*, which may consist of olives, sausage, oysters, shrimps, or a type of calamari.

Spain produces many fine wines, and available everywhere is that nectar of the gods, *sangria*, a concoction made from red wine, brandy, mineral water, orange and lemon juice, and heaps of sugar, and served with fruit and ice cubes - don't miss it!

The cuisines of every Spanish province are available in Madrid, but its own specialties are *cocido*, a soup/stew made from chick peas, meats and vegetables, and *callos* a highly-seasoned tripe dish. Of course, all the traditional Spanish dishes are available, such as *gazpacho* and *paella*.

Meals are usually eaten quite late in Spain. Lunch is between 1.30 and 2.30pm and dinner between 8.30 and 9pm. Keep an eye out for the fixed-price tourist menu, which must consist of three courses plus bread and wine.

Shopping

The busiest shopping area is along Calle de Preciados, between Puerta del Sol and the Plaza de Callao, much of which is a pedestrian mall. The large department stores are here, including **Celso Garcia**, **Cortefiel**, **El Corte Ingles** and **Galerias Preciados**. Do not expect the staff in department stores to be able to speak English, and unless you make an effort to speak Spanish, don't expect them to go out of their way to help you.

For upmarket and expensive boutiques, it is hard to go past Calle de Serrano, between Calle Diego de Leon and the Plaza de la Independencia. Calle Goya, between the Plaza de Colon and Calle del Conde de Penalver is another popular area with its share of department stores, and leather outlets.

Young people would be best to head for Calle de la Princesa, near the University City.

Sightseeing

Ayuntamiento

The centre of the city is **Puerta del Sol**, where all the main roads converge, and where the main Metro station is found. The name means "Gate of the Sun", as it was once one of the main entrances to the town, and it has witnessed some important historic occasions. On May 2, 1808 the Spanish resistance to Napoleon began here; in 1835 the Liberals took possession of the Post Office building; in 1912 Canalejas, the then Prime Minister, was assassinated by anarchists; and in 1931, from the balcony of the Old Post Office, the Second Republic was proclaimed.

The **Old Post Office**, now the police headquarters, was built in the 18th century and its construction caused the demolition of two whole blocks of houses. The building is of granite, white limestone and red brick, and has two arcaded inner courtyards. The clock tower was a later addition, and so was the iron cage that contains the gilded ball that announces the beginning of the New Year to the enormous crowds that gather in the square.

The cafes and bookshops for which Puerta del Sol was famous have disappeared, but there are still many specialty shops, confectioners and people that make it one of the liveliest places in Madrid.

From Puerta del Sol, walk about 400m north along Calle del Preciados or Calle Montera to the **Gran Via**, which runs from the Calle de Alcala to the Plaza de Espana. A street of office blocks, banks, department stores, cafes, cinemas, Metro stations and underground parking stations and Bingo halls, the Gran Via is the centre of modern and commercial life.

Spain

The **Plaza de Espana** is a green expanse where old meets new: the old quarters of the Habsburg and Bourbon regimes meet the Gran Via of the 1930s and the high rise of the 1950s. The square is dominated by the monument in its centre. It is dedicated to Cervantes who is seated looking down on statues of his characters *Don Quixote* and *Sancho Panza*, who in turn are looking out over a lake. It is a very attractive edifice, and the park is very popular with workers at lunchtime, and with people going to or coming from the many nearby cinemas.

The **Palacio Real** (Royal Palace) is in Calle de Bailen, a short walk from the Plaza Espana, although the main facade is on the south side, facing the Plaza de la Armeria.

The palace is ☉open Mon-Sat 10am-1.30pm, 4-6.15pm and Sun 10am-1.30pm (summer); Mon-Sat 10am-12.45pm, 3.30-5.15pm and Sun 10am-1.30pm (winter) and conducted tours are available in English, French, German and Spanish.

Worth seeing are the apartments occupied by Charles III, the throne room and the incomparable tapestry collection.

From Plaza de Espana Metro station it is possible to catch a train to **Casa de Campo**, a 1700ha park that houses a swimming pool, an amusement park, a cableway, and the **Parque Zoologico** (Zoo). Previously a royal hunting ground closed to the public, the park is now visited by an average of 50,000 cars and 500,000 people every week. The zoo is ☉open daily 2-7pm.

If you are not interested in visiting the zoo, from Calle de Bailen take Calle Mayor to the **Plaza Mayor**, which has been

Nuestra Senora de la Almudena

an important part of the city since the 17th century. Not only was it the commercial centre, but it was also the site of royal proclamations, canonizations, and a few executions, as well as bullfights and dramatic plays. The statue of Philip III in the middle of the square now presides over the Christmas fair, and the many people who congregate in the pavement cafes, or at the stamp market.

The Plaza Mayor is a pedestrian area, and has two exits on each side leading to the Calle de Toledo, Calle Mayor and Calle Postas. Near the Casa de la Carniceria there are steep steps leading down to the **Cava de San Miguel** quarter, a fascinating part of old Madrid with plenty of restaurants, cafes and tascas.

From Plaza Mayor exit onto Calle Mayor, continue to Carrera de San Jeronimo then to Plaza Canovas del Castillo and from there you will see the **Museo del Prado** on Paseo del Prado.

King Charles III wanted to urbanise the Spanish capital, and part of his dream was a new plan for the Prado de San Jeronimo, or St Jerome's Meadow. The meadow consisted of the gardens of the former San Jeronimo monastery, and the gardens of the Buen Retiro Palace, which was a popular picnic spot for the locals at that time. The outstanding figure in Spanish architecture at that time was the Neo-Classical Juan de Villaneuva (1739-1811), so he was given the brief and designed the Botanical Gardens, the Astronomical Observatory, and in 1785, the present Prado.

The building was not opened until 1819, during the reign of Ferdinand VII, and was called the Museum of the Royal Picture Collection. That was the beginning of one of the greatest art collections in the world, housed in one of the greatest galleries. If anyone is visiting Madrid for one day, they should forget the rest and head for the Prado. True lovers of art who are in Madrid for five days could happily spend their whole time in the Prado. There is not room here to describe the whole collection, and to choose one section would not do justice to the rest, so the only advice given here is not to miss visiting. It is ☺open Mon-Sat 9am-7pm, Sun and public holidays 9am-2pm, and there is a cafe and a bookshop.

The Best of Madrid in Brief

Royal Palace (Palacio Real). One of Europe's premier palaces, This superb building was commissioned by King Phillip V and its construction began in 1738. It contains an amazing 2000 rooms, all overflowing with artistic treasures and decorative grandeur. Many tours are available and this opulent attraction should not be missed. *Plaza de Oriente, Calle de Bailen 2.*

Palacio Real

Prado Museum (Museo del Prado). Thousands of notable paintings are on display here in one of the world's most important museums. It houses the best collection of the Spanish masters, with Velazquez leading a distinguished field, followed closely by El Greco and de Goya. Flemish and Italian art is also represented. Famous names are splashed across every wall and fill entire rooms, names such as Rubens, Bosch, Botticelli, Raphael and many more. An art lover's paradise. *Paseo del Prado*.

Thyssen-Bornemisza Museum. If you're not worn out by the Prado musuem, head over to the adjacent building to see the excellent collection of Baron von Thyssen, which features works by all the masters seen in the Prado next-door, although of a slightly inferior calibre. It also has an excellent section covering the Impressionists. A visit to these two museums will provide a nice balance and complete your appreciation of Spain's best art museums. *Palacio de Villahermosa, Paseo del Prado 8*.

Museo Nacional Centro Reina Sofia. Perhaps your interests incline more towards modern art. This huge museum contains contemporary works of the twentieth century. The most notable is Picasso's *Guernica* with its antiwar theme, one of the country's most prestigous and prized paintings. *Santa Isabel 52*.

Bullfight. Not for everyone, the traditional Spanish bullfight is nevertheless an integral part of Spanish culture, although it is increasingly becoming more of a tourist exhibition. Head to Plaza de Toros and expect to see the exploits of accomplished matadors and the drawn-out death of a raging bull.

Retiro Park (Parque del Retiro). This is a great place to experience the city's vibrant people and culture. The sprawling grounds occupy 350 acres and contain a huge lake, statues, monuments, fountains, rose gardens and pleasant eateries. *Off Calle de Alfonso XII*.

Spain

Alphonso XII Monument

Chapel San Antonio de la Florida, Goya's Tomb (Panteon de Goya). The frescoes which surround Goya's tomb were created by the hands of the artist himself, taking him four months of arduous daily work to complete. *Glorieta San Antonio de la Florida*.

Royal Tapestry Factory (Real Fabrica de Tapices). Good exhibitions illustrate the process of tapestry-making. *Calle Fuenterrabia 2*.

Monasterio de las Descalzas Reales. This former convent has a torrid history and now displays its valuable collection of art, accumulated back in the sixteenth century. Titian and Breugel feature among other relics. *Plaza de las Descalzas Reales*.

Fine Arts Museum (Museo de la Real Academia de Bellas Artes). More paintings and scultures make up this vast museum and all the usual famous contributors appear. *Alcala 13*.

Museo Lazaro Galdiano. In addition to some interesting paintings there are some fascinating pieces of jewellery and weaponry drawn from many historical eras. *Serrano 122*.

Barcelona

Positioned on the Mediterranean coast, Barcelona is an important European port and the second city of Spain. It is known not only for its famous soccer side - *el Barsa* - but also as a commercial and industrial centre for Spain. As the capital of Catalunya (Catalonia) it is also the centre of the Catalan culture. Catalan, along with Castilian, are the official languages (you see both on signposts).

Catalonia is one of 17 semi-autonomous regions of Spain with their own regional government. Catalonia consists of four provinces, is home to around 15% of Spain's total population, and covers 6% of the country's area. The provinces are Lleida, Girona, Tarragona and Barcelona, and their inhabitants have their own language, Catalan.

Barcelona city has a population of around 1,715,000, and was the site of the 1992 Summer Olympics.

History

Very early in time, Barcelona's shores were visited by Phoenician and Greek traders. Carthaginians established a settlement called Barcino, named after their General. A Roman garrison and town dates from the second century BC, and excavations beneath the Museu d'Historia de la Ciutat and the Placa del Rei have brought ruins of that town to light.

Control of the town passed from the Romans to the Visigoths, then the Moors, then the Franks, who in the 870s founded the House of the Counts of Barcelona.

The political history of Barcelona has always involved the participation of nobles, the wealthy business sector and the Church.

Entrance to Sagrada Familia

Since the fourteenth century there had been count kings, of which Peter IV was famous for his building projects. The House of Barcelona ended with the death of Martin I in 1410, and Catalonia became associated with the kingdom of Castile, although retaining its rights and constitutions that limited the king's control.

The city hit troubled times, with the annexation by Castile, then the War of Succession. During the War of the Spanish Succession (1700-1714), Catalonia was against the Bourbon Felipe V, so when he took control he punished Catalonia by revoking its constitution, which was not restored until 1932. (It was short-lived though, and was again revoked in 1939. In a referendum in 1979 the people of Catalonia voted in favour of self-government, and autonomy was granted soon after.) Trouble continued with Napolean's romp through the area, then with the anarchy at the turn of the century and late last century. Tragic Week in 1909, when more than 70 religious buildings were razed to the ground, was symptomatic of the times. The turbulence of the republic and the Spanish Civil War in the 1930s followed. Since 1939 it has enjoyed relative calm.

However, with two Universal Exhibitions in 1888 and 1929, Barcelona made a name for itself as a European city of note. Over two million people visited in 1888, and by 1929 Barcelona was a much larger city with plenty of impressive Modernist architecture on display.

In recent years, the city has taken advantage of staging the 1992 Olympic Games and rebuilt parts of the city, highlighting its many cultural and physical attractions.

Its art and the influence of modernism is instantly noticeable and gives the city a distinctive air. There are some 40 museums and art galleries of note, and buildings reflecting the inspiration of Gaudi, Ricardo Bofill and others. For those interested in groundbreaking urban design, Barcelona is a 'must see' city.

When you arrive in Barcelona, you find yourself in a new swish-glassed funnel of an airport terminal. The city is determined to impress from the outset with this creative building. From here you can take a train from the terminal to the centre of the city on a fairly efficient metro system, or you can catch a taxi.

The city of Barcelona has the Montjuic on its southwest side and the sea to its south with a newly refurbished port and waterfront. To the north is the mountain of Tibidabo which limits development of the city's boudaries. A tunnel through the mountain takes travellers to satellite towns beyond.

Las Ramblas stretches from Avenida Diagonal right down to the sea. It is a wide street with two lanes of traffic on either side and a wide paseo or 'park' in the middle. Here bird sellers, artists, and other merchants sell their wares. Seats grace both sides of this walkway, and believe it or not, you have to pay to use them. Hotels face on to this area which is also lined with many trees affording shade and adding to the pleasant environment.

Tourist Information

There is an information office at the airport that is ☉open Mon-Sat 9.30am-8pm, Sun 9.30am-3pm. There is also one at the Estacio Barcelona Central Sants (railway station - access from Platform 6) that is ☉open daily 8am-8pm, ✆(93) 491 4431.

Local Transport

The Metropolitan Transport Corporation produce a booklet called *"Guia del Transporte Publico de Barcelona y su Area Metropolitana"* which is available at their offices at Sants station; Placa de Catalunya; the Universitat metro station; Ronda Sant Pau 43; and Avinguda

Borbo 12. These are ☼open daily 8am-7pm, and can also advise on special deal fares and tickets.

Tickets can also be purchased at metro stations, savings banks and some buses. For information, ✆(93) 336 0000.

The very good bus service operates ☼daily from 5.30am-10.30pm, plus a few night services. From June 23 to September 16, the Bus Turistic (no. 100) runs on an "explorer" route. It stops at 15 main attractions and passengers can get on and off at any or all of its stops. The ticket can also be used on the Tramvia Blau (tram), and the funiculars to Tibidabo and Montjuic.

The Metro has four underground lines, 1, 3, 4 and 5, that connect with above and underground train services run by the Generalitat which extend beyond the city. All stations have maps of the network displayed. The Metro operates ☼Mon-Fri 5am-11pm, Sat-Sun and Holidays 5am-1am.

Accommodation

The accommodation given below is not your normal American-style, business-type hotels, costing a mere US$400 per night, but rather a group of individual hotels used to catering for tourists watching their budget. Prices listed are for double room and also include the IVA (tax). The tax varies according to what you are buying - a service or a good. It is around 7% for accommodation. The hotels listed take major credit cards. Rooms normally have ensuite and telephone.

Cataluna, Santa Anna 24, 08002, ✆93-301 9150, fax 93-302 7870, 50 rooms, 16 single. A block from Las Ramblas - upper end. This used to be a modest hotel that has been refurbished with ensuites, elevator, breakfast room and a restaurant next door. Metro: Plaça de Catalunya - ✪15,000Ptas.

Jardi, Plaça Sant Josep Oriol 1, 08002, Barcelona, ✆93-301 5900, fax 93-318 3664, email ✎sg110sa@retemail.es. 42 rooms, varying in size. Overlooks a delightful plaza which is fronted by the church of

Santa Maria del Pi . The bar downstairs is fairly popular. Metro: Liceu - ✪10,000Ptas, breakfast 1000Ptas.

Granvia, Gran Via de les Corts Catalanes 642, 08007, ✆93-318 1900, fax 93-318 9997. 53 units of various sizes. Its grand entrance, wood panelling and marble finishes appearing in the oddest places, gives the impression that the building is out of another era. Metro: Passeig de Gràcia - ✪15,000Ptas, breakfast 1000Ptas.

Neutral, Rambla de Catalunya 42, 08007, ✆93-487 6390. 28 units, 10 with ensuite. Entrance on the mezzanine level of the building. A budget hotel in a fashionable area. Metro: Passeig de Gràcia - ✪7,000Ptas.

Windsor, Rambla de Catalunya 84, 08008, ✆93-215 1198. 15 units. The english sign at the front cannot be missed. A nice place to base your stay, with a reasonable price. Metro: Passeig de Gràcia - ✪8,000Ptas.

Internacional, La Rambla 78-80, 08002, ✆93-302 2566, fax 93-917 6190, ⊛www.husa.es. 60 units. Part of the HUSA chain and includes a number of function rooms. Many German tourists seem to frequent this place. There is a nice a breakfast room. Breakfast is included in the price during winter, but an extra 100Ptas is charged at other times of the year. Overall this hotel is a bit pricey for what you receive. Metro: Liceu - ✪20,000Ptas.

Wilson, Avenida Diagonal 568, 08021, ✆93-209 2511, fax 93-200 8370, ✆www.husa.es. 57 rooms, bar, business facilities. Rooms have a TV, minibar, safe and telephone, with ensuite facilities. The hotel is nothing special but it is comfortable, and you have a concierge, a lift (it is 7 storeys) and a laundry service at your disposal. 20 minute walk to Las Ramblas. Metro: Diagonal - ✪18,700Ptas.

Ritz Hotel, Gran Via De Las Cortes, Catalanes, Barcelona, ℰ(93) 318 5200, fax 318 0148 (✎travelweb@hotelbook.com(02890)). Deluxe hotel with 161 rooms, restaurant, bar/lounge - ✪27,000-50,000Ptas.

Hilton Barcelona

Avenida Diagonal, 589-591, ℰ93-495 7777, fax 93-495 7700, ℰwww.hilton.com. 286 rooms. Situated in the middle of the commercial and shopping district of Barcelona. Typical Hilton - with a Bistro, Cristal Restaurant on the ground floor, Le Hiedra Terrace restaurant (open in summer only), and the Atrium Bar which offers drinks and light snacks. The Hilton is famous for one thing - Sophia Loren slipped and fell here as she was leaving to go to dinner with the wonderful Alec Guinness. Covered in mud and slush she picked herself up, returned to her room, and 20 minutes later rejoined Sir Alec in a new outfit with a little plaster on her chin as though nothing had happened. All class. An average meal will cost ✪2,500Ptas, drinks (non alcoholic) 615Ptas, whiskey 1,200Ptas - book your room on the web and get a good deal: ✪27,500Ptas with extras.

Diplomatic Hotel, 122 Pau Claris, Barcelona, ℰ(93) 272 3810, fax 272 3811 (✎travelweb@hotelbook.com(20618)). A Superior First Class hotel in the city centre. 211 rooms, restaurant, bar/lounge, pool gym, sauna - ✪25,000-36,000Ptas.

Colon Hotel, 7 Avenida Catedral, Barcelona, ℰ(93) 301 1404, fax 317 2915 (✎travelweb@hotelbook.com(28893)). First Class hotel in the Gothic Quarter. 147 rooms, coffee shop, bar/lounge - ✪1700-31,500Ptas.

Taber Hotel, Aragon 256, Barcelona, ©(93) 487 3887, fax 488 1350 (✓travelweb@hotelbook.com(27574). Situated in the heart of the shopping/business district. 91 rooms, restaurant, bar/lounge - ✪14,900-24,500Ptas.

There are four **Youth Hostels** in Barcelona:
Mare de Deu de Montserrat, Passeig Mare de Deu del Coll 41-51, ©phone/fax (93) 210 5151.
Hostal de Joves, Passeig Pujades 29, ©(93) 300 3104.
Pere Tarres, Numancia 149-151, ©(93) 410 2309, fax 419 6268.
Studio, Duquesa d'Orleans 58, ©(93) 205 0961.

Food and Drink

As with any place that is close to the sea, fish is frequently on the Barcelona menu with cod being the most common. The favourite meat is pork, closely followed by lamb. Pasta is widely used, and replaces rice in many of the traditional dishes, such as paella.

Some of the local specialties: *Espinacs a la Catalana* is spinach with pine nuts and raisins; *Arros negre* is rice cooked in squid ink; and *Pilotas* are spongy meat balls flavoured with pine nuts, cinnamon, parsley and garlic.

Barcelona has eight wine producing areas, so there is quite a choice of both whites and reds. Generally speaking they are very good. Drinks are actually less expensive here, not that they cost less, but the measures are larger.

Following are a few restaurants, to give some idea of the price of meals in this part of the world.

Agut, Trinidad, 3 (corner Avinyo, 8), ©(93) 302 6034 Open Tues-Sat. The Agut family (3rd generation) make a popular Catalan meat dish. Popular restaurant. ✪5000Ptas average meal. Amex, Diners, Visa, MC.

Giardinetto Notte, La Granada del Penedes, 22, ©218 7536. Closed Sundays and all of August. Excellent salmon dishes, Italian and whatever you want. Good place to meet. ✪4000Ptas average meal. Amex, Diners, Visa, MC.

Eldorado Petit, Dolores Monserda, 51, ©204 5153. One of the better restaurants in Barcelona. ✪7500Ptas average meal. Amex, Diners, Visa, MC.

Shopping

Barcelona is not really a place for shopping. Of course there are shops, and plenty of them, but everything is so expensive that it is better to save your money for somewhere else.

Sightseeing

The Harbour is one of the largest and most modern in Spain, which services commercial and passenger ships.

In the Placa de Portal de la Pau, adjacent to the waterfront, is the **Christopher Columbus Monument**. Built in 1888, the base is decorated with scenes from Columbus' life and voyages, and the column is topped by an 8m bronze statue of the man himself. A lift, on the harbour side, can take visitors to the top, but the view is not great.

There is also a reproduction of the *Santa Maria*, Columbus' flagship on his voyage of discovery to America in 1492, on the harbour side of the monument. The ship is ☺open daily 9am-2pm, 3pm-dusk.

Also on Placa del Portal de la Pau is the **Maritime Museum** (Museu Maritim), housed in the halls of the old Royal Shipyard.

The shipyard was established in the 13th century, and was declared a national monument in 1976. (There are the remains of some of the old town walls on the south side.) The exhibits are continually being added to and cover all facets of shipping and sailors, from full scale replicas of olden day ships, to models in glass bottles. A visit is recommended and the museum is ☉open Tues-Sat 10am-2pm, 4-7pm; Sun 10am-2pm.

A **Cableway** runs from the slopes of Montjuic, to Torre de Jaime 1, then on to Torre de San Sebastian, a steel pylon on the New Mole. The cablecars run from ☉11.30am until 8pm daily.

The **Passeig de Colom**, a wide tree-lined avenue, runs north-east from the Columbus Monument to the Head Post Office, which is close to the Lonja (the Exchange).

The Ramblas

They are a series of main tree-lined streets that run north-west from the Columbus Monument to, and through, the Placa de Catalunya, the biggest square in Barcelona, to the Avinguda de la Diagonal, a wide main street of the new town. The Ramblas have many pavement cafes and news stands, and attractions include:

Rambla de Santa Monica - **Wax Museum** ☉open Mon-Fri 10am-1.30pm, 4-7.30pm, Sat-Sun 10am-1.30pm, 4.30-8pm.

Carrer Nou de la Rambla (west of Rambla dels Caputxins) - **Museum of the Theatre** (Museu de les Arts de l'Espectacle) housed in a building designed by Antoni Gaudi. It is ☉open Tues-Fri 11am-2pm, 5-8pm.

Carrer de Sant Pau - **Sant Pau del Camp** (St Paul in the Fields), a Romanesque church built in 1117, outside the town walls.

Rambla de Sant Josep - flower market held every morning. The Mercat (Market Hall) is on the left, with a fish market in the centre. Near the Market is the former Palace of the Vicereine, with two bronze horses guarding the entrance. Built between 1772 and 1777 for the Viceroy of Peru, it was occupied by his widow until 1791, but now it is the home of the **Museum of Decorative Art**, ⏰open Tues-Sat 10am-2pm, 4.30-9pm, Sun 9am-2pm. Also in residence is the Postal Museum.

Placa de Catalunya - the end of the Ramblas, and also the Old Town quarter. The square is very large and has gardens and ponds. Many of the leading banks are found around here. To the east, in Carrer Sant Pere Mes Alt, is the **Palace of Catalan Music**, another Modernismo building, this time designed by Domenech i Muntaner. **Barcelona University** is on the Placa de la Universitat, which is reached by following Carrer de Pelai from the south corner of the Placa de Catalunya.

Passeig de Gracia, a very wide street with four rows of plane-trees, runs parallel to the Rambla for just over a kilometre. There are two buildings in the street that were designed by Antoni Gaudi: no. 43 **Casa Battlo**, which was inspired by the story of St George; and no. 92 **Casa Mila**, which is a great example of his work but not apparently inspired by anything but the Art Nouveau Movement, which the Spanish called Modernismo. The Casa Mila has guided tours ⏰Mon-Fri at 10am, 11am, noon, 1pm, 5pm and 6pm, Sat at 11am noon and 1pm (except in August). For those interested in Antoni Gaudi, there is a museum devoted to him in the Parc Guell, which is in the section on the north of the city.

Also in the Passeig de Gracia, at no. 35, is **Casa Lleo-Morera** which was completed by Domenech i Montaner in 1905, with a bit of help from the leading artists of the day. The building has been refurbished and on the first floor is the headquarters of the local tourism office called the **Patronat Municipal de Turisme**. It is ⏰open Mon-Sat 9am-2.30pm, 3.30-5.30pm.

The Old Town (Gothic Quarter or Barri Gotic) is basically between the Ramblas and Via Layetana, and is the surviving part of the medieval town. It is a collection of narrow streets, mostly pedestrian, with all kinds of shops, bars and restaurants.

The **Town Hall** is on the Placa de Sant Jaum, north-east of the Rambla dels Caputxins. The building dates from the 14th century, but the main part of the front is from 1847. The sides of the building, however, still have some Gothic parts. Inside the building, the Council Chamber is from the 14th century, and the Salon de las Cronicas has murals by Jose Maria Sert.

Opposite is the **Palau de la Generalitat**, which was built in the 15th century to house the Estates of Catalonia. It now has the offices of the provincial government, and a beautiful inner courtyard in the Gothic style.

The **Cathedral** is situated on Monte Tabor, the highest point of the Old Town, and was built on the site of a Romanesque church which itself had been built on the site of an early Christian basilica. The present Gothic building was started in 1298, but it was not finished until 1448 so most of the building dates from around the 14th century.

Inside the church there is a feeling of great space, and that is typical of the Catalan Gothic style. There are 29 side chapels, one of which has the historic "Christ of Lepanto". It was used as a figurehead on the flagship of Don John of Austria's fleet that defeated the Turks in 1571. Also in this chapel is the tomb of the sainted Bishop Olegarius who died in 1136. In the last chapel on the north there is a black Virgin similar to the famous Virgin of Montserrat. Other features not to be missed are the stained glass, the choir-stalls in the nave, and the pulpit, all from the 15th century, and the 16th century retablo in the Capilla Mayor. Steps from the **Capilla Mayor** lead down to the crypt where there is the chapel of St Eulalia, one of the city's patron saints, to whom the cathedral is dedicated. Her alabaster sarcophagus is the work of an Italian artist in the 14th century.

The Cloister is on the western side of the Cathedral. It was built between 1380 and 1451, and is surrounded by numerous chapels dedicated to different saints. At the south-west corner, in the Chapterhouse (Sala Capitular) is the Cathedral Museum, which is ☉open daily 11am-1pm.

South-east of the Cathedral is Placa del Rei, and in that square is the Casa Padellas, a replica of a medieval mansion built in 1931. When excavating for the foundations workmen came across many Roman remains. The Casa Padellas houses part of the **Historical Museum** (Museu d'Historia), the remainder is in the nearby former church of Santa Agata, and in the Salon de Tinell, a large hall that is part of the former royal palace where Colombus met with Ferdinand and Isabella when he returned from his first trip to America. The museum is ☉open Tues-Sat 10am-2pm, 4-8pm, Sun 10am-2pm (July, Aug, Sept 10am-8pm).

Take Carrer de la Princesa from the square to Carrer Montcada, then look for no. 15, the Palau Berenguer de Aguilar, a Late Gothic mansion that houses the **Picasso Museum**. ☉Open Tues-Sat 10am-8pm, Sun 10am-3pm. The works are arranged in chronological order and include paintings, drawings, lithographs and etchings from all of the various periods. Not to be missed if you are at all interested in modern art.

Montjuic

It means "Hill of the Jews", is on the south side of the city, and was so named because of the large Jewish cemetery that once existed on the site. Some of the gravestones are now in the Archaeological Museum in Passeig Santa Madrona, with the Parc de Montjuic.

The northern side of the 213m hill has been progressively developed since the late 19th century, and for the 1929 Universal Exhibition, the 202ha park acquired pavilions, sports facilities and exhibition halls, together with gardens and fountains. Added to these were the Anella

Olimpica (Olympic Ring) that was the principal site of the 1992 Olympic Games.

Access from the harbour is by cableway to the Parc de Miramar on the north-east slope. From Avinguda del Parallel, there is a funicular, with the first section underground, that meets up with a cableway that goes up to the castle. The funicular operates ⊙noon-2.50pm, 4.30-9.15pm.

The **Castle** (Castell de Montjuic) has a Military Museum in its centre, but its main attractions are the city views obtained from the bastions at its corners. There are also great views from the flat roof of the citadel.

On the northern slopes of the hill is found a **Parc de Atraccions**, or amusement park, with sideshows, a Ferris wheel, a theatre and restaurants. This park is ⊙open Mon-Fri 6.15pm-12.15am, Sat to 1.15am, Sun noon-12.15am.

The north-west side of the hill has many pavilions that were built for the 1929 Exhibition and are now used as museums.

North of the City

Carrer de Mallorca runs off Avinguda Diagonal at Plaza Mossen Verdaguer, and its most fascinating building is the **Templo de la Sagrada Familia** (Church of the Holy Family). Experts say it is the principal work of Antoni Gaudi (1825-1926), who unfortunately died before it was completed, without leaving behind a set of plans. He did leave a scale model, but this was badly damaged when anarchists attacked the building in 1935. So it remains unfinished, although Jordi Bonet Armengol, son of one of Gaudi's collaborators, is now the chief architect and he believes that one day the building will be completed. Work moves very slowly.

Some try to describe the church by saying that it is Gothic and Neo-Gothic combined with Art Nouveau, but whatever you like to call it, it seems to be a hotchpotch of real and fairy-tale architecture. (Is there any truth in the rumour that the English word "gaudy" derives from the name of this Spanish architect?)

The building is ☉open daily 9am-7pm, and there is an audio-visual presentation on the history of the project near the entrance. There are parts of the building that are open to the public daily 9am-7pm.

If you want to see more of Gaudi's work, head for **Parc Guell**, in the north-west of the city (Metro station Vallcarca - Line 3). The park was designed by Gaudi and worked on between 1900 and 1914. It contains the house where he was born, which is now a museum (☉open daily 10am-2pm, 4-7pm), and many other Gaudi buildings and details for buildings.

The Best of Barcelona in Brief

Barcelona Cathedral (Catedral de Barcelona). This thirteenth century Catalan Gothic cathedral has simply massive proportions. Highlights are the side chapels, cloister, naves, high altar and arches. *Placa de la Seu.*

Gothic Quarters (Barri Gotic). The narrow streets of this district are flanked by some buildings still preserved since medieval days. Few particular attractions glare at walkers, but there is a certain collective ambience that lends the area its charm.

Catalonian Art Museum (Museu Nacional d'Art de Catalunya). This sumptuous museum displays the best in rare Classic Romanesque and Gothic art, with many drawcards. *Palau Nacional building, Parc de Montjuic.*

Spain

Sacred Family Church (La Sagrada Familia). You will either be impressed or repulsed at first glance by Gaudi's strange and striking incomplete architectural creation; parts of its exterior look like hot wax has been poured over them. Gaudi died in 1926 and strong arguments have suggested that the ongoing work steers away considerably from his original conception. *Mallorca 401.*

Picasso Museum (Museo Picasso). The best chance to see some of Picasso's earliest works and to trace the development of his unique tone and form. The most popular piece here is his 1897 work *Science and Charity. Montcada 15-19.*

Frederic Mares Museum (Museu Frederic Mares). The sculptures here represent periods over a range of 2000 years or more, but the highlight is the comprehensive medieval section. *Placa de Sant lu 5-6.*

Fundacio Joan Miro. Houses the best collection of Miro's abstract modern art and accompanies it with selected works by some of his contemporaries. *Placa de Neptu, Parc de Montjuic*.

Fundacio Antoni Tapies. This museum is dedicated to the modern art of Antoni Tapies, most particularly his exploration of abstract impressionism. *Arago 255*.

Modern Art Museum (Museu d'Art Modern). Contains modern art by notable figures, in various forms from paintings to furniture. *Placa d'Armes, Parc de la Ciutadella*.

Palau Guell. A park with good views of the city and examples of Gaudi art imitating nature.

Barcelona Museum of Contemporary Art (Museu d'Art Contemporareo de Barcelona). An interesting if not brilliant collection of modern art, somewhat outshined by the architectural accomplishment of the building in which they are kept. *Placa dels Angels*.

Columbus Monument (Monument a Colom). This complex monument, consisting of bronze and iron and containing an internal elevator, stands 50 metres high. *Portal de la Pau*.

Sant Josep Market . This is a bustling market selling a wide array of food items, from the adventurous (*toro* testicles) to the extravagent (olives in 25 distinct

Base of Columbus Monument

varieties). There is a lot to be gained from mingling with locals in such an environment and trying different traditional flavours - and it also makes a healthy and perhaps welcome change from wandering through museums. *Off La Rambla*.

Museu de la Ciencia. A hands-on museum illustrating the subtleties of science in a practical environment. *Teodor Roviralta 55.*

Maritime Museum (Museu Maritim). Although there are a couple of rare artifacts kept here and some interesting models, they are really not sufficient to warrant a visit on a short stay in Barcelona. *Avinguda de las Drassanes.*

Casa Mila (La Pedrera). More of Gaudi's idiosyncratic architectural flourishes can be appreciated in this extroverted building.

Castle of Montjuic. There are good scenic vistas from this castle and a large but only mildly interesting military museum.

Fountains (Fonts Lluminoses). The fountains in this mountain park are very picturesque, and their lights and music make for a very soothing place to relax for a while in the evening.

Spain

Seville

The fourth-largest city in Spain and capital of Andalusia, Seville lies on the left bank of the Rio Guadalquivir at an altitude of 10m. It has a population of around 800,000, and one of the hottest climates in mainland Europe, sometimes reaching 48C.

The 1992 International Exhibition was held in Seville, at the same time as the Olympics were in Barcelona.

Andalucians speak Castilian, the 'normal' Spanish.

History

There was already an established town on the site when the Romans arrived in 205BC, but by the time of Caesar it was a very important port called Colonia Julia Romula. During the 5th century AD it was ruled firstly by the Vandals, then by the Visigoths. The 8th century saw the Moors take over, then the Umayyads, the Almoravids and the Almohads from 1147. In the latter half of the 12th century many fine buildings were erected, and the city had a larger population than Cordoba.

In 1248 the town was recaptured by Ferdinand III of Castile, who made it his capital for the remaining four years of his life. After his discovery of the New World, Colombus was given a ceremonial reception in Seville. Voyages by Amerigo Vespucci and Magellan were orchestrated from Seville and it became the world's busiest and most important port.

In 1717 Seville lost its trade monopoly to Cadiz, mainly because the Rio Guadalquivir had a constant problem with silting, and facilities at Cadiz had drastically improved.

Tourist Information

The city tourist office is located at Costurero de la Reina, Paseo de las Delicias 9, ✆(95) 423 4465; and the provincial tourist office is at Avenida de la Constitucion 21B, ✆(95) 422 1404.

There is also an information desk at San Pablo Airport, ✆(95) 425 5046.

Local Transport

The city's bus service is operated by Tussam and there are route maps at bus stops. A complete map of the network - *Plano de Red Lineas* - can be picked up at tourist offices. Single journey fares are purchased on board the bus, but Bonobus saver tickets for ten trips are available at tobacconists (*estancos*).

Horse-drawn carriages operate around the central sightseeing area, and will take up to four people. Always settle on a price before getting into the carriage.

Accommodation

Here the prices are for a double with an ensuite. Rooms are air-conditioned. Major credit cards are accepted at these places.

Principe de Asturias

Isla de la Cartuja, 41092 Sevilla, ✆95-446 2222, fax 95-445 0428, email ✉principe@sevillaonline.com. Near the World Exhibition site of 1992. 295 rooms, tropical gardens, swimming pools, transport available to the city centre, fountains - a delight. Regarded as a 5 star hotel - ✪14,500Ptas.

America, Plaza de Duque, 41002 Sevilla, ✆95-422 0351, fax 95-421-0626, email ✉hotel-america@sol.com. 100 rooms, bar, dining room, good location. Classed as 3 star in a 1970s building - ✪15,000Ptas.

La Hosteria del Laurel, Plaza de los Venerables 5, 41004 Sevilla, ✆95-422 0299, fax 95-421 0450, email ✉laurel@sol.com. 21 rooms behind a very popular restaurant in the middle of the Barrio. This is a popular little hostel because of its ambience - ✪9,500Ptas.

Hotel Fernando

San Jose 21, 41004 Sevilla, ✆95-421 7307, fax 95-422 0246, email ✉nj.10386@autovia.es. 157 rooms, 24 hour service, swimming pool on fourth floor, restaurant, lounge. Classed as 4 star hotel. A very comfortable stay - ✪17,000 Ptas.

Europa, Jimios 5, 41001 Sevilla, ©95-450 0443, 421 4305, fax 95-421-0016, email ✎hotel-europa@sol.com. 30 rooms in an 18th century building whose walls are adorned with the most delightful paneling. Elevator for convenience, dining room. Located in the cultural and commercial heart of the city - ✪10,000Ptas.

Giralda Hotel, Sierra Nevada 3, Seville, ©(95) 441 6661, fax 441 9352 (✎travelweb@hotelbook.com(14691)). Near the tower of the same name. 96 rooms, restaurant, bar/lounge - ✪24,000-30,000Ptas.

Cuidad de Seville, Av Manuel Siurot 25, Seville, ©(95) 423 0505, fax 423 8539 (✎travelweb@hotelbook.com(17924)). A first class hotel in the downtown area. 94 rooms with facilities including restaurant, bar, coffee shop, health club, swimming pool, shops - ✪14,000-35,000Ptas.

Gran Hotel Lar, Plaza De Carmen Benitez 3, Seville, ©(95) 441 0361, fax 441 0451 (✎travelweb@hotelbook.com(02344)). A first class hotel in the downtown area. Facilities include restaurant, bar, coffee shop, health club, shops and beauty salon - standard room ✪9000-14,500Ptas, deluxe room 14,500-18,000Ptas.

Inglaterra Hotel, 7 Plaza Neuva, Seville, ©(95) 422 4970, fax 456 1336 (✎travelweb@hotelbook.com(21553)). Situated 500m from the Cathedral. 113 rooms, 2 restaurants, barbecue, bar/lounge - ✪12,580-19,000Ptas.

Seville's **Youth Hostel** is at Isaac Peral 2, ©(95) 461 3150, fax (95) 461 3158.

Food and Drink

A good thing to remember when you are in a Seville restaurant is that *callos a la andaluza* means "tripe stew", which may not titillate your taste buds.

During the 1992 Expo many restaurants realised that it would be a good idea to have menu translations, and that practice has continued.

Spain

The area around Seville is an important producer of rice, so expect to see many dishes incorporating that grain. Obviously seafood also features widely.

Following is a selection of eateries that are popular with the locals.

El Burladers, Canalejas, 1, ✆(95) 422 2900 - in the Hotel Colon - the house specialty is Bull's Tail.

La Isla, Arfe, ✆(95) 421 2631 - in Arenal district near the bullring. Traditional Seville cuisine and seafood.

La Dorada, Ramon y Cajal, Viapol Building, ✆(95) 492 1066 - Andalusian cuisine - specialties are fried fish platters, gilthead baked in salt and gazpacho.

Egena-Oriza, San Fernando 41, ✆(95) 422 7254 - very fine Basque restaurant - overlooks Murillo Gardens.

El Rincon de Curro, Virgen de Lujan, 45, ✆(95) 445 0238 - Andalusian cuisine.

Florencia, Eduardo Dato, 49, ✆(95) 457 0040 - in Hotel Porta Coeli - menu constantly changes with the seasons and the available produce.

Shopping

Don't expect to pick up any bargains in Seville. The shops are very attractive, but do your sums with the exchange rates and leave your credit card firmly in your wallet.

Department stores are: **El Cortes Ingles**, Plaza Duque de la Victoria, ✆422 09 31; and the less expensive **Galerias Preciados**, Plaza de la Magdalena, ✆422 20 14. The main shopping area is around the pedestrians-only *Calle Sierpes*.

Sightseeing

Seville Cathedral

Seville Cathedral was built on the site of the city's principal mosque during the period 1402 to 1506, and it is the fourth largest in the world. In fact it is the largest and richest Gothic cathedral in the world, and has the largest interior space of all cathedrals. Having said all that, it must be added that it is also probably the gloomiest church on earth.

When inside the cathedral it is hard to really appreciate its size because the view is restricted by the choir and the high altar, but it measures 83m wide, 95m long and 30m high.

The **Capilla Mayor** (high altar) has 36 tableaux on gilded hardwood depicting the life of Christ. It was constructed between 1482 and 1564. The **Coro** (choir) has wrought-iron grilles similar to those of the main altar, and ebony wood stalls in the Mudejar-Renaissance style.

The **Capilla Real** (Royal Chapel) was completed in 1575 and contains the tombs of many royal personages. Traditionally, the monarchs of Spain are buried here. It also has a 13th century carving depicting *La Virgen de los Reyes*, patron of Seville, made from larch wood.

In the south transept, near the Puerta de San Cristobal, is the **Monument of Christopher Columbus**, which was originally in Havana Cathedral and brought to Seville after the loss of Cuba in the Spanish-American War of 1898. Although the monument is often referred to as "Columbus' Tomb", he is not buried here, but his son's tomb is at the west end of the nave.

Spain

Throughout the church there is a plethora of priceless works of art and gold and silverware, in fact a visit is quite exhausting.

On the east side of the Cathedral is the **Giralda** (Weathercock), probably the world's most beautiful minaret and the landmark of Seville. Originally the minaret of the Great Mosque, the tower was built in 1184-1196. The bell-chamber was added in 1568 and is topped by a weathervane (*giraldilla*) 4m high in the shape of a female representing Faith and carrying the banner of Constantine. From the first gallery, at 70m, there are great views of the city, and of the Cathedral which can't really be viewed from anywhere else because of the surrounding buildings. Before you begin your ascent, though, make sure that the gallery's 24 bells are not due to be rung. The Giralda is ☉open Mon-Sat 11am-5pm, Sun 2-6pm.

South of the Cathedral

South of the Cathedral is the Plaza del Triunfo, and the Casa Lonja, the former Exchange which now houses the **General Archive of the Indies**. The archive has more than four million documents relating to the discovery of, and Spanish settlement in, America. Much of the material is now on computer and can be accessed by researchers, but there is a changing exhibition of actual records, usually including pages from the diaries of Christopher Columbus. It is ☉open Mon-Fri 10am-1.00pm.

At 5 Calle Santo Tomas, on the south side of the Casa Lonja, is the Old Chapterhouse (Cilla del Cabildo Catedral) which now houses the **Museo de Arte Contemporaneo**, ☉open Tues-Fri 10am-2pm, 5-8pm; Sat-Sun 10am-2pm. The museum has works by Miro, Tapies, Saura and Chillida, as well as local artists.

The Alcazar

The **Alcazar** is on the south-east side of the Plaza del Triunfo, and it was the stronghold of the Moorish and the later Christian kings. The present building is from the second half of the 14th century. Enter through the Puerta Principal and take the narrow passageway to the left. This leads to the *Patio de las Doncellas* (Court of the Maids of Honour), built 1369-1379, but the glazed gallery was added in the 16th century.

On the north side of the Patio is the *Salon de Carlos V*, with a beautiful ceiling. Next are the apartments of a favourite lady of Pedro the Cruel (Maria de Padilla), then the Dining Room (Comedor), then the oldest room in the Alcazar, the **Salon de Embajadores** (Hall of the Ambassadors) which dates from 1420. The rest of the ground floor is taken up with royal apartments.

The magnificent staircase from the Patio de la Monteria leads to the first floor which has the apartments of the Catholic Monarchs and some fine chapels.

The **Jardines del Alcazar** (gardens) were laid out by Charles V, and are divided by a rocaille wall. Their main attractions are an underground bath-house and the **Pabellon de Carlos V** (Pavilion) to which Felipe V added the **Apeadero** which is used for exhibitions. The Alcazares is ☉open Mon-Sat 9am-12.45pm, 3-5pm; Sun 9am-12.45pm.

The Centre of Town
To the north of the Cathedral is the centre of town, the **Plaza San Francisco**, where bullfights, tournaments and executions were once held. The west side of the square has the Renaissance **Ayuntamiento** (Town Hall), which was commenced in 1527 and finished in 1564. The front of the building is one of the best examples of the Plateresque style.

On the west side of the Town Hall is the Plaza Nueva, and on its north side is the narrow **Calle de las Sierpes** (Street of the Snakes), the main shopping street and a pedestrian zone.

Calle Jovellanos Gallegos runs off Calle de las Sierpes, on the right, and has the church of **San Salvador** from the 16th century but remodelled in Churrigueresque style in the late 18th century. The church has works by Montañes, including an *Ecce Homo*, and a painting by Murillo.

Take Calle de Aguilas from San Salvador east to the Plaza de Pilatos, and the 16th century **Casa de Pilatos**. Legend has it that whilst in the Holy Land the Marquis of Tarifa, Don Fabrique Enriquez de Ribera, visited the ruins of Pilate's house in Jerusalem. When the Marquis returned to Seville in 1521 he decided to model his home on his own idea of what the ruins represented. It is now considered to be the grandest private residence in Seville, and is owned by the Duke of Medinaceli. Much of the house and grounds are open to the public (☉Mon-Fri 10am-6pm, Sat 10am-2pm) and it gives an insight into the lifestyles of the different ages.

Calle de las Sierpes as it travels north becomes Calle Amor de Dios then passes the Plaza del Duque and continues to the **Alameda de Hercules**, a wide and shady avenue with gardens and, at its south end, two granite columns from a Roman temple with statues of Hercules and Julius Caesar. These two are important to Sevillan mythology. Hercules is credited as the founder of the city; Julius Caesar with building its protective **walls**, part of which can be seen on the north side of the old town between the Puerta de Cordoba and the Puerta de la Macarena.

From the Plaza del Duque take Calle de Alfonso XII to the **Museo de Bellas Artes**. Sevillans believe this museum has the greatest art collection in Spain, which makes it painfully obvious that none of them have visited the Prado in Madrid. Nevertheless it does have a good collection, particularly of the works of the 17th century Spanish painters. Artists represented include El Greco, Pacheco, de Roelas, Zurbaran, Murillo, Velazquez and Carreno.

South of the City

To the south of the city, on the Paseo de las Delicias and leading from the Puente del Generalisimo, is the **Parque de Maria Luisa**. It is named after Maria Luisa Fernanda, sister of Queen Isabel II and duchess of the Montpensier family, who presented the gardens to the city in 1893.

The Ibero-American Exhibition of 1929-30 was held in the park, and some of the buildings remain: the Palacio Centrale, with its two 82m towers at the corners, in the **Plaza de Espana**; the Pabellon Mudejar, Pabellon Real and Palacio del Rinacimiento in the **Plaza de America**.

The Pabellon Mudejar houses the **Museum of Folk Art and Costume**, and another building in the Plaza de America houses the **Archaeological Museum**.

The International Exhibition of 1992 celebrated the 500th anniversary of the discovery of America, and was held on an island between the Guadalquivir and the Canal de Alfonso XIII, to the north of the suburb of Barrio de Triana.

The central feature of the Expo was the Carthusian monastery of Santa Maria de las Cuevas, founded in 1401. It was there that Columbus planned his voyage across the Atlantic.

The Best of Seville in Brief

Cathedral (Catedral). This fifteenth century Gothic church is the third largest in Europe and took 120 years to complete. The main attractions of its interior are the amazing altarpiece contained in the sanctuary, the thousands of precious stones displayed in the treasury and the place where Columbus is allegedly laid to rest. *Plaza del Triunfo, Avenida de la Constitcion.*

Giralda Tower. The top of this twelfth century Moorish structure has a stunning panorama over Seville and is reached by a series of ramps which spiral 100 yards upwards. It functions as the Cathedral's bell tower.

Alcazar. For 600 years, this palace has been the residence of the Spanish royal family. It does not rank as one of Europe's greats, but there are some aspects worth seeing if you are seeing the sights of Seville, including the throne room, the Sevillian craftmanship of the interior, the Hall of Ambassadors (Salon de Embajadores) and the tropical gardens. *Plaza del Triunfo*.

Barrio de Santa Cruz. Filled with narrow lanes made for strolling, this old Jewish quarter contains a couple of little art museums, good cafes, small plazas, and attractive Spanish architecture everywhere.

Plaza de Espana. This pleasant square is always filled with people and contains tiles that record episodes of historical significance.

Mueum of Fine Arts (Museo de Bellas Artes). One of Spain's most important galleries, Sevilles Museo de Bellas Artes houses works on two floors by El Greco, Velazquez, Murillo and others. *Plaza de Museo 9*.

Basilica Macarena. The exquisite statue of the Weeping Virgin (Virgen de la Macarena) is kept by the altar. *Puerta Macarena*.

Hospital de la Caridad. This charity hospital has a few notable elements - the courtyard, the seventeenth century exterior and the paintings on display in the chapel. *Temprado 3*.

Tower of Gold (Torro del Oro). An historic building which long ago lost its namesake (the golden tiles that graced its exterior). The tower now acts as the site for a small and unarresting Naval Museum (Museo Nautico). *Paseo de Cristobal Colon.*

Driving Through Spain

Catalonia

Itinerary - 8 Days - Distance 814kms

Barcelona, the capital of Catalonia, is the second largest city in Spain, and was the host of the 1992 Olympic Games. As well as being an imposrtant port, it also has many historical buildings and museums. South of Barcelona, drive along the coast road to **Tarragona**. This city dates back to Roman times and there are many sites still remaining.

Drive inland to **Lerida**, in the hills, with its citadel and medieval cathedral. From Lerida, head north to the state of **Andorra**, notable for its duty free goods. Head back towards the coast through the scenic route over the mountains. You pass through the towns of **Puig Cerda** and **Ripoli** to **Gerona**. Gerona is one of the oldest cities in this state and is very picturesque. Just north of Gerona is **Figueras**, where the home of Salvadore Dali is now a museum.

Make your way to the Mediterranean coast, and **Roses**, the start of the Costa Brava. Drive back down along the Costa Brava, through towns such as **L'escala**, **Palamos**, **S. Feliu de Guixois** to **Blanes**. From here it is a short drive back to Barcelona.

Andalusia

Itinerary - 10 Days - Distance 1035kms

Seville, Spain's third largest city, and home of the 1992 World Expo, is situated on the Guadalquivir River. There are many reminders that this city was originally an Arab settlement, and many interesting buildings can be seen. From Seville, head north to **Cordoba**, one of the most ancient cities in Spain. It was the capital during the Moorish settlement, and for many centuries Muslim, Christian and Jewish communities intertwined. The city is also famous for its bullfights.

Turn south from Cordoba, and drive down to **Granada**, which was the centre of another Muslim state. It is at the foot of the Sierra Nevada where snow skiing is popular in winter. Granada also boasts a Moorish Palace - Ahlambra, which is worth seeing. From Granada, head east to **Guadix**, another ancient town with many historic buildings. Of particular interest is **Las Cuevas**, where houses are dug out of the ground.

South on the coast lies **Almeria**, another city rich in Arab history. The citadel Alcazaba, is particularly impressive. There are many tourist spots here, but it is also possible to find quiet beaches. Turn west, and follow the Mediterranean coast towards **Motril**, passing through holiday resorts such as **Roquetas De Mar** and **La Rabita**. As well as being a holiday resort it is also important as a fruit and vegetable growing region.

Further along the coast you reach **Malaga**, again passing through resort towns. This whole stretch of coastline, the Costa de Sol, is given over to the tourist trade, with such places as **Torremolinos** and **Marbella** - big resorts. The entrance to the Mediterannean lies at **Algeciras** which is a port town, and is a popular stepping stone to Africa. The rock of Gibraltar is under British influence, and stands guardian over the straits of Gibraltar. Head north to **Cadiz**, one of the oldest cities in Spain, founded in 1100 BC. Again there are many interesting buildings and monuments to see.

Toledo, 67km southwest of Madrid, is perfect for a day trip

Jerez de la Frontera is the home of sherry, and there are many vineyards and wineries in this region. It is also the home of the Royal Andalusian riding school, and this can be visited also. From here, head back to Seville, where the tour ends.

Switzerland

L AND-LOCKED SWITZERLAND has an area of 41,288 sq km and a population of around 6,675,000 people, whose language depends on which part of the country they inhabit. Around 70% speak a dialect of German, but those who live between the French border and the Matterhorn speak French, and account for another 20%. The remaining 10% is divided between the southern-most Canton of Ticino where Italian is spoken, and the Engadine and Upper Rhine Valley where people speak Romansch, an ancient language of Roman origin. Most people in the hospitality industry speak English.

The government is a Confederation of twenty-three Cantons that have their own government and administration. The Federal Government is responsible for defence, foreign affairs, and transport and postal systems.

Climate

Average temperatures for Zurich are: Jan max 2C, min -3C; July max 25C, min 14C. July and August are the peak tourist months, when it is necessary to queue for every attraction and service, but June and September have roughly the same weather, less crowds, and cheaper hotel tariffs.

Entry Regulations

Visitors must have a valid passport, but a visa is not required for visits up to 90 days.

The duty free allowance is 200 cigarettes or 50 cigars or 250 gm pipe tobacco; alcoholic beverages up to 15% proof 2 litres, over 15% proof 1 litre; perfumery 0.5 litre, films unrestricted if for personal use. There is no restriction on the import or export of currency. No vaccinations are required.

Currency

The currency of the land is the Swiss Franc (SFr), which is divided into 100 centimes or rappen. Approximate exchange rates, which should be used as a guide only, are:

A$	=	0.95SFr
Can$	=	1.13SFr
NZ$	=	0.77SFr
S$	=	1.00SFr
UK£	=	2.52SFr
US$	=	1.66SFr
Euro	=	1.55SFr

Notes are in denominations of 1000, 500, 100, 50, 20 and 10 Swiss Francs, and coins are 5, 2 and 1 Franc and 50, 20, 10 and 5 centimes.

Banks are ☉open Mon-Fri 8.30am-noon, 2-4.30pm. There are no currency restrictions and at exchange offices (Bureaux de Change or Geldwechsel) most currencies can be bought or sold.

Switzerland

Shopping hours are ☉Mon-Fri 8am-12.30pm, 1.30-6.30pm, Sat 8am-12.30pm, 1.30-4pm, although in the big cities the shops tend to stay open at lunchtime.

Post offices are ☉open Mon-Fri 7.30am-noon, 1.45-6pm, Sat 8.30-11am.

Credit cards are widely accepted, though it is better to have some cash when travelling through the smaller towns. There is a Goods and Services Tax (MWST) of 6% on most items.

Telephone

International direct dialling is available and the International code is 00, the country code 41.

It is expensive to make international calls from hotels.

Driving

It is necessary to have an international driving licence to hire a car. Driving is on the right. In this country traffic coming from the right has priority, as have trams in the cities and post-buses on mountain roads.

Speed limits are:

Motorways	-	130km/h
Open roads	-	100km/h
Built-up areas	-	50km/h

On-the-spot fines can be imposed for speeding.

Miscellaneous

Local time is GMT + 1 (Central European Time). Daylight saving operates from late March to late September.

Electricity is 220v AC, with round, two-pin plugs.

Health - Switzerland has an excellent health system, but it is wise to have insurance cover.

Lucerne

Lucerne (Luzern) is the scenic capital of Central Switzerland (Zentralschweiz), which is the most-visited region of the country. Consequently there is no shortage of hotels and restaurants in this part of the world, and getting to Lucerne by road or rail is easy and picturesque.

The city is attractively situated on the banks of the Reuss River as it begins its journey from the Vierwaldstattersee (also called Lake Lucerne).

History

Central Switzerland, in particular the areas around Vierwaldstattersee, is William Tell country. This legendary national hero leapt into the lake from the wicked Gessler's boat and escaped. His story has been told in drama and music, and even if he did not actually exist, as historians believe, the events taking place in the story did.

The Rutli meadow, on the western shores of the lake, is where representatives of the Confederates of Schwyz, Uri and Unterwald met in 1291 to compose the Oath of Eternal Alliance, which formed the world's oldest still-existing democracy.

Tourist Information

The Tourist Board Luzern has its office at Bahnhofstrasse 3, ✆(41) 227 1717, fax 227 1718, and is ⊙open Mon-Fri 8am-noon 2-5.30pm, closed Sat-Sun.

A Tourist Information Centre is found at Zentralstrasse 5 (in the train station/West building), ✆(41) 227 1717, fax 227 1720. The centre is ⊙open Mon-Fri 8.30am-7.30pm, Sat-Sun 9am-7.30pm (summer); Mon-Fri 8.30am-8.30pm, Sat-Sun 9am-8.30pm (June 16-Sept 15); Mon-Fri 8.30am-6pm, Sat 9am-6pm, Sun 9am-1pm (winter).

Local Transport

There are efficient bus and trolley bus services.

Accommodation

Following is a selection of accommodation with prices for a double room per night, which should be used as a guide only.

Chateau Gutsch

Kanonenstrasse, Lucerne, ✆(041) 249 4100, fax (041) 249 4191 (✎travelweb@ hotelbook.com(00913)).Built as an hotel in 1888, but you could be forgiven for thinking that it was originally a castle. 31 rooms, restaurant, bar/lounge - ✪Sfr250-450 including breakfast.

Wilden Mann Romantik Hotel, Bahnhofstrasse 30, Lucerne, ✆(041) 210 1666, fax 210 1629 (✎travelweb@hotelbook.com(00271)). 43

rooms situated in the Old Town, its facilities include 2 restaurants and a bar/lounge - ✪SFr155-420.

Grand Hotel Europe, Haldenstrasse 59, Lucerne, ✆(041) 370 0011, fax 370 1031 (✉grand-hotel-europe@bluewin.ch). Within walking distance of the town and the lake. 178 rooms, restaurant, bar/lounge - ✪SFr160-270.

Art Deco Hotel Montana, Adligenswilerstrasse 22, Lucerne, ✆(041) 410 6565, fax 410 6676 (✉travelweb@hotelbook.com(01894)). Situated 1 km from city centre with wonderful views over the Lake. Take a cable car from the lake shores to the lobby. 65 rooms, restaurant, bar/lounge - ✪SFr135-440.

Johanniter TOP Hotel, Bundesplatz 18, Lucerne, ✆(041) 231 8555, fax 210 1650 (✉travelweb@hotelbook.com(00614)). Situated 3 minutes from the railway station. Has 65 rooms, coffee lounge, bar/lounge - ✪SFr99-240.

Food and Drink

The specialty of Lucerne is *Kugelipaschtetli*, puff-pastry filled with chicken, veal or sweetbreads, mushrooms and cream sauce. Fish is also prominent on the city's menus, usually sauteed and served with tomato, mushroom and caper sauce.

Restaurants around here are not cheap, although the food is very good and so you often feel the price is justified. Here are a few at the lower end of the price scale.

Zur Pfistern, Kornmarkt 4 -a 14th century guildhall on the old-town waterfront -fish dishes are recommended - credit cards accepted.

Rebstock/Hofstube, St Leodegarstrasse 3 (next to the Hofkirche) - international cuisine in brasserie and the more formal restaurant, reservations necessary, credit cards accepted.

Galliker, Schutzenstrasse 1. Real traditional Luzerner cuisine. Popular with locals and visitors. Reservations are a good idea. Credit cards accepted. Note: this restaurant is ☉closed on Sunday and Monday from mid-July to mid-August.

Shopping

Lucerne is the main shopping venue for the entire region, so the shops tend to remain open longer than in other cities.

The main department store is *Jelmoli*, Pilatusstrasse 4; and the chain stores are **Nordmann**, Weggisgasse 5, and *EPA*, Rossligasse 20.

Lucerne was once a major producer of lace and embroidery goods, but although this is no longer the case, it is still one of the best places to buy Swiss handiwork. Watches are also high on people's shopping lists.

For lace and embroidered goods try:

Sturzenegger, Schwanenplatz 7.

Schmid-Linder, Denkmalstrasse 9.

Innerschweizer Heimatwerk, Franziskanerplatz 14.

For watches try:

Bucherer, Schwanenplatz, who represent Piaget and Rolex; and *Gubelin*, Schweizerhofquai, who represent Philippe, Patek, and Audemars Piguet as well as its own brand.

Sightseeing

A walking tour can begin at the **Altes Rathaus** (Old Town Hall) which

was built in the late Renaissance style between 1599 and 1606, and has been used by the town council for its meet-ings since 1606. It is on Rathausquai, facing the modern bridge, **Rathaus-Steg**.

On the right of the Town Hall, in Furrengasse, is the **Am Rhyn Haus**, which has a good collection of Picasso paintings from his late period. It is ⊙open daily 10am-6pm (Jan-Oct); 11am-1pm, 2-4pm (Nov-Mar).

Take the stairs on the right, and pass the Zunfthaus zu Pfistern, a guildhall and restaurant, to the Kornmarkt. Cross the square and go to the left into the **Weinmarkt**, the most picturesque of the city's squares. During the 15th, 16th and 17th centuries people came from all over Europe to see the famous passion plays presented in this square, which before that time was the site of the wine market. The fountain in the centre portrays St Mauritius, the patron saint of warriors.

Now walk towards the **Spreuerbrucke**, the narrow wooden bridge that runs off Muhlenplatz. The bridge dates from 1408 and its inside gables have a series of 17th century paintings by Kaspar Meglinger of the *Dance of Death*. They are well preserved, but certainly not to everyone's taste.

The other end of the bridge brings you to the **Natur-Museum** and next to it the **Historisches Museum**. The Natural History Museum has very modern exhibits and even some live animals. It is in Kasernenplatz, and is ⊙open Tues-Sat 10-noon, 2-5pm; Sun 10am-5pm. The Historical Museum, in Pfistergasse, is not really very interesting to anyone who is not Swiss, but nevertheless it is ⊙open Tues-Fri 10am-noon, 2-5pm; Sat-Sun 10am-5pm.

Continue along Pfistergasse in the direction of the lake until you get to Bahnhofstrasse, turn left, then right into Munzgasse. Continue on to Franziskanerplatz and the **Franziskanerkirche** (Franciscan Church), which is more than 700 years old although it has been renovated more than a few times and lost a lot of its original style.

Go back to Bahnhofstrasse, turn right and walk past the Government Building (**Regierungsgebaude**), the home of the cantonal government, to the **Jesuitenkirche** (Jesuit Church). This church was built between 1667 and 1678, and is worth a visit. The enormous interior has been completely restored and it is a brilliant example of the Rococo style. Next door, in Theaterstrasse, is the **Stadttheater** (City Theatre). On the waterfront there is a fish market every Friday morning.

Next we cross the 14th century **Kapellbrucke** (Chapel Bridge), the oldest wooden bridge in Europe. Bridges usually go across rivers in a straight line, but not this one - it crosses diagonally. This is because it originally was a division between the river and the lake. The bridge is the symbol of Lucerne - its stone water tower, its shingled roof and its shape making it instantly recognizable, much as the Golden Gate to San Francisco and the Harbour Bridge to Sydney.

When you walk across you will notice the gables painted by Heinrich Wagman in the 17th century, but some will be empty. There were 112 panels depicting local history, legends and coats of arms, but during a fire in 1993, 78 of the paintings were completely destroyed, and some others are being carefully restored and will be replaced. The bill for rebuilding and restoring the bridge came to around 3 million Swiss francs.

From the bridge, veer towards your right through the Schwanenplatz and along Schweizerhofquai, passing the *Hotel Schweizerhof*, which has had as guests Napoleon III, Mark Twain, Leo Tolstoy and Richard Wagner.

Continue to Zurichstrasse, turn left and continue to Lowenplatz where you can't miss the **Bourbaki-Panorama**. A conical structure built as a tourist attraction and nothing else, it has a panoramic painting of the French Army retreating into Switzerland during the Franco-Prussian War. As you walk around, the painting seems to become 3-D with things coming out towards to you. There is also a recorded commentary in several languages and the whole complex is ☉open daily 9am-6pm (May-Sept), 9am-5pm (March-April and October).

The well-known restaurant, the **Old Swiss House**, is next door to the Panorama, but check out the prices before you wander in.

Lowendenkmal

From Lowenplatz take Denkmalstrasse to the **Lowendenkmal** (Lion Monument), another symbol of Lucerne that should not be missed under any circumstances. It is carved out of a sheer sandstone face and is of a dying lion, with a broken spear in his side and his chin sagging on his shield. Carved by Lucas Ahorn of Konstanz, from a design by Danish sculptor Berthel Thorwaldsen, it commemorates 760 Swiss guards, and their officers, who were killed defending Louis XVI at the Tuileries in Paris in 1792. There is a Latin inscription that translates: "To the bravery and fidelity of the Swiss". When you are there, standing near the pond in front of the monument, take a moment to look at people around you. Many will have tears in their eyes, not because they feel any affinity with some brave men who died over two hundred years ago, but simply because of the spirit evoked by the carving itself.

Next to the park that houses the Lion is the **Gletschergarten** (Glacier Garden), where excavations between 1872 and 1875 revealed bedrock that had been polished and pocked by glaciers during the Ice Age. A small museum on site has impressive relief maps of Switzerland, but admission times vary dramatically so ask at the Tourist Information Office for current times.

To get back to the city centre, return to Lowenplatz, get back onto Zurichstrasse, then turn right onto Museggstrasse and follow it all the way. It actually goes through one of the 15th century city gates, and gives some good views of the old town.

The Best of Lucerne in Brief

Old City. Bordered by mountains and the lake, this medieval district boasts attractive squares including the Kornmarkt, Weinmarkt and the Hirschenplatz. There are many beautiful buildings such as the Town Hall and Pfistern guildhall.

 **Dying Lion Monument**. This famous monument was carved to commemorate the valiant efforts of Swiss mercenaries who died protecting French royalty in Tuileries in 1792. Mark Twain described the evocative work as the "saddest and most moving piece of rock in the world".

Glacier Garden. This "prehistoric" garden preserves and displays blocks of ice that are remnants of the Ice Age 15,000 to 20,000 years ago, and fossils which are more than 20 million years old.

Chapel Bridge. The Water Tower attached to the bridge, with its distinct octagonal shape, has become the city's landmark. The bridge itself was built in the fourteenth century and contains paintings depicting episodes from Lucerne's history.

Wasserturm and Kapellbrucke. These structures are remants of the town's original fortifications and date back to the fourteenth century. They are the country's landmarks, said to be its most photographed subjects.

Picasso Museum. Kept in an old and picturesque historical building, Am-Rhyn-House, are a collection of Picasso's late works, created in the 20 years leading up to his death. The gallery of 200 photographs capturing the artist is a welcome complement to his featured works.

Swiss Museum of Transport. Planes, trains and automobiles feature in Europe's most comprehensive transport museum. The history and development of different modes of travel and also of communication technology is expounded with the use of hundreds of visual exhibits. There are many old vehicles and other nostalgic memorabilia.

The Jesuit Church. A great Baroque building, this church was built by Father Vogler in the seventeenth century and was the first of its architectural kind in the country.

Town Hall. An attractive seventeenth century building contructed in the Italian Renaissance style.

Zurich

The largest city in Switzerland, Zurich has a population of around 400,000 and is situated on the Limmat River and along the shores of the northern tip of the Zurichsee (*see* = lake).

Zurich is a very beautiful city, and a commercial, industrial and university centre. One could be forgiven for wondering why it is not the capital of Switzerland, but that honour goes to Bern.

History

It is known that the area was inhabited as early as 4500BC, for land and marine archaeologists have discovered artifacts from many Stone Age and Iron Age settlements around the lake.

The Romans, ever on the lookout for a good, central location, built a customs house on a hill overlooking the river in the 1st century BC. The customs house became a fortress, and remains of it can still be seen. Legend has it that the Romans were also responsible for providing Zurich with its patron saints. During the Roman occupation, the Roman governor beheaded a brother and sister, Felix and Regula, because they were Christians. That part is historically correct, but the rest has yet to be proven. After their execution they picked up their heads, waded through the water, and marched up a hill before succumbing at a spot where the Grossmunster now stands.

The Romans were ousted in the 5th century by the ancestors of the present occupants, but the importance of the town dwindled until four hundred years later when the Carolingians built an imperial palace on the banks of the Limmat. Then Louis the German, grandson of Charlemagne, had an abbey built where the Fraumunster now stands.

Zurich's flair for trade and commerce was evident by the 12th century, and the merchants became very powerful. This was not appreciated by the tradesmen and labourers who, led by an aristocrat named Rudolf Brun, took the merchants on, and defeated the town council. They then established the guilds for which Zurich is famous, and in fact the original thirteen guilds retained their power until the French Revolution. They still have their prestige, shown by the annual festival when businessmen don medieval costumes for the procession through the city to the guildhalls.

During the Reformation, a leader named Huldrych Zwingli preached in the Grossmunster, exhorting the populace to thrift and hard work. His success can be measured by the fact that the Zurich stock exchange is the fourth most important in the world (after New York, London and Tokyo) and turns over on average 636 billion Swiss Francs each year.

Tourist Information

The tourist information office is in the Main Railway Station, ✆(01) 215 4000, fax 215 4099, and it is ⊙open Mon-Fri 8.30am-9.30pm,

Sat-Sun 8.30am-8.30pm (April-October; Mon-Fri 8.30am-7.30pm, Sat-Sun 8.30am-6.30pm (November-March). (☞www.zurichtourism.ch)

Local Transport

Zurich has a very efficient tram service from 5.15am to midnight. Tickets must be purchased from vending machines before boarding.

Taxis are not really an alternative as they are very expensive - ✪10SFr minimum.

Accommodation

Following is a selection of accommodation with prices for a double room per night, which should be used as a guide only.

Arabella Sheraton Atlantis Hotel, Doeltschiweg 234, Zurich, ✆(01) 454 5454, fax 454 5400. Set in forested parkland 10 minutes from the city centre. 2 restaurants, bar/lounges - standard room ✪SFr270-395, deluxe room SFr325-475.

Hotel Schweizerhof, Bahnhof Platz 7, Zurich, ✆(01) 218 8888, fax 218 8181. Centrally located Superior First Class hotel. 147 rooms, restaurant, cafe, bar/lounge - ✪SFr270-490.

Arabella Sheraton Neues Schloss, Stockerstrasse 17, ✆(01) 286 9400, fax 286 9445. Situated in the business district. 58 rooms, restaurant, bar/lounge - standard room ✪SFr240-380, deluxe room SFr264-410.

Rigihof TOP Hotel, Universitatstrasse 101, Zurich, ✆(01) 361 1685, fax 361 1617 (✉travelweb@hotelbook.com(00620)). Only 1km from the city centre. 65 rooms, restaurant, bar/lounge - ✪SFr200-270.

Zurich's **Youth Hostel** is *Wollishofen*, Mutschellenstrasse 114, ✆(01) 482 3544, fax (01) 481 9992.

Food and Drink

A few dishes spring to mind when thinking of Switzerland - cheese fondue, rosti and veal in cream and white wine sauce. Everyone knows of the first and last, but *rosti* might be new to some. It is a cake of hash-brown potatoes crisped in a skillet and flavoured with bacon, herbs or cheese. And it is delicious.

The Swiss use a lot of cheese in their main courses, and a lot of chocolate in their desserts. Speaking of chocolate, it is available everywhere and is simply the best, though it is not cheap. Actually, eating anything in Switzerland, and in Zurich particularly, is an expensive exercise. Probably the best bet is to have the main meal at lunch-time and take advantage of the reduced prices for business lunches. Here are a few restaurants that won't charge an arm and leg:

Zeughauskeller, Bahnhofstrasse 23, ✆(01) 211 2690 - 15th century building that is popular with locals and visitors alike - reservations necessary for lunch - no credit cards accepted.

Mere Catherine, Nagelihof 3, ✆(01) 262 2250 - bistro with a varied menu and an interesting clientele - no credit cards accepted.

Rheinfelder Bierhaus, Marktgasse 19, ✆(01) 251 2991 - somewhat dreary decor but excellent home-made meals. They do not accept credit cards.

Shopping

The main department stores are **Jelmoli**, Bahnhofstrasse at Seidengasse, ✆(01) 220 4411, and **Globus**, Bahnhofstrasse at Lowen-platz, ✆(01) 221 3311. Smaller chain stores are **Vilan**, Bahnhofstrasse 75, ✆229 5111 and **ABM**, Bellevueplatz, ✆261 4484.

The main shopping street, as you may have worked out for yourself, is **Bahnhofstrasse** and the Paradeplatz end, towards the lake, has the more exclusive shops and boutiques.

A **flea market** is held ⊙every Saturday 6am-3.30pm at Burkliplatz, which is at the lake end of Bahnhofstrasse.

Switzerland

Sightseeing

The main sights of Zurich are easily seen on a walking tour and the best place to begin is the **Hauptbahnhof** (Main Railway Station). When the enormous station was first built, in the 1800s, it was considered to be a work of beauty. Time has taken its toll. The current restoration program has been going on for some time. It is expected to be even grander than before.

The **Schweizerisches Landesmuseum** (Swiss National Museum) is at Museumstrasse 2, behind the station, in a huge Gothic building. Exhibits include Stone Age objects, early watches, dress and furniture from earlier times, and models of military battles. A mural by Ferdinand Hodler entitled *Retreat of the Swiss Confederates at Marignano* is in the Hall of Arms. The museum is ☉open Tues-Sun 10am-5pm and admission is free.

The statue in the centre of Bahnhofplatz is of **Alfred Escher**, a financial wizard and politician who was responsible for Zurich becoming a major banking centre. He was also involved in the development of the city's university, the Federal Railways and the tunnel under the St Gotthard Pass.

There is a subterranean passage under Bahnhofplatz that comes out at **Bahnhofstrasse**, the city's main street and principal shopping strip.

Continue along this street until you come to Rennweg, on the left. Turn into it and then left again onto Fortunagasse, then continue on to the **Lindenhof Square**. Here there are remains of the Roman fortress and a medieval imperial residence. There is also a fountain that commemorates the women of Zurich who, in 1292, saved the town from the Habsburgs. Apparently the town was all but defeated when the women donned uniforms and armour and marched to the Lindenhof. When the enemy saw them coming they assumed that it was a second, fresh army and so fled the scene.

A short walk from here to your right takes you to the St Peterhof and **St Peterskirche**, the oldest parish church in Zurich. There has been a church on this site since the 9th century, but the present building dates only from the 13th century. In the tower is the largest clock face in Europe. Again walking to your right, turn into Schlusselgasse, then into an alley named Thermengasse. Through grates you will be able to see beneath you the ruins of **Roman baths**, which have been excavated. There are signs giving details of the dig. Continue on to **Weinplatz** which has some excellent shops, and opens onto the riverside. After checking out the shops, continue on your way, crossing the Rathaus Bridge over the river.

The street that runs along the riverbank on this side is called **Limmat Quai** and near here at nos. 40, 42 and 54 there are some interesting guildhalls (*zunfthausen*) that are now restaurants. No. 40 is **Zunfthaus zur Zimmerleuten** which dates from 1708 and was for carpenters; no. 42 is **Gesellschaftshaus zum Ruden** a 13th century noblemen's hall; and no. 54 is **Zunfthaus zur Saffran** a 14th century haberdashers' meeting place.

Across from no. 54 is the 17th century Baroque **Rathaus** (Town Hall), which can only be visited by people attending the cantonal Parliament Monday morning meeting, or the city Parliament Wednesday afternoon meeting. The interior is in good condition and the stucco ceiling in the Banquet Hall is worth a look.

Further along Limmat Quai is the 15th century **Wasserkirche** (Water Church) built in the late-Gothic style with stained glass by Giacometti. Attached to the church is the **Helmhaus** which dates from the 18th century. Here a linen market was once held, but now it has changing contemporary art exhibitions. It is ☉open Tues-Sun 10am-6pm (until 9pm Thurs), and for more information ✆251 7166. Both these buildings were once on an island, the one where Felix and Regula lost their heads.

Continuing towards the lake the next stop is the very grand **Grossmunster**. The church was built on the site of a Carolingian church which was dedicated to Felix and Regula, as this was as far as they carried their heads, and where they were buried. Legend has it that Charlemagne decided that a church should be built on the spot when his horse stumbled over their graves. There is a huge statue of Charlemagne near the south tower, but it is only a copy - the original is in the crypt for safe-keeping. The inside of the church is very austere, but remember that this was where Zwingli preached his 'thrift and hard work' sermons.

Follow Limmat Quai to Ramistrasse, and if you are interested in art, turn left and continue on to the **Kunsthaus** (Art Gallery) on Heimplatz. It is ☉open Tues-Thurs 10am-9pm, Sat-Sun 10am-5pm, ©251 6755. Also on Heimplatz is the **Schauspielhaus** (Theatre), which was the only German-language theatre in the world that was not controlled from Berlin during the Second World War.

If you are not interested in art, turn right onto Ramistrasse, and on Bellevueplatz is the **Opern Haus** (Opera House), built in 1890 and renovated between 1980 and 1984.

As you continue across **Quai Brucke** (Bridge) take time to notice the great views both to the right of the city, and to the left of the lake. The views are particularly good at night, so a return visit is a good idea.

At the end of the bridge veer to the right, then take the second street on the right, Fraumunsterstrasse, which leads, of course, to the **Fraumunster**. Built on the site of a 9th century abbey, whose remains can be seen, the Fraumunster was originally Gothic in style, then in 1732 the beautiful narrow spires were added. The Romanesque choir has stained-glass windows by Marc Chagall.

At Munsterhof 20 is the Baroque **Zunfthaus zur Meisen**, an 18th century guildhall for the wine merchants that now houses the

Switzerland

Landesmuseum's ceramics collection, ☏221 2144. ☺Open Tues-Fri and Sun 10am-noon, 2-5pm, Sat 10am-noon, 2-4pm. Also in this square is the **Zunfthaus zur Waag**, a 17th century guildhall for the linen weavers and hat makers.

Walk along Poststrasse to Paradeplatz, a major crossroads and centre on Bahnhofstrasse, from where you can catch a train back to the railway station, or wherever you are staying.

The Best of Zurich in Brief

Grossmunster. This is the city's most famous landmarks - its distinct dual towers are responsible for establishing this honour. The building now functions as part of the University, appropriately containing the theological faculty. Romanesque architecture can be identified in the cloisters, which were built in the twelfth century. Sculptures from this period are housed inside.

Fraumunster. The highlight of this church is the stained glass windows, added in 1970 at the hands of Chagall. The church foundations are thought to date back to the ninth century A.D.

Lindenhof. Preserved from Roman times, this area contains a Roman tombstone, customs post and small fort. There are great views from its elevated position.

Zunfthaus zum Meisen. Porcelain displays and the rococo interior decoration make this wonderful 18th century Baroque building worth visiting.

St. Peter's Church. St. Peter's is the city's oldest church and bears Europe's largest clock face, spanning 8.7 metres.

Tonhalle. This superb concert hall, renowned for its fine acoustics, plays host to the talents of the Zurich Chamber

Orchestra and the Tonhalle Orchestra. It is more than a century old. *Gotthardstrasse 5*.

Schauspielhaus. This is Zurich's largest and most famous theater. It became something of a sanctuary during WWII, frequented by such talents as Bertolt Brecht. *Raemistrasse 34*.

 **Opera House**. World-class performances are on show for most of the year and include symphonies, ballets and, naturally, operas, all covering a refreshing array of different styles. The auditorium is crafted in a wonderful Neo-baroque style. *Falkenstrasse 1*.

Swiss National Museum. Traces the interesting history of Switzerland and exhibits many pieces of national interest.

Niederdorff. When the sun drops, locals and tourists flock to Niederdorff to become part of the vibrant nightlife.

Kunsthaus. Modern and nineteenth century art in various forms is displayed in the city's top gallery. *Heimplatz*.

Bahnhofstrasse. The place to shop, or at least to window shop. This retail stretch is popular and picturesque.

Museum Rietberg. For something different, this museum contains interesting exhibits from Asia and the African continent.

Urania Observatory. The tower at this observatory stands almost 50 metres high and the complex has a bar with superb views over the city below.

Driving Through Switzerland

A Scenic Tour of Switzerland by Road

Itinerary - 8 Days - Distance 666kms

Geneva is the second city in Switzerland, and is situated at the western end of Lake Geneva. This city is the European headquarters of the United Nations, and of the Red Cross. The old part of the city has buildings dating from the 12th century. From Geneva head north along the shores of Lake Geneva through **Nyon** and **Morges**, little towns on the shores of the lake. From here you reach **Lausanne**, a university town on the northern shore of Lake Geneva. Lausanne is the headquarters of the International Olympic Committee, and houses an interesting Olympic museum.

Drive north towards Neuchatel Lake. **Yverdon** is a spa and resort town at the southern end of the lake. The town of **Neuchatel** is very picturesque. From here, drive through **Biel/Bienne**, a tourist town, with many interesting old buildings. Close by is **Berne**, the capital of the Swiss confederation of states. The Parliament Buildings are here, as is the famous Bear Pit. There are many historic buildings here.

From Berne drive east towards **Lucerne**. Lucerne is a very scenic town on the shores of Lake Lucerne, with buildings dating from Gothic and Renaissance times. Head south from Lucerne to **Altdorf** through a mountain tunnel. At Altdorf you can see the William Tell Memorial and museum. Further south you drive through some scenic but mountainous roads to **Brig**. This town is the starting point for travel to Zermatt and the Matterhorn. To reach Zermatt you can leave your car in the car park, and take the mountain railway up to the town.

From the town of **Sion** you can see the tallest dam in the world on Grand Dixience Lake. Head back to **Montreux** through little villages, all popular for winter sports, such as skiing. Montreux is on the eastern end of Lake Geneva and is famous for its music festivals.

Continue back to Geneva along the southern shores of the lake (through France) through the resort towns of **Evian** and **Thonon**.

United Kingdom

THE COUNTRIES THAT MAKE UP the United Kingdom, also called Great Britain, are England, Scotland, Wales and Northern Ireland. They cover an area of 244,100 sq km and have a total population of 58,123,000.

Not much is known about the history of England before the invasion by Julius Caesar, in 55BC, which made it a Roman province. The last Roman legions were withdrawn in 442AD leaving behind many temples, baths, forums, walls and paved highways that can still be seen today.

Peace was short-lived. The warring Picts and Scots from the north continually invaded, as did the Welsh from the west.

King Edward I of England subdued the Welsh and his son, the first Prince of Wales, was born at Caernarvon in 1284. This did not quell the rebellions but Henry VIII finally joined the two countries under the same system of laws and government.

The island of Rockall not shown.

0 75 150 km
0 75 150 mi

North Atlantic Ocean

Voe. Shetland Islands

Orkney Islands

Hebrides

Scotland

Aberdeen

Dundee.

North Sea

Grangemouth
Glasgow. Edinburgh

.Londonderry
Northern Ireland .Belfast

Newcastle upon Tyne
Middlesbrough

Isle of Man (U.K.)
Irish Sea Liverpool.
Kingston upon Hull
Manchester

IRELAND

England

Wales Birmingham

LONDON

Cardiff. Bristol

Dover.

Celtic Sea

Channel Tunnel

English Channel

Guernsey (U.K.)
Jersey (U.K.)
FRANCE

United Kingdom

The Romans tried unsucc-essfully to capture Scotland but finally gave up and built a wall across the north of England. Scotland became united with England in 1603 when Mary Queen of Scots' son, James VI of Scotland became James I of England.

England, Scotland and Wales became united in 1707 under Queen Anne to form Great Britain.

Religious disputes have plagued Ireland since its beginning. Northern Ireland is largely Protestant, as a result of English migration. The rebellion of 1641 lasted eight years and paved the way for Oliver Cromwell to decimate the entire island, which had been ruled from London in oppressive fashion. In 1916 Sin Fein declared southern Ireland an independent state. After an impossible conflict for the British, Britain withdrew her troops and in 1921 the Irish Free State was proclaimed. Later the south became the Republic of Ireland and the north remained under British rule with a guaranteed protestant majority in political life.

Latest available population figures are: England 46,382,050, Scotland 4,962,152, Wales 2,811,865. English is spoken throughout the United

Kingdom. However, Gaelic is also spoken in some parts of Scotland. The Welsh also maintain their ancient Celtic tongue.

Climate

On the whole Britain has a cool climate. January is the coldest month with temperatures of 4C (39F). July and August are the warmest 16C (60F). The highest rainfall is in November with 97 mm. September is considered by many to be the best time of the year to visit. The temperature is 57F (14C), rainfall 3.2 ins (83 mm); there are less tourists to compete with; and prices fall. Tourist attractions and some hotels close at the end of September until Easter. April and May are also good months to visit. The spring flowers are in bloom and the temperature is reasonable.

Entry Regulations

All visitors must produce a valid passport. Commonwealth visitors staying less than six months do not require a visa. No vaccinations are required. The duty free allowance is 200 cigarettes or 100 cigarillos or 50 cigars or 250gm tobacco. Alcoholic drinks: 2 litres of still wine plus 1 litre of drinks over 22% vol, or 2 litres of alcoholic drinks under 22% vol or a further 2 litres of still wine. 60cc perfume, 250cc of toilet water. Other goods worth £145.

Currency

The currency of the land is the British Pound (£), which is divided into 100 pence. Approximate exchange rates, which should be used as a guide only, are:

A$	=	0.36£
Can$	=	0.48£
NZ$	=	0.31£
S$	=	0.40£
US$	=	0.66£

United Kingdom

Notes are in denominations of £50, £20, £10, £5, andcoins are £2 £1, 50p, 20p, 10p, 5p, 2p and 1p. Scotland has its own notes and although English pounds are accepted in Scotland, you must change your Scottish pounds before you leave that part of the country. They are the same value and denomination as the English.

Major credit cards are widely accepted, but not by some leading stores (eg Marks & Spencer, John Lewis). You can obtain money from certain banks with your card. Check before leaving home as to which bank takes your card.

Changing travellers cheques can be expensive. There is a £4 commission charge at most banks and money exchanges. American Express travellers cheques can be changed free of commission at Lloyds and the Bank of Scotland. Thomas Cooks cheques at Thomas Cook outlets.

Banks are ☺open Mon-Fri 9.30am-4.30pm (Northern Ireland 10am-3.30pm). Some major banks open on Saturdays and for a few hours on Sundays, but all are closed on Public Holidays. Some banks in Scotland and Northern Ireland close for an hour at lunchtime.

Post offices are ☺open Mon-Fri 9am-5.30pm, and the main ones on Sat 9am-1pm (Northern Island until 12.30pm).

If you don't have a mailing address in the UK, it is best to have your mail sent to Poste Restante, Trafalgar Square Branch, 24-28 William IV Street, London WC2N 4DL. They will hold your mail for four weeks, and you must show proof of identity to collect it.

Most *shops* ☺open at 9.30am and close at 5.30pm, Mon-Sat. Small shops usually open at 9am. Late night shopping is Thursday when shops stay open until 8pm. Harrods opens at 10am and closes at 7pm. In suburbs many shops close for a half day on Wednesday or Thursday. In the country they often close for lunch.

United Kingdom

Tax

VAT (value added tax) of 17.5% is charged on most goods and services. Non-EC residents may reclaim VAT but it has to be arranged through shops. Not all retailers participate and the value of the item is also considered. The goods must be shown to customs at your port of exit from Europe along with a form which the store will have given you. Shops usually charge a fee for the service. In other words, unless you have done some very expensive shopping it is not worth the trouble.

Telephone

It will cost more to phone from your hotel, so go to a pay phone. As a considerable amount of small change is needed to make even a local call, it is better to buy a phonecard. These are available from any British Tourist Information Centre, post offices and shops displaying the green phonecard sign. They come in £2, £5, £10 and £20 credit. For Overseas calls dial ✆010 then the country code, the area code, then the number. Check the time difference in the phone book.

Driving

Driving is on the left-hand side of the road. The wearing of seat belts is compulsory. There are strong penalties for driving while under the influence of alcohol. Take your driving licence with you. People from certain countries only require their current licence. They can drive on it for one year. Countries not exempt need an International Driving Permit obtainable in your home town. Check before you leave home.

Road signs are almost all international. A copy of the highway code is obtainable from the AA, RAC, airports and car rental firms. The speed limits are as follows.

built up areas	-	30mph (48kph)
suburban areas	-	40mph (64kph)
motorways	-	70mph (113kph)
other roads	-	60mph (97kph)

Parking can be a headache. It is not allowed where there is an unbroken yellow line. Broken yellow or red lines indicate no stopping. As there are few parking meters, it is safer to go into a parking area where you put your money in a machine. If you park illegally, the authorities will clamp your wheels and you will have to pay a hefty fine - and suffer twenty-four hours of inconvenience!

Miscellaneous

Local time is GMT. Daylight saving operates from late March to late September.

Electricity is 240v AC. Take an adaptor or converter with you as the plugs are a different shape to those in other countries.

Health - Take any medication you require with you. It is also advisable to photocopy your prescriptions. Ask your doctor to give you a letter listing all medications you are on and any ailment from which you may suffer. Keep all medication in your overnight bag. It is essential to be covered for health insurance. It is also advisable to carry full insurance in case of emergencies.

Disabled facilities - Britain caters for the disabled. Most hotels and B&Bs have walk-in showers and ground floor rooms. British Rail and London Underground assist passengers on and off trains. With British Rail you must notify them the day before you travel. In the Underground simply ask one of the staff for assistance. Advice can be obtained from Holiday Care Service, 2 Old Bank Chambers, Station Road, Horley, Surry, ✆(0293) 774 535. Ask the British Tourist Authority for a Holiday Care enquiry form.

Pubs

Drinking hours in England and Wales are ☺11am-11pm weekdays, Sun midday-10.30pm; in Northern Ireland, Mon-Sat 11.30am-11pm, Sun 12.30pm-10pm; in Scotland, Mon-Sat 11am-11pm, Sun 12.30-2.30pm and 6.30-11pm.

United Kingdom

All pubs serve food ranging from sandwiches and snacks to full hot dinners. There is no VAT on pub food which is usually of excellent quality.

Restaurants usually have a menu outside with the prices, and it is advisable to check this before entering or you could be in for a nasty shock. Remember to add the VAT and, in most cases, there is also a service charge.

Tipping

If a hotel or restaurant adds a service charge to your bill, there is no need to tip. Taxi drivers expect 10%, porters 50p a bag. Tipping is not so popular as in the past and is more confined to those who give extra service.

London

London is a huge metropolis with a permanent population of about 7,000,000 plus a floating population of workers and tourists. It really has something for everyone.

History

The oldest part in the city of London is a small square-mile patch, that was the original Roman Londinium. Although it is now the banking and commercial sector it also has some of the main tourist attractions. The City of Westminster is also another sector where many attractions can be found. Next there is the West End where the theatres and shops are located, and away from these main areas there is London, stretching out in all directions.

The Romans built their city at the highest point of the Thames, on Cornhills and Ludgate Hill. It was sacked by Bodicea in AD 61, and later attacked by the Vikings.

William the Conqueror built the White Tower of the Tower of London in the 11th century. The church and the 'guilds' sponsored building during the Middle Ages - St Bartholomew the Great 1123, St John of Jerusalem, Clerkenwell 1150, Temple Church 1185. Westminster Abbey was commenced in the 11th century. Southwick Cathedral, Westminster Hall, Lambeth Palace and the Guildhall were all built during this century.

By the 16th century, London had started to expand and St James Palace was erected. Queens House, Greenwich 1619-35. Banqueting Hall, Whitehall 1619-22, which has ceilings painted by Rubens. St Pauls Cathedral was built in 1665 and destroyed by fire in 1666. The Cathedral was replaced by Wren.

The 17th and 18th century saw more expansion with numerous squares designed by the Adams Brothers. These included Adelphi, Strand and Portland Place.

London was badly bombed during World War II but the damage has been repaired, with some historical buildings having been replaced by modern office blocks.

Tourist Information

British Tourist Authority has its head office at 1 Lower Regent Street. You can make reservations for transport, accommodation and theatre; change money, buy phonecards or shop for souvenirs. BTA information centres are located at all major railway stations.

Local Transport

You can go almost anywhere on the Underground, and easy to read maps show which route to take. Buses are frequent but because of the traffic, are not as fast. There are also Green Line buses to places outside the metropolitan area. Trains go in every direction. **Visitor Travelcards** are available for travel on the Underground and bus networks. They are available in 2, 3, 4 and 7-day formats, and must be purchased before you leave home. Available in the UK are: **One Day**

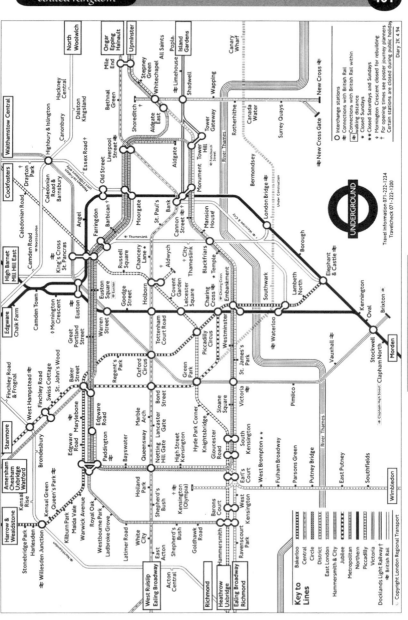

Travelcards (valid after 9.30am) which cost - ✪2 zones £3.80; 4 zones £4; all 6 zones £6.70 (children £1.90 all types); **Weekend Travelcards** (Sat and Sun) cost - ✪2 zones £5.70, 4 zones £6, zones 2-6 £4.90, all 6 zones £6.70 (children £2.80 all types) - a 25% saving on two one-day cards.

Family Travelcards are also available and can be used by any group of two adults and between one and four children travelling together, irrespective of whether they are related or not.

The **Carnet** pack buys 10 single tickets for zone 1 only and costs ✪£10 (a saving of £4).

For long term visitors there are weekly and monthly **Travelcards**. These can be obtained at Underground stations, but a passport size photograph is required.

Taxis are plentiful, and can be hired in the street, but a journey of a few miles within the central area will probably cost around ✪£6 (plus a 10% tip).

One of the best ways for a visitor to see London is by taking **The Original London Sightseeing Tour**. This is a hop-on/hop-off tour in an open topped double decker bus that has 90 stops, and offers a choice between a live guided tour in English, or recorded commentaries that are available in a wide choice of languages. Open-dated vouchers can be purchased before arriving in the UK and costs are ✪£12.50 adult, £7.50 child 5-15.

Accommodation

Following is a selection of accommodation with prices for a double room per night, which should be used as a guide only.

Ritz, Piccadilly WIV 9D6, ©(0171) 493-8181, fax(071) 493-2687 (✉ travelweb@hotelbook.com(00702). 129 rooms. Stately, luxury hotel (noted for afternoon tea) decorated in the French style. Restaurant, bars, romantic Italian al fresco dining room. Handy distance to everything, transport at the door - ✪£290-385.

United Kingdom

Sheraton Park Tower, 101 Knightsbridge, London, SW1X 7RN, ✆(171) 235 8050, fax 235 8231. A deluxe hotel situated in the heart of London with all the facilities expected of a 5-star hotel. For those who want to splurge. Three classes of accommodation - Classic ✪£221-280, Executive £264-380, Butler £660-1450.

Hotel Inter-Continental, 1 Hamilton Place, Hyde Park, London, W1V 0QY, ✆(0171) 409 3131, fax 493 3476. 460 room, bars, restaurants, everything the discerning traveller can possible need - ✪£195-330.

Amsterdam Hotel, 7 Trebovir Road, Earl's Court, London, SW5 9LS, ✆(0207) 370 5084, fax 244 7408 (✎reservations@amsterdam-hotel.com). Centrally located hotel with bar, restaurant and usual facilities. 27 rooms - ✪£80-160.

Comfort Inn Kings Cross, 2-5 Chad's Street, London, WC1H 8BD, ✆(0207) 837 1940, fax 278 5033. Centrally located with all amenities, plus continental breakfast - ✪£71-120.

Park Lodge Hotel

73 Queensborough Terrace, Bayswater, London, W2 3SU, ✆(0171) 229 6424, fax 221 4772 (✎travelweb@hotelbook.com(27512)). A peaceful residential terrace with 29 rooms situated close to Hyde Park - ✪£45-85.

Best Western Phoenix Hotel, 1-8 Kensington Gardens Square, London, ✆(0207) 229 2494, fax 727 1419. 125 rooms. A 3-star hotel within walking distance of Hyde Park, Oxford Street and city centre - ✪£63-86.

Stuart Hotel, 110-112 Cromwell Road, Kensington, London, SW7 4ES, ✆(0171) 373 1004, fax 370 2548 (✎travelweb@hotelbook.com(17032)). A tourist hotel with 50 rooms. A short walk from Albert Hall and Gloucester Road Underground.

Lime Grove Hotel, 32 Lime Grove, Hammersmith, W12 8EA, ✆(01817) 435 243, fax 400 364. A town house hotel with 15 rooms located 2 miles from Earl's Court. Cold buffet breakfast provided - ✪£48-75.

Food and Drink

Think of dining out in London and you will probably think of fish and chips, or bangers and mash, washed down with a pint of ale. These are still available, of course, but every other type of food you can imagine can also be found in London.

Beware of restaurants, though, with well-known names such as the ***Savoy***, ***Suntory***, or the ***Ivy***. They are all excruciatingly expensive, so it is best to investigate the menu outside before you enter. For best value go to the pubs, or British Home Stores and Littlewoods have cafeterias at reasonable prices.

Sightseeing

Among the main sights in the **City of London** is **St Paul's Cathedral**, which was designed by Sir Christopher Wren after the Great Fire of London destroyed its predecessor in 1666. Attractions in the Cathedral include the *Whispering Gallery*, the *Stone Gallery*, and the *Golden Gallery*, which offers superb views over London, and the tombs of the famous in the crypt. Take the underground to St Paul's Station. ⊙Open Mon-Sat 8.30am-4pm; Galleries 9.30am-4pm, admission to the Cathedral and crypt is ✪£4 adult, £2 child; to galleries £3.50 adult, £1.50 child. Guided tours are available and cost £10 per person, which includes admission fees. For more information contact ✆(0171) 246 8348 (☞stpauls.london.anglican.org).

The **Old Bailey**, built on the site of the infamous **Newgate Prison** is where most of the famous British criminals have been brought to justice. Seats in the public galleries are very much sort after so be early. Close to the Old Bailey is the **"Old Lady of Threadneedle Street"**, more formally known as the Bank of England. In this vicinity you can see the lane where the fire of London started; visit pubs frequented by Bacon, Dickens and many more; but the most impressive building in the city is the **Tower of London**.

The *White Tower* was built in the time of William the Conqueror. The *Bloody Tower* is where the young Princes were murdered by King Richard III. *Traitor's Gate* lives up to its murky reputation, and visitors can gaze on the spot where Ann Boleyn and Catherine Howard kept their appointments with the executioner. On the brighter side you can see the crown jewels displayed in well illuminated glass cases. The Underground is the quickest way to the Tower - use Tower Station. ⊙Open Mon-Sat 9am-5pm, Sun 10am-5pm, and admission is ✪£10.50 adult, £6.90 child, ✆(0171) 709 0765 (☞www.hrp.org.uk).

By contrast, the **City of Westminster** has wide streets with lots of parklands. Here are found the **Houses of Parliament**, and the spot where Charles I was condemned to death in the **Palace of Westminster** next door (use Westminster Station).

Westminster Abbey stands across the road. Here all the kings and queens except Edward V and Edward VIII have been crowned. Many famous royals, statesmen and poets have been buried here (use St James Station). ⊙Open Mon-Sat with last admissions 3.45pm Mon-Fri, 1.45pm Sat. Admission is £5 adult, £2 child, ✆(0171) 222 5152 (☞www.westminster-abbey.org). Guided Tours are available, and are well-worth taking - ✪£3 per person, ✆(0171) 222 7110.

Stroll up **Northumberland Avenue**, past the many offices that house the Admiralty, War Office and Foreign Office, to the **Cenotaph** and then into **Downing Street** where the Prime Minister lives. In the last street on the right, just before **Trafalgar Square** there is a pub called the *Sherlock Holmes* which serves excellent meals. It also has a museum of Sherlock Homes memorabilia.

Once in Trafalgar Square you will see the tall column with **Lord Nelson** on the top. **St Martin's-in-the-Fields** church, the **National Gallery** and the **Reference Library** are all in this vicinity. Passing through the **Admiralty Arch** leads to **The Mall** with **Buckingham**

Palace at the end. The palace's state rooms are open seven days a week to tourists when the Queen is away on her summer break, usually from early August to late September or early October. Admission prices are high, and there are always long queues, but it is still worth a visit. Tickets can be purchased at the booth in the park opposite, or ✆(0171) 321 2233 and use a credit card. The **Changing of the Guard** is held at ⊙11.30am every day in summer and every second day in winter. In order to get a good view it is imperative to get there at least an hour before it starts, but again, the wait is worth it. For more information, ✆(0171) 414 2353.

Those interested in World War II, should visit the **Cabinet War Rooms**, Clive Steps, King Charles Street, ✆(0171) 930 6961 (✇www.iwm.org.uk). This is where Winston Churchill and his advisors made their decisions and planned their strategies. There are 21 underground rooms presented as they were in the 1940s (use Westminster Station). ⊙Open 10am-6pm, admission ✪£4.80 adult, children free.

Take the Underground to Baker Street, turn into Marylebone Road and visit **Madame Tussaud's Waxworks**, ✆(0171) 935 6861, and **London Planetarium**, ✆(0171) 486 1121. Both establishments are usually ⊙open Mon-Fri 10am-5.30pm, Sat-Sun 9.30am-5.30pm, but

United Kingdom

it is best to ring and confirm. Admission to the waxworks is ✪£10.50 adult, £7 child, and to the Planetarium, £6 adult, £4 child, but there are combined tickets available for £12.25 adult, £8.50 child.

Madame Tussaud's is one of those places that you can visit every time you are in the neighbourhood, because new 'people' are always being displayed, or old 'people' are returning after a bit of rejuvenation. In the Planetarium audiences can embark on a journey through time, or watch the feature *Planetary Quest* which lasts for 40 minutes and shows ⊙daily from 9.30am during school holidays and from 12.20pm at other times, with the last show commencing 5pm.

Museums
The British Museum and British Library, Great Russell Street, ✐(0171) 636 1555 (✎www.british-museum.ac.uk). Take the Underground to Tottenham Court Road or Russell Square. ⊙Open Mon-Sat 10am-5pm, Sun noon-6pm, and there is no admission fee, but guided tours are available from ✪£5-7. This is the world's oldest museum (1753) and one of its most fascinating. There are 2.5 miles of galleries with artefacts from almost every aspect of international cultural history. Anyone interested in Egyptology could spend a week in this museum. There is the Rosetta Stone; the recent addition of Roxie Walker Galleries of Egyptian Funerary Archaeology presenting an unparalleled collection of mummies; and dear old *Ginger*, a predynastic man who died pre-3100BC, befores the practice of mummification, but is here in all his glory.

Dickens House Museum, 48 Doughty Street, ✐(0171) 405 2127 (✎www.rmplc.co.uk/orgs/dickens). Although Charles Dickens and his family only lived here for two years or more (1837-1839), it was during that time that he wrote *The Pickwick Papers*, *Oliver Twist* and *Nicholas Nickleby*, and made his name in English literature. The house has probably the most comprehensive Dickens library in the world, and is ⊙open Mon-Sat 10am-5pm. Admission is ✪£4 adult, £2 child (Russell Square Station).

The Museum of London, London Wall, ✆(0171) 600 3699 (✆www.museumoflondon.org.uk) traces the growth of the city from prehistoric times to the present day (use St Paul's Station). ⊙Open Mon-Sat 10am-5.50pm, Sun noon-5.50pm. Admission is ✪£5 adult, children free.

Victoria and Albert Museum, Cromwell Road, ✆(0171) 938 8500 (✆www.vam.ac.uk) is ⊙open daily 10am-5.45pm and admission is £5 adult, child under 18 free (4.30-5.45pm admission free). This is a museum of decorative arts, with 146 galleries exhibiting: a collection of over 400 years of European fashion; the Raphael Gallery; the Silver Galleries; and the Canon Photography Gallery. (Use South Kensington Station.)

Kensington Palace State Apartments, Kensington Gardens, ✆(0171) 937 9561 (✆www.hrp.org.uk). ⊙Open Wed-Sun 10am-3pm, and admission is ✪£8.50 adult, £6.10 child. William III and Mary acquired the palace in 1689 as a country retreat, but it is better known now as the home of the late Diana, Princess of Wales. There are changing displays, but often they are of special occasion clothes worn by the present Royals. (Use Queensway or High Street Kensington Stations.)

Shakespeare's Globe Exhibition, New Globe Walk, Bankside, ✆(0171) 902 1500 (✆www.shakespeares-globe.org), is ⊙open daily 10am-5pm, and admission is ✪£7.50 adult, £5 child (subject to change). While not strictly a museum, the exhibition features the story of the Globe Theatre, the *in* place in Shakespeare's day. All aspects of Elizabethan theatre are covered, including the roles of the playwright, the actor, the audience, and the architects and craftsmen who built the playhouses of that time. Not to be missed by fans of the Bard of Avon.

United Kingdom

Walking in London

Walking allows the visitor to discover places that are not found on the 'tourist routes'. In almost every street there are houses with plaques that commemorate the famous people who lived there. Sundays are never dull in London. You can take the Underground to **Hampstead**, walk up the hill towards the heath and look at the pavement artists. Then have lunch at one of the famous pubs, for example *Jack Straws Castle* which was a favourite watering hole of Dick Turpin the Highwayman, or stroll across the heath to the *Spaniards*, also the haunt of highwaymen. The *Bull and Bush*, immortalized in song, has been rebuilt, and across the road is **Anna Pavlova's house** in Golders Hill Park where deer roam free. Museums, art galleries and many other attractions are all open on Sundays.

Covent Garden is at its liveliest at weekends, and singers and other artists entertain in front of **St Paul's Church**. This is known as the Actors' church and many memorials are found inside. The former wholesale fruit and vegetable market now has shops and a market which has some interesting goods at reasonable prices. The **London Transport Museum** and the **Theatre Museum** are both nearby, and just around the corner stands the **Royal Opera House** and **Drury Lane** theatre. Those who prefer horticulture can take the Underground to Kew and wander around **Kew Gardens**, ☉open daily 9.30am-5pm, ☻£5 adult, £2.50 child, ✆(0181) 940 1171.

Sights Further Afield

It is possible to go by Green line bus, or train, to visit **Windsor Castle**, but the best way is to take a tour that includes a visit to nearby **Eton School** and **Runnymede**, where King John signed the Magna Carter in 1215. Windsor Castle is quite breathtaking when you first lay eyes on it, and in fact, it covers 13 acres. The Queen lives here for part of the year, usually Christmas, Easter and Ascot week, but even so some of the royal apartments are open to the public, as are the Round Tower, St George's Chapel, where Henry VIII and Charles I are buried, and the Royal Dolls House. Admission is ✪£10 adult, which is pretty steep, but remember they have to pay for the £80 million restoration work that followed the 1992 fire.

Hampton Court Palace, Surrey, ✆(0181) 781 9500 (✇www.hrp.org .uk) is a must-see. It is ☺open Mon 10.15am-4.30pm, Tues-Sun 9.30am-4.30pm. Admission to State Apartments, Maze and Privy Garden is ✪£10 adult, £6.60 child; to the Maze only £2.30 adult, £1.50 child; to Privy Garden only £2.10 adult, £1.30 child. Cardinal Wolsey, Archbishop of York commenced building the palace in 1514, but later thought it prudent to make a gift of it to his sovereign, Henry VIII, who added the Chapel Royal's magnificent roof. Make sure you don't miss the tennis court, and incredibly old grapevine, and of course, try your luck with the Maze. Allow plenty of time here as there is plenty to see and do.

Canterbury and Woburn Abbey are also within easy reach of London.

The Best of London in Brief

Westminster Abbey. Built in 1065, the Abbey has been the site of every royal coronation save two since that of William the Conquerer in 1066. It contains the remains of 29 monarchs and houses 3,000 tombs. Highlights of a walk through this majestic building and through its 900 years of history include the shrine of Edward the Confessor, the Coronation Chair,

Henry VII Chapel, Poet's Corner, the Tomb of Queen Elizabeth I and Mary I, and the Nave. Although crowds are always heavy, this is without question one of Great Britain's premier attractions. *Broad Sanctuary*.

 **Tower of London**. Bursting at the seams with visitors, this historical fortress is well-worth a wait in the queues. The White Tower with its thick walls was built by William the Conquerer in the twelfth century, not only for defence but also as a signature of strength. While torture certainly took place here, it was not quite the order of the day. Plenty of heads belonging to famous traitors, wives whose husbands grew tired of them, or stoic Catholics, made their way onto the cold stone floor without a shoulder to lean on. The Crown Jewels, of which St. Edwards's Crown is the oldest piece (1061) and the Sovereign's Scepter bears a 530-carat diamond, are kept here. Other highlights of the fortress include the Bloody Tower where prisoners were kept, the Medieval Palace and the picturesque Tower Bridge. *Tower Hill*.

British Museum. The best insight into the history of civilisation, from the ancient worlds of Egypt, Greece, Assyria Asia, Mexico and Africa to modern worlds. Highlights include the Rosetta Stone, part of a huge statue of Ramses II, Egyptian mummies, the Elgin Marbles, the Sutton Hoo Anglo-Saxon burial ship and countless other scultpures and relics. *Great Russel Street*.

Buckingham Palace. This colossal residence is always high on the itinerary of visitors to London, particularly on days when the Changing of the Guard ceremony is scheduled. *The Mall*.

St. Paul's Cathedral. England's national church took 35 years to build. This architectural masterpiece was completed in 1710. Its main dome rises 365-feet into the air and is the world's second largest. Wellington, Nelson, Nightingale and the church's designer, Sir Christopher Wren are among those laid to rest in the crypt. *St Paul's Churchyard*.

Houses of Parliament. The Houses of Parliament are contained in the former residence of British royalty, the Palace of Westminster, which was largely destroyed in a fire in 1834 and rebuilt in Gothic Revival style. Both the House of Commons and House of Lords can be visited within when in session. Highlights inside are the Westminster Hall and Jewel Tower. The sight of this 1000-room building lining the bank of the Thames, with its clock tower containing the Big ben bell soaring above, is the quintessential image of London. *Parliament Square*.

Cabinet War Rooms. The underground headquarters of the British government, as used by Churchill and his advisors during World War II, has been left in its 1945 state. *King Charles Street*.

National Gallery. Displaying Britain's best offering of European art from the thirteenth century to modern Impressionism, this great gallery has works by da Vinci, Botticelli, Michelangelo, Leonardo, Bruegel, Titian, van Gogh, Rembrandt, Monet, Cezanne, and many others, which are wonderfully explained in an audio tour. *Trafalgar Square*.

Victoria and Albert Museum. A gallery of Decorative Arts, with rooms devoted to English fashion, the work of Raphael and Donatello, medieval European art, legitimate copies of famous art and some notorious forgeries. *Cromwell Road*.

Harrods. Europe's most extravagent department store is in Knightbridge. It has a staggering array of goods and an amazing food court that should be visited. Beware that it also has some of the most eye-popping price tags you will find. *87-135 Brompton Road.*

Trafalgar Square. Located in the centre of London, this famous square is a bustling hive of activity. Sit on the steps and take in your surrounds; the statue of Lord Nelson, the lions, the milling pedestrians and the many hungry pigeons.

Globe Theatre. Shakespeare fans should head to the master wordsmith's home ground, faithfully recreated to appear as it did in his day, which contains details of his life and work and also puts on performances. *Near Southwark Bridge.*

Tate Gallery of British Art. Covering five centuries of British art, the highlights of the gallery are pieces by Turner, Blake, Gainsborough and Hogarth. *Millbank.*

Tate Gallery of Modern Art. This terrific museum features the twentieth century works of Picasso, Warhol, Monet and their contemporaries. *Near Globe Theatre.*

Piccadilly Circus. Like Trafalgar Square, Piccadilly is brimming with people, the difference being that most of them here are tourists. Segaworld, an IMAX theatre and Chinatown are attractions in the area.

National Portrait Gallery. Famous British faces are captured here on canvas, from Henry VIII to Shakespeare to Princess Diana. *St. Martin's Place.*

Covent Garden. Overrated shopping precinct that has the interesting London Transport Museum nearby.

United Kingdom

Hyde Park. Covering more than 600 acres, famous Hyde Park, once the hunting grounds of Henry VIII, contain Speakers' Corner, Serpentine Lake, comfortable benches and plenty of grass.

British Library. An invaluable collection of old maps, Bibles, the original Magna Carta, manuscripts from early English literature including Shakespeare's folios, and selections of important music lyrics. *96 Euston Road.*

Natural History Museum. A fascinating look at the two worlds of biology and geology, covering the human body and evolution, and our planet's development and natural disasters. *Cromwell Road.*

Madame Tussaud's Waxworks. A famous gallery of well-known wax bodies with their well-known wax heads. *Marylebone Road.*

Apsley House. The displays in the Wellington Museum were collected by the Duke of Welligton, who defeated Napolean at Waterloo, and include artworks by Velazquez and Canova. *149 Piccadilly, Hyde Park Corner.*

Museum of London. If you are interested in the history of the city, stretching back before the days of Roman occupation, this capable museum will quench your thirst. *150 London Wall.*

Millenium Bridge. A new sleek pedestrian bridge crossing the Thames.

British Airways London Eye. An enormous Ferris wheel providing the highest possible viewpoint in the city without the aid of an aircraft.

Kenwood House. Its stunning interior is enhanced by an art collection including works by Rembrant and Gainsborough. *Hampstead Lane.*

Imperial War Museum. Covers warfare of the last century in great detail, offering insights into the monumental events that wracked the world and defined the tumultuous history of the 1900s. *Lambeth Road.*

York

North-west of London is the walled city of York with a population of around 100,000. Cars are not permitted inside the city walls.

York was founded by the Romans in 71AD and its Roman name was Eboracum, however Viking remains have been excavated and are now on show in the Jorvik Viking museum.

Tourist Information

British Tourist Authority have an office at the railway station and another in Tower Street, City centre.

The Yorkshire Tourist Board is at 312 Tadcaster Road, York, ©(01904) 707 070, fax 701 414 (☜www.ytb.org.uk).

Local Transport

The best way to see the sights is to take the Sightseeing Bus, which you can get off and on as often as you like.

Accommodation

The Parsonage Country House Hotel Escrick, York, ©(01904) 728 111, fax 728 151. Close to all major link roads, but only 10 minutes from the centre of York. 22 cosy rooms with ensuites - ✪£66-80 per person.

The Grange Hotel, 1 Clifton, York, ©(01904) 644 744, fax 612 453 (✎info@grangehotel.co.uk), 5 minutes from the Minster and city walls. 30 rooms with en-suites, licensed, 3 restaurants - ✪£50-66 per person.

Midway House Hotel, 145 Fulford Road, York, ©/fax (01904) 659 272. Located on A19 south of city centre. 12 en-suite bedrooms, full English breakfast, no smoking - ✪£36-50 per person.

Self Catering

Abbey House Self Catering Apartments, 7 St Mary's, York, ©(01904) 636 154, fax 612 340. Situated in the heart of York. 20 units sleeping 1-6, bed linen, towels, heating, colour TV - ✪£125-385 per unit per week.

Cloisters Walk, 1 St Mary's, York, ©(01904) 638 915. Close to the Minster. 2 units sleeping 2-4. Well equipped, electricity and linen included, no smoking - £200-340.

The Wasps Nest Holiday Cottages, Green Hammerton, York, ©(01423) 330 153, fax 331 204. Central for exploring the Dales and moors, towns, abbeys and stately homes. 4 units sleeping 1-5, owner supervised - ✪£150-390 per unit per week.

Food and Drink

You cannot really claim to have been to York unless you have sampled Yorkshire pudding, made as only the locals can. The batter is formed into a deep circle with a base and filled with cooked beef and onion gravy.

There are plenty of cafes and other eating houses that serve reasonably priced food. Most restaurants serve good wholesome English food. Tea houses are popular.

United Kingdom

Sightseeing

The **Gothic Minster** is the most famous building in York. It has an 11 tonne bell, known as Big Peter, which tolls every day at noon.s

Take the time to look at the soaring columns, the choir screen portraying the kings of England and the rose window which commemorates the marriage of King Henry VII to Elizabeth of York.

Visit the Chapter House built in the 13th century.

The narrow streets of York are full of surprises and are well worth wandering through. **Clifford's Tower** stands perched on a grassy mound. Museums abound: **York Castle**, **National Railway**, **Friargate**, **Regimental**, **Bar Convent**, **Museum of Automata** and the **York Dungeon**, an animated horror museum.

You can walk along the 13th century walls, and look at the medieval half wooden shops and houses in the centre of the city called the **Shambles**.

York also has the most fashionable shopping centre in the north of England.

Sights Further Afield

Within easy reach, and well worth seeing, are **The Yorkshire Dales**. Apart from the beauty of the scenery, this is James Herriott (*All Creatures Great and Small*) country. You will see where the real surgery was, the church where he was married and the locations for the TV show.

Another great tour is to **Castle Howard**. This was the stately home used in the TV series *Brideshead Revisited*. The castle was built between 1699 and 1759, and the state rooms are lavish, the chapel interesting and the costume museum well worth seeing. The grounds are beautiful and time should be made to wander through them. The house is occupied by the Howard family.

Yet another interesting tour is to Bronte Country and **Emmerdale**. On this tour you can watch traditional clogs being made.

It will be easy to understand how the countryside inspired Emily Bronte to write *Wuthering Heights*.

The Best of York in Brief

York Minster. Built on an historic site which once bore a Roman fort, then a Norman church and now this huge Gothic cathderal, York Minster has great views from its Central Tower and provides interesting details of its construction in the Foundations Museum. Its magnificent interior is replete with Gothic and Romanesque art and architecture. This is one of York's top attractions. *Deangate*.

York Castle Museum. A terrific museum, one of Europe's best, with a recreation of the streets and shops of old York, World War II memorabilia, a lively history of household appliances and much more. *The Eye of York*.

National Railway Museum. A comprehensive look at 150 years of rail history in a world-class museum. Photographs, interactive exhibitions, wonderful models and displays make this a fascinating experience. *Leeman Road*.

Merchant Adventurers' Hall. This old Guild Hall is a national treasure with plenty of historical significance. First built in the fourteenth century and rebuilt in the fifteenth century, it

United Kingdom

contains the Great Hall where meetings and business were conducted, the Undercroft where charity and medical help were administered and the Chapel where prayers were taken. Even the wood, stone and bricks used as building materials are themselves significant. *Fossgate*.

Jorvik Viking City. Archaelogical evidence found on this site inspired the detailed recreation of Jorvik, a tenth century Viking city. Astonishing depth has gone into the production, designed to transport the visitor back to this age in every possible way. *Coppergate*.

City Walls. Part of York's medieval walls still stand and you can walk along them for fine views of the city while reflecting on the centuries they stood protecting it.

Yorkshire Museum. 1000 years of the city's heritage are captured here in a good collection of Roman, Viking, Anglo-Saxon, Norman and Gothic artifacts. *Museum Gardens*.

Yorkshire Air Museum. For those interested in wartime aircraft, the focus of this musuem is on World War II, with reconstructions of several planes, a Control Tower and a Squadron Room. These are accompanied by a detailed history of several wartime inventions. *Halifax Way Elvington*.

York Dungeon. Recounts York's bloody Viking past and Guy Fawkes' 'Gunpowder Plot'. *12 Clifford Street*.

The Shambles. A popular pedestrian street whose people and ambience attracts the tourists.

Castle Howard. Situated on over 1000 acres of natural and landscaped parkland, this beautiful palace was built in the eighteenth century and is the largest residence (still occupied by the Howard family) in Yorkshire.

The Lake District

The Lake District is a beautiful slice of England. The lakes are separated by rugged hills rising about 900m - high by English standards. The scenery is soft and has a soothing effect. It's no wonder it was home to so many poets and writers. To appreciate the area you really need to do a lot of walking.

William Wordsworth lived from 1799 to 1808 at Dove Cottage in the town of Grasmere. The cottage and an adjoining museum are open to the public (✓ww@dovecott.demon.co.uk). Wordsworth spent the last 17 years of his life at nearby Rydal Mount which is also open to the public. He died in 1850 and was buried in Grasmere churchyard where his grave can be seen.

Windermere is the largest lake in England and also the name of the tourist town that lies on its east bank. It is popular with yachtsmen and boaters. Regular trips around the lake are run by the Iron Steamboat Company.

Wast Water has the most spectacular mountains in the district but is not accessible by road. **Keswick** has the Fitz Park Museum which has manuscripts and letters written by some of the famous authors who lived and wrote some of their best known works while living in the area. Samuel Coleridge moved here in 1800 and lived at Greta Hall. Other writers whose work is displayed include Robert Southey and John Ruskin. Sir Hugh Walpole wrote his famous *Herries Saga* when living in the district. His works are also on display.

Hawkeshead has the building where Wordsworth went to school. It is open to the public. You can also see Ann Tyson's cottage where Wordsworth stayed when a schoolboy.

Sawrey is where Beatrix Potter lived in a country house at Hill Top. The house, with her original manuscripts and drawings, is open to the public from Easter to the end of October.

Tourist Information

Cumbria Tourist Board, Ashleigh, Holly Road, Windermere, ©(015394) 44 444, fax 44 041 (☞www.cumbria-the-lake-district.co .uk, ✎mail@cumbria-tourist-board.co.uk).

Accommodation

Following is a selection of accommodation with prices for a double room per night, which should be used as a guide only.

Gilpin Lodge Hotel

Crook Road, Windermere, ©(015394) 88 818, fax 88 058 (✎hotel@gilpin-lodge. co.uk). Situated 2 miles from Lake Windermere and 12 miles from M6. 14 rooms with en-suite, licensed, good restaurant - ✪£66-80.

Storrs Hall, Windermere, ℂ(015394) 47 111, fax 47 555. Georgian hall set on the shores of Lake Windermere. 4 rooms with en-suite, restaurant with great views - ✪£80+.

Low Wood Hotel, Windermere, ℂ(015394) 33 338, fax 34 072 (✆www.elh.co.uk, ✎lowwood@elh.co.uk). 117 rooms with en-suite situated on shore of Lake Windermere, 2 restaurants, 3 bars, watersport centre, leisure club - ✪£50-66.

The Fairfield, Bowness-on-Windermere, ℂ/fax (015394) 46 565 (✎ray&barb@the-fairfield.co.uk). 200 year-old-house close to village and lake. Licensed, leisure club, great hospitality - ✪£26-36.

Holly Lodge, 6 College Road, Windermere, ℂ/fax (015394) 43 873. 6 rooms with en-suite situated close to shops, restaurants and transport. Good English breakfast - ✪£16-26.

The Best of The Lake District in Brief

Derwentwater. This very picturesque lake is best for a leisurely sail on its waters or a stroll along its shores.

Keswick. This town rests against the north eastern part of Derwentwater and is the place where graphite was first discovered and the famous Derwent pencils are now made. There is a Pencil Museum in town which traces this history.

Buttermere. A relatively small but beautiful lake, Buttermere has a 6.5km perimeter which can be followed on an idyllic walk.

Castlerigg Stone Circle. One of those inexplicable sights that pops up in the United Kingdom, this one comprises stones that are over three milleniums old and which seem to have strange geometric links with the surrounding landscape.

Dove Cottage. This is the former residence of the famous English poet William Wordsworth, who occupied the country retreat while in his creative prime. It is a good way to see the environment in which he worked and gain an understanding of his appreciation for nature. There is a good little museum adjacent.

Beatrix Potter's Farm. Peter Rabbit and Jemima Puddleduck were among those famous creations who sprung to life in this seventeenth century cottage. The cluttered rooms contain original drawings and details of the author's life.

Hikes and Walks. The Lakes District takes in some of Britain's most attractive countryside. Walking or hiking is the best way to immerse yourself in it, and there are innumerable trails to tread.

Manchester

Manchester is situated on the River Irwell which is linked to the Mersey estuary by the Manchester ship canal, built in 1894. It is a main port and the second biggest commercial city in England with a population of around 450,000.

Probably the most famous things that Manchester has produced are the television series *Coronation Street*, and the champion soccer team, Manchester United.

History

Originally it was the Roman fort of Mancuniom, and during the mid-eighteenth century, it became the cotton capital of the world, although most of the cotton mills are outside the city. Today it is a thriving industrial centre producing chemicals, clothing, printed goods, publishing, paper, food products, rubber and electrical goods.

The airport is less congested than Heathrow and passengers can take the fast rail link and be in the city in 20 minutes. It is a good starting point for touring the various regional areas of Britain outside of London.

Machester claims to be the city where the first atom was split; the first passenger railway station was built; the first test-tube baby was born; the first public library was opened; the first British plane was flown; and the first commercial computer was developed. Quite an achievement for a place that was a village 200 years ago.

Tourist Information

British Tourist Authority has an office at the railway station.

The North West Tourist Board is at Swan House, Swan Meadow Road, Wigan Pier, Wigan, ©(01942) 821 222, fax 820 002 (✆www.visitbritain.com/north-west-england, email ✎info@nwrb.u-net.com)

Local Transport

There are buses and trains to wherever you wish to go. Manchester is not really a tourist city, so it does not have the usual infrastructure.

Accommodation

Following is a selection of accommodation with prices for a double room per night, which should be used as a guide only.

Crowne Plaza Manchester-The Midland, Peter Street, Manchester, ©(0161) 236 3333, fax 932 4100 (✆www.crowneplaza.co.uk). Set in the heart of the city close to theatres, Granada Studios, Old Trafford and shopping areas - 303 rooms with en-suite, restaurants, bars - ✪£80+.

Portland Thistle Hotel, 3-5 Portland Street, Piccadilly Gardens, Manchester, ©(0161) 228 3400, fax 228 6347. Located in the heart of the city. 205 rooms with en-suite, restaurants, bars - ✪£66-80.

United Kingdom

The Princess Hotel, 101 Portland Street, Manchester, ℂ(0161) 236 5122, fax 236 4468. Situated in city centre close to shopping area and theatres. 85 rooms with ensuite, restaurant, bars - ✪£26-36.

Food and Drink

There are plenty of places to eat and drink in Manchester, but there are no special dishes that the city can call its own. Check the menus outside restaurants before entering.

Sightseeing

Although it has been transformed into a modern go-ahead city, many of Manchester's Victorian buildings have been restored.

Manchester Cathedral, built as a church in the 15th century, is well worth a visit.

Some of the best known features of this city are the *Guardian*, first published in 1821 as the Manchester Guardian; The Halle Orchestra; the Grammar School; the Institute of Science and Technology; and the University, all established in the 19th century. Cricket fans know Manchester from Test Matches played at **Old Trafford** and soccer fans either love or hate *Manchester United*.

The Best of Manchester in Brief

The Currier Gallery of Art. This great little musem has paintings, sculptures and decorative arts from America and Europe spanning the era from the Renaissance to modern times. Highlights are the pieces by Monet and Picasso. Tours can be taken through Zimmerman House, listed on the National Register of Historic Houses and designed by American architect Wright in 1950. *201 Myrtle Way*.

Pump House People's History Museum. Traces Manchester's social working culture and some of the highs and lows of its historical events. *Left Bank, Bridge Street*.

Manchester Cathedral. Noted for its wood carvings from the fifteenth century and the fact that it contains the country's widest nave. *Cathedral Yard*.

Manchester Historic Association. A library and museum detail the industrial history of this working town. They also provide maps for heritage walking tours past the city's eighteenth century buildings and distinct row houses. *129 Amherst St*.

The Museum of Science & Industry. This is a large museum occupying five buildings (actually a former passenger railway station - the oldest in the world) with a variety of exhibits that interpret the human body, the earth, space and much more. There are also changing seasonal programs. *Liverpool Road*.

Chester

The quaint, old city of Chester stands on the River Dee. Although it is the capital of the county of Cheshire, its population is only around 59,000.

History

In 70AD the Romans built a fortress called Deva where Chester now stands. They used it when they were endeavouring to conquer the north, and it was occupied by the 20th Legion for 300 years. Chester was the last town in England to yield to William the Conqueror in 1070, so he repaid the people of the area by confiscating their land. After the Norman conquest, Cheshire was made a palatine - province of a feudal lord - under the Earl of Chester. It had its own parliament but the Earl owned all the land except that belonging to the church. This situation remained the same until the reign of Henry VIII.

Cheshire is rich in literary traditions. Raphael Holinshed was the chief author of a history of Britain, on which Shakespeare based fourteen of his plays. Charles Lutwidge Dodgson, better known as Lewis Carroll, author of *Alice in Wonderland*, was born in a vicarage near Warrington. Elizabeth Gaskell immortalised the village of Knutsford in her book *Cranford*. William Congreve, the Restoration dramatist, also lived in the area. Religious figures linked with Chester include hymn writer Bishop Heber and missionary explorer Sir Wilfred Grenfell.

Tourist Information

The British Tourist Authority has an office at the station.

The Chester Visitor and Craft Centre is in Vicars Lane, Chester, ✆(01244) 603 127, fax 602 2620 (✉g.tattum@chestercc.gov.uk).

Local Transport

The best way to see Chester is on the Explorer bus. It is a double decker and can be boarded anywhere. Fares can be paid on the bus but you save ✪£1 if you buy it in advance from BTA.

Keep your ticket as this entitles you to another reduction if you take an explorer trip in another city.

Accommodation

Following are a couple of accommodation possibilities with prices for a double room per night, which should be used as a guide only.

The Grosvenor-Pulford Hotel, Wrexham Road, Pulford, ✆(01244) 570 560, fax 570 809 (✐www.grosvenorpulfordhotel.co.uk, email ✉grosvenor@btinternet.com). Situated 3 miles from the city of Chester in magnificent countryside. 70 rooms with en-suite, swimming pool, health club, restaurant, bar - ✪£36-50.

United Kingdom

> **Forest Hills Hotel**
>
> Bellemonte Road, Overton Hill, Frodsham,
> ©(01928) 735 255, fax 735 517
> (✄113002.1271@compuserve.com).
> Close to M56 in scenic countryside. 57 rooms with ensuite.
> Swimming pool, sauna, steam room, squash courts, restaurant,
> bar - ❾£36-50.

Food and Drink

There are plenty of restaurants, tea shops and pubs where you can have a good English meal.

Sightseeing

The main attractions of Chester are its ancient buildings. The **city walls**, built by the Romans and reinforced by the Normans, still stand, and, in fact, Chester is the only British city where the walls are wholly intact. Roman remains visible today are the ruins of an **amphitheatre** and the foundations of a large Roman building in the cellar of the shop at 28 Northgate Street. On the north and east side of the city, the walls follow the original Roman construction and incorporate their work. The north-eastern medieval tower is called the **King Charles Tower** because Charles I stood there to watch a Civil War battle in 1645.

The narrow streets in the city are called **Rows**. This is because there are rows of half timbered two-tiered shops all in a line that were built in the 1200s. If you follow Forgate Street eastwards and take the right fork at the roundabout, just beyond the Engine House pub, you will see an **ecumenical monument**. It marks the spot where Protestant George Marsh was burned to death by the Catholics in 1555. It also commemorates Saint John Plessington who was hanged, drawn and quartered in 1679 by the Protestants. His relics are venerated at the Franciscan church in Chester. Chester has a Cathedral and several churches. It also boasts the smallest racecourse in England. There is a wharf where you can hire a boat and explore the River Dee.

Sights Further Afield

Chester is close to North Wales and there is a good road along the coast. The model manufacturing village of **Sunshine,** built in 1888, is a short distance. William, Lord Leverhulme and his brother James, started a soap manufacturing company known to this day as Lever Bros. He introduced profit-sharing, pensions, medical care and other benefits for his employees.

The Best of Chester in Brief

Chester Cathedral. The original Norman church dates back to the early twelfth century and the Gothic Cathedral standing here was constructed in the fifteenth century. Highlights of the cathedral are its elegant and famous choir stalls, the refectory, the monastic cloisters and surrounding gardens. *St Werburgh Street.*

Grosvenor Museum. Delving into the days of Roman rule in the city, Chester's top musuem has exhibits which vividly depict the social and military history of those times, with reconstructed buildings and a cemetery. Other drawcards are the art and craft galleries, Period House and the interactive displays. Keep an eye out for changing exhibitions. *27 Grosvenor Street.*

Chester Zoo. This is an award-winning regional zoo with some impressive facts and figures: it is Great Britain's largest garden zoo encompassing 50 hectares; contains 6000 animals representing more than 500 species, over half of which are on the endangered list; has a breeding colony for chimpanzees and a large herd of Asiatic elephants; and also has a Twilight Zone

Bat Cave, a Monkey Island exhibit, a Tropical Realm and a Zoofari Overhead Railway. *Upton-by-Chester*.

Chester Toy and Doll Museum. Children's toys of all kinds from the nineteenth and twentieth centuries fill five rooms. The museum is most famous for having the largest collection of Matchbox toys in the world. *13a Lower Bridge Street*.

Dewa Roman Experience. Focusing soley on Roman Chester, this museum goes to great lengths to show what it was like when the Romans walked the streets, with reconstructions filling in every detail of life. There is also an archaelogical exhibit. *Pierpoint Lane, Bridge Street*.

Bath

Bath is a quiet, sleepy city resting on the banks of the River Avon in South West England. It has a population of around 80,000.

History

The Romans founded a settlement here and named it Aquae Sulis because of its mineral springs. They turned it into a spa resort covering six acres with pools reaching temperatures of 49C (120F). They are still intact today.

After the Romans left, the Britons neglected the town and even built over some of the spa pools. The Roman baths were rediscovered in 1879. Bath became fashionable in the 18th century when famous people went there to "take the waters". Dickens, Swinburne, Defoe, Jane Austen and scores of other people of note found the soothing atmosphere conducive to inspiration.

Tourist Information

The Tourist Information Office is in the Abbey Churchyard, just south of the Abbey, and it is ☺open Mon-Sat 9.30am-5pm, Sun 10am-4pm, ✆(01225) 477 101 (rarely answered personally).

The office has a City Trail guidebook available for ✪£1.50, and it is worth its weight in gold for the serious visitor.

Local Transport

There are plenty of local buses that will take you to different points in the city, or you can take a tour bus to ensure that you will see all the points of interest.

Accommodation

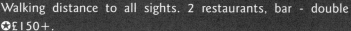

Bath Spa

Sydney Road, BA2 6JF, ✆(01225) 444 424, fax 444 006. 98 rooms with all facilities. Georgian mansion built in 1850, renovated. Parking. Walking distance to all sights. 2 restaurants, bar - double ✪£150+.

The Francis on The Square, Queen Square, BA1 2HH, ✆(01225) 424 257, fax 319 715. 98 rooms with bath. Built in 1729. Overlooking Georgian Square, situated between Royal Crescent and the Abbey. Restaurant, bar - double ✪£100-150.

Athelney Guest House, 5 Marlborough Lane, Bath, ✆(01225) 312 031. 3 rooms, good meals - ✪£36-40.

Food and Drink

There are plenty of cafes and small restaurants, not to mention the pubs where food is served. The only alleged local delicacy is the Bath Bun, a type of sweet bread cake. It is available at many bakeries in the city, but the most popular place is rumoured to be *Mountstevens* on Westgate Street.

United Kingdom

Bath Olivers are a biscuit that was originally invented to be eaten whilst "taking the waters", but the local factory that produced them was bombed during the war. Production has recommenced in Leamington Spa, and it is still recommended that they are at their best when eaten in a hot bath, even though they are now covered with chocolate. You can buy them from Waitrose supermarket in the Podium.

There is a cafe in North Parade Passage called **Sally Lunns** where they still bake the bun with the same name.

Since October 1997, Bath has again been brewing its own local beer, Abbey Ales. It is available from the Farmhouse on Lansdown Road.

Sightseeing

The Georgian nobles built elegant houses mostly in sweeping curves. The best example of this distinctive architecture is the **Royal Crescent**, an arc of thirty houses overlooking extensive lawns. House No. 1 is open to the public; No. 15 is the fictional home of Sir Percy Blakeney, the Scarlet Pimpernel. **The Circus**, where the houses are built in a circle is close by. Dr Livingstone lived at No. 13, and the painter Gainsborough at No. 17, where he painted the famous *Blue Boy*. As it is uphill, it is best to take a bus up to Royal Crescent and walk back down.

The ancient attractions are all in the centre of the city.

Next to the Roman baths are the **Pump Rooms**. Here you can have morning or afternoon tea served as one would imagine it being done in the 18th century. A string quartet plays music by the old masters. Thakeray used the Pump Room as one of the locations in *Vanity Fair*. The Roman Baths are ☉open Mon-Sat 9.30am-5pm, and there is an admission fee.

Bath Abbey, built in the 16th century, is famous for the stone angels on the facade. The carvings represent a dream of Bishop Oliver

King who built this last Tudor church before the Reformation. In his vision, angels climbed up and down ladders to heaven, but the only way the stonemasons could distinguish between the two was to make the ones descending do it head-first, which tends to make them look like 'fallen angels'. Inside, Australians would be interested in a memorial to Governor Philip who lived just off the Circus at 19 Bennett Street. The house bears a plaque.

Don't miss the **Pulteney Bridge**, with its elegant horseshoe-shaped weir. The bridge is one of only three in the world with shops on both its sides, and was designed by Robert Adam.

The **Museum of Costume**, which houses original garments since the late 1500s, is of interest to everyone not just those with an eye for fashion. It is housed in the *Assembly Rooms*, frequently mentioned by Jane Austen in her novels of early 19th century life.

Across the Avon in another 18th century building is the **Holbourne Museum and Crafts Study Centre**. It has a superb collection of 17th and 18th century art.

Sights Further Afield

For those with the time, a tour to Longleat, the home of the Marquise of Bath is worth a visit. The house is the finest example of Elizabethan architecture in the country. Built in 1550 it burnt down in 1567 and was rebuilt in 1572. The house is open all year round. There is also a lion safari park in the grounds.

The Best of Bath in Brief

Museum of Costume. This wonderful museum allows you to inspect the development of fashion from the sixteenth century to the present, decade by decade, with over 200 models dressed in detail down to jewelery and accessories. It is one of

United Kingdom

the top museums in Europe and arguably the best of its kind in the world. *Assembly Rooms, Bennett Street.*

Roman Baths. These baths mark the origins of the city, where Romans discovered hot springs, were astonished by their soothing effects, and created their version of a resort town almost two thousand years ago. The great Roman temple, ancient uncovered treasures and the baths themselves are a must-see for a fascinating return to a past era. *Pump Room, Abbey Church Yard.*

Bath Abbey. This late fifteenth century abbey is built on the historical site where England's first King was crowned in an Anglo-Saxon abbey. Stained glass, fan vaulting and perpendicular Gothic architecture make it worth a second glance. *Abbey Church Yard.*

Industrial Heritage Cottage. A great collection of Victorian memorabilia.

Pump Room. Overlooking the King's Spring, the Grand Pump Room is an eighteenth century Georgian Hall in whose elegant interior you can sip your tea while relaxing to music played by the oldest resident trio in Europe. *Abbey Church Yard.*

Jane Austen Centre. Fans can retrace the esteemed author's daily footsteps, through her Georgian town house and along her favourite city paths, past sights made famous in her novels. *40 Gay Street, Queen Square.*

Assembly Rooms. This National Trust building functioned as a meeting and recreation hall in the eighteenth century. The chandeliers are originals from this time. *Bennett Street.*

Herschel House Museum. For astronomy buffs, this house was where Uranus was discovered back in 1781, on William Herschel's hand-made telescope. The NASA photographs here are offset by the preserved eighteenth century furniture. *19 New King Street*.

No 1 Royal Crescent. This restored Georgian house, with its fine Palladian architecture, dates back to 1774. It contains a museum highlighting some interesting features of Georgian life.

Stonehenge. Dated as far back as 3000BC, these mysterious stones, some weighing over 50 tonnes each, are thought to have been placed here by a neolithic people. The reasons for their circular placement and the method used to transport them are speculative. The dominant theory is that they form an ancient type of calendar and were rolled to the site on logs all the way from the Preseli Mountains in Wales, but nobody knows for sure. The engineering feat is staggering considering their age, and these mysterious stones have a unsettling and awe-inspiring ambience. *Located south east of Bath in Amesbury, Wiltshire*.

Edinburgh

The city of Edinburgh is the capital of Scotland and the second largest city, with a population of around 420,000. Nowadays it is a cultural centre thanks in the main to the very popular *Edinburgh Festival*.

History

Strategically placed on the shores of the Firth of Forth, Edinburgh played an important part in the wars between England and Scotland in medieval times. After the death of Elizabeth I of England, James VI of

Scotland also became James I of England and moved his court south, causing Edinburgh to lose some of its importance. In recent years this has been regained by its contribution to learning.

Tourist Information

Scottish Tourist Board, 23 Ravelston Terrace, Edinburgh, ℰ(0131) 332 2433, fax 315 4545 (☜www.holiday.scotland.net/os).

Local Transport

There are plenty of buses to all parts of the city. In the city centre it is better to walk.

Accommodation

Following is a selection of accommodation with prices for a double room per night, which should be used as a guide only.

Best Western Apex International, 31-35 Grassmarket, Edinburgh, EH1 2HS, ℰ(0131) 300 3456, fax 220 5345. Located in historic Old Town. 175 rooms, rooftop restaurant with great views of the castle, bar, lounge - ✪£120-180.

Carlton Highland Hotel, North Bridge, Edinburgh, EH1 1SD, ℰ(0131) 472 3000, fax 556 2691 (✎travelweb@hotelbook.com(08504)). In the heart of the Royal Mile. 4-star facilities including a restaurant and night club - ✪£75-193.

Albany Town House Hotel

39 Albany Street, Edinburgh, EH1 3QY, ℰ(0131) 556 0397, fax 557 6633 (✎travelweb@hotelbook.com(28770)). A superior first class hotel situated in the New Town. Has a restaurant and bar - ✪£75-185.

United Kingdom

Quality Hotel Commodore-Edinburgh, Marine Drive, Edinburgh, EH4 5EP, ©(0131) 336 1700, fax 336 4934. Restaurant, cocktail bar - ✪£75-108.

Best Western Braid Hills Hotel, 134 Braid Road, Edinburgh, EH10 6JD, ©(0131) 447 8888, fax 452 8477. Built in 1886 for golfers visiting Braid Hills Courses nearby. Good location for visiting all the attractions of Edinburgh. 67 rooms, bar/lounge, restaurant - ✪£70-110.

Tulip Jarvis Learmonth, 18-20 Learmonth Terrace, Edinburgh, EH4 1PW, ©(0131) 343 2671, fax 315 2232 (✓travelweb@hotelbook. com(25854)). Situated half a mile from the city centre, one and a half miles from the Castle. 62 rooms, restaurant with extensive menu, terrace bar - £65-119.

Quality Hotel Edinburgh Airport, 1 Ingliston, Edinburgh, EH28 8NF, ©(0131) 333 4331, fax 333 4124. Bar/lounge, restaurant - ✪£55-105.

Simpsons Hotel, 79 Lauriston Place, Edinburgh, ©(0131) 622 7979, fax 622 7900 (✓travelweb@hotelbook.com(29540)). Centrally situated with 57 rooms, bar - ✪£49-100.

Food and Drink

The Scots have a dish called *haggis* which is delicious although some people steer clear of it because of the recipe. It consists of oatmeal, minced offal, suet and seasoning, cooked in maw (the stomach of a sheep).

Seafood is one specialty and oyster bars are plentiful. Others are Scotch whisky, smoked haddock, salmon, kippers, herrings, and cock-a-leekie soup, which is made from a whole fowl and leeks with other seasonings. Dunlop Cheese has a rich, mellow flavour. Another very local dish is "tatties an' herrin" (spotatoes and herring boiled together).

Shopping

The best buys are tweed materials. Tweed made into garments is very popular and quite unique. Fine woollen items, silk shawls, worsteds and linen are also popular.

Sightseeing

Taking a tour on the jump on/jump off double-decker buses is always a good way to get your bearings in a new city. The tour of Edinburgh takes about an hour in total, and buses leave from central locations about every 15 minutes.

Edinburgh Castle dominates the city, and the best view of it is from Princes Street. Inside the castle you can inspect the apartments occupied by Mary Queen of Scots, including the room where she gave birth to James I. The **Crown Jewels**, which were recovered by Sir Walter Scott, are also kept here. There is also a collection of antique weapons, the banqueting hall and a military museum. At ☉1pm each day a cannon is fired, a 150 year tradition. Other attractions within the castle are the 11th century **St Margaret's Chapel**, **Old Parliament Hall**, and the small cemetery containing the remains of military mascots (dogs). There is a changing of the guard ceremony, but it is the antithesis of those that take place at Buckingham Palace, being instead very relaxed, with the participants obviously enjoying themselves.

The **National War Memorial** stands close by. The **Royal Mile** is a cobbled street lined with interesting shops and houses, including one that was occupied by John Knox, founder of the Calvinist Presbyterian Church in Scotland in 1560. Below the Castle is a wide parade ground where the Edinburgh Tattoo is held.

United Kingdom

At the end of the road stands the palace of **Holyrood House**. It is the Queen's official residence but visitors can inspect it when she is not staying there. Inside there are many antiquities including needlework done by Mary Queen of Scots. A plaque commemorates the place where her secretary Rizzio was murdered on the instructions of Queen Mary's husband, Lord Darnley.

There are many small streets running off the Royal Mile.

In **Lawnmarket** stands the six storey tenement house built in 1620, and known as Gladstone's Land. It is furnished in the style of a merchant's house of the time, and the ceilings are magnificently painted. Nearby is **Lady Stair's House** a town dwelling of 1622. It has exhibits by Sir Walter Scott, Robert Louis Stevenson and Robbie Burns. In High Street the Cathedral called **The High Kirk of St Giles** dates from the 12th century.

Canongate was once a separate burgh outside the walls of Edinburgh.

Huntley House, built in 1520, is a museum featuring Edinburgh's history and social life. The most impressive structure along **Princes Street** is the 60m statue of Sir Walter Scott. Not far away are the **National Gallery**, **Zoological Park**, **Parliament House**, **Greyfriars Churchyard**, **Museum of Childhood** and the **Royal Scottish Museum**.

Sights Further Afield

Three miles from the city is **Craigmillar Castle**, while not far from the city is the ancient seaport and castle of **Dunbar** and the fashionable resort of **North Berwick**.

The Best of Edinburgh in Brief

Royal Mile. This historic stretch makes for a wonderful walk for any visitor to Edinburgh. Highlights are the Castle Esplanade at the bottom of which is a site where many witches were burnt at the stake for about two-and-a-half centuries; Gladstone's Land, a sixteenth century merchant's house; Writers' Museum, in a sixteenth century house called Lady Stair's House which displays manuscripts by some famous Scottish authors and poets; St Giles Cathedral, the most important church in the country; Tron Kirk, housing an historical display of the city; John Knox House, containing a museum of the life of the Presbyterian Church's founder; People's Story, an exhibition dedicated to the working class produced by the Industrial Revolution; and Holyrood Palace, the once-a-year residence of the Queen when she visits Scotland.

Edinburgh Castle. The 1300-year-old fortress dominating the skyline atop the hill and overlooking sprawling Edinburgh below has some wonderful views and must-see attractions inside. The Great Hall, the Scottish National War Memorial, St. Margaret's Chapel and the Scottish Crown Jewels are not to be missed. *Castlehill*.

Walter Scott Monument. This soaring monument,with great views from its peak, is topped by a marble statue of the Scottish author and decorated with the likenesses of actual poets and fictional characters. *East Princes Street Gardens*.

National Gallery of Scotland. The best collection of Scottish paintings anywhere, and also some surprising masterpeices by European greats such as Raphael and Titian. *2 The Mound*.

Scottish National Gallery of Modern Art. A plethora of twentieth century art from a varied and terrific selection of well-known modern artists. Belford Road.

Glasgow

Glasgow on the River Clyde, is the largest city in Scotland and the third largest city in the United Kingdom, with a population of around 760,000. It is a relatively modern city, and not many buildings pre-date the Victorian era. Its once depressed areas, including the Gorbals, have long been levelled and replaced.

History

Glasgow was a religious and learning centre in the 12th century. Shipbuilding was always one of its major industries, but it has now declined. Both the great ships the *Queen Mary* and the *Queen Elizabeth* were built along the River Clyde. Other industries include engineering, textiles, brewing, chemicals and whisky blending. Glasgow grew rapidly after 1707 when Scotland was united with England. It was the chief port for the importation of tobacco and sugar from the New World.

The city survived the industrial revolution with its deposits of coal and iron ore nearby.

Tourist Information

The Greater Glasgow & Clyde Valley Tourist Board, 11 George Square, Glasgow G2 1DY, ©(0141) 204 4400, fax 221 3524, (☞www. seeglasgow.com, ✁tourismglasgow@ggcvth.org.uk).

Local Transport

Buses are plentiful. Tours are also available.

Accommodation

Following is a selection of accommodation with prices for a double room per night, which should be used as a guide only.

> **Copthorne Glasgow**
>
> George Square, Glasgow, GS 1DS, ©(0141) 332 6711, fax 332 4264 (✓travelweb@ hotelbook.com(03847)). A good location, situated in the centre of the city and convenient for sightseers and business travellers with a tight schedule. 140 rooms, restaurant, bar. It is a stylish hotel with an attractive facade and an interior to match. Room decor and facilities are not overly luxurious, but they are adequate and suited to the price range - ✪£107-135.

Thistle Glasgow, 36 Cambridge Street, Glasgow, G2 3HN, ©(0141) 332 3311, fax 332 4050 (✓glasgow@thistle.co.uk). Scotland's largest conference hotel. 302 rooms, 2 restaurants, 2 bars - ✪£105-140.

Jarvis Ingram Hotel, 201 Ingram Street, Glasgow, G1 1DQ, ©(0141) 248 4401, fax 226 5913 (✓travelweb@hotelbook.com(29571)). In the city centre near the Cathedral. 91 rooms, bar and grill with an extensive menu - ✪£86-94.

Quality Hotel Central-Glasgow, 99 Gordon Street, Glasgow, G1 3SF, ©(0141) 221 9680, fax 226 3948. Bar/lounge, restaurant, indoor pool - ✪£75-108.

Black Bull Thistle Hotel, Main Street, Glasgow, G62, 6BH, ©(0141) 956 2291, fax 956 1896 (✓reservations@thistle.co.uk). Situated outside Glasgow in proximity to Loch Lomond and the Trossachs. 27 rooms, restaurant, 3 bars - ✪£77-93.

Buchanan Hotel, 185 Buchanan Street, Glasgow, G1 2JY, ✆(0141) 332 7284, fax 333 0635. Situated in the heart of the city, only yards from Royal Concert Hall. 59 rooms, bar/lounge, restaurant - ✪£60-95.

Bruce Hotel, Cornwall Street, East Kilbride, Glasgow, G74 1AF, ✆(01355) 229 771, fax 242 216 (✉travelweb@hotelbook.com (28856)). In the city centre adjoining the Plaza Shopping Centre. 110 rooms - ✪£60-90.

Food and Drink
Good wholesome food is readily available. Some restaurants serve continental fare. Seafood, smoked and fresh salmon, and haggis are local specialties.

Shopping
Glasgow has one of the finest shopping thoroughfares in Britain - **Sauchiehall Street**. You can buy almost anything there.

Sightseeing
St Munro's Cathedral dates from the 12th century. **Glasgow University** was built in 1451. Other places of interest are: **Kelvingrove Art Gallery and Museum** houses a fine collection of European art including Salvador Dali's famous painting of the *Crucifixion*; **The Museum of Transport** includes a re-creation of a 1938 street; **The Glasgow School of Art** was designed by Charles Rennie Mackintosh and contains much of his work. The **Burrell Art Collection** is housed in a gallery in Pollock Park.

Glasgow also has the biggest football stadium in Britain, **Hampden Park**. In 1989, at **Culcreuch Castle**, a short distance north of Glasgow, Tom Moody, an Australian cricketer, won a haggis-throwing competition with a throw of 67m, beating the local record of 50m.

Sights Further Afield

A short distance from Glasgow are some of the most scenic areas in the whole of Scotland. **Loch Lomond**, is one of the most beautiful lakes in Europe. It can be reached in less than an hour. Trips are usually extended into the loch and mountainous country of **Argyle**. The road travels through the charming little town of **Inveraray** where the Duke of Argyle, Chief of the Clan Campbell, has his castle.

On the Atlantic side of Glasgow, the sea-lochs cleave deep into the mountains. The wild scenery of **Loch Long**, one of the longest, deepest and most beautiful fjords is easily accessible. Charming **Loch Goil** is right on Glasgow's doorstep.

The Best of Glasgow in Brief

Bothwell Castle. Scotland's greatest thirteenth century stone castle is set attractively above the Clyde and has a tumultuous history. *Castle Avenue, Uddington.*

Burrell Collection. This collection has a variety of artifacts, including sculpture and tapestries, representing chiefly the ancient, classical and medieval eras. *2060 Pollockshaws Road.*

Gallery of Modern Art. A unique contemporary gallery whose four floors are divided thematically into the four natural elements. *Queen Street.*

Glasgow Botanic Gardens. Highlights in these gardens are the many tropical plants and the Victorian Kibble Palace with its marble statues. *730 Great Western Road.*

Glasgow Cathedral. The city's patron saint, St Mungo, is buried in the crypt of this twelfth century Gothic cathedral. *Castle Street.*

Hunterian Art Gallery. An outstanding collection of works from the seventeenth century onwards, taking in paintings by Rembrandt, portraits, Scottish works, American art and modern sculpture. *University of Glasgow, 82 Hillhead Street*.

Hunterian Museum. Scotland's oldest museum, this musuem has a great array of pieces including the Bearsden Shark which is 330 million years old, dinosaur bones, coins, archaelogical treasures, scientific instruments, medals, maps and much more. *University of Glasgow, University Avenue*.

Museum of Transport. All modes of transport are represented in this rare collection of transport memorabilia. *Kelvin Hall, 1 Bunhouse Road*.

People's Palace Museum. Two hundred years of Glaswegian history and culture is recounted in a vibrant and modern style. *Glasgow Green*.

University of Glasgow Visitor Centre. The Visitors Centre of the fourth oldest university in the United Kingdom contains interactive displays with cutting-edge technology. *University Avenue*.

Belfast

Belfast, the Capital of Northern Ireland, is situated on the banks of the River Lagan, where it flows into the Belfast Lough on the border of Counties Antrim and Down. The surrounding hills are soft and green, so typical of the scenery of Northern Ireland. It has a population of around 400,000.

History

Belfast became a city in 1888. Around the turn of the century it was the biggest ship-building centre in the world, one of its most famous vessels being the *Titanic*. In 1921 it became the capital of the newly created Northern Ireland. In 1969, due to sectarian violence, the British sent the military in, and tourists stayed away in their thousands. It is only in the last few years, mainly since the Good Friday peace Accord in 1998, that Belfast is back on travel itineraries.

Tourist Information

The Tourism Development Office, Belfast City Council, The Cecil Ward Building, 4-10 Linenhall Street, Belfast, BT2 8BP, ©(01232) 320 202 ext 3585.

Local Transport

Local public transport is good. Ask at your hotel or the local tourist information.

Accommodation

Following is a selection of accommodation with prices for a double room per night, which should be used as a guide only.

Belfast Hilton International Hotel, 4 Lanyon Place, Belfast, BT1 2LP, ©(01232) 277000, fax 277 277 (✎ travelweb@hotelbook.com (28732)). A 5-star hotel situated in the heart of the city overlooking the River Lagan. 195 rooms, restaurant, bar/lounge - ✪£155-203.

Europa Hotel, Great Victoria Street, Belfast, BT2 7AP, ©(01232) 327 000, fax 327 800 (✎ travelweb@hotelbook.com(00047)). Famous hotel in the heart of Belfast. 184 rooms, restaurant, lounge/bar, brasserie - ✪£99-140.

Quality Hotel Fergus, 75 Belfast Road, Carrickfergus, BT 38 8PH, ©(02893) 364 556, fax 351 620. Restaurant, bar/lounge - ✪£85-150.

United Kingdom

Stormont Hotel, 587 Upper Newtownards Road, County Down, Belfast, BT4 34P, ✆(01232) 658 621, fax 480 240 (✉travelweb@ hotelbook.com(20778)). Situated half a mile from Stormont Castle, and 4 miles from Belfast city centre. 109 rooms, 2 restaurants, bar/ lounge - ✪£60-130.

Jury's Belfast Inn, Great Victoria Street, Belfast Antrim, Belfast, BT2 7AP, ✆(01232) 533 500, fax 533 511 (✉travelweb@hotelbook. com(25814)). Situated opposite the Opera House and City Hall. 191 rooms, coffee shop, lounge - ✪£55-63.

Food and Drink
Main restaurants offer continental and British specialties but the Irish prefer plain hearty meals of meat, bread and vegetables. Fish and chips and home baked bread made from whole-wheat flour are specialities. Try the pubs for a good meal at a reasonable price.

Shopping
Best buys are Belfast linen and Irish whiskey.

Men's shirts and collars made in Londonderry are world renowned for their quality.

Sightseeing
The city centre is dominated by the copper dome of the **City Hall**, in Donegall Square, which was modelled on St Paul's Cathedral in London. Free guided tours are available ⊙Oct-May Mon-Sat 2.30pm, June-Sept Mon-Fri 10.30am, 11.30am, 2.30pm, Sat 2.30pm only, ✆(01232) 270 405 for recorded information.

Another landmark of the city is **Belfast Castle**, which is 400 ft above sea level on the slopes of Cave Hill. The first castle on this site was built by the Normans in the late 12th century, then in 1611 a stone and timber castle was erected. The present building was commenced in 1862 by the 3rd Marquis of Donegall, but his fortune had dwindled dramatically before the building was finished, and his son-in-law, Lord Ashley, heir to the title Earl of Shaftesbury, had to step in and meet the shortfall. In 1884 the 3rd Marquis died, and in 1885 the 7th Earl of Shaftesbury followed, and Lord Ashley and his wife inherited the Shaftesbury title and the Donegall home.

The castle was presented to the City of Belfast in 1934, and from the end of the 2nd World War to the 1970s, it was a venue for wedding receptions, dances and afternoon teas. In 1978, the Belfast City Council began a major refurbishment program, and the building was officially re-opened to the public in 1988.

The castle's cellars were opened in 1990, having been transformed into a Victorian atmosphere of narrow streets, shop fronts, gas lights, and the like. Visitors can now enjoy an antique and craft shop, the **Castle Tavern** bar and the **Castle Kitchen** - a bistro that is ☼open daily and serves everything from light snacks to full meals.

From the summit of **Cave Hill**, on a clear day, you can see the Isle of Man and the Ayreshire coast.

Belfast Zoo, Antrim Road, on the side of Cave Hill, offers great views of the city. It has all the usual animals, and is ☼open April-Sept daily 10am-5pm, Oct-March Sat-Thurs 10am-3.30pm, Fri 10am-2.30pm. There is an entry fee, ✆(01232) 776 277.

Linenhall Library, Donegall Square, opposite City Hall, has been lending books out since 1788. It is ☼open Mon-Wed, Fri 9.30am-5.30pm, Thurs 9.30am-8.30pm, Sat 9.30am-4.30pm, ✆(01232) 321 707. Even if you don't want to borrow a book, you can enjoy a quiet cup of coffee upstairs.

Parliament met in Belfast from 1921-1972 then moved to **Stormont**, five miles outside the city. The dignified building where it now meets is made of Portland stone and was opened in 1932 by the then Prince of Wales. Nearby is the Prime Minister's House.

The **Queen's University** received a Royal Charter in 1909, and is situated in the south of Belfast, near the **Botanic Gardens**, the **Palm House**, which has many exotic plants, and the **Ulster Museum**, ☾open Mon-Fri 10am-5pm, Sat 1-5pm, Sun 2-5pm, ✆(01232) 383 000. The centrepiece of the museum is the *Girona Treasure*, which consists of relics recovered in the 1960s from three Spanish Armada vessels which sank of the coast in 1588. Admission is free.

The **Ulster Folk Museum** consists of farmhouses, watermills, a whole village, shops and church, all moved from the countryside and reassembled here. Across the road is the **Transport Museum**. For opening hours of both museums, ✆(01232) 428 428.

Mount Stewart House and Gardens are rated by the National Trust in the top six in the UK.

Along the north bank of **Belfast Lough** stands a small community called **Carrickfergus**. Here the ancestors of Andrew Jackson, President of the USA, kept an inn. On the waterfront stands an inscribed stone to commemorate the landing of King William III who was on his way to defeat James I at the Battle of the Boyne. Within sight of Carrickfergus' ancient castle and in the Belfast Lough, Captain John Paul Jones, a Scottish gardener ran up his colours on the *Ranger* and fought it out with HMS *Drake*. He was one of the founders of the US Navy.

Giant's Ring is a circular rampart 200m in diameter that may be as much as 4000 years old. It is a mile south of Shaw's Bridge, off the N23.

Sights Further Afield

One of the most picturesque and scenic highways in Europe is a winding road running north from Belfast along the coast. At times the road is so close to the water that the windscreen is covered with spray. The highway crosses rocky peninsulas with views of basalt highlands and the deep waters of the Irish Sea. Well worth the time it takes.

The Best of Belfast in Brief

City Hall. Constructed at the turn of the nineteenth century, this proud building contains a statue of Queen Victoria, a marble staircase, the original charter of Belfast from the early seventeenth century, and the Great Hall. *Howard Street*.

Falls Road. Although things have certainly calmed down by comparison with former days, a visitor to this corner of town can sense (or imagine) the tension of sectarian violence and discontent still crackling in the air. The area has the Peace Line, the headquarters of Sinn Fein and a commemorative IRA cemetery.

Botanic Gardens. A lovely park setting with a Tropical Ravine and Palm House on the grounds.

Ulster Museum. Apart from an Egyptian mummy, the Girona Treasure and a medieval exhibit, there is little else to thrill visitors to this museum. *University Road*.

Driving Through The U.K.

You could easily spend a month touring around England, Scotland and Wales.

England

Itinerary - 12 Days - Distance 1450kms

After spending time exploring **London**, head north east to **Cambridge**. Cambridge is a famous university town, with many historic buildings. From here, drive north to **Lincoln**. This city dates from Roman times, and there are many interesting ruins. The cathedral is spectacular.

Further north of Lincoln, you reach **York**, a preserved medieval walled city, and famous for the York Minster. There are also interesting museums here. Head north, through the Yorkshire Dales, stopping at small towns such as **Ripon** and **Richmond**. Richmond is a good starting point for visiting the National Park. Continue on to **Hexham**, which is close to Hadrians Wall. This was started in the 1st century. The Northumberland Dales are also near here.

Continue on to **Edinburgh**, the capital of Scotland. Here there are many things to see and do, including making a visit to the famous Edinburgh Castle. Each August the Edinburgh Festival is held, and the Military Tattoo is popular. From Edinburgh head south towards the Lake District. On the way you pass through towns such as **Peebles**, famous for its salmon fishing, and **Selkirk**, with its links to Queen Victoria and Sir Walter Scott.

On the border, **Gretna Green** used to be a popular place for eloping couples to marry. **Windermere**, **Keswick** and **Grasmere** all lie in the heart of the Lake District. This picturesque area is very popular as a holiday destination. The poet Wordsworth lived at Grasmere, and you can visit the museum in his honour. Drive south from here until you reach **Blackpool**, a typical English seaside resort.

Continue south to **Chester**, a medieval walled city with relics dating from Roman times. There are many historic buildings here. From Chester, head west along the north coast of Wales, stopping at coastal towns such as **Colwyn Bay** and **Bangor**. **Caernavon** is famous for its castle, dating from the 13th century. The Snowdonia National Park is ideal for day and longer walks, and is accessible from here.

Head south east over the Cambrian Mountains to **Shrewesbury**. This town is located on both sides of the Severn River, and is an appealing sight with its black and white timbered houses. From here, drive to **Stratford-Upon-Avon**, Shakespeare's birth place and a very

United Kingdom

popular tourist destination. You must book well in advance for theatre bookings at the Royal Shakespeare Theatre.

Further south, you reach **Oxford**, another famous old university town, with many historic buildings still in use today. Make your way back through the picturesque Chilterns to London where your tour finishes.

The South of England

Itinerary - 10 Days - Distance 1002kms

From **London**, drive west to **Windsor**, famous for the castle - home of the Royal Family. Many parts of the castle are open for public entry. Windsor is also noted for its Safari Park, and Eton Public School, one of the oldest in England. Head south west to **Salisbury**. Salisbury Cathedral is well known as one of the most beautiful cathedrals in the United Kingdom. A copy of the Magna Carta is held here. Close by Salisbury lies **Stonehenge**, with ancient stone circles dating from 2200 BC. It is no longer possible to wander through these huge stone pillars. From here head north to **Bath** and **Bristol**. Bath is an elegant spa town, with relics dating from Roman times. Bristol is a lively city, situated on the river Severn.

United Kingdom

Stonehenge, southwest of Bath

Make your way south through the cathedral city of **Wells** to **Glastonbury**. This town is famous for being the first place where Christianity was practised in England, in AD 700. **Exeter** lies on the southern coast. This is a good starting point for touring Devon and Cornwall. Exeter, an old Roman town was overrun by Norman troops, and the remains of William the Conqueror's castle can still be seen. The Maritime Museum is a reminder of the towns naval history.

Travel east now along the south coast, through seaside resorts such as **Lyme Regis** and **Bournemouth**. Drive through the New Forest town of **Lyndhurst**. Wild horses still run free in the forest. The port cities of **Southampton** and **Portsmouth** provide access to the Isle of Wight. Make a detour to **Winchester**, once the capital of England, with its beautiful cathedral. The Great Hall of the castle reputedly contains King Arthur's round table.

Continue along the coast to **Brighton**, another popular holiday destination. The Indian inspired Royal Palace is worth visiting. **Folkestone** and **Dover** are important ferry ports for crossing to the continent. Head north from Dover to **Canterbury**. The first Canterbury Cathedral was started in the 11th century. The town is full of history and there are many interesting museums. Head back to London through the pleasant Kent countryside.

The Highlands of Scotland

Itinerary - 11 Days - Distance 1447kms

After spending time in **Edinburgh**, head north to the coast and the famous **St Andrews** golf course. Unless you have reciprocal club membership, tourists must go into a ballot to be entitled to play golf on this course. Drive north to **Perth**, the old capital of Scotland, with its historic buildings. From Perth head towards **Braemar**, where the Highland Games are held each August. Balmoral Castle, summer residence of the Royal Family is nearby.

Aberdeen lies on the east coast of Scotland, and is associated with the North Sea oil industry. To the north west of Aberdeen, in the

Speyside region, you find the centre of the whisky industry. Many of the distilleries are open to the public. Continue on to Inverness, where the nearby Loch Ness is well known for its monster. From **Inverness**, take the coastal road to **John O'Groats**, the northern most point of Scotland. From here you can see across to the Orkney Islands.

Head west along the coast to the remote town of **Durness**, and then down the rugged western coastline to **Ullapool**, where ferries depart for the Outer Hebrides. Another ferry port leading to the Isle of Skye is at **Kyle of Lochalsh**. From here make your way south to **Fort William** at the foot of Ben Nevis, and **Glencoe**, the site of the massacre of the McDonald clan by the Campbells. Head back past Loch Lomond to **Stirling**, where the restored castle is impressive, to complete your trip in Edinburgh.

United Kingdom

Index

Index

Index

OTHER TRAVEL TITLES FROM LITTLE HILLS PRESS

Prices listed are recommended retail only, include GST, and were correct at time of printing.

AUSTRALIAN TITLES

186315146X	Australia's Great Barrier Reef	$16.95
1863151524	Doing the Coast	$21.95
1863151125	Outback Australia	$21.95
1863151095	Small Hotels of Sydney	$9.95
1863151451	Sydney: Short Stay Guide	$16.95
1863151419	Tasmania: Short Stay Guide	$18.95

Australian Pocket Guidebooks

1863150900	Melbourne	$5.95
18631510lX	Brisbane & Gold/Sunshine Coasts	$13.95

Australian Driving Guides

1863150617	Australia's Central & Western Outback	$9.95
1863151109	Australia's Eastern Outback	$9.95
1863151338	Australia's South East	$19.95
1863151109	Australia's Wet Tropics & North-Eastern Outback	$9.95
1863151303	Outback Western Queensland	$9.95

OVERSEAS TITLES

1863151192	California	$19.95
18631 5132X	Cambodia: Short Stay Guide	$18.95
18631 5129X	Fiji	$9.95
1863151478	Hong Kong & Macau: Short Stay Guide	$16.95
1863150552	London Pocket Guidebook	$6.50
1863151141	New Zealand	$19.95
1863151265	Singapore	$9.95
1863150455	Singapore Pocket Guidebook	$6.50
1863150889	South Korea	$19.95
1863151036	South Pacific Islands	$19.95
1863151184	Thailand	$19.95

OTHER

1863151044	Travel Diary	$18.65

LITTLE HILLS PRESS ORDER FORM

Your details:

Name:_____

Address (of delivery):

_____

_____

Phone Number:_____

Email:_____

ISBN	TITLE	PRICE	QTY	TOTAL

TOTAL BOOKS*_____

TOTAL PRICE*_____

How To Order

By Fax: 61 2 9838 7929

By Post: 3/18 Bearing Road, Seven Hills NSW 2147 Sydney, Australia

By Email: ✗ info@littlehills.com

👁www.littlehills.com

*An additional freight charge applies to orders containing less than 5 books in total and orders to be sent outside Australia